Deutsch Aktuell

Deutsch Aktuell 2

Deutsch Aktuell 1

Completely Revised Program!

Includes Spelling Changes in the German Language!

The Best

German

Program

Just Got

Better!

Now

The all-new fourth edition of *Deutsch Aktuell* is a totally rewritten textbook series that continues the tradition of success. The *Deutsch Aktuell* textbook program has become the ultimate for successful German language instruction since its inception. *Deutsch Aktuell* offers the most exciting and up-to-date approach available for teaching German. This new program features an abundance of proficiency-based situational and communicative activities to help your students "live the language and culture."

Deutsch Aktuell

Deutsch Aktuell is a totally new three-level textbook program with unique communicative features that will get your students excited about learning German! Taking a truly functional approach to learning German makes language learning relevant and personal. While developing cultural sensitivity to the everyday activities of German-speaking people, students acquire proficiency in listening to, speaking, reading and writing German. From day one, students practice communicating easily and confidently with their peers in paired or cooperative learning groups.

Flexible

The goal of *Deutsch Aktuell* is to meet the needs of the wide range of ability levels in your classroom. Because most classes are diverse, you need to provide students with opportunities to interact in small groups and work together toward communicative competency. *Deutsch Aktuell* offers a variety of options and approaches for teaching students at multiple ability levels and with diverse learning styles.

Proficiency Based

The *Deutsch Aktuell* program provides a series of proficiency activities in which students can experience situations in a range of contexts that they would most likely encounter in German culture. These activities help students begin to internalize and master German. This ability to interact with others using listening, speaking, reading and writing skills, all integrated with culture, gives students the confidence to use the language "on their feet."

Broad Cultural Coverage

In-depth coverage of various German cultures in *Deutsch Aktuell* gives students a solid understanding of and appreciation for the language within its multicultural, diverse context. Authentic cultural situations, used as the vehicle for proficiency-based role-playing and creative expression, appear throughout the program to encourage students to widen their cultural horizons as they develop their proficiency in German.

Uniquely Balanced

Listening, speaking, reading and writing are all important skills in learning a language, and *Deutsch Aktuell* offers the most balanced approach to developing these skills. Each lesson carefully blends creative oral and written exercises to build expressive skills, while culture-based reading and listening exercises provide listening

practice to develop receptive skills. Presentation of each of the four language skills within an authentic cultural context helps your students function proficiently in the language. *Deutsch Aktuell* has a carefully controlled vocabulary and bridging of structures that allow for constant recycling of basic information to form the foundation for developing proficiency.

Student-Friendly

Extensive research on factual and real-life situational content was done to make sure *Deutsch Aktuell*'s abundance of interesting topics will appeal to students. *Deutsch Aktuell* features role-playing activities, cooperative learning activities, group activities and a variety of other suggested classroom activities and games that make language learning fun for students. This program also introduces an innovative, lighthearted cartoon series— *Willi und Milli*—that students will look forward to reading while reinforcing their German language skills.

Textbook

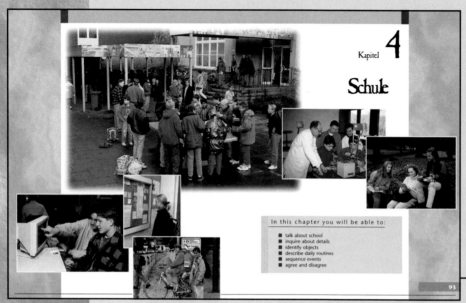

Preceding the chapter text are two photo-illustrated **Chapter Opener** pages that visually prepare students for the general cultural content of the particular chapter. Functions reflecting what students will be able to do are also listed here.

Deutsch Aktuell uses an eclectic mix of activities to integrate the four basic skills with culture. With *Deutsch Aktuell,* your students will begin to use German immediately in authentic contexts while having fun building their communicative competency from the first day of class.

There are two *Aktuelles* sections in each chapter, presenting a cross-cultural approach in a mini-social studies format. An activity follows each *Aktuelles* section so that the students can measure their understanding of the cultural content.

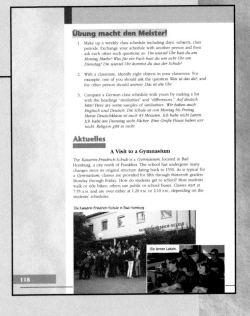

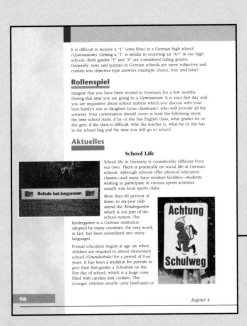

The *Rollenspiel* section contains role-playing activities that engage students in meaningful conversations that reflect real-life situations.

The *Praktische Situation* section in each chapter provides students with a cooperative learning experience as each activity engages students within a group to perform certain tasks and helps them in meeting the goal of that activity.

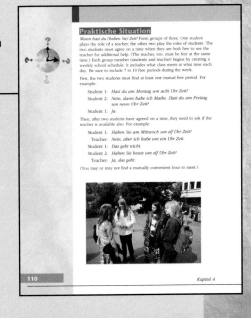

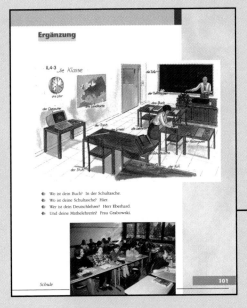

The *Ergänzung* sections in each chapter reinforce and expand the topic of the chapter theme and provide additional language and cultural information.

A unique feature to each textbook chapter is the original, humorous **Willi und Milli** cartoon series that uses only the vocabulary and structure with which students are familiar.

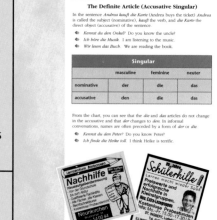

An explanation of the structure or grammar leads off each *Sprache* section, followed by speaking and writing activities illustrating the specific grammar point.

The **Lesestück** reading section introduces additional cultural situations that occur in everyday German life through a mixture of narrative- or conversational-style reading passages.

Wie findest du die da drüben?

Kennst du sie?

Michael: Wie findest du die da drüben?
Goran: Ganz toll! Ich kenne sie sehr gut.
Michael: Wirklich? Wie alt ist sie denn?
Goran: Fünfzehn. Ivana, komm mal her!

Ivana: Hallo, Goran. Was gibt's?
Goran: Das ist Michael, mein Freund.
Michael: Tag, Ivana. Bist du Gorans Freundin?
Ivana: Aber nein. Goran ist mein Bruder.

1. *Falsch!* The following statements are incorrect. Provide the correct statements in German.
   1. Goran kennt das Mädchen nicht gut.
   2. Ivana ist sechzehn.
   3. Gorans Freund heißt Mark.
   4. Goran ist Ivanas Freund.

Hallo, Goran. Was gibt's?

Tag, Ivana.

42   *Kapitel 2*

Opening Dialogs are at the beginning of each chapter and feature short conversations dramatizing situations of interest to students and depicting common everyday life in German-speaking countries to ensure better retention and understanding of the language. These dialogs are followed by comprehension check-up activities to measure the students' understanding in a step-by-step manner.

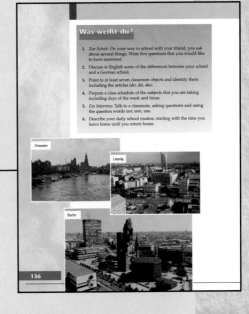

Was weißt du?

1. *Zur Schule.* On your way to school with your friend, you ask about several things. Write five questions that you would like to have answered.
2. Discuss in English some of the differences between your school and a German school.
3. Point to at least seven classroom objects and identify them including the articles (*der, die, das*).
4. Prepare a class schedule of the subjects that you are taking including days of the week and times.
5. *Ein Interview.* Talk to a classmate, asking questions and using the question words *wer, wen, was*.
6. Describe your daily school routine, starting with the time you leave home until you return home.

Dresden

Leipzig

Berlin

136

The *Was weißt du?* section at the end of each chapter gives students a chance to measure their understanding of the chapter content. It also serves as an excellent review prior to giving the chapter tests.

Land und Leute

Österreich

Österreich ist eine Republik. Das Land liegt in der Mitte° von Europa. Österreich ist ungefähr so groß wie der Staat Maine.

Es hat mehr als sieben Millionen Einwohner. Ungefähr 99% (Prozent) sprechen deutsch. Österreichs Nationalfahne° ist rot-weiß-rot.

Das Land liegt zum größten Teil° in den Alpen. Der höchste° Berg ist der Großglockner. Die Donau ist der längste Fluß°. Sie fließt° von Westen nach Osten.

Die Hauptstadt von Österreich ist Wien. Mehr als 20% der Österreicher wohnen in der Hauptstadt. Wien liegt im Osten Österreichs. Da ist das Land flach°. Die Donau fließt

durch° Wien. Im Süden liegt Graz, auch eine große Stadt. Linz liegt im Nordosten. Die Donau fließt auch durch Linz. Nach Wien, Graz, und Linz kommt Salzburg im Nordwesten. Salzburg ist eine beliebte° Stadt. Viele Touristen kommen im Sommer zum Musikfest° nach Salzburg. Innsbruck ist die fünftgrößte Stadt in Österreich. Diese Stadt liegt im Westen und ist während jeder Jahreszeit° beliebt. Besonders schön ist es da im Winter.

Welche Städte möchtest du in Österreich besuchen? Wien, Graz, Linz, Salzburg oder Innsbruck? Warum möchtest du sie gern sehen?

in der Mitte in the center; *die Nationalfahne* national flag; *zum größten Teil* for the most part; *höchst-* highest; *der längste Fluß* the longest river; *fließt* flows; *flach* flat; *durch* through; *beliebt-* popular; *das Musikfest* music festival; *während jeder Jahreszeit* during every season

Graz

Salzburg

Wien

259

The *Land und Leute* reading selection (beginning with *Kapitel 4* and in every fourth chapter thereafter) familiarizes students with geographical and cultural features of Germany, Austria and Switzerland.

Supplementary Materials

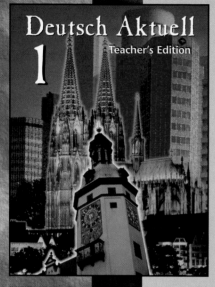

Deutsch Aktuell
1
Teacher's Edition

Teacher's Edition

The annotated **Teacher's Edition** includes the student pages with practical teaching suggestions in the margin as well as answers to the activities. An introduction to the Teacher's Edition provides a Scope and Sequence Chart, lesson plans for a model unit that covers both regular class periods and block scheduling, teaching suggestions, games and activities. Easy-to-use marginal notes suggest when to use ancillary materials and offer suggestions for expanding the lesson content. The Teacher's Edition features cross-curricular activities covering such topics as mathematics, geography and history to help students expand their knowledge.

The *Deutsch Aktuell* Teacher's Edition contains numerous activities on various topics corresponding to and supporting the material students are studying in each chapter, including the following:

- Critical thinking
- Paired activities
- Cooperative learning
- Ideas for modifying and expanding activities
- Games
- Language through action/ total physical response
- Activities for students with multiple intelligences

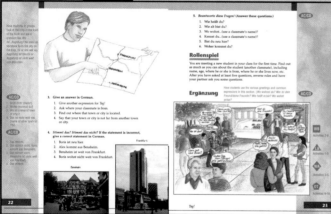

There are icons that cross-reference all of the *Deutsch Aktuell* components.

Deutsch Aktuell
2
Workbook

Workbook

Innovative activities correlated to each section in the textbook help students become proficient in written German as they practice the functions, vocabulary and structures in each chapter. The **Workbook** recombines previously learned language concepts and broadens students' understanding. Realia-based activities prepare students to use the language in authentic situations.

Workbook Teacher's Edition

The **Workbook Teacher's Edition** contains the answers for all of the exercises in the student workbook. The Teacher's Edition contains icons that explain where each workbook activity best fits into your lesson plan.

Teacher's Resource Kit

The **Teacher's Resource Kit** contains a variety of useful and practical tools to help you make your daily lesson plans. This easy-to-use kit includes additional listening and writing comprehension activities on reproducible blackline masters (with answer key/teacher's edition), audiocassettes or CDs with listening activities, a teacher's edition of the workbook, an audiocassette/audio CD program manual and a map of Germany.

Audiocassette/Audio CD Program

The **Audiocassette/Audio CD Program** is an integral part of *Deutsch Aktuell*. Appropriate icons in the Teacher's Edition designate which material in the textbook has been recorded on audiocassettes or CDs by native speakers of all ages. This program will help your students develop an ear for the many nuances of the German language.

Recorded material in each chapter includes:

- *Dialoge*
- *Übungen*
- *Ergänzung*
- *Lesestück*
- *Sag's mal*
- *Erweiterung*

The Audiocassette/Audio CD Program Manual includes the complete script of the recorded material for each chapter in the textbook.

Testing/Assessment Program

A complete **Testing/Assessment Program** that tests all language skills offers you an easy-to-use method for measuring students' understanding of the material. The testing program provides tests for each chapter of the textbook, as well as semester and final examinations.

The Testing/Assessment Program includes: audiocassettes or CDs for listening comprehension, a test booklet, a test booklet teacher's edition, an oral proficiency evaluation manual, and portfolio assessment.

Components of the Testing/Assessment Program

Audiocassettes or CDs

The **Audiocassettes and CDs** for listening comprehension test students' understanding of the chapter content. The Audiocassettes and CDs for listening comprehension are included in the Testing/Assessment Program.

Components of the Testing/Assessment Program

Test Booklet

Included in the **Test Booklet** are listening and written tests for each chapter to measure the students' understanding of the chapter content. Achievement Tests for midyear and for year-end are valuable tools in measuring students' progress. The Test Booklet and Test Booklet Teacher's Edition are included within the Testing/Assessment Program.

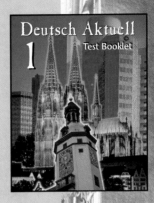

Portfolio Assessment

In addition to traditional testing and evaluation tools, the **Portfolio Assessment** includes activities for monitoring students' progress. The Porfolio Assessment is included within the Testing/Assessment Program.

Oral Proficiency Evaluation Manual

Measuring your students' oral proficiency is a difficult task. This **Oral Proficiency Evaluation Manual** offers you guidelines, correlated to the themes and content of the textbook, for comprehensive oral proficiency evaluation. The numerous activities provide varied situations that students will encounter as they use German to communicate in everyday life. This allows teachers the flexibility of using the manual for formal oral testing or for providing students with additional practice using German in realistic contexts. The Oral Proficiency Evaluation Manual is included within the Testing/Assessment Program.

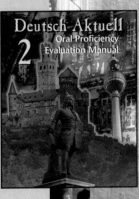

Video Program

Filmed entirely on location in Berlin, Germany, with professional actors, this exciting **Video Program** with a continuous story line is closely coordinated with the functions, vocabulary and structures of each chapter in the textbook. The videos enable students to see authentic situations and hear conversational dialog in German. The accompanying Video Manual contains transcripts of the video units and numerous activities related to the video episodes.

Students become involved with their German-speaking contemporaries and can't wait to discover what happens in the next episode.

Overhead Transparencies

Full-color **Overhead Transparencies**, correlated to the content of each chapter, offer illustrations of scenes, objects and maps to provide an outstanding method of visually reinforcing the chapter's content. These creatively designed transparencies can be used to teach or review the chapter's content in a creative, communicative manner. The Teacher's Edition contains icons that note where each transparency best fits into your lesson plan.

Computer Software

The **Computer Software Program** (Macintosh and IBM), closely coordinated with the textbook, is ideal for reviewing and reinforcing each chapter's structural information. At the end of each chapter, a comprehensive chapter quiz checks students' understanding of each concept. The Computer Software Program Manual provides additional details on how to use the program effectively.

CD-ROM Program

EMC/Paradigm's *Deutsch Aktuell* series features a highly interactive, multimedia **CD-ROM Program** designed to enhance students' skills in speaking, listening, writing and reading within a functional and cultural context. As interns at a publication in the German-speaking world, students face the many communicative challenges of reporters. This business setting allows students to solve meaningful, real-world problems as they improve their proficiency in German.

Interactive Dialogs

- Native German speakers engage students in conversations on a variety of topics.
- An innovative recording feature allows students to record conversations for playback.
- Students can check their speaking ability and fluency by listening to models of native speakers.

Innovative Assignments

- Observation and listening skills are honed as students watch videos and gather information to solve problems encountered by journalists.
- Vocabulary and fluency improve as students become immersed in authentic, animated conversations.

Publication Pages

- Engaging assignments motivate students to do research and write about the geography, history and culture of German-speaking countries and cities.
- Reading and writing skills improve as students read faxes and encyclopedia articles to prepare the pages for publication.

- Futuristic online reference materials allow immediate access to a dictionary, a colorful atlas, and an encyclopedia for all cultural and publication activities.

The *Deutsch Aktuell* Program

Choose the Best German Program That Just Got Better for You and Your Students!

Deutsch Aktuell will make your students' experiences with German an exciting adventure and your job easier and more rewarding!

- Teacher-friendly to minimize your preparation time

- Flexible to meet the needs of students at all ability levels

- Proficiency based to enhance students' real-world skills

- Up-to-date broad cultural coverage

- Balanced approach to skills development

- Comprehensive and numerous supplementary materials

Completely Revised Program

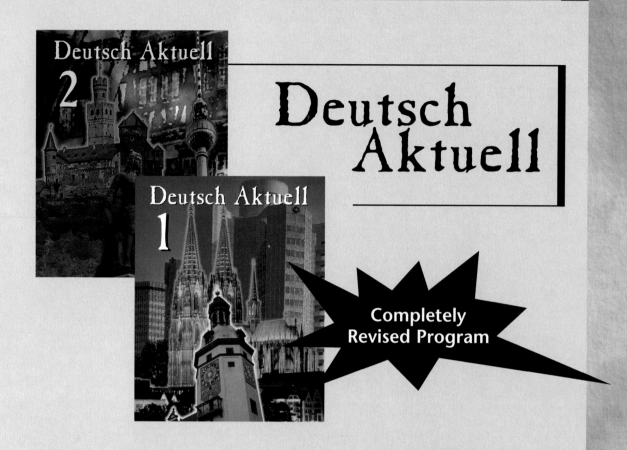

Deutsch Aktuell 1
Fourth Edition

Teacher's Edition

Wolfgang S. Kraft

EMC/Paradigm Publishing, Saint Paul, Minnesota

Credits

Desktop Production Specialists
Bradley J. Olsen
Rita Westerhaus

Designer
Tim Heitman

Illustrator
Hetty Mitchell

Cartoon Illustrator
Steve Mark

ISBN 0-8219-1475-8

Published by EMC/Paradigm Publishing
875 Montreal Way
St. Paul, Minnesota 55102

Printed in the United States of America
1 2 3 4 5 6 7 8 9 10 XXX 03 02 01 00 99 98

About the Cover

The collage of buildings assembled on the cover of *Deutsch Aktuell 1* is particularly appropriate for a first-level language textbook. One can't build anything lasting without first laying a good foundation. The science-art architecture is a paradigm for the study of a foreign language. The functions, vocabulary and structures of language resemble the bricks and mortar of a Gothic cathedral, the girders and rivets of a modern skyscraper, the timbers and plaster of a *Fachwerkhaus*. The architect finds limitless creative expression within the confines of the laws of physics and available materials. So, too, the student of German will find infinite capacity for expression and communication once the functions, vocabulary and structures of German are understood and practiced. A building with a good foundation will stand for possibly hundreds of years. Likewise, a student with a good foundation will be able to develop and use those skills for a lifetime.

The front cover's three main visual elements illustrate European history's three great social movements lead by church, state and commerce. The foreground is of the newly restored *Rathaus* clock tower in Leipzig. Behind the clock tower is the *Kölner Dom*. In the background looms the cityscape of downtown Frankfurt's business district. The monuments of the past are living reminders of the best that German culture has to offer, and continue to inspire future generations.

Tim Heitman
Graphic Artist

About the Author

Wolfgang S. Kraft, a native of Germany, is Director of Foreign Languages at EMC/Paradigm Publishing. He graduated from the University of Minnesota with B.A., B.S., and M.A. degrees, and has taught German at University High School, Minneapolis, Minnesota; White Bear Senior High School, White Bear Lake, Minnesota; Bethel College, St. Paul, Minnesota; and for several adult education programs.

Kraft also has participated as Native Informant at NDEA Foreign Language Institutes, has served on various foreign language panels, and has conducted many workshops in the United States as well as abroad.

Besides writing and taking most of the photographs for *Deutsch Aktuell*, Kraft has authored several other German programs, among them *So sind die Deutschen* and *Passport to Germany*.

To keep the textbook series fresh and exciting for students, Kraft travels extensively throughout German-speaking countries gathering interesting facts and information about the language and culture.

Contents

Kapitel	Communicative Functions	Dialog	Topics	Aktuelles
Einführung *Also, los!*	greeting and saying farewell to someone asking and telling someone's name introducing someone else asking and telling someone's age giving telephone numbers		greetings identifying people names numbers 0-20 addition/subtraction cognates alphabet letter *ß*	General Greetings
1 *Tag!*	introducing yourself and others greeting people asking and telling how things are going giving information asking where someone lives	*Hallo!* *Woher kommst du?*	greetings introductions where a person lives	*Du oder Sie?* Greetings, Farewells and Introductions
2 *Meine Familie*	describing people answering a telephone call asking what time it is pointing out family members asking for and giving information introducing someone else	*Kennst du sie?* *Hast du Zeit?*	family relations age days of week numbers 10-1,000 time of day	The Telephone What Time Is It?
3 *Was machst du?*	asking and telling what someone is doing talking about what interests you expressing likes and dislikes giving opinions reporting information	*Heike möchte zum Rockkonzert* *Sie hören CDs und Kassetten*	directions time of day interests	Youth Activities Leisure-Time Activit
4 *Schule*	talking about school inquiring about details identifying objects describing daily routines sequencing events agreeing and disagreeing	*Wer ist klug?* *Was ist zu Hause?*	classroom objects school subjects grades class schedule	School Life A Visit to a *Gymnasi*
5 *Zu Besuch*	talking about the weather writing a letter identifying countries and languages spoken there asking where someone is from giving information	*Monika kommt zu Besuch* *Wohin fahren alle?*	additional family relations months seasons weather countries, languages	Visiting Germans The Weather
6 *Wie schmeckt's?*	choosing from a menu and ordering at a café offering something to eat and drink expressing likes and dislikes making requests giving advice talking about what to do today	*Matthias hat Hunger* *Was bringt die Kellnerin?*	beverages foods ice cream flavors	From the *Ratskeller* t the *Schnellimbiss* Eating Out

Ergänzung	Sprache	Lesestück	Erweiterung	Land und Leute	Rückblick
Wie heißt du? greetings names numbers 0-20 *Wie alt bist du?* alphabet	cognates				
greetings	familiar and formal forms *(du, ihr, Sie)* personal pronouns present tense verb forms		agreement numbers 0-20 *richtig / falsch* personal questions		
Die Familie numbers 10-1,000 time days of week	formation of questions *der, die, das*	*Zu Hause*	numbers time of day dialog completion missing words		
Was machst du gern? *Wie viel Uhr ist es?* directions	*haben* (present tense) word order *zu Hause/nach Hause*	*Bastian und Uli gehen nach Hause*	personal questions missing words dialog completion TV schedule		present tense *Wann? Was? Wie? Wo? Woher? Wohin?* sentence formation time of day family reading a letter
Die Klasse school subjects *Stundenplan*	definite article (accusative) *Wer? Wen? Was?* *sein* (present tense)	*Ein Tag bei Jochen*	personal questions dialog completion missing words	*Deutschland*	
Die Monate und Jahreszeiten *Wie ist das Wetter?* *Länder und Sprachen*	indefinite article (nominative and accusative) plural nouns (nominative and accusative) *Wie viel? Wie viele?*	*Tina besucht ihren Cousin*	categorizing words personal questions missing words developing dialog		
ice cream flavors beverages eating places foods	modal auxiliaries: *mögen* (*möchten*), *müssen*, *wollen* negation *wissen* (present tense)	*Gehen wir in die Pizzeria!*	dialog completion missing words writing a paragraph		verb forms *Wer? Was? Wo? Wohin? Wie viel? Wie viele?* *kennen/ wissen* opposites paragraph completion sentence formation

Kapitel	Communicative Functions	Dialog	Topics	Aktuelles
7 *Wie gefällt dir das?*	making suggestions asking about prices describing and choosing clothing items writing a letter and a card talking about a department store	*Der Pulli steht Christine gut* *Alex will Jeans kaufen*	colors clothing items	The Ins and Outs of Shopping *Das Kaufhaus*
8 *Geburtstag*	talking about birthday presents offering and accepting gifts congratulating someone identifying rooms and furniture describing daily activities expressing intentions telling someone to do something	*Was für ein Geschenk hat Rainer?* *Wer geht zur Party?*	rooms of house gift ideas	Special Occasions Common Courtesies
9 *Unterhaltung*	talking about a film expressing likes and dislikes describing weekend activities and hobbies pointing out tasks and obligations making plans	*Gehen wir ins Kino!*	hobbies leisure-time activities entertainment obligations at home	Entertainment Music: Classical to P●
10 *Sport*	talking about sports expressing likes and dislikes restating information inquiring about personal preferences identifying parts of the body	*Sie spielen Tennis*	sports parts of body	*Sport für alle* *Fußball*
11 *Reisen*	talking about traveling asking for and giving directions identifying important places in a city describing a trip asking for information	*Wohin reisen sie?*	means of transportation places in city directions (additional)	*Der Bahnhof* Traveling by Train
12 *Das macht Spaß!*	talking about weekend activities accepting or refusing an invitation describing talents and abilities ordering from a menu talking about past events	*Wer geht zum Tanz?*	musical instruments foods (additional)	Foreign Influence in Germany Metric Measurement●

Ergänzung	Sprache	Lesestück	Erweiterung	Land und Leute	Rückblick
Die Farben clothing items	modal auxiliaries: *dürfen, können, sollen* future tense words used for emphasis	*Heike und Natascha werden nach Österreich fahren*	dialog completion personal questions reading a letter developing dialog		
dates (ordinal numbers) presents *die Wohnung oder das Haus*	verbs with stem vowel change personal pronouns (nominative, accusative) command forms	*Angelika hat Geburtstag*	dialog completion missing words categorizing words developing dialog		
entertainment hobbies home chores	verbs with separable prefixes accusative propositions compound nouns	*Die Pilos Puntos Schülerrockband*	dialog completion missing words personal questions	*Österreich*	categorizing words verb formation rooms in house/apartment personal pronouns compound nouns
Sportarten *Körperteile*	dative (indirect object) dative (prepositions) verbs followed by the dative case	*Ein großer Tag*	categorizing words personal questions verb formation description of a sport missing words dialog completion		
Verkehrsmittel places in city and directions	present perfect tense (regular verbs) dative (personal pronouns)	*Auf dem Bahnhof*	giving instructions dialog completion missing words personal questions word description		
musical instruments foods and beverages	present perfect tense (irregular verbs) possessive adjectives	*In der Tanzschule*	sentence formation developing dialog or reading a paragraph meaning of words sentence completion personal questions	*Die Schweiz*	present perfect tense dative case categorizing words dialog completion interview sentence formation paragraph completion

Introduction

The fourth edition of *Deutsch Aktuell* is not just a revised edition, but a totally rewritten text that continues the tradition of a successful textbook series that has become the flagship of German language instruction for more than 15 years.

The new edition is the result of extensive research involving hundreds of teachers who have used the previous editions, numerous discussions at professional workshops and focus groups as well as the application of recent trends in foreign language instruction.

The strength of the new edition of *Deutsch Aktuell* becomes apparent in the variety of communicative activities (cooperative learning, role-playing, pair and group) and the new sections added, as well as the cultural coverage of German-speaking countries (Germany, Austria and Switzerland).

This new edition of *Deutsch Aktuell*, with its innovative content and components, will move students well into the next century. The major improvements include the use of an abundance of full-color photos and illustrations that make the content come alive and more meaningful. Besides the realistic dialogs and conversations as well as the numerous situational and communicative activities found in each chapter, sections such as *Rollenspiel, Praktische Situation, Übung macht den Meister! and Sag's mal!* provide additional language practice and application in a proficiency-based format. A unique feature to each textbook chapter is the original *Willi und Milli* cartoon series that uses vocabulary and structure with which students are familiar. Finally, two cultural sections titled *Aktuelles* are part of each chapter so that students will expand their understanding of the cultural subtleties that are part of German life.

The purpose of the front section of this teacher's edition is to provide a complete overview of *Deutsch Aktuell 1* (Scope and Sequence Chart), describe the philosophy and goals, outline the components and main features of the program, suggest a lesson plan for one of the chapters (for both 50-minute and 90-minute classes in a block scheduling system), introduce additional classroom expressions, provide a list of organizations representing German-speaking countries and give additional teaching suggestions—including additional activities and games. Finally, this front section includes a summary of the major changes in German spelling rules that are reflected in all of the *Deutsch Aktuell* print materials.

This teacher's edition contains an annotated version of the student textbook. Marginal notes, printed in another color, include numerous comments and suggestions to expand the material and provide additional information that may be useful to the teacher. The answers to all activities are also included in this teacher's edition. Finally, the activities that are part of the following ancillaries are coordinated with the chapter content and coded as such: audiocassettes/audio CDs, workbook, listening and written activities, end-of-chapter tests, oral proficiency evaluation, portfolio assessment, overhead transparencies, video program, computer software and CD-ROM.

Philosophy and Goals

Since the National Standards in Foreign Language Education have become accepted among foreign language teachers, it is imperative that the *Deutsch Aktuell* textbook series also addresses those issues. These national standards clearly define the need that today's students must become effective communicators, keen observers of global cultures, insightful about themselves and their learning, informed and knowledgeable across disciplines, and participants in the community and global marketplace. Furthermore, the national standards document five important goal areas of foreign language education that need to be addressed in implementing a successful program. These goal areas are called the five C's of foreign language education. They are as follows:

- *Communication* Communicate in languages other than English
- *Cultures* Gain knowledge and understanding of other cultures
- *Connections* Connect with other disciplines and acquire new information
- *Comparisons* Develop insight into the nature of language and culture
- *Communities* Participate in multilingual communities at home and around the world

Extensive research has shown that a teacher needs to use a variety of student-centered activities and approaches to maximize learner outcomes and minimize the teacher's involvement. This ensures that students and not the teacher are at the center of the learning process. Consequently, a variety of techniques have been implemented for optimal achievement of language proficiency that cater to all learning abilities.

The following material describes the various techniques and learning strategies that have been incorporated in the *Deutsch Aktuell* textbook series throughout to maximize learner outcomes and to offer numerous opportunities in creating authentic experiences.

Cooperative Learning

As the teacher-centered classroom has shifted to a more effective student-centered environment, cooperative learning has become an important part of student participation. In cooperative learning students work together to share their knowledge, increase their skill level and attempt to meet the goals that they themselves have set. Cooperative learning happens when both the students and the teacher are actively engaged in the teaching and learning situation that incorporates these five elements: positive interdependence, individual accountability, face-to-face interaction, interpersonal and small group skills, and group processing.

Groups should contain a maximum of four students with varied abilities. The teacher should provide specific tasks and explain the criteria for success. When assigning roles in groups, the teacher should divide responsibilities to ensure interdependence and cooperation. One possible division of responsibilities is to appoint a discussion leader/facilitator, a recorder, and a reporter. Upon each group's completion of the assigned cooperative learning activity, the final activity should be shared with the rest of the class and the entire class and teacher should assess the quality of the group's activity.

The section in each chapter titled *Praktische Situation* provides students with a cooperative learning experience. Each activity engages students within a group to perform certain tasks and helps them meet the objective or goal of that activity.

Group Activities

Besides cooperative learning activities, students have other opportunities to work together in groups in order to strengthen their language skills. By dividing students into smaller groups, the teacher will realize more effective and productive use of class time, and students will enjoy the social and friendly atmosphere as they exchange ideas and discuss topics in German that are part of the chapter content. Suggestions for group activities are provided in this front section as well as in the annotations throughout this teacher's edition.

Paired Activities

Many activities in each chapter suggest that the class be divided into pairs as smaller groups can maximize their time to practice all language skills, their oral skills in particular. The paired activities come in the form of interviews, question-answers, role-play situations and developed conversations and/or narratives that relate to real-life, and meaningful cultural situations. Paired activities are particularly effective as they (1) increase practice time, (2) provide students with greater self-confidence through less threatening situations, (3) provide a more realistic, communicative setting, (4) increase student involvement and motivation, (5) vary classroom routine, (6) encourage student cooperation with others to achieve goals and (7) allow the teacher to circulate and spot problems. Besides numerous paired activities suggested in the textbook, there are over 100 additional activities in the accompanying Oral Proficiency Evaluation Manual.

TPR Activities

TPR (Total Physical Response) activities encourage students to perform certain tasks after listening to directions given by the teacher or any of the classmates. TPR activities clearly demonstrate the students' understanding when requests are made and students are asked to follow the instructions accordingly. These activities may create some commotion in the classroom since there is a certain amount of student mobility involved. The following is a sample TPR activity:

> Teacher: *Monika, steh auf und geh zu Rainer!*
> (Monika should get up and go to Rainer.)
> *Rainer hat ein Buch. Zeig es der Klasse!*
> (Monika should pick up Rainer's book and show it to the class.)
> *Geh zu dem Stuhl zurück!*
> (Monika should return to her chair.)

The advantage of such a TPR activity is that the student is following directions and physically performs a given task. Such a performance enhances learning and becomes more meaningful in the learning process.

Cross-curricular Activities

A language and culture cannot be isolated in itself, but must be interwoven with other subject areas or curricula that form part of the students' everyday learning experience. As students are exposed to *Deutsch Aktuell*, they will be confronted with topics related not just to the language and culture, but also to various cross-curricular activities that include such subjects as social studies, mathematics, geography, history and psychology. These activities will help maximize and expand global understanding and provide a bridge to further communication that encompasses curricula beyond the German language and culture.

Games

Games can serve as motivational tools that encourage students to participate in fun-filled activities while reviewing and reinforcing previously introduced material. Furthermore, they ensure that communicative competence is achieved and help students to further expand their language skills. Suggested games coordinated with the chapter content are described in the "Teaching Suggestions" of this front section.

Activities for Students with Multiple Intelligences

Every class consists of students with different abilities and learning styles. Consequently, it is important to provide activities that cater to the needs of all students, those who need additional practice and those who want to be challenged more. The teacher will find many such activities, particularly in the sections titled *Praktische Situation, Übung macht den Meister* and *Erweiterung*.

Portfolio Assessment

A portfolio is a systematic and organized collection of evidence used by the teacher and student to monitor growth of a student's knowledge and skills developed in a specific subject area, in this case German. The collected information should include authentic forms of assessment because they represent real learning activities going on in the classroom. Portfolios, similar to performance-based activities, offer a chance to better measure what students really know and can do.

Portfolios should include a random sampling of what students are expected to do at various levels of instruction. They may include oral work that has been recorded (audiocassette) or videotaped (videocassette) to provide information about the students' ability to communicate. Furthermore, portfolios may contain writing samples such as guided or original narratives, and descriptions or observations that recombine, review and expand material learned in the classroom.

A portfolio should be structured both physically and conceptually. The physical structure of the portfolio could include chronological order (listing in sequence of chapters or topics covered). The conceptual structure deals with the goals and functions for student learning. Both physical and conceptual items should be documented by the teacher with selected student work.

Throughout this teacher's edition, specific activities have been noted that are ideal for portfolio assessment. In addition, a separate Portfolio Assessment Manual details how to set up and administer a student's portfolio.

Components

Deutsch Aktuell 1 is the first of a comprehensive three-level German language series designed to meet the needs of language students well into the next century. This first-level textbook program includes the following components:

- Textbook
- Teacher's Edition
- Workbook
- Workbook Teacher's Edition
- Teacher's Resource Kit
  - Listening Activities on Audiocassettes or Audio CDs
  - Listening Activities on Duplicating Masters
  - Written Activities on Duplicating Masters
  - Additional Activities Teacher's Edition (listening and written activities)
  - Workbook Teacher's Edition
  - Audiocassette/CD Program Manual
  - Map of Germany
- Testing/Assessment Program
  - Audiocassettes or Audio CDs (listening comprehension tests)
  - Student Test Booklet
  - Test Booklet Teacher's Edition
  - Oral Proficiency Evaluation
  - Portfolio Assessment
- Audiocassette / CD Program
  - Chapter Audiocassettes or Audio CDs (*Einführung, Kapitel 1-12*)
  - Manual
- Video Program
  - Videos
  - Manual
- Overhead Transparencies
- Computer Software (IBM or Mac)
  - Disks
  - Manual
- CD-ROM (IBM or Mac)

Textbook

This completely revised and rewritten fourth edition textbook contains a total of 13 chapters (*Einführung, Kapitel 1-12*), a grammar summary, an end vocabulary section (German-English and English-German) and an index. All the chapters (except the *Einführung*) have been designed and structured in a similar manner so that students will become accustomed to the various sections and know what to expect.

Chapter Format

Chapter Opener—Preceding the chapter text are two photo-illustrated that visually prepare students, for the general cultural content of the particular chapter. Communicative functions, also listed here, express the tasks that students will be expected to perform.

Dialogs—The chapter begins with short conversations dramatizing situations of interest to students, but also depicting common everyday life in German-speaking countries. The speakers in these dialogs represent a cross section of age groups, although the emphasis is on scenes centered around young adults. At the beginning of each of the first eight chapters (*Kapitel 1-8*) are two dialogs that include different groups of people, whereas each of the last four chapters (*Kapitel 9-12*) has three dialogs that are continuous in theme dealing with the same groups. In all chapters, the short opening dialogs have been divided to ensure better retention and understanding. These mini-dialogs are followed by comprehension check-up activities to measure the students' understanding in a step-by-step manner.

Each dialog has been carefully designed not only to be authentic, but also to include the language structure taught in the chapter. The introduction of new words has been kept to a minimum so that students will not be burdened by excessive vocabulary.

Following the mini-dialogs are various types of activities ranging from questions to recombination narratives, matching, true/false statements or supplying the missing information.

Sprichwort—A proverb ties together the topic of the chapter.

Für dich!—This is a short section pointing out specific language or cultural subtleties that appear in the opening dialogs.

Rollenspiel—A role-playing activity engages students in meaningful conversations that reflect real-life situations.

Aktuelles—There are two such sections in each chapter that present, in a mini-social studies format, a cross-cultural approach. The text is presented in English so that students, from the very beginning, can be exposed to important cultural information. An activity follows each *Aktuelles* section so that students can measure their understanding of the cultural content.

Ergänzung—Two or three of these colorfully illustrated sections appear in each chapter. The accompanying activities reinforce and expand the topic of the chapter theme and provide additional language and cultural information.

Sag's mal!—This feature includes practical, communicative-oriented and up-to-date words and/or expressions selected to highlight the general topic of the chapter. Students are encouraged to make use of these words to express their opinions or feelings on specific and commonly asked questions. Although some of these words and/or expressions are used in context within the chapter, there are several additional phrases that further expand the students' ability to express themselves. These additional vocabulary items are indicated by an asterisk (*).

Sprache—An explanation of the structure or grammar leads off each section followed by oral and written activities illustrating the specific grammar point. Most of the activities that follow the explanation of the language structure have been designed to be communicative in nature for functional and practical application. The *du* form has been used in most activities. The teacher may wish to change the instructions and/or question-answer activities using *Sie*, depending on the circumstances. Each chapter contains two or three *Sprache* sections.

Kombiniere—This activity provides opportunities for students to create sentences using words and phrases in various combinations.

Praktische Situation—This cooperative learning activity involves students in group activities in which they have to create meaningful real-life situations that involve them actively by using the language within a communicative setting.

Lesestück—A reading selection (beginning with *Kapitel 2*) introduces additional cultural situations that occur in everyday German life. These reading passages employ a mixture of narrative or conversational style so that students can effectively use the material to communicate. The new vocabulary is found at the end of each *Lesestück*. New words and phrases are indicated by the degree symbol (°). A variety of different types of activities testing the students' comprehension follow each reading selection.

Willi und Milli—This original cartoon series offers a lighthearted and humorous approach utilizing the vocabulary and structures that can easily be understood.

Übung macht den Meister!—The purpose of this section is to provide students with opportunities to practice their oral skills and to recall information in an open-ended format. The individual tasks challenge and involve students at all ability levels. Students will be able to express themselves with as little or as much vocabulary as their abilities allow, and to expound on given topics in a free and creative manner. Various group activities are encouraged, ranging from pair/role-playing to small and large group activities.

Erweiterung—A variety of additional activities are presented in this section to expand and reinforce the students' understanding of the grammatical and cultural content of the chapter. It also provides numerous opportunities for students to become involved creatively in language expression.

Land und Leute—This reading selection (included in *Kapitel 4, 8, 12*) familiarizes students with geographical and cultural features of Germany, Austria and Switzerland. The new vocabulary, which is indicated by the degree symbol, is found at the end of each section. It is considered passive and, therefore, is important only for reading comprehension but not necessary for effective use in communication oriented activities. Passive words are also indicated in the end-of-book vocabulary by an asterisk. Following these reading selections are activities testing the students' understanding of the content.

Rückblick—The review section (included in *Kapitel 3, 6, 9, 12*) reviews the various grammatical structures learned in previous chapters. The *Rückblick* ensures better retention and reinforcement of previously learned material.

Was weißt du?—This section gives students an opportunity to measure their understanding of the chapter content. It also serves as an excellent review prior to taking the chapter test.

Vokabeln—The vocabulary section gives the students an easy reference source to the new words introduced in each chapter. The plural forms have been listed from the first chapter on, even though the plural as a grammatical structure is not formally introduced until *Kapitel 5*. The vocabulary meaning is confined strictly to the context in which it is used in that particular chapter. In cases where the meaning of the same German word changes, the word is listed again in subsequent chapters. All words at the end of each chapter are intended as active vocabulary.

Grammar Summary—The grammar introduced in this book has been summarized in this section for convenient reference.

End Vocabulary—The complete vocabulary is listed here for easy reference. Each word or phrase is followed by a number indicating the chapter in which it appears for the first time. For convenient and flexible use, both German-English and English-German vocabularies are included. New passive vocabulary items, usually following the *Land und Leute* reading section, are marked by an asterisk in the end-of-book vocabulary.

Index—A complete index of all the grammar and cultural material is provided at the end of the book for easy reference to the chapter in which they were introduced.

Teacher's Edition

This teacher's edition contains the following sections:

Front Section

- scope and sequence chart
- philosophy and goals
- description of all textbook components

- teaching approaches of model chapter for 50-minute periods and 90-minute block schedule
- classroom expressions (including those listed in the *Einführung* of the student edition)
- useful addresses for organizations representing German-speaking countries
- teaching suggestions (including *Allerlei*—suggested games, activities and projects)

Text Annotations and References

Numerous suggestions for variation, expansion and reinforcement have been provided for practical and functional classroom use of the material presented.

An audiocassette/CD symbol is printed for all those sections recorded on the audiocassette/audio CD program for convenient reference. Although the text for these oral activities is contained in the textbook itself, a separate manual accompanying the audiocassettes and audio CDs is available including the additional text for student-directed instructions.

The following ancillaries have been cross-referenced and marked with icons that indicate the most convenient place to use these supplementary materials, wherever appropriate:

AC/CD Audiocassette/CD Program   **OT** Overhead Transparency

WB Workbook   **VP** Video Program

LA Listening Activity   **S** Computer Software (IBM or Mac)

WA Written Activity   **TP** Testing/Assessment Program

OP Oral Proficiency Evaluation   **CD-ROM** CD-ROM (IBM or Mac)

PA Portfolio Assessment

For example, the reference " **WB** , Activity 1" located in the margin means that Workbook Activity 1 is used best in connection with this particular section.

Scope and Sequence

The scope and sequence chart lists the main topics (functional, cultural and grammatical) presented in each chapter.

Philosophy and Goals

The philosophy and goals outline the various techniques, strategies and activities employed in providing students with valuable tools that will make the language come alive in the classroom.

Description of Components

A detailed description of all the components accompanying *Deutsch Aktuell 1* informs teachers of the type of support available in successfully implementing this program.

Teaching Approaches of Model Chapter

50-Minute Periods

Many school districts center around 45- to 55-minute periods. The first chart (pages TE24-25) following this section provides a detailed outline for spreading a complete chapter (*Kapitel 3*) over a period, utilizing the specified time frame.

Block Scheduling

Many school districts have implemented a block scheduling system that can include blocks of time ranging from 75- to 110-minute periods. Furthermore, block schedules can involve consecutive days for a whole semester, alternate days for a year or many other variations. Our model (pages TE26-27) is based on a 90-minute class period.

Classroom Expressions

We recommend that the teacher employ a communication-oriented approach using such methods as TPR (Total Physical Response). Although the textbook includes an abundance of such activities, the suggested classroom phrases should be used right from the beginning so that students become accustomed to phrases and expressions that will become part of the daily language experience. Thus, we have listed some of the most frequently used expressions in this front section as well as in the *Einführung* in the textbook.

Useful Names and Addresses

Many of the listed organizations (pages TE30-33) representing the German-speaking countries (Germany, Austria, and Switzerland) will assist teachers by providing information, free materials and so on.

Teaching Suggestions

This section includes the *Allerlei* section which, offers a variety of creative classroom activities such as games, and individual and group performances. These activities play an important part in ensuring that students achieve communicative competence. Individual and group projects also help ensure that students can further expand their language skills.

Workbook

The workbook reviews, reinforces and expands the material covered in the textbook. The various activities are coordinated with the chapter content and, therefore, follow the same sequence. Additional activities provide the students with opportunities to test their understanding of authentic realia collected in Germany, Austria and Switzerland. Students should be made aware that they do not have to understand every word, but simply should get the gist or idea of the material presented. A crossword puzzle, the culminating activity of each chapter, reviews contextually some of the key vocabulary from the chapter. This teacher's edition also makes reference to the individual workbook activities as they relate to the textbook material.

Workbook Teacher's Edition

A teacher's edition to the workbook containing the answer key is also available.

Teacher's Resource Kit

The teacher's resource kit puts a variety of useful materials right at the teacher's fingertips and assists him or her in daily lesson planning. The following components are part of the resource kit:

Listening Activities on Audiocassettes or Audio CDs

These listening activities are an excellent bridge to the numerous listening and oral activities in the textbook. In addition, they will prepare students for communicating well in the classroom, and ultimately for the listening tests that are part of the testing/assessment program.

Listening Activities on Duplicating Masters

These activities for additional listening comprehension offer students an opportunity to test their understanding of vocabulary and structure-controlled material in an authentic setting. Students can follow along on sheets. These activities are used in conjunction with the audiocassettes/audio CDs.

Written Activities on Duplicating Masters

Additional written activities are provided for convenient and flexible use. There are about 12 activities per chapter, which are coordinated and sequenced with the chapter content.

Additional Activities Teacher's Edition

A complete answer key is also available for the recorded listening comprehension activities as well as for the written activities.

Workbook Teacher's Edition

This student annotated edition includes the answers to all the workbook activities.

Audiocassette/CD Program Manual

This manual contains the complete script to the recorded material from the introductory chapter *(Einführung)* and Chapters 1-12 *(Kapitel 1-12)*. Furthermore, this manual also includes the timings for all the recorded audiocassette and audio CD sections.

Map of Germany

A map of German-speaking countries is an important part of this program. It represents the various geographical features discussed in *Deutsch Aktuell*. This map is especially useful for geographical review and discussion in conjunction with the various chapter activities and the *Land und Leute* reading sections.

Testing/Assessment Program

The testing/assessment program includes audiocassettes or audio CDs, a student test booklet, a test booklet teacher's edition, an oral proficiency evaluation, and portfolio assessment.

Audiocassettes or Audio CDs

The audiocassettes or audio CDs present the recorded sound track for the listening comprehension tests.

Student Test Booklet

End-of-Chapter Tests

The test booklet contains two sections: (1) the student answer sheets for the listening comprehension tests, and (2) the written tests for each chapter. For convenience and ease of scoring, the two tests (listening comprehension and written) for each chapter total 100 points. These tests should be given after the completion of each chapter. Students use the answer sheets while listening to the audiocassettes or audio CDs, which direct them step-by-step to follow along and complete specific tasks as described. The test activities include true/false *(ja/nein)* and other multiple-choice statements as well as fill-in-the-blank sections based on the recorded material. Wherever appropriate, picture cues further assist students to select appropriate choices as directed by the speakers. The written tests are intended to measure the students' understanding of the language and cultural content of each chapter.

Achievement Tests

There are two achievement tests included in the testing program. Achievement Test I follows *Kapitel 6*, and Achievement Test II follows *Kapitel 12*. The tests contain 150 points each and should be given at the end of the semester. The material covered in the achievement tests focuses on the previous six chapters and tests the students' understanding of that material. Both listening comprehension and written tests are included.

Test Booklet Teacher's Edition

This teacher's edition includes a complete answer key to the listening comprehension (including audiocassette/audio CD script) and written tests (Chapters 1-12 and Achievement Tests I and II).

Oral Proficiency Evaluation

Various oral activities for each chapter are coordinated with the chapter content and measure proficiency in the communicative functions. Their flexibility allows them to be used during regular class sessions and provides additional paired or small group practice. There are three basic types of oral proficiency activities: oral interview, paired role-play situations and visual identification and description or discussion.

Portfolio Assessment

Portfolio assessment materials are designed to evaluate and assess student performance. The communicative functions at the beginning of each chapter can be used as goals against which the student's progress can be measured. This manual provides valuable information for evaluating and assessing student performance.

Audiocassette/CD Program

The audiocassette/CD program is an integral part of *Deutsch Aktuell 1*. The audiocassettes/CDs are coordinated with the *Einführung* (introduction) and Chapters 1-12. The recorded material for all chapters has been indicated by an audiocassette/CD symbol. Numerous opportunities are provided for students to be actively involved in practicing the material as presented in the textbook. A separate manual containing the text of the audiocassettes/CDs is also available.

Video Program

Filmed on location in Berlin, Germany, with professional actors, these live-action videos are carefully coordinated with the vocabulary and language structure of the twelve chapters, thus enabling students to understand authentic situations of everyday German life. A continuous story line weaves throughout the various episodes. Students will follow and identify with the characters as they encounter various experiences. A separate manual contains the printed video text as well as many additional activities.

Overhead Transparencies

A set of full-color overhead transparencies, coordinated with the 12 chapters, is also available. Many of these transparencies depict real-life situations and challenge students to describe, act out or narrate the scene as shown. Other transparencies can be used in a flexible manner, either reviewing or reinforcing the chapter material.

Computer Software

A software program (IBM and Mac), ideal for reviewing, reinforcing and expanding upon the grammatical information, is available. An accompanying manual provides additional details on effective program use.

CD-ROM

This innovative interactive multimedia program is designed to enhance the language skills within a functional and cultural context. As journalistic interns for a publication, students enter a microworld of German-speaking countries. In this microworld, students face the many communicative challenges of news reporters. Also included are learner and teacher reports that assess students' proficiency in the language. Authentic video clips of German speakers engage students in verbal conversations on a variety of topics. An innovative recording feature allows students to record the entire conversation for playback. The students' vocabulary and fluency improves as they become immersed in authentic, animated conversations. An abundance of geographic, historic and cultural information further expands the students' understanding of German-speaking countries.

Teaching Approaches of Model Chapter

Because instructional objectives and the length of classes vary greatly, and since ability levels among students are usually considerably different within one class, it would be impossible to provide a detailed lesson plan that would suit all teachers and students using *Deutsch Aktuell*.

Based on a national survey, class length can vary anywhere from 40 to 110 minutes. Consequently, two different plans have been provided based on a 50-minute class period as well as on a block schedule system with a 90-minute class period.

This Teacher's Edition contains correlationss of all the ancillary materials to the textbook (audiocassettes/CDs; workbook; additional activities on duplicating masters; oral proficiency evaluation; portfolio assessment; overhead transparencies; video program; computer software; testing/assessment program, and CD-ROM program). These notations occur in the text once all information necessary to complete a specific activity has been presented. They are numbered consecutively in the textbook. However, the model chapter plan (written with attention to variety and reentry) does not necessarily refer to these activities in the sequence in which they appear in the text.

Regular Class Period (50 minutes)

	Textbook	Support Materials

Day 1	Review: *Kapitel 2*
	Chapter Focus: Discussion of chapter opener, pp. 66-67
	Dialog 1: *Heike möchte zum Rockkonzert*, p. 68
	    Activities 1-2, p. 69
	Ergänzung: Was machst du gern?, p. 74
	    Activities 6-7, pp. 75-76
		AC/CD, Dialog 1
		AC/CD, Activity 1
		AC/CD, *Ergänzung*
		AC/CD, Activities 6-7
		Workbook, Activities 3-4
		Listening Activity 1
		Written Activity 3
		Oral Proficiency Evaluation, Activity 2

Day 2	Review: Dialog 1, p. 68
	    Ergänzung: Was machst du gern?, p. 74
	Activity 8, p. 76
	Dialog 2: *Sie hören CDs und Kassetten*, p. 69
	    Activities 3-4, p. 70
	
	Sprichwort, p. 70
	Für dich, p. 71
	Aktuelles: Youth Activities, pp. 72-73
	Was passt hier?, p. 73
		AC/CD, Dialog 1
		AC/CD, *Ergänzung*
		Overhead Transparency 22
		AC/CD, Dialog 2
		AC/CD, Activity 3
		Workbook, Activities 1-2
		Written Activity 1
		Oral Proficiency Evaluation, Activity 1
		Overhead Transparencies 23-24
		
		Written Activity 2

Day 3	Review: Dialogs 1-2, pp. 68-69 *Rollenspiel*, p. 71 Activity 5, p. 71 *Sag's mal!: Wie ist die Rockmusik?*, p. 77 *Übung macht den Meister!:* Activity 1, p. 89 *Sprache:* Present Tense of *haben*, p. 78 Activities 9-10, pp. 78-79	AC/CD, Dialogs 1-2 AC/CD, Activity 5 AC/CD, *Sag's mal!* Oral Proficiency Evaluation, Activity 8 AC/CD, Activities 9-10 Workbook, Activity 5 Written Activity 4 Computer Software, Activity 2
Day 4	Review: *Sprache*, p. 78 *Praktische Situation*, p. 77 *Kombiniere:* Activity 11, p. 79 *Ergänzung: Wie viel Uhr ist es?*, pp. 80-81 Class Activity: *Wie viel Uhr ist es?*, p. TE37	AC/CD, *Ergänzung* Workbook, Activities 6-7 Written Activity 5 Oral Proficiency Evaluation, Activities 4-5 Overhead Transparencies 25-26
Day 5	Review: *Ergänzung: Wie viel Uhr ist es?*, pp. 80-81 *Übung macht den Meister!:* Activity 2, p. 89 *Sprache:* Word Order, p. 81 Activities 12-14, pp. 82-84 Game: *Ratet mal!*, p. TE37	AC/CD, Activities 12 and 14 Workbook, Activity 8 Computer Software, Activity 4

	Textbook	Support Materials

Day 6	Review: Word Order, p. 81
	Lesestück: Bastian und Uli gehen nach Hause, pp. 85-86
	          Activities 16-17, p. 87
	
	Willi und Milli, p. 88
	Ergänzung: cities and directions, p. 88
	          Activities 18-19, p. 89
		AC/CD, *Lesestück*
		AC/CD, Activity 17
		Workbook, Activities 10-12
		Listening Activity 2
		Written Activity 6
		Video Program (including activities)
		
		AC/CD, *Ergänzung*
		AC/CD, Activity18
		Workbook, Activities 13-14
		Computer Software, Activity 3

Day 7	Review: *Ergänzung*: cities and directions, p. 88
	
	Sprache: zu Hause and *nach Hause*, p. 84
	          Activity 15, p. 84
	
	Übung macht den Meister!: Activities 3-4, p. 89
	
	Erweiterung: Activity 20, p. 93
		Listening Activity 3
		Written Activity 7
		Oral Proficiency Evaluation,
		     Activities 3 and 6
		Workbook, Activity 9
		AC/CD, Activity 15
		Oral Proficiency Evaluation, Activity 7
		Computer Software, Activity 5
		Oral Proficiency Evaluation, Activity 9
		Workbook, Activity 15
		AC/CD, Activity 20
		Workbook, Activities 16-18

Day 8	Review: Telling time and geographic locations, *Ergänzung*, pp. 80 and 88 *Aktuelles:* Leisure-Time Activities, pp. 90-91 *Was passt hier?*, p. 92 *Praktische Situation*, p. 92 *Erweiterung:* Activities 21-22, pp. 93-94	Listening Activity 4 Written Activities 8-10 Video Program (including activities)
Day 9	Review: Leisure-Time Activities, pp. 90-91 *Erweiterung:* Activities 23-24, p. 94 Class Activity: German Popular Music, pp. TE37 *Rückblick:* Activities 1-3, pp. 95-96	Oral Proficiency Evaluation, Activity 10 Computer Software, Activity 1
Day 10	Review: Time expressions, p. 80 *Rückblick:* Activities 4-7, pp. 96-99	Workbook, Activity 19 Written Activity 11 Computer Software, Activity 6 Video Program (including activities)
Day 11	Review: All *Erweiterung* and *Rückblick* sections, pp. 93-99 *Was weißt du?*, p. 100 Review: Complete chapter including *Vokabeln*	Portfolio Assessment
Day 12	Chapter Test Student Test Booklet, Test Booklet Teacher's Edition, Audiocassette/CD (including listening comprehension tests), Oral Proficiency Evaluation Manual, Portfolio Assessment	

Block Schedule (90 minutes)

	Textbook	Support Materials
Day 1	Review: *Kapitel 2* Chapter Focus: Discussion of chapter opener, pp. 66-67 Dialog 1: *Heike möchte zum Rockkonzert*, p. 68 　　　Activities 1-2, p. 69 *Ergänzung: Was machst du gern?*, p. 74 　　　Activities 6-7, pp. 75-76 *Sprichwort*, p. 70 *Für dich*, p. 71 *Aktuelles:* Youth Activities, pp. 72-73 *Was passt hier?*, p. 73	AC/CD, Dialog 1 AC/CD, Activity 1 AC/CD, *Ergänzung* AC/CD, Activities 6-7 Workbook, Activities 3-4 Listening Activity 1 Written Activity 3 Oral Proficiency Evaluation, Activity 2 Written Activity 2
Day 2	Review:　Dialog 1, p. 68 　　　*Ergänzung: Was machst du gern?*, p. 74 Activity 8, p. 76 Dialog 2:　*Sie hören CDs und Kassetten*, p. 69 　　　Activities 3-4, p. 70 *Rollenspiel*, p. 71 Activity 5, p. 71 *Sag's mal!: Wie ist die Rockmusik?*, p. 77 *Übung macht den Meister!:* Activity 1, p. 89 *Sprache:* Present Tense of *haben*, p. 78 　　　Activities 9-10, pp. 78-79	AC/CD, Dialog 1 AC/CD, *Ergänzung* Overhead Transparencies 23-24 AC/CD, Dialog 2 AC/CD, Activity 3 Workbook, Activities 1-2 Written Activity 1 Oral Proficiency Evaluation, Activity 1 Overhead Transparency 22 AC/CD, Activity 5 AC/CD, *Sag's mal!* Oral Proficiency Evaluation, Activity 8 AC/CD, Activities 9-10 Workbook, Activity 5 Written Activity 4 Computer Software, Activity 2
Day 3	Review: Dialogs 1-2, pp. 68-69 　　　*Sprache*, p. 78 *Praktische Situation*, p. 77 *Kombiniere:* Activity 11, p. 79 *Ergänzung: Wie viel Uhr ist es?*, pp. 80-81 *Lesestück: Bastian und Uli gehen nach Hause*, pp. 85-86 　　　Activities 16-17, p. 87 Class Activity: *Wie viel Uhr ist es?*, p. TE37 *Übung macht den Meister!:* Activity 2, p. 89 *Sprache:* Word Order, p. 81 　　　Activities 12-14, pp. 82-84 Game: *Ratet mal!*, p. TE37	AC/CD, Dialogs 1-2 AC/CD, *Ergänzung* Workbook, Activities 6-7 Written Activity 5 Oral Proficiency Evaluation, Activities 4-5 Overhead Transparencies 25-26 AC/CD, *Lesestück* AC/CD, Activity 17 Workbook, Activities 10-12 Listening Activity 2 Written Activity 6 Video Program (including activities) AC/CD, Activities 12 and 14 Workbook, Activity 8 Computer Software, Activity 4

	Textbook	Support Materials

Day 4	Review: *Ergänzung: Wie viel Uhr ist es?*, pp. 80-81
	    Word Order, p. 81
	Willi und Milli, p. 88
	Ergänzung: cities and directions, p. 88
	    Activities 18-19, p. 89
	
	Sprache: zu Hause and *nach Hause*, p. 84
	    Activity 15, p. 84
	
	Übung macht den Meister!: Activities 3-4, p. 89
	
	Erweiterung, Activity 20, p. 93
		AC/CD, *Ergänzung*
		AC/CD, Activity 18
		Workbook, Activities 13-14
		Computer Software, Activity 3
		Workbook, Activity 9
		AC/CD, Activity 15
		Oral Proficiency Evaluation, Activity 7
		Computer Software, Activity 5
		Oral Proficiency Evaluation, Activity 9
		Workbook, Activity 15
		AC/CD, Activity 20
		Workbook, Activities 16-18

Day 5	Review: *Ergänzung:* cities and directions, p. 88 Telling time and geographic locations, *Ergänzung*, pp. 80 and 88 *Aktuelles:* Leisure-Time Activities, pp. 90-92 *Was passt hier?*, p. 92 *Erweiterung*, Activities 23-24, p. 94 *Praktische Situation*, p. 92 *Erweiterung:* Activities 21-22, pp. 93-94 Class Activity: German Popular Music, p. TE37 *Rückblick:* Activities 1-3, p. 95-96	Listening Activity 3 Written Activity 7 Oral Proficiency Evaluation, Activities 3 & 6 Oral Proficiency Evaluation, Activity 10 Listening Activity 4 Written Activities 8-10 Computer Software, Activity 1 Video Program (including activities)
Day 6	Review: Time expressions, p. 80 *Rückblick:* Activities 4-7, pp. 96-99 Review: All *Erweiterung* and *Rückblick* sections, pp. 93-99 *Was weißt du?*, p. 100	Workbook, Activity 19 Written Activity 11 Computer Software, Activity 6 Portfolio Assessment Video Program (including activities)
Day 7	Review: Highlights of chapter Chapter Test Student Test Booklet, Test Booklet Teacher's Edition, Audiocassette/CD, Oral Proficiency Evaluation Manual, Portfolio Assessment	

Classroom Expressions

From the first day of instruction, the teacher may want to introduce students to frequently used classroom expressions so that students get used to the spoken language right away. The following is a suggested list (including those listed in the *Einführung* of the student textbook) of some of the more useful expressions:

Hört (gut) zu!	Listen (well!)
Wiederholt!	Repeat!
Alle zusammen!	Everybody!
Noch einmal!	Once more!
Lauter, bitte!	Louder, please!
Passt auf!	Pay attention!
Antwortet!	Answer!
Beantwortet die/diese Frage!	Answer the/this question!
Fragt!	Ask!
Macht eure Bücher auf, Seite...!	Open your books to page...!
Macht eure Hefte auf, Seite...!	Open your notebooks/workbooks to page...!
Nehmt ein Stück Papier 'raus!	Take out a sheet of paper!
Nehmt einen Bleistift oder Kuli!	Take a pencil or pen!
Schreibt!	Write!
Lest!	Read!
Fangt jetzt an!	Start now!
Weiter.	Continue.
Macht eure Bücher zu!	Close your books!
Macht eure Hefte zu!	Close your notebooks/workbooks!
Geht an die Tafel!	Go to the board!
Seht an die Tafel!	Look at the board!
Schreibt...an die Tafel!	Write...on the board!
Seht mich an!	Look at me!
Seht euch den Videoteil (die Bildfolien) an!	Look at the video segment! (overhead transparencies)!
Steckt die Diskette in den Computer!	Insert the diskette into the computer!
Das ist richtig.	That's right.
Das ist falsch.	That's wrong.
Das ist sehr gut.	That's very good.
Gut.	Good.

Prima.	Great.
Ausgezeichnet.	Excellent.
Wo ist der Fehler?	Where's the mistake?
Buchstabiert das!	Spell that!
Wie heißt das auf Deutsch (Englisch)?	What is that in German (English)?
Danke.	Thank you.
Hausaufgaben/Schularbeit.	Homework.
Für morgen...	For tomorrow...
Gebt mir eure Hausaufgaben! (Schularbeit)!	Give me your homework!
Wir schreiben eine Klassenarbeit.	We're having a test.
Wer weiß es?	Who knows it?
Auf Deutsch, bitte!	In German, please.
Seid ihr fertig?	Are you finished?
Ruhe, bitte.	Quiet, please.

To express themselves in class, students may want to learn the following basic expressions.

Ich weiß es nicht.	I don't know.
Nochmal, bitte.	Repeat, please.
Ich verstehe das nicht.	I don't understand that.
Was bedeutet...?	What does...mean?
Wie sagt man...?	How do you say...?
Ich habe eine Frage.	I have a question.

Useful Names and Addresses

A number of organizations provide assistance to students and teachers in matters relating to German-speaking countries. This assistance ranges from answering questions about entry of the country (embassies/consulate general) to supplying travel information, brochures and posters (tourist offices). The list below represents some of the more important sources of contact. There also may be additional local or regional organizations in your area. Contact any of the following organizations for specific information.

Germany

Embassy of the Federal Republic of Germany
Attn.: Cultural Section
4645 Reservoir Road NW
Washington, D.C. 20007-1998
Phone: (202) 298-4000
Fax: (202) 298-4317
e-mail: ge-embus@ix.netcom.com

∎∎∎

Regional Consulates:

Consulate General of the Federal Republic of Germany
Marquis Two Tower, Suite 901
Peachtree Center Avenue NE
Atlanta, GA 30303-1221
Phone: (404) 659-4760
Fax: (404) 659-1280

Consular district: Alabama, Georgia, Mississippi, North Carolina, South Carolina, Tennessee

∎∎∎

Consulate General of the Federal Republic of Germany
100 N. Biscayne Boulevard
Miami, FL 33132
Phone: (305) 358-0290
Fax: (305) 358-0307

Consular district: Florida, Puerto Rico and the Virgin Islands

∎∎∎

Consulate General of the Federal Republic of Germany
Three Copley Place, Suite 500
Boston, MA 02116
Phone: (617) 536-4414
Fax: (617) 536-8573

Consular district: Connecticut (with the exception of Fairfield County), Maine, Massachusetts, New Hampshire, Rhode Island, Vermont

Consulate General of the Federal Republic of Germany
676 N. Michigan Avenue, Suite 3200
Chicago, IL 60611
Phone: (312) 580-1190
Fax: (312) 580-0099

Consular district: Illinois, Iowa, Kansas, Minnesota, Missouri, Nebraska, North Dakota, South Dakota, Wisconsin

∎∎∎

Consulate General of the Federal Republic of Germany
Edison Plaza, Suite 2100
660 Plaza Drive
Detroit, MI 48226-1271
Phone: (313) 962-6526
Fax: (313) 962-7345

Consular district: Indiana, Kentucky, Michigan, Ohio

∎∎∎

Consulate General of the Federal Republic of Germany
1330 Post Oak Boulevard, Suite 1850
Houston, TX 77056-3018
Phone: (713) 627-7770/71
Fax: (713) 627-0506

Consular district: Arkansas, Louisiana, New Mexico, Oklahoma, Texas

∎∎∎

Consulate General of the Federal Republic of Germany
6222 Wilshire Boulevard, Suite 500
Los Angeles, CA 90048
Phone: (213) 930-2703
Fax: (213) 930-2805

Consular district: Arizona; California counties of Imperial, Kern, Los Angeles, Orange, Riverside, San Bernardino, San Diego, San Louis Obispo, Santa Barbara, Ventura

Consulate General of the Federal Republic of Germany
460 Park Avenue, 18th Floor
New York, NY 10022
Phone: (212) 308-8700
Fax: (212) 308-3422

Consular district: Connecticut (Fairfield County only), New Jersey, New York, Pennsylvania

■■■

Consulate General of the Federal Republic of Germany
1960 Jackson Street
San Francisco, CA 94109-1061
Phone: (415) 775-1061
Fax: (415) 775-0187
Consular district: California (excluding counties listed above under Los Angeles consulate), Colorado, Hawaii, Nevada, Utah, Wyoming, Island of Canton, Midway Islands

Consulate General of the Federal Republic of Germany
2500 One Union Square Building
600 University Street
Seattle, WA 98101
Phone: (206) 682-4312
Fax: (206) 682-3724

Consular district: Alaska, Idaho, Montana, Oregon, Washington

■■■

(assisting with travel plans)
German National Tourist Office
122 East 42nd Street
New York, NY 10168
Phone: (212) 661-7200
Fax: (212) 661-7174

German National Tourist Office
11766 Wilshire Blvd., Suite 750
Los Angeles, CA 90025
Phone: (310) 575-9799
Fax: (310) 575-1565

(providing information and materials)
German Information Center
950 Third Avenue
New York, NY 10022
Phone: (212) 888-9840
Fax: (212) 752-6691

Deutsche Zentrale für Tourismus
e.V. (DZT)
Beethovenstr. 69
60325 Frankfurt (Main)
Germany

(providing political & general information)
Inter Nationes
Kennedyallee 91-103
53175 Bonn
Germany

(providing information on German government)
Presse- und Informationsamt der Bundesregierung (BPA)
Auslandsabteilung
Friedrich-Ebert-Allee 45
53113 Bonn
Germany

(providing information on the postal system)
Deutsche Bundespost
Posttechnisches Zentralamt
Postfach 1180
64283 Darmstadt
Germany

(providing tickets and flight information on Lufthansa routes)
Lufthansa German Airlines
680 5th Avenue
New York, NY 10019
Phone: 1-800-645-3880

(providing professional service and information to German teachers)
American Association of Teachers of German, Inc. (AATG)
112 Heddentowne Court, Suite 104
Cherry Hill, NJ 08034
Phone: (609) 795-5553
Fax: (609) 795-9398
e-mail:
73740.32310@Compuserve.com

(providing information about Germany, strengthening cultural ties between Germany and the U.S., and promoting the teaching of the German language)

Goethe House Milwaukee
814 W. Wisconsin Avenue
Milwaukee, WI 53233
Phone: (414) 276-7435
Fax: (312) 329-2487
(Chicago area)

Goethe House New York
1014 Fifth Avenue
New York, NY 10028
Phone: (212) 439-8700
            (general information)
Fax: (212) 439-8705
e-mail:
ghny@goethenewyork.org
(director)

Goethe-Institut Ann Arbor
City Center Building, Suite 210
220 E. Huron
Ann Arbor, MI 48104
Phone: (313) 996-8600
Fax: (313) 996-0777
e-mail:
goethe@goethe-annarbor.org

Goethe-Institut Atlanta
Colony Square, Plaza Level
1197 Peachtree Street NE
Atlanta, GA 30361-2401
Phone: (404) 892-2388
Fax: (404) 892-3832
e-mail: goethe@post-peach.net

Goethe-Institut Boston
170 Beacon Street
Boston, MA 02116
Phone: (617) 262-6050
Fax: (617) 262-2615
e-mail:
100627.1010@compuserve.com

Goethe-Institut Chicago
401 N. Michigan Avenue
Chicago, IL 60611
Phone: (312) 329-0915
              (general information)
Fax: (312) 329-2487
e-mail: goethe@interaccess.com
              (director)

Goethe-Institut Cincinnati
559 Liberty Hill
Cincinnati, OH 45210-1548
Phone: (513) 721-2777
Fax: (513) 721-4136
e-mail: goethe@uc.edu

Goethe-Institut Houston
3120 Southwest Freeway, Suite 100
Houston, TX 77098
Phone: (713) 528-2787
              (general information)
Fax: (713) 528-4023
e-mail: goethehou@aol.com
              (director)

Goethe-Institut Los Angeles
5700 Wilshire Boulevard, Suite 110
Los Angeles, CA 90036
Phone: (213) 525-3388
Fax: (213) 934-3597
e-mail: vclark@artnet.net
              (director)

Goethe-Institut St. Louis
326 N. Euclid Avenue
St. Louis, MO 63108
Phone: (314) 367-2452
Fax: (314) 367-9439
e-mail: goethcsl@attmail.com

Goethe-Institut San Francisco
530 Bush Street
San Francisco, CA 94108
Phone: (415) 391-0370
              (general information)
Fax: (415) 391-8715
e-mail: gisfprog@aol.com
(director)

Goethe-Institut Seattle
605 First Avenue, Suite 401
Seattle, WA 98104
Phone: (206) 622-9694
Fax: (206) 623-7930
e-mail: goethe@eskimo.com
              (director)

Goethe-Institut Washington
810 Seventh Street NW
Washington, D.C. 20001
Phone: (202) 289-1200
Fax: (202) 289-3535
e-mail: goethedc@artswire.org

*(assisting in student exchange
programs)*
German American Partnership
Program (GAPP)
c/o Goethe House New York
1014 Fifth Avenue
New York, NY 10028
Phone: (212) 439-8700
Fax: (212) 439-8705

AFS Intercultural Programs/USA
220 E. 42nd Street
New York, NY 10017
Phone: (212) 949-4242
Fax: (212) 949-9379

Youth for Understanding (YFU)
3501 Newark Street NW
Washington, D.C. 20016
Phone: (202) 966-6800
Fax: (202) 895-1104

Informationsbüro für deutsch-
amerikanischen Austausch
Hechtgraben 6-8
14195 Berlin
Germany

Informationsbüro für den deutsch-
amerikanischen Jugendaustausch
auf kommunaler Ebene (YOU)
Berliner Promenade 15
66111 Saarbrücken
Germany

Gesellschaft für internationale
Jugendkontakte (GIJK)
Ubierstr. 94
53173 Bonn
Germany

Pädagogischer Austauschdienst
(PAD)
Nassestr. 8
53113 Bonn
Germany

The Congress-Bundestag Youth
Exchange Program
3501 Newark Street, NW
Washington, D.C. 20016
Phone: (202) 966-6800
Fax: (202) 895-1104

German Academic Exchange
Service (DAAD)
950 Third Avenue, 19th Floor
New York, NY 10022
Phone: (212) 758-3223
Fax: (212) 755-5780
e-mail: daadny@daad.org
Website: http://www.daad.org

Open Door Student Exchanges
839D Stewart Avenue
Garden City, NY 11530
Phone: (516) 745-6232
Fax: (516) 745-6233

Organisation für Internationale
Kontakte (OIK)
Alte Bahnhofstr. 26
53173 Bonn
Germany

Partnership International e.V. (PI)
Frankstr. 26
50676 Köln
Germany

NACEL Cultural Exchanges
3460 Washington Drive, Suite 109
St. Paul, MN 55122
Phone: (612) 686-0080
Fax: (612) 686-9601

*(providing opportunities to
communicate with pen pals)*
Euro-Briefclub "Der Blütenzweig"
Enniskiller Str. 130
33647 Bielefeld
Germany

Internationaler Katholischer
Korrespondenz- und
Austauschdienst Veilchenweg 2
66798 Wallerfangen
Germany

People-to-People International
Letter Exchange Program
501 E. Armour Boulevard
Kansas City, MO 64109
Phone: (816) 531-4701
Fax: (816) 561-7502

Student Letter Exchange
Attn.: Mary or Wayne Dankert
215 Fifth Avenue SE
Waseca, MN 56093
Phone: (212) 557-3312
          (New York office)
Fax: (507) 835-3217

World Pen Pals
International Institute of Minnesota
1694 Como Avenue
St. Paul, MN 55108
Phone: (612) 647-0191
Fax: (612) 647-9268

(providing information on camping)
Deutscher Camping-Club e.V.
Postfach 400428
Mandlstraße 28
80802 München
Germany

*(providing information on youth
hostels)*
Deutsches Jugendherbergswerk
Bismarckstr. 8
32756 Detmold
Germany

*(offering magazine of interest to
teenagers)*
JUMA (Das Jugendmagazin)
Frankfurter Str. 40
51065 Köln
Germany

Austria

Embassy of Austria
2343 Massachusetts Avenue NW
Washington, D.C. 20008
Phone: (202) 895-6700
Fax: (202) 895-6747

(providing travel information)
Austrian National Tourist Office
PO Box 1142
Timesquare, NY 10110
Phone: (212) 944-6880
Fax: (212) 730-4568

*(providing brochures and cultural
information)*
Austrian Institute
11 E. 52nd Street
New York, NY 10022
Phone: (212) 759-5165
Fax: (212) 319-9636

Switzerland

Embassy of Switzerland
2900 Cathedral Avenue NW
Washington, D.C. 20008
Phone: (202) 745-7900
Fax: (202) 387-2564

*(providing travel information and
materials)*
Swiss Tourism
608 Fifth Avenue
New York, NY 10020-2303
Phone: (212) 757-5944
Fax: (212) 262-6116
Website:
http://www.switzerlandtourism.ch/na
Switzerland Tourism
150 N. Michigan Avenue, Suite 2930
Chicago, IL 60601-7525
Phone: (312) 332-9900
Fax: (212) 262-6116
Automated Fax: (212) 757-4733
Website:http://
www.switzerlandtourism.ch

Switzerland Tourism
737 N. Michigan Avenue, Suite 2301
Chicago, IL 60611
Phone: (312) 915-0061
Fax: (312) 915-0388

*(providing tickets and flight
information on Swiss Airlines route)*
Swissair Airlines
Chicago Office
150 N. Michigan Avenue, Suite 2900
Chicago, IL 60601
Phone: 1-800- 221-4750

Teaching Suggestions

Einführung

ALLERLEI

1. Game—*Tippen*

You might play this game, using the vocabulary from the introductory chapter, once you have presented the German alphabet and the class has practiced it. Use the *Alphabet* section for practice. The *Tippen* (typing/keyboarding) game strengthens spelling accuracy in German. To set up the game, divide the class into two teams. Then assign a letter of the alphabet—including letters *ä, ö, ü* and *ß*—to members of each team. Make sure that each team has enough members to represent the entire alphabet. If the class is small, then assign several letters to each player.

Start the game by giving one team a word from the chapter to spell orally. They must spell out the word so quickly that they sound like they are typing the word on a computer keyboard. You may set a time limit for calling out letters, say one or two seconds. Let's take one example. The word is *heißen*. The student with the letter *h* calls out that letter in German and teammates with the appropriate letters complete, in turn, the spelling of *heißen*. By doing this, the team earns one point. Then the other team gets their shot at a word. Whenever a team fails, its rival gets a chance to spell the word and win another point. The game can last as long as you allow it to go on.

2. Game—*Buchstabiert es*!

Divide the class into teams. Each team challenges the other(s) by asking them to spell a word. At first, you may want to limit each word to five or six letters.

3. Class Activity—Greetings

Divide the class into small groups (two to four students) and have them practice the expressions from this chapter: *Tag!, Wie heißt du (er, sie)?, Wer ist das?, Wie alt bist du?*, and so on.

Kapitel 1

ALLERLEI

1. Game—*Woher kommst du?*

Prepare an index card for every student. Write a name and a location on each card and give one to each student. Instruct your students that they will assume the identity of the person on the card and that they are from the city as noted on the card. After students have learned their name and city of origin, all cards are collected. Then pass out a sheet to each student that lists all of the names (on the cards) in alphabetical order. You may want to divide them into *Jungen* and *Mädchen* categories. Each student moves around the classroom with his or her list and asking others, *Wie heißt du?* and *Woher kommst du?* The object is to complete the list by identifying as many names and cities of origin as possible.

To make this game more interesting, you may want to offer a prize to students who complete their list first. For additional learning experience, you may ask students to locate their hometown on a map (at the front of this textbook, or another map in the classroom).

2. Class Activity—Greetings

After practicing the greetings in the *Dialoge* and *Ergänzung* and reading about them in the *Aktuelles* section, act them out. Divide the class into groups of three. Have one group member introduce a second member to the third one. It might go something like this: *Heike, das ist Stefan.* Heike responds, *Tag, Stefan!* (or *Grüß dich, Stefan!* or *Hallo, Stefan!*). As part of their greetings, students should shake hands in the German manner.

3. Group Activity-Asking about Others

Have students cut out photographs of well-known people from newspapers and magazines and bring them to class. You may want to divide the class into small groups. Each group shares their photos and asks such questions as *Wer ist das? Kennst du...? Wo wohnt er oder sie?* One person acts as the recorder for the group and makes a list of people. After a certain number of photos (designated by you) have been reviewed and discussed, the recorder presents three to five of these well-known people to the rest of the class. (1. *Das ist...*, 2. [student's name in group] *kennt* [name of person in photo], 3. [student's name in group] *kennt* [name of person in photo] *nicht*, 4. *Er oder sie wohnt in* [name of city]).

4. Class Project—Pen Pals

A number of organizations will make arrangements to get pen pals from German-speaking countries for American students based on the students' sex, age and interests. You may want to contact some of the organizations listed in this front section for assistance. Exchanging letters with German-speaking people will give students a chance to communicate with their peers overseas. At first the students will correspond mostly in English, but this project should encourage them to write more in German.

With the more recent international communication opportunities like Internet, a number of schools have developed a more direct communication link by searching for schools, teachers and students via this international network. You may want to check with your school district about such opportunities.

Kapitel 2

ALLERLEI

1. Game—*Ich telefoniere*

Divide the class into several teams. Whisper a sentence to the first person on each team who in turn whispers it to the next person, until the sentence gets to the last person on the team. The last person announces what he or she heard. The team that has the closest version of the original sentence scores a point.

2. Game—Lotto

After presenting and practicing the numbers from 0 to 100, you might hand out cards (or have students make up their own) bearing these numbers (you may decide to use fewer numbers) and play the German version of Bingo.

3. Game—*Summ!*

After presenting and practicing numbers 0 to 100, you might play this game. Similar to the English game called Buzz, *Summ!* drills the students' knowledge of numbers in German. The game starts with all students on their feet, and ends when one student remains standing. Students count off in German. The first student says *null*, the second *eins*, the third *zwei* and so on. They must watch out when an arbitrarily chosen number or its multiple comes up. Traditionally, the number 7 is used, although the game plays well with numbers like 5, 6 or 8. Students must also be alert when it's their turn to give either a number containing 7 (e.g., 17, 27, 37) or a multiple of 7 (e.g., 14, 21, 28).

The student says *Summ!* in lieu of *sieben* or any number related to it. You spot those students responding incorrectly and ask each to sit down. Of course, a student can slip up and be seated even when the number to be given has nothing to do with 7. The count picks up after the next student in line corrects the error by saying *Summ!* or the right number, depending on the type of mistake made. Though students compete against each other, the whole class will take pride in keeping this game going for longer and longer stretches. If more of a challenge is needed, you may want to include numbers above 100 and see how far students can go.

4. Game—*Wer weiß die Antwort?*

Divide the class into two or more teams. Have each team prepare a few math problems, using the material from the chapter. One team states the problem orally to the other team(s). The object is to find out how fast and accurate the answer can be given.

5. Class Activity—*Wer ruft an?*

Have students bring two telephones to class (students could also improvise using another object). Ask one student to answer the phone. Give the caller a name (see list in *Einführung*, the introductory chapter). Improvise the phone ringing. You may also want to provide some additional words for students to use in their conversation. (Examples are: *sagen, wie viele, Buchstaben, beginnen*.) The activity could go like this: Student A = caller; Student B = person receiving call and disguising his or her voice.

Student B:	*Hier Uwe Meier. Wer da?*
Student A:	*Ich sage das nicht.*
Student B:	*Bist du ein Junge oder ein Mädchen?*
Student A:	*Ein Junge.*
Student B:	*Wie viele Buchstaben hat dein Name?*
Student A:	*Fünf.*
Student B:	*Beginnt dein Name mit A...? B...? C...?*

(Student A says *Nein* each time until the letter *P* comes up, at which time Student A can guess. If he or she doesn't get it, another student takes over with the second letter, another with the third letter, until the fifth—if needed.)

Student B (or C-E):	*Heißt du Peter?*
Student A:	*Richtig.*

Kapitel 3

ALLERLEI

1. Game—*Ratet mal!*

This game is similar to Hangman. The object of this game is to guess a word. Confine words to categories like nouns, verbs, adjectives and so on. A student from one team goes to the board and thinks of a word. He or she writes blanks for each letter on the board. The other team (or the whole class) now guesses each letter in German (good review of the German alphabet!). If the correct letter is guessed, the student writes that letter on the first blank. If it's incorrect, he or she draws the first part of the hanged person. This game goes on until either the complete word has been guessed or the hanged person has been completed.

2. Class Activity—*Wie viel Uhr ist es?*

Divide the class into small groups. Ask each student to write down five different times (of day) on a piece of paper. Each student in turn asks others in their group, *Wie viel Uhr ist es?* while pointing to a specific time on the paper. This activity gives everyone a chance to be involved orally and practice time telling.

3. Class Activity—German Popular Music

Your students will enjoy listening to currently popular German songs. Choose a recording with words that are fairly clear and easy to understand, perhaps a slow song such as a ballad. Before playing it in class, give a little background information on the singer and song. Next, you might hand out to each student a sheet with the lyrics. Leave blank spaces on the sheets for words that students already know. Ask students to write in the missing words while you play the selection several times. To cap off this activity, you might translate the whole song for the class. If you want to plan ahead, you could play the Pilos Puntos song *"Europa"* which is introduced in the *Lesestück* of *Kapitel 9*.

Kapitel 4

ALLERLEI

1. Game—*Fragen und Antworten*

Write questions and answers on separate index cards or sheets of paper, using known vocabulary and structures. The questions should be phrased with and without question words *(wer, wen, was)*. You may want to use different-colored paper for questions and answers for easy identification. Mix all questions and answers in a bag or box. Then have each student take a card or piece of paper. Be sure that you have exactly as many questions and answers as the number of students in your class.

The object of the game is to have each student that draws a question find the student who has the answer to the question, and vice versa. You may want to limit this game to three or five minutes.

2. Game—*Wie heißt das Wort?*

Divide the class into teams. Each student is given a word in either German or English and asked to supply the equivalent in the other language to score a point for his or her team.

3. Class Project—*Stundenplan*

Have students make up a school schedule (either real or imaginary), including school days, class time(s), subjects and activities. Once every student has his or her own schedule, have students ask each other such questions as: *Wie viele Fächer hast du?*, *Was hast du am Montag?*, *Hast du Physik?*, *Wann?*, *Was für ein Fach hast du am Montag um zehn Uhr?*

Kapitel 5

ALLERLEI

1. Game—*Wer ist das in der Familie?*

Make up four decks of cards, each with the following words: *Vater, Mutter, Großvater, Großmutter, Bruder, Schwester, Onkel, Tante, Cousin, Cousine, Sohn, Tochter*. On the back of each card write such questions as: *Wie heißt er oder sie? Wie alt ist er oder sie? Wo wohnt er oder sie? Wer ist das in deiner Familie?* You may want to add some additional questions.

Divide the class into groups of four. One student from each group shuffles a deck of cards. Each player asks another player a question. If the answer is *ja*, he or she gets the card; if the answer is *nein*, the card is passed to the next player. The first group member to have all 12 cards wins.

2. Game—*Das nächste Wort?*

Divide the class into two teams. A player from each team calls out any day, month, number, etc., that is part of a definite sequence. The corresponding person from the other team has to say the next item in the sequence. For example, Player 1 from Team A says *Mai*. Player 1 from Team B will have to respond *Juni*. The same rules apply to other categories. A point is scored for each correct answer. As an alternate activity, teams may want to do the sequences in reverse order.

3. Individual Project—Map

After learning the names of the neighboring countries in the *Ergänzung* and additional information from *Land und Leute (Deutschland)* in *Kapitel 4*, each student could make a map of Germany. You might also have students locate the capitals of the 16 *Länder* (found on the map that is part of the Teacher's Resource Kit) and draw the boundaries for each *Land*. For this assignment, students may have to contact some of the German organizations (listed on pages TE30-33).

4. Group Activity—*Wie ist das Wetter in...?*

Have students pick at least 10 cities from the weather section of your local newspaper. These cities can be national as well as international. Ask students to either cut out the weather report or jot down the cities and temperatures on a piece of paper. In their individual groups, students ask each other at least three questions about place names. Sample questions are: *Wie ist das Wetter in New York?*, *Ist es heiß, warm, kühl oder kalt?*, *Wie ist das Wetter morgen?*

5. Class Project—Calendars

Now that the students have learned the days of the week *(Kapitel 2)*, and the months of the year *(Kapitel 5)*, you might have them make German calendars. Some students could make a calendar of the entire year, while others could make a monthly calendar listing the holidays, special school events, tests, etc. for that particular month. A monthly calendar could be placed in a prominent location in the classroom. The rest of the students could make calendars for upcoming months. All students should work on these projects as part of a team.

Kapitel 6

ALLERLEI

1. Game—*Wie viele Wörter kannst du bilden?*

Give students (individual students or teams) a fairly long word. The object is to use its letters to form as many new words as possible. Example: *Restaurant—er, Tante, aus.*

2. Game—*Wie lang ist der Satz?*

Divide the class into two or three sections, with at least six students in each section. Write the beginning of a sentence on the board or say it to the whole class. The first student in each group repeats your sentence and adds another noun. The second student repeats what the first student said and adds another noun. If a student fails to say the complete sentence (remembering all the words), he or she is out of the game for this round.

Example:

Teacher:	*Zum Mittagessen möchte ich...*
Student 1:	*Zum Mittagessen möchte ich Wiener Schnitzel.*
Student 2:	*Zum Mittagessen möchte ich Wiener Schnitzel und Kartoffeln.*
Student 3:	*Zum Mittagessen möchte ich Wiener Schnitzel, Kartoffeln und eine Cola.*

You may decide to play this game with the whole class, and also add names of beverages.

3. Group Activity—*Was gibt's zum Abendessen?*

Divide the class into groups of three or four. Each group prepares an imaginary dinner menu that could also be used for a German club activity. A spokesperson presents each group's suggested menu. Then the class votes on the menu that is the most original.

4. Individual Project—American vs. German Eating Establishments

Have students make a list of differences and similarities between American and German eating establishments and customs associated with them. Which do your students prefer, and why?

Kapitel 7

ALLERLEI

1. Game—*Ich gehe einkaufen*

The object of the game is to remember what was said before, and to add another item. For example, the first person says, *Ich gehe einkaufen. Ich kaufe ein Hemd.* The second person might say, *Ich gehe einkaufen. Ich kaufe ein Hemd und eine Hose.* The third person repeats everything the second person said and adds another clothing item. A student who cannot repeat what was previously said (or makes a mistake) is out of the game for this round.

2. Game—*Konzentration*

You might play this game to review the conjugation of verbs, modal auxiliaries and the use of *werden*. It resembles the English game of the same name (Concentration). For each student, you write out a different verb (including modal auxiliaries) on an 8 1/2x11-inch sheet of paper. Tape one of the sheets to each student's desktop of each student. It must hang over the desk edge. Students should move their desks into a circle, allowing them full view of the sheets.

Now the game begins. All students hit the tops of their desks with the palms of their hands twice and clap their hands twice. One assigned student (or the teacher) then calls out one of the verbs plus a subject in this basic "1-2" rhythm *(wissen-du)*. Keeping the "1-2" beat, all students hit their desks twice, clap twice and the student who has the verb *wissen* calls out *du weißt.* Then all students again hit their desks twice, clap twice and the student with the verb *wissen* calls out another verb subject *(e.g., müssen-ihr)*. This sets off another round of desk-tapping, hand-clapping and verb-calling. If a student misses his or her turn, mispronounces the verb or responds out of rhythm, the student flips up his or her verb sheet to signify he or she is out of the game. Continue playing, at as lively a pace as possible, until one student remains. This game may strike senior high students as silly, but it's a challenge to play especially when it moves at a fast pace.

3. Class Activity—Clothing and Colors

After students have learned the terms for clothing items and colors, you might have them do this activity. Ask students to bring magazines or advertising brochures to class that contain photos of the latest styles. The pictures they collect should display a wide variety of clothes in various colors. Next, they should write captions in German that name the items and colors depicted. For example, *Der Herr hat einen Anzug an. Er ist braun.* Finally, you might have students present their work to the class, both showing their pictures and reading the captions.

4. Class Activity—Going to the Department Store

Ask students to make some paper money and coins, and have them bring different clothing items to school. Improvise a shopping scene by setting up a clothing store. Have students select roles (customers, clerk and/or cashier). Students should be free to act out a shopping situation according to their own ideas. Depending on the caliber of your class, you may or may not decide to have students prepare beforehand. This is an excellent role-playing activity.

5. Class *Activity-Zeig mir, was du hast!*

Cut out pictures of clothing items and distribute them among your students. Then say to your students, *Zeigt mir ein Kleid!* The student(s) with the appropriate picture holds it up and says, *Hier ist ein Kleid.* Another question might be *Hast du ein gelbes Kleidungsstück.* The response could be *Ja, hier ist ein Pulli. Er ist gelb.*

Kapitel 8

ALLERLEI

1. Game—*Wann hast du Geburtstag?*

Ask students to write their name and birthday (day and month) on a card. (Example: *Peter Hauser, 15. Mai*) Collect all cards, shuffle them and place the pile of cards upside down. Draw the top card from the pile and read the student's birthday aloud. The student whose birthday is read says: *Das ist mein Geburtstag. Mein Geburtstag ist am 15. (fünfzehnten) Mai.* After you have gone through the complete stack of cards, you may want to go through it once more. This time, have all students write down all the names and birthdays. At the end, find out who jotted down all the birthdays correctly.

2. Game—*Ein Buchstabe, aber wie viele Wörter?*

Give students (or teams) a letter and have them come up with as many words as possible that begin with that letter. Example: The letter "g" (*gehen, Geburtstag, groß, Geld, Glück*). You may want to limit a more frequently appearing letter to nouns, verbs or adjectives.

3. Class Activity—*Ein typischer Tag*

Have students write one or two paragraphs about a typical day. They should be as creative as possible, using the vocabulary and structure learned up to this point. Upon completion of this short essay, you may want to divide the class into small groups and have everyone in each group read his or her own version. To keep the listeners active, ask them to write down three sentences of the highlights from each person's report.

4. Individual Project—Map

Have students draw a map of Austria including such items as neighboring countries, major cities, rivers, etc. These maps could be displayed in the classroom for motivational appeal.

Kapitel 9

ALLERLEI

1. Game—*Wer ist der Rockstar?*

Have each student write down the names of three well-known rock stars or groups and three to five questions to ask their classmates about their celebrities. Then divide the class into small groups. Each student gets a turn to ask another student in the group about the rock star/group that he or she has named. Students should ask questions such as: *Ist der Rockstar ein Mann oder eine Frau?, Wie alt ist er oder sie?, Wo wohnt er oder sie?, Wie heißt ein Hit?* and so on. The object is to guess the identity of as many stars/groups as possible.

2. Game—*Wie lange kannst du sprechen?*

Give students a specific topic and ask them to talk about this subject for as long as they can. You may want to have students work in pairs or teams to keep the momentum. Allow students to stop for only about five seconds. Either you or another student could keep track of the time. The person or team that speaks for the longest time wins.

3. Class Project—Invite a Native Speaker

Have students find out if there are native speakers in town or people who have recently been in German-speaking countries. You may even have an exchange student at your school. If such a person can be located, ask him or her about coming to your class. Before the speaker arrives, either you or your students should find out about this person. Depending upon his or her background, ask students to prepare questions beforehand in German (if the speaker is from a German-speaking country). You should prepare students as much as possible to make the visit worthwhile.

Kapitel 10

ALLERLEI

1. Game—*Erzähl eine Geschichte!*

Begin telling a story. Have each student add a sentence until the story has been completed. It might be fun to record the story and play it back.

2. Game—*Ich sehe etwas, was du nicht siehst...*

You may want to start this game by saying, *Ich sehe etwas, was du nicht siehst. Es beginnt mit 'B'.* The class guesses what it is. The student who has guessed the right answer selects the next mystery word.

3. Individual Project—*Welche Sportart treibst du gern?*

Have students write a short essay based on their experience in participating in sports. If some students are not active in sports, have them substitute such topics as *Was für ein Hobby hast du? Beschreibe es!*

Kapitel 11

ALLERLEI

1. Game—*Wo sind diese Gebäude?*

Give each student a map with several blocks and street names indicated, and several labeled miniature sketches or illustrations of specific buildings such as *Schule, Bahnhof, Restaurant, Post, Café, Kaufhaus, Rathaus, Museum.* One location (example: *Park*) can be marked on each map and then becomes the starting point for giving directions. The object of the game is to follow your instruction and place the building in the correct location. Here is an example: *Der Bahnhof ist drei Ecken vom Park. Er ist auf der rechten Seite zwischen der Goethestraße und der Frankfurter Allee.* Students then place the sketch or illustration of the train station accordingly. Students should be allowed to ask questions at any time if they are not sure of the building's location. However, they must ask questions only in German.

2. Game—*Wir fahren nach Deutschland*

The object of this game is to remember what was said before. The first student says, *Wir fahren nach Deutschland. Wir nehmen ein Buch mit.* The second student repeats the first sentence and might say, *Wir nehmen ein Buch und eine Landkarte mit.* The third student repeats what the second one said and adds another word. A student who cannot repeat what was previously said and makes a mistake is out of the game. If you don't want to play this game, you may want to substitute German place names instead. For example, *Wir fahren nach Bonn.* The next might say, *Wir fahren nach Bonn und dann nach Hamburg.* The third student adds another place name and the game continues in the same manner.

3. Group Activity—*Was nehmen wir mit?*

Divide the class into groups of three or four. Have each group prepare for an imaginary trip. You may want to prepare some specific questions that must be part of each group's description such as: *Von welcher Stadt fahrt ihr ab? Wann geht's los? Mit welchem Verkehrsmittel fahrt ihr? Was nehmt ihr mit? Wer kommt mit? Wie lange dauert die Reise? Wie lange bleibt ihr dort? Was macht ihr da? Wann kommt ihr wieder zurück?*

Kapitel 12

ALLERLEI

1. Game—*Zwanzig Fragen*

Have one student think of an object, a person or a place. The other students ask him or her questions that are answered with *ja* or *nein*. The goal of the game is to guess the object, person or place in 20 questions.

2. Class Activity—*Eine Party*

Have students describe a party (real or imaginary) orally or in writing. They can use either dialog or narrative form. To create a more vivid, meaningful description, you may help students with some additional vocabulary. Have them make up a short list (in English) so that you can give them the words in German. Students could act out a party, or you may even turn this activity into an after-school event (a good German club activity!).

3. Individual Project—*Wer kann ein Musikinstrument spielen?*

Find out who can play a musical instrument. Select some well-known German folksongs or some popular German hits for which written texts are available for handouts. Ask one or two of these students to prepare one or two songs. Read the text before singing it to practice pronunciation. When the musicians are ready and the rest of the class knows the pronunciation, have everybody participate in singing these songs.

4. Individual Activity—Switzerland

After students have read and studied *Land und Leute (Die Schweiz),* tell them to pretend they are going to Switzerland. Have them plan what they want to see there. Ask them to write down their travel plans (in English) after they decide what type of trip they prefer—a wide-ranging tour, an extended stay at one favorite site, visits to one attraction (e.g., a ski resort and so on). Students can find some valuable information through your school or local library, travel agents (with free brochures) or the Swiss National Tourist Office (see address on page TE33).

REFORM OF SPELLING RULES

Major changes in German spelling rules have been made and implemented in print materials throughout German-speaking countries. According to a commission that met in Vienna in July 1996, these new changes must be made during the period of August 1998, and no later than July 2005.

For specific information and details of the spelling changes, you may want to refer to any of the following reference books:

DUDEN—Die neue deutsche Rechtschreibung, Bibliographisches Institut & F.A. Brockhaus AG, Mannheim 1996

Die neue deutsche Rechtschreibung, Bertelsmann Lexikon Verlag GmbH, Lexikographisches Institut, München 1996

Wahrig—Deutsche Wörterbuch, Bertelsmann Lexikon Verlag GmbH, Gütersloh 1996

Rechtschreibung 2000—Die aktuelle Reform, Ernst Klett Verlag GmbH, Stuttgart 1996

For your convenience and reference, the most important changes that affect the printed text of the *Deutsch Aktuell* (textbooks and ancillaries) have been summarized below.

1. **The ß following a short vowel no longer exists.**

old spelling	new spelling
muß, mußt, müßt	*muss, musst, müsst*
ißt, eßt	*isst, esst*
daß	*dass*

However, the ß remains in words with preceding long vowels or double vowels as in *Straße, draußen, Maß*.

2. **The word *wieviel* becomes *wie viel*.**

Similar to the old spelling of *wie viele* and *so viele*, the rule now dictates that *wie viel* must be spelled as two words.

3. Specific time designations related to *heute* and daily or weekly times are capitalized.

old spelling	new spelling
heute mittag	*heute Mittag*
gestern abend	*gestern Abend*
am Sonntag abend	*am Sonntagabend*

4. Words related to colors amd language designation are capitalized.

old spelling	new spelling
auf deutsch	*auf Deutsch*

5. The familiar forms *du* and *ihr* as well as other related forms are now written in small letters.

Under the old rule, friends and relatives were address in correspondence with *Du, Dich*, etc.

old spelling	new spelling
Du, Dein, Dich, Dir	*du, dein, dich, dir*
Ihr, Euer, Euch	*ihr, euer, euch*

The most following rule changes will most likely appear in more advanced German texts. However, for your convenience and reference, they have been listed here as well.

6. Words with the same three consecutive consonants remain as they appear.

When the same three consonants come together (*Schiff + Fahrt*), they all remain.

old spelling	new spelling
Schiffahrt	*Schifffahrt*
Schrittempo	*Schritttempo*

7. **Nouns connected with prepositions are capitalized.**

old spelling	new spelling
haltmachen	*Halt machen*
radfahren	*Rad fahren*

8. **Anglicized words follow the same rules as for German compound nouns. Sometimes they can be separated with a hyphen.**

old spelling	new spelling
Compact Disc	*Compactdisc*
Swimming Pool	*Swimming-Pool*

9. **Words that take the form of nouns are capitalized.**

old spelling	new spelling
in bezug auf	*in Bezug auf*
schuld geben	*Schuld geben*
der, die, das letzte	*der, die, das Letzte*
es ist das beste	*es ist das Beste*
jung und alt	*Jung und Alt*
aufs herzlichste	*aufs Herzlichste*

10. **Hyphenation is determined by syllables.**

old spelling	new spelling
We-sten	*Wes-ten*
bak-ken	*ba-cken*
Ofen	*O-fen*

Deutsch Aktuell 1
Fourth Edition

Wolfgang S. Kraft

Chief Consultants

Shawn Cecilia Jarvis
St. Cloud State University
St. Cloud, Minnesota

Hans J. König
The Blake Schools
Hopkins, Minnesota

Roland Specht
Ruhr Universität Bochum
Bochum, Germany

Consultants

Thomas Keith Cothrun
Las Cruces High School
Las Cruces, New Mexico

Ingrid M. May
Harding High School
River Valley High School
Marion, Ohio

Helga Schmitz
Overland High School
Aurora, Colorado

Margaret E. Durham
St. Paul Academy
St. Paul, Minnesota

Jo Ann D. Nelson
Jacksonville High School
Jacksonville, Illinois

Marcia K. Slosser
Lloyd C. Bird High School
Chesterfield, Virginia

Richard Jones
Fallston High School
Fallston, Maryland

Ron Porotsky
Whitehall High School
Whitehall, Pennsylvania

EMC/Paradigm, Publishing, Saint Paul, Minnesota

About the Cover

The collage of buildings assembled on the cover of *Deutsch Aktuell 1* is particularly appropriate for a first-level language textbook. One can't build anything lasting without first laying a good foundation. The science-art architecture is a paradigm for the study of a foreign language. The functions, vocabulary and structures of language resemble the bricks and mortar of a Gothic cathedral, the girders and rivets of a modern skyscraper, the timbers and plaster of a *Fachwerkhaus*. The architect finds limitless creative expression within the confines of the laws of physics and available materials. So, too, the student of German will find infinite capacity for expression and communication once the functions, vocabulary and structures of German are understood and practiced. A building with a poor foundation will not stand for long. A student with a good foundation will be able to develop and use those skills for a lifetime.

The front cover's three main visual elements illustrate European history's three great social movements lead by Church, State and Commerce. The foreground is of the newly restored *Rathaus* clock tower in Leipzig. Behind the clock tower is the *Kölner Dom*. In the background looms the cityscape of downtown Frankfurt's business district. The monuments of the past are living reminders of the best that German culture has to offer and continue to inspire future generations.

Tim Heitman
Graphic Artist

Credits

Desktop Production Specialists
Bradley J. Olsen
Rita Westerhaus

Illustrator
Hetty Mitchell

Designer
Tim Heitman

Cartoon Illustrator
Steve Mark

ISBN 0-8219-1449-9

Published by EMC/Paradigm Publishing
875 Montreal Way
St. Paul, Minnesota 55102

Printed in the United States of America
1 2 3 4 5 6 7 8 9 10 XXX 03 02 01 00 99 98

Willkommen!

Welcome to an exciting, new language and culture! As the title *Deutsch Aktuell* suggests, you will become familiar with a language that mirrors today's contemporary everyday-life of teenagers in German-speaking countries. By being exposed to numerous real-life situations you will be able to better relate to your own surroundings and make comparisons between the cultures of German-speaking countries and your own.

"Why should I study German? What do I need it for?" you may ask yourself. Did you know these facts?

- More than one-fourth of the population in this country claims German ancestry.
- Germany is the world's largest exporter and a major trading partner of the United States.
- Over 200 million Europeans speak German as their first foreign language.
- German is an international language in the fields of technology, chemistry, medicine, music, philosophy, and art.
- More Germans travel per capita than any other national group in the world—you're likely to meet them everywhere!
- One out of every ten books published in the world is written in German.
- A knowledge of German improves your job opportunities.
- Knowing German also improves your understanding of English; German students are likely to score higher on college entrance exams than others.

You will learn skills that will help you to communicate on many topics. As you begin learning German, you will initially listen, then gradually learn to speak about topics that interest you. Don't be afraid to express yourself. It's natural to make mistakes, but your language skills and cultural understanding will gradually become stronger each time you use German. In short time your confidence will increase as you experience success communicating German.

The best of success and have lots of fun!

Viel Erfolg und viel Spaß!

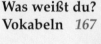

Kapitel 12
Das macht Spaß! 355

Reference 386

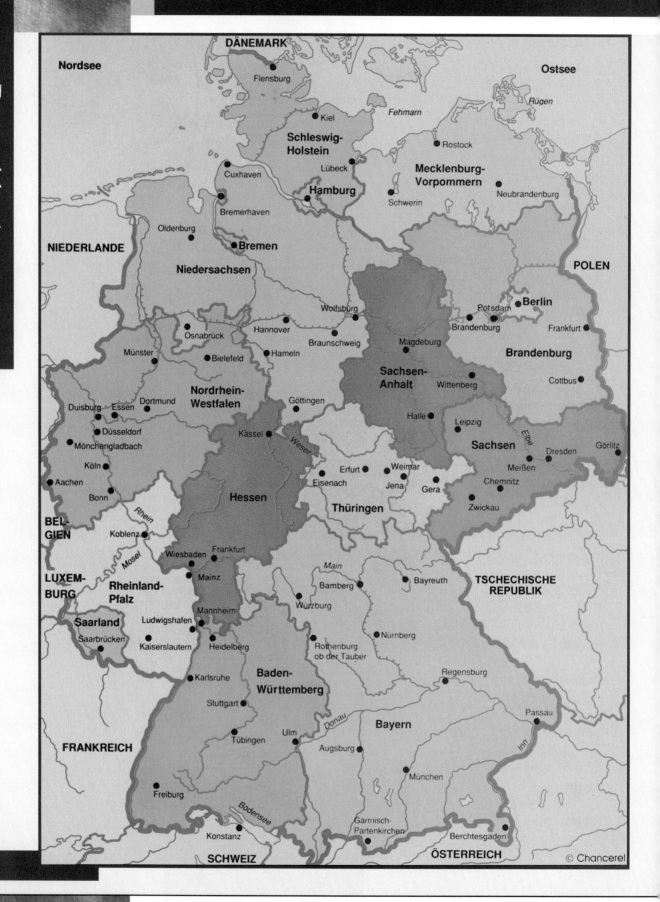

Deutschland

Nordsee

DÄNEMARK

Ostsee

Flensburg

Rügen

Kiel

Fehmarn

Schleswig-
Holstein

Rostock

Lübeck

Mecklenburg-
Vorpommern

Cuxhaven

Hamburg

Schwerin

Neubrandenburg

Bremerhaven

Oldenburg

NIEDERLANDE

Bremen

Niedersachsen

POLEN

Berlin

Wolfsburg

Potsdam

Hannover

Brandenburg

Frankfurt

Osnabrück

Braunschweig

Magdeburg

Brandenburg

Münster

Hameln

Bielefeld

Sachsen-
Anhalt

Wittenberg

Cottbus

Nordrhein-
Westfalen

Göttingen

Duisburg

Essen

Dortmund

Halle

Leipzig

Elbe

Görlitz

Düsseldorf

Kassel

Sachsen

Dresden

Mönchengladbach

Weser

Meißen

Köln

Erfurt

Weimar

Chemnitz

Aachen

Eisenach

Jena

Gera

Bonn

Hessen

Thüringen

Zwickau

Rhein

BEL-
GIEN

Koblenz

Mosel

Wiesbaden

Frankfurt

Main

LUXEM-
BURG

Mainz

Bamberg

Bayreuth

TSCHECHISCHE
REPUBLIK

Rheinland-
Pfalz

Mannheim

Würzburg

Saarland

Ludwigshafen

Saarbrücken

Kaiserslautern

Heidelberg

Nürnberg

Rothenburg
ob der Tauber

Karlsruhe

Baden-
Württemberg

Regensburg

Stuttgart

Passau

FRANKREICH

Donau

Bayern

Tübingen

Ulm

Inn

Augsburg

München

Freiburg

Bodensee

Garmisch-
Partenkirchen

Berchtesgaden

Konstanz

SCHWEIZ

ÖSTERREICH

© Chancerel

x

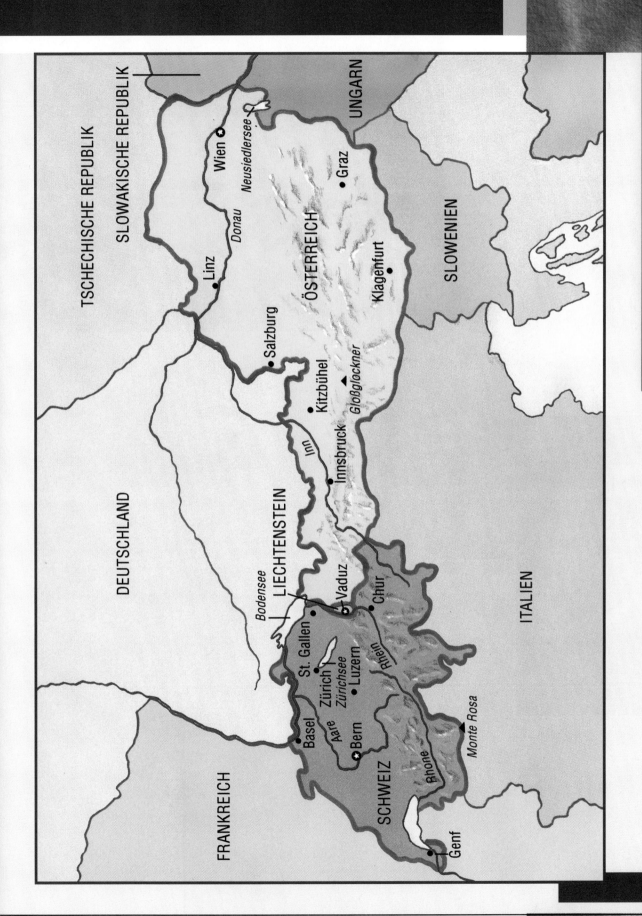

TSCHECHISCHE REPUBLIK

SLOWAKISCHE REPUBLIK

UNGARN

Wien

Neusiedlersee

Graz

Donau

Linz

ÖSTERREICH

Klagenfurt

SLOWENIEN

Salzburg

Kitzbühel

Gloßglockner

Innsbruck

DEUTSCHLAND

Inn

LIECHTENSTEIN

Bodensee

Vaduz

Chur

ITALIEN

St. Gallen

Zürich

Zürichsee

Rhein

Luzern

Monte Rosa

Basel

Aare

Bern

SCHWEIZ

Rhone

FRANKREICH

Genf

Deutschland

Bad Mergentheim

Karneval
in Köln

Augsburg

auf dem Brandenburger Tor
(Berlin)

auf einem See in Blankenheim

Kleinwalsertal

Wo ist das Museum?

Segelboote in Hamburg

Deutschland

die Kongresshalle in Coburg

Schloss Bückeburg

auf einem Markt in Koblenz

Cochem an der Mosel

auf dem Lande
(Menzenschwand)

Drachenfliegen (Goslar)

Kinder in Ruhpolding

Kajakfahren

Kassel

vor dem Rathaus in Leipzig

Österreich

Velden

Kinder auf einem Bauernhof

Macht das Spaß?

Rodeln

Das Parlament (Wien)

Mountainbiking

Was spielt sie?

Skilaufen

xvii

Schweiz

Bergwanderer im
Berner Oberland

Sonntagstrachten
in der Ostschweiz

Kindertrachten in St. Gallen

Luzern

Snowboardfahren

Rhein, in der Nähe
von Schaffhausen

Was machen
sie in den
Bergen?

Eiskunstlaufen in Graubünden

xix

Einführung

Also, los!

In this chapter you will be able to:

- greet and say farewell to someone
- ask and tell someone's name
- introduce someone else
- ask and tell someone's age
- give telephone numbers

Martina

Alex

Sven

Ich heiße Martina. Und du?
Ich bin Alex.

Wie heißt du?
Ich heiße Sven.

Wie heißen Sie?
Ich heiße Frau Tauber.
Und ich heiße Herr Polinski.

Wie heißt er?
Wie heißt sie?

Wer ist das?
Das ist Gisela.

Uli

Herr Polinski

Frau Tauber

Anne

Natascha

OT Activities 5-6

Aktuelles

Hallo!, Tag! and *Grüß dich!* all mean "Hello" or "Hi." Although *Hallo!* is commonly heard throughout Germany, *Grüß dich!* is more often heard in southern Germany and *Tag!* in the rest of the country. All three are informal greetings and are used among young people, friends and relatives. Additional greetings that often can be heard for "Hello" are *Grüß Gott!* in southern Germany and *Guten Tag!* in other parts of the country.

Tschüs! is a casual form of *Auf Wiedersehen!*, both meaning "good-bye." It's quite common for people to drop the first word and simply say *Wiedersehen!*

Guten Tag!

Also, los!

1. ***Wer ist das?*** **With a partner look at the photos below and identify each person by answering your partner's question *Wer ist das?* Be sure to take turns and point to the various people out of sequence.**

   ◆ Wer ist das?
   Das ist Thomas.

Thomas

1.

Timo

2.

Katja

3.

Ilona

4.

Karsten

5.

Nils

6.

Christine

7.

Sabrina

8.

Udo

2. *Wie heißt er? Wie heißt sie?* It's your first day in school. Ask the person next to you about different students in your class and then introduce yourself to that person. Use either *Tag* or *Grüß dich.*

◆ Wie heißt sie? (Monika)
Sie heißt Monika.
Tag, Monika!

◆ Wie heißt er? (Peter)
Er heißt Peter.
Grüß dich, Peter!

ein Mädchen–
Sie heißt
Tanja.

ein Junge–
Er heißt
Thomas.

Namen für Jungen		Namen für Mädchen	
Achim	Jörg	Alexandria	Judith
Alexander	Jürgen	Andrea	Julia
Ali	Kai	Angelika	Jutta
Andreas	Karl	Anja	Karin
Axel	Karsten	Anna	Katharina
Benjamin	Kevin	Anne	Katja
Bernd	Klaus	Annette	Katrin
Bernhard	Kurt	Ariane	Kerstin
Björn	Lars	Astrid	Laura
Boris	Lukas	Barbara	Lisa
Carsten	Manfred	Bärbel	Manuela
Christian	Manuel	Beate	Maren
Christoph	Marc	Bettina	Maria
Christopher	Marcel	Bianca	Martina
Daniel	Marco	Birgit	Melanie
David	Marcus	Brigitte	Michaela
Dennis	Mark	Britta	Miriam
Dieter	Matthias	Carmen	Monika
Detlef	Maximilian	Christa	Nadine
Dirk	Michael	Christiane	Natalie
Erich	Oliver	Christine	Natascha
Erik	Patrick	Claudia	Nina
Felix	Peter	Cornelia	Nora
Florian	Philipp	Dagmar	Olivia
Frank	Rainer	Daniela	Petra
Franz	Ralf	Diana	Regina
Friedrich	Robert	Doris	Renate
Fritz	Rolf	Elfriede	Rita
Georg	Rudolf	Elisabeth	Ruth
Gerd	Rüdiger	Elke	Sabine
Gerhard	Sebastian	Erika	Sabrina
Günter	Simon	Eva	Sandra
Hans	Stefan	Franziska	Sara
Harald	Steffen	Frieda	Sarah
Hartmut	Sven	Gabi	Sibylle
Heiko	Thomas	Gabriele	Silke
Heinrich	Thorsten	Gerda	Silvia
Heinz	Timo	Gisela	Simone
Helmut	Tobias	Gudrun	Sonja
Herbert	Toni	Heide	Sophie
Hermann	Torsten	Heidi	Stefanie
Holger	Udo	Heike	Susanne
Horst	Uli	Helga	Susi
Ingo	Uwe	Ilona	Tanja
Jan	Volker	Ilse	Tina
Jens	Walter	Inge	Ulla
Joachim	Werner	Ingrid	Ulrike
Jochen	Willi	Irene	Ursula
Johann	Wolf	Jana	Vanessa
Johannes	Wolfgang	Jessica	Yvonne

Namen

3. Manfred wants to invite seven of his friends to his birthday party. His friends are eager to find out who will be there. Manfred gives them a challenge by writing all the syllables of the names on a piece of paper. Can you help Manfred's friends figure out who will be at his party? If you figure out who is coming, the beginning letters of the seven names when put in the right sequence, will spell the German word for "correct."

AS   LA
BI   NA
CHRI   RE
GI   RID
GO   PHER
HEI   SE
IN   TE
ING   TO
KE   STO

RENATE
INGRID
CHRISTOPHER
HEIKE
TOBIAS
INGO
GISELA

(Correct = RICHTIG)

4. *Junge oder Mädchen? Folge den Beispielen!* (Follow the examples.)

AC/CD

◆ Britta
   Andreas ist ein Junge.

◆ Andreas
   Britta ist ein Mädchen.

Mädchen

1. Carmen
2. Florian
3. Marco
4. Jana
5. Nadine
6. Karsten
7. Bianca
8. Kai

1. Carmen ist ein Mädchen.
2. Florian ist ein Junge.
3. Marco ist ein Junge.
4. Jana ist ein Mädchen.
5. Nadine ist ein Mädchen.
6. Karsten ist ein Junge.
7. Bianca ist ein Mädchen.
8. Kai ist ein Junge.

Jungen

Also, los!

AC/CD

Ich heiße Claudia.
Ich bin achtzehn.
Ich heiße Timo.
Ich bin fünfzehn.

Practice these numbers in sequence (forward and backward). Write the numbers on cards or on the chalkboard, asking students to identify each. Numbers 21-1,000 are taught in Chapter 2. Students can make up their own cards and practice with classmates.

Ask students to say their phone numbers out loud. Then invite the class to play bingo. You call out the numbers in German while your students cross them off a bingo card. At this point, you can only use numbers 0-20. If you want to play with all the numbers, you may want to wait until Chapter 2 in which numbers through 100 are introduced. Point out the way Germans write numbers "1" and "7." See also the *Aktuelles* section in the Einführung of *Deutsch Aktuell 2*.

OT Activities 7-8

0 null 1 eins 2 zwei 3 drei 4 vier

5 fünf 6 sechs 7 sieben 8 acht 9 neun

10 zehn 11 elf 12 zwölf 13 dreizehn 14 vierzehn

15 fünfzehn 16 sechzehn 17 siebzehn 18 achtzehn 19 neunzehn

20 zwanzig

Wie alt ist Peter? Er ist vierzehn.

5. **Wie alt ist er? Wie alt ist sie? Imagine a German student is staying with you for a while. You introduce him or her to several people in your neighborhood. Your German guest asks you about the ages of the various people he or she is meeting. Respond accordingly.** *Folge den Beispielen!*

◆ Tina / 13
   Das ist Tina.

◆ Wie alt ist Tina?
   Sie ist dreizehn.

1. Susanne / 16
2. Heidi / 18
3. Ali / 12
4. Robert / 19
5. Bärbel / 8
6. Christine / 15

Susi ist siebzehn.

Also, los!

AC/CD

1. Das ist Susanne.
   Wie alt ist Susanne?
   Sie ist sechzehn.
2. Das ist Heidi.
   Wie alt ist Heidi?
   Sie ist achtzehn.
3. Das ist Ali.
   Wie alt ist Ali?
   Er ist zwölf.
4. Das ist Robert.
   Wie alt ist Robert?
   Er ist neunzehn.
5. Das ist Bärbel.
   Wie alt ist Bärbel?
   Sie ist acht.
6. Das ist Christine.
   Wie alt ist Christine?
   Sie ist fünfzehn.

Rollenspiel

Carry on a brief conversation with the person next to you asking questions as: *Wie heißt du? Wie alt bist du?* (Point to others in your *Wer ist das? Wie heißt er? Wie heißt sie? Wie alt ist er? Wie alt ist sie?*

Wie heißt du?

1. Acht plus elf ist neunzehn.
2. Dreizehn minus eins ist zwölf.
3. Fünf plus zwei ist sieben.
4. Zwanzig minus sechs ist vierzehn.
5. Sechzehn minus fünf ist elf.
6. Sieben plus neun ist sechzehn.

6. **Wie viel ist...?**

   ◆ 1 + 3 = ?
   Eins plus drei ist vier.

   ◆ 10 - 1 = ?
   Zehn minus eins ist neun.

   1. 8 + 11 = ?
   2. 13 - 1 = ?
   3. 5 + 2 = ?
   4. 20 - 6 = ?
   5. 16 - 5 = ?
   6. 7 + 9 = ?

A ah
B beh
C tseh
D deh
E eh
F eff
G geh
H hah
I ih
J jott

K kah
L ell
M emm
N en
O oh
P peh
Q kuh
R err
S ess
T teh

U uh
V fau
W weh
X iks
Y üpsilon
Z tset
Ä äh
Ö öh
Ü üh
ß ess-tset

AC/CD

Have a spelling bee. Ask students to spell their names (first and last) while classmates write them down. Then check their spelling. You also may ask students to say a German word and have others spell it.

Für dich

You probably noticed that there are four additional letters in the German language: *ß, ä, ö, ü*.

The letter *ß* is equivalent to *ss* but cannot necessarily be substituted. The *ß* is used after a long vowel *(Straße)* or vowel combination *(heißen)*.

The *ß* is never used when all the letters in a word are capitalized *(Straße, but STRASSE)*.

Barfüßerstraße

Führt zum alten Barfüßer-
(Franziskaner-) Kloster,
jetzt Stadtkirche

Teacher's Note:

You may want to point out to your students that new spelling rules are in effect as of August 1998. Until these rules are fully implemented (no later than 2005), your students may still be exposed to old rules in various publications. For additional reference, see pages TE46-48 of the front section of this Teacher's Edition.

Also, los!

Sprichwort

Ich lese das Buch von A bis Z.
(I'm reading the book from cover to cover.)

7. *Wie buchstabiert man...? Mündlich, bitte!* **(How do you spell...? Orally, please.)**

   1. alt
   2. Katja
   3. fünf
   4. Tag
   5. Mädchen
   6. Frau
   7. sie
   8. plus

Wie buchstabiert man „Willkommen"?

8. Take a look at a section taken from a German telephone book. Pick eight different entries and read them aloud, including their first and last names as well as their telephone numbers; then spell each first and last name.

```
Dasche Elise Paul-Heyse Str.29         3 22 6o o4
Daschek Gottfried Lindenallee 5        6 26 44 75
Dase Adam Buckower Damm 288            3 04 53 91
DaSilva Pierre Neuheimer Weg 17        7 81 02 40
Daske Birgit Holzminder Str. 59        5 93 66 32
Daskiewicz Fritz Am Grüngürtel 2       2 62 15 74
Dasovic Ljilljana Klausenburger Pfad 43  5 89 91 05
Dasse Ilona Hermsdorfer Damm 23        9 37 17 42
Dassel Karin Hildburghauser Str. 118   2 96 32 01
Dassler Joachim Grabbeallee 87         4 89 31 18
Dassow Edeltraud Ansbacher Str. 66     3 20 17 59
Dastani Ali Winfriedallee 13           8 52 11 72
Dasualopoulos Dimitros Mondstr. 113    6 05 28 09
Dath Wolfgang Nahmitzer Damm 14        2 08 65 58
Dathe Klaus Seesener Str. 51           8 91 53 98
Datow Käthe Germersheimer Weg 8        7 90 62 43
Datzmann Frieda Rockenhauser-Str. 44   6 21 39 08
Dau Magdalena Momsner Platz 20         5 29 01 78
Daub Max  Eichenweg 51            90 38
```

Nützliche Ausdrücke in der Klasse

The following is a list of expressions that you might use and hear in your classroom:

◆ *Hört (gut) zu!* Listen (well)!
◆ *Wiederholt!* Repeat!
◆ *Noch einmal.* Once more.
◆ *Öffnet eure Bücher (Arbeitshefte) auf Seite...!* Open your books (workbooks) to page...!
◆ *Nehmt ein Stück Papier raus!* Take out a sheet of paper!
◆ *Nehmt einen Bleistift (Kuli)!* Take a pencil (pen)!
◆ *Schreibt!* Write!
◆ *Lest!* Read!
◆ *Weiter.* Continue.
◆ *Geht an die Tafel!* Go to the chalk(board)!

From the first day of instruction, the teacher may want to introduce students to frequently used classroom expressions. These, as well as other suggested classroom expressions, are also listed in the front section of this teacher's edition.

Also, los!

Wer weiß es?

- *Das ist richtig.* That's right (correct).
- *Das ist falsch.* That's wrong.
- *Das ist sehr gut.* That's very good.
- *Gut.* Good.
- *Prima.* Great.
- *Ausgezeichnet.* Excellent.
- *Buchstabiert das!* Spell that!
- *Wer weiß es?* Who knows it?
- *Auf Deutsch, bitte.* In German, please.

You may want to learn the following basic expressions when talking to your classmates or your teacher:

- *Ich weiß es nicht.* I don't know.
- *Ich verstehe das nicht.* I don't understand that.
- *Was bedeutet...?* What does...mean?
- *Wie sagt man...?* How do you say...?
- *Ich habe eine Frage.* I have a question.

9. **Complete each statement by selecting an appropriate word from the list below.**

| Guten | Wie | dich | Auf | Junge |
| Sie | viel | Mädchen | Tschüs | minus |

1. dich
2. Junge
3. Sie
4. Wie
5. Auf
6. minus
7. Guten
8. Mädchen
9. viel
10. Tschüs

1. Grüß ____, Natascha!
2. Alexander ist ein ____.
3. Wie heißen ____?
4. ____ alt ist Monika?
5. ____ Wiedersehen!
6. Neun ____ drei ist sechs.
7. ____ Tag, Frau Neumann!
8. Britta ist ein ____.
9. Wie ____ ist drei plus vier?
10. ____, Dieter.

Tag!

10. **You are trying to demonstrate to your friend that you know some German. Your friend starts to say something, and you finish the sentence.**

◆ Wie alt bist ____?
Wie alt bist du?

1. Guten ____!
2. Bis ____.
3. Auf ____!
4. Grüß ____!
5. Wie heißen ____?
6. Martina ist ein ____.
7. Vier plus sieben ist ____.
8. Wer ist ____?

Hallo, Jochen!

1. Tag
2. später
3. Wiedersehen
4. dich (Gott)
5. Sie
6. Mädchen
7. elf
8. das

AC/CD

11. **You are talking to another student. What are the logical statements to complete this short conversation? You may want to use some of the cues listed below for possible answers.**

Ich bin... / Ich heiße... / Tschüs... / Tag / Sie ist...

Tag!

____

Wie heißt du?

____

Wer ist das?

____

Wie alt ist sie?

____

Tschüs!

____

Guten Tag!

Tschüs!

Willi und Milli is an original cartoon series written specifically for this book. The vocabulary and structure have been carefully coordinated with the content of each chapter.

Übung macht den Meister!

1. Ask five classmates their names and phone numbers. Write this information on a piece of paper. Your classmates will collect the same information from others. Alternating with a partner, say each name and phone number one at a time, and write them down. After each of you has written down all five names and phone numbers, compare your sheets to make sure the information is correct.

2. Write down three addition and/or subtraction problems. Then ask your partner to give you the answers to each problem. Give all three problems at one time, or alternate. *Beispiel: Wie viel ist sieben plus drei?* Answer: Sieben plus drei ist zehn.

Sprache

Have students go through a German newspaper or magazine to see how many cognates they can find. This activity is strictly for word recognition.

There are many German words that look the same or are similar to English words. These words are called *cognates*. The word "**cogn**ate" comes from "re**cogn**ize." If you recognize a word in German because there is a similar word in English, it may be a cognate. You won't have any problems identifying the cognates that are part of the following photos. Unfortunately, there are words in German that are *false cognates*. A false cognate is a German word that looks like an English word but means something quite different. For example, if you would like to send a gift to someone in Germany, don't mark your package with the word "gift." The word *Gift* in German means "poison."

Für dich

The following words and expressions will help you understand the content for this introductory chapter.

- ◆ *Wer ist das?* Who is that?
- ◆ *Das ist...* That is...
- ◆ *Wie heißt er/sie?* What's his/her name?
- ◆ *Er/Sie heißt...* His/Her name is...
- ◆ *Wie heißt du?* What's your name? (informal)
- ◆ *Wie heißen Sie?* What's your name? (formal)
- ◆ *Ich heiße...* My name is...
- ◆ *Wie alt bist du?* How old are you?
- ◆ *Ich bin...* I am...
- ◆ *Wie alt ist...?* How old is...?
- ◆ *Wie viel ist...?* How much is...?
- ◆ *ein Junge* a boy
- ◆ *ein Mädchen* a girl

Also, los!

Der Himmel über Saarbrücken um einiges klarer.

Auf Wiedersehen in
Meißen

Tag!

In this chapter you will be able to:

- introduce yourself and others
- greet people
- ask and tell how things are going
- give information
- ask where someone lives

Hallo!

Tanja: Tag, Gülten!

Gülten: Hallo, Tanja! Ist das Jens?

Tanja: Nein, Klaus.

Gülten: Und wo wohnt Klaus?

Tanja: Der wohnt da drüben.

Gülten: Kennst du Klaus?

Tanja: Nicht sehr gut.

Klaus wohnt da drüben.

1. ***Wer ist diese Person?*** **(Who is this person?) Identify the person. You may need to know these two verb forms:** *sagt* **(says) and** *fragt* **(asks).** *Diese Person...*

   1. kennt Klaus nicht sehr gut.
   2. wohnt da drüben.
   3. sagt: „Hallo!"
   4. fragt, wo Klaus wohnt.

2. **What do you say in German when you...**

1. greet someone?
2. ask a student his or her name?
3. ask where someone else lives?
4. ask someone if he or she knows a person?

Für dich

In informal conversations in which a person has been identified and is immediately referred to again, Germans often use the article *der* or *die* with or without their respective names rather than *er* or *sie* (Example: *Und wo wohnt Klaus? Der wohnt da drüben.*)

Germans use the word *denn* quite frequently in conversations. In this context the word itself has no meaning and is used strictly for emphasis.

Woher kommst du?

Alex:	Grüß dich! Du bist neu hier, nicht wahr?
Boris:	Ja, das stimmt.
Alex:	Woher kommst du denn?
Boris:	Aus Bensheim.
Alex:	Wo ist das denn?
Boris:	Nicht weit von Frankfurt.

Grüß dich!

Tag!

AC/CD

1. Hallo! (Grüß dich!, Tag!)
2. Wie heißt du?
3. Wo wohnt [die] Christine ([der] Robert)?
4. Kennst du (name of person)?

AC/CD

Ask students to greet each other with *Tag!* or *Grüß dich!* and shake hands.

Alex

WB Activity 2

WA Activity 2

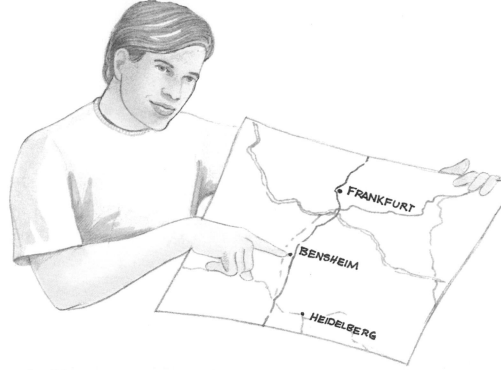

AC/CD

AC/CD

3. **Give an answer in German.**

   1. Give another expression for *Tag!*
   2. Ask where your classmate is from.
   3. Find out where that town or city is located.
   4. Say that your town or city is not far from another town or city.

4. *Stimmt das? Stimmt das nicht?* **If the statement is incorrect, give a correct statement in German.**

   1. Boris ist neu hier.
   2. Alex kommt aus Bensheim.
   3. Bensheim ist weit von Frankfurt.
   4. Boris wohnt nicht weit von Frankfurt.

Frankfurt

Bensheim

5. *Beantworte diese Fragen!* (Answer these questions.)

1. Wie heißt du?
2. Wie alt bist du?
3. Wo wohnt...(use a classmate's name)?
4. Kennst du...(use a classmate's name)?
5. Bist du neu hier?
6. Woher kommst du?

Rollenspiel

You are meeting a new student in your class for the first time. Find out as much as you can about the student (another classmate), including name, age, where he or she is from, where he or she lives now, etc. After you have asked at least five questions, reverse roles and have your partner ask you some questions.

Ergänzung

Have students use the various greetings and common expressions in this section. (*Wo wohnst du? Wer ist dein Freund/deine Freundin? Wie heißt er/sie? Wo wohnt er/sie?*)

WB
Activities 3-6

LA
Activities 1-3

WA
Activities 3-5

OT
Activities 9-10

WB Activities 7-9

OT Activities 11-12

Sag's mal!   Wo wohnst du?

da drüben

gleich gegenüber vom Spielplatz*

mitten in der Stadt*

beim Park

da

in Frankfurt

in der Stadt

gleich um die Ecke

in der Mozartstraße*

nicht weit weg von der Schule*

in einer Hauptstraße*

nicht weit von hier

da hinten*

hier

* You have not seen this expression before. If you cannot figure out its meaning, you may want to ask your teacher.

Wo wohnst du?

Sprichwort

Es geht drunter und drüber.

(It's topsy-turvy.)

Aktuelles

Du oder Sie?

Both *du* and *Sie* mean "you." However, *du* is considered the informal mode of address. Family members always say *du* to refer to one another. Children are always addressed with *du* until mid-adolescence. The *du* form is also used in prayers and church services. Finally, *du* is used to address animals.

For Germans, there is nothing stiff about *Sie*. For instance, people may work in the same office for years and still call each other *Sie*, yet the atmosphere can be

Sie wohnen in der Stadt.

Tag!

Critical Thinking: Ask students to think of ways that English speakers differentiate between the concept of *du* and *Sie*. (Possible answers: register levels, tone of voice, forms of address, body language, etc.) Then discuss with students the benefits of being able to distinguish this in German because of the two different words for "you."

25

Do they use du or Sie?

very friendly and pleasant. So, who else uses *du*? Primarily blue-collar workers, students and military personnel or police officers say *du* to each other.

People you know well socially—called *Bekannte* (acquaintances)—are addressed with *Sie*, while close personal friends—called *Freunde*—are addressed with *du*. Young people, too, quickly tend to use the *du* form for one other.

WB Activity 10

S Activity 3

AC/CD

1. Sie
2. Sie
3. Sie
4. du
5. du
6. Sie
7. du
8. du
9. du
10. Sie

6. *Du oder Sie?* **Indicate which form you as a student in Germany would use if you were to talk to these people or animals.**

1. an acquaintance your own age
2. your doctor
3. a police officer
4. your friend
5. your father or mother
6. a teacher
7. a six-year-old child
8. your cat
9. your aunt
10. your friend's uncle

7. *Kombiniere...* **(Combine...) How many sentences can you make using the following words in various combinations? Choose one word or phrase from each column.**

Ich	ist	ein Mädchen
Ali	bin	Gisela
Tina	wohnst	da drüben
Du	kennt	hier
		mein Freund
		in der Stadt

Sprache

The Familiar Form: *du* and *ihr*

The familiar forms *du* and *ihr* are used when speaking to relatives, close friends, children and animals.

> (Mrs. Schmidt is speaking to a child.)

◆ *Wo wohnst du?* Where do you live?

> (Andreas is talking to his new classmates.)

◆ *Woher kommt ihr?* Where do you come from?

Note that *du* is used to address one person and *ihr* is used for two or more people.

> (Andreas and Petra are asked by Kerstin.)

◆ *Wohnt ihr in der Stadt?* Do you live downtown?

The Formal Form: *Sie*

The formal form *Sie* is used when speaking to adults and to those not addressed by their first name.

> (Thomas is talking to his teacher.)

◆ *Wo wohnen Sie, Herr Schulz?* Where do you live, Mr. Schulz?

> (Mrs. Müller talks to her neighbors.)

◆ *Kennen Sie die Hoffmanns, Herr und Frau Meier?* Do you know the Hoffmanns, Mr. and Mrs. Meier?

The formal form *Sie*, in both singular and plural, is always capitalized.

WB Activities 11-12

8. ***Du, ihr, Sie?*** **Which of these forms would you use in the following situations? You are talking to your...**

AC/CD

1. uncle
2. parents
3. teacher
4. dog
5. doctor
6. brother
7. girlfriend
8. pet rabbits
9. friend's aunts
10. school principal

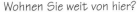

Wohnen Sie weit von hier?

1. du
2. ihr
3. Sie
4. du
5. Sie
6. du
7. du
8. ihr
9. Sie
10. Sie

Tag!

Sprache

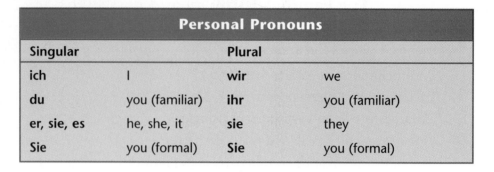

Personal Pronouns			
Singular		**Plural**	
ich	I	**wir**	we
du	you (familiar)	**ihr**	you (familiar)
er, sie, es	he, she, it	**sie**	they
Sie	you (formal)	**Sie**	you (formal)

Present Tense Verb Forms

In the present tense in English, there are basically two different verb forms for all persons. For example, "live" is used for all persons, except after "he," "she" or "it" where it is "live(s)." In German, however, the verb has more forms, as can be seen in the chart.

To use the proper form, you need to know the infinitive of the particular verb. The infinitive of the English verb forms "came" or "comes" is "to come." The infinitive of a German verb ends with *-en* as in *gehen, kommen* or *wohnen* (in a few cases *-n*). The infinitive is a combination of the stem of the verb and the ending (infinitive = stem + ending).

When the stem of a verb is known, you need to know the appropriate ending for the particular singular or plural form.

The present tense of regular verbs requires the endings indicated on the next page.

Wir heißen Sven und Tina.

Kapitel 1

	Stem + Ending	Meaning
Singular ich	geh + *e*	I go, I am going, I do go
du	geh + *st*	you go, you are going, you do go
er		he goes, he is going, he does go
sie	geh + *t*	she goes, she is going, she does go
es		it goes, it is going, it does go
Plural wir	geh + *en*	we go, we are going, we do go
ihr	geh + *t*	you go, you are going, you do go
sie	geh + *en*	they go, they are going, they do go
Sie	geh + *en*	you go, you are going, you do go (sg. & pl.)

 Activities 6-7

NOTE: Should the stem of the verb for *du* end in *s* or *ß*, then the *s* of the ending is dropped.

 Activity 1

◆ *Heißt du Martina?* Is your name Martina?

Praktische Situation

Divide the class into pairs. Ask your partner his or her name, age and where he or she lives. Then get together with another pair of students and tell them the information you have learned about your partner.

Example:

Student 1: *Wie heißt du?*

Student 2: *Ich heiße Heidi.*

Student 1: *Wie alt bist du?*

Student 2: *Ich bin 16.*

Student 1: *Wo wohnst du?*

Student 2: *Ich wohne in Chicago.*

After Student 2 has asked the same questions, the following sample conversation might take place:

Student 1 talks to Students 3 and 4: *Sie heißt Heidi. Heidi ist 16. Sie wohnt in Chicago.*

Students 2, 3 and 4 also present their partner to the others.

Finally, your teacher may select one of you to present the other three to the entire class.

 Activity 13

 Activity 8

Tag!

1. Nein, ich wohne da drüben.
2. Nein, ich wohne gleich um die Ecke.
3. Nein, ich wohne in der Stadt.
4. Nein, ich wohne nicht weit von hier.

1. Ich wohne da. Und du?
2. Ich wohne um die Ecke. Und du?
3. Ich wohne beim Park. Und du?
4. Ich wohne nur fünf Minuten von hier. Und du?
5. Ich wohne in der Stadt. Und du?

9. **Wo wohnst du?** **Assume that you are being asked if you live in a certain location. How might you answer the following questions?**

   ◆ Wohnst du hier? (beim Park)
   ◆ Nein, ich wohne beim Park.

   1. Wohnst du in der Stadt? (da drüben)
   2. Wohnst du hier? (gleich um die Ecke)
   3. Wohnst du beim Park? (in der Stadt)
   4. Wohnst du in Frankfurt? (nicht weit von hier)

10. **Several people are asking you where you live. Answer them with the provided cues and also inquire where they live.**

    ◆ Wo wohnst du? (da drüben)
    ◆ Ich wohne da drüben. Und du?

    1. Wo wohnst du? (da)
    2. Wo wohnst du? (um die Ecke)
    3. Wo wohnst du? (beim Park)
    4. Wo wohnst du? (nur fünf Minuten von hier)
    5. Wo wohnst du? (in der Stadt)

Wir wohnen in Köln.

11. *Wie heißt sie? Wie heißt er?* **Your friend is interested in getting to know some students in your school. Tell your friend their names.**

AC/CD

Natascha

Boris

◆ Wie heißt sie?
Sie heißt Natascha.

◆ Wie heißt er?
Er heißt Boris.

To further practice the expression *Wie heißt er/sie?*, have each student point to a classmate and ask a third student to answer the question. Example: A student points to Patrick while asking Maria, both of whom are classmates, *Wie heißt er, Maria? Er heißt Patrick.*

1. Sie heißt Tina.
2. Sie heißt Britta.
3. Er heißt Ingo.
4. Er heißt Manfred.
5. Er heißt Michael.
6. Sie heißt Julia.

1. Tina

2. Britta

3. Ingo

4. Manfred

5. Michael

6. Julia

Tag!

Übung macht den Meister!

1. Ask the person next to you what his or her name is, where he or she lives and whom he or she knows among your classmates.

2. Greet one of your classmates. Make sure that the greeting includes saying "hello," but also an appropriate handshake.

3. Count off numbers 1-20 in your class by saying the numbers first in sequence, then backward and, finally, skipping either the even or the odd numbers.

After students have worked with individual partners asking questions, have them reverse roles so that they can now answer or respond to questions. For additional activities and games, see the front section of this teacher's edition.

AC/CD

1. Sie heißt Christine.
2. Gabi ist fünfzehn.
3. Ali wohnt gleich um die Ecke.
4. Nein, das ist Bärbel.
5. Ich kenne Peter nicht sehr gut.
6. Er heißt Robert.

AC/CD

1. Wie heißen Sie?
2. Wohnen Sie weit von hier?
3. Wie geht es Ihnen?
4. Kennen Sie Frau Krüger?
5. Kommen Sie aus Frankfurt?

AC/CD

12. **Use the cues to answer each question.**

    1. Wie heißt sie? (Christine)
    2. Wie alt ist Gabi? (fünfzehn)
    3. Wo wohnt Ali? (gleich um die Ecke)
    4. Ist das Angelika? (Bärbel)
    5. Kennst du Peter? (nicht sehr gut)
    6. Wie heißt er? (Robert)

13. **Change each of the following questions from the familiar (du) to the formal (Sie) form.**

    1. Wie heißt du?
    2. Wohnst du weit von hier?
    3. Wie geht's?
    4. Kennst du Frau Krüger?
    5. Kommst du aus Frankfurt?

14. *Ein Interview.* **A German exchange student is meeting you for the first time. Answer the various questions.**

    1. Wie geht's?
    2. Wie heißt du?
    3. Wie alt bist du?
    4. Wo wohnst du?
    5. Wer ist das?

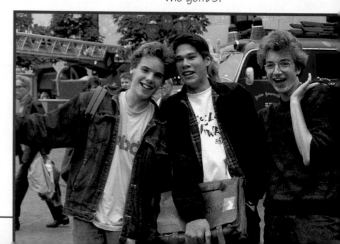

Wie geht's?

15. **Was fehlt hier? (What's missing here?) Select one of the words from the list to complete the dialog.**

gut	Tschüs	Tag	ist	kommt
Wie	du	Ecke	alt	neu

Heidi: ____, Christine!

Christine: ____ geht's, Heidi?

Heidi: Ganz ____.

Christine: Ist Jens ____ hier?

Heidi: Ja, er ____ aus Hamburg.

Christine: Kennst ____ Jens?

Heidi: Ja, er wohnt gleich um die ____.

Christine: Wie ____ ist er?

Heidi: Er ____ sechzehn.

Christine: ____, Heidi.

Tag, Wie, gut, neu, kommt, du, Ecke, alt, ist, Tschüs

16. **Pretend that one of your classmates is meeting you for the first time. He or she is talking to you in German. Can you respond?**

Classmate: Tag!

Du: ____

Classmate: Wie heißt du?

Du: ____

Classmate: Wo wohnst du?

Du: ____

Classmate: Ist das deine Freundin?

Du: ____

Classmate: Wie heißt sie?

Du: ____

Wie heißt du?

Tag!

Aktuelles

Greetings, Farewells and Introductions

The American expressions "Hello!" and "Hi!" have become international greetings, and many younger Germans use them when greeting one another. Their own language, however, did not originally include such short, informal greetings. The normal German greeting is *Guten Tag!* Often the first word is dropped and you'll simply hear *Tag!*

Hallo!

or people just mumble *'n Tag!* In southern Germany you will rarely hear *Guten Tag!* but rather *Grüß Gott!* Young people in that region will also greet each other with *Grüß dich!* In Austria, people often greet each other with *Servus!* Many young people in Germany today are also greeting each other with a simple *Hallo!* which is similar to our "Hi!"

In the morning, most Germans say *Guten Morgen!* or simply *Morgen!* whereas in the evening they say *Guten Abend!* or again just mumble *'n Abend!* When entering a town or city, the visitors are often greeted with a sign that says *Willkommen!*

Auf Wiedersehen! (literally: "Until we see again") or simply *Wiedersehen!* means "good-bye." *Tschüs!* is a very casual form of "good-bye," primarily used in northern Germany. It comes closest to the American "See you!" or "So long!"

Servus!

Germans do a lot more handshaking than Americans. Germans not only shake hands when being introduced, but many still consider a handshake as part of the everyday greeting. To a German, it means little more than saying "Hello." A nod of the head usually accompanies the handshake. When meeting acquaintances in the street, in shops or elsewhere in public, Germans usually shake hands only if they intend to chat.

WB Activity 14

WA Activity 9

17. **Was *weißt du*? (What do you know?)** Complete each statement with the appropriate German phrase or expression based on the *Aktuelles* section.

1. ____! is a more formal form of good-bye than ____!
2. The standard greeting in the morning is ____!
3. In southern Germany, people in the street will greet each other with ____!; however, young people in that region will say ____!
4. The normal German greeting during the day is ____!
5. ____! is the typical good-bye phrase.
6. Austrians will often greet one another with ____!

1 *Auf Wiedersehen / Tschüs*
2. *Guten Morgen*
3. *Grüß Gott / Grüß dich*
4. *Guten Tag*
5. *Auf Wiedersehen*
6. *Servus*

This section, here and in subsequent chapters, is optional. You may wish to use all or part of it for additional reinforcement and practice of the different language skills.

Erweiterung

18. **Ja, *das stimmt.*** You are agreeing with everything you are asked.

◆ Wohnst du hier?
◆ Ja, ich wohne hier.

1. Wohnst du in der Stadt?
2. Kennst du Gisela?
3. Ist das Dieter?
4. Ist er neu hier?
5. Ist Boris vierzehn?
6. Ist vier plus neun dreizehn?
7. Heißt sie Frau Lehmann?
8. Wohnt Tanja beim Park?

1. Ja, ich wohne in der Stadt.
2. Ja, ich kenne Gisela.
3. Ja, das ist Dieter.
4. Ja, er ist neu hier.
5. Ja, Boris ist vierzehn.
6. Ja, vier plus neun ist dreizehn.
7. Ja, sie heißt Frau Lehmann.
8. Ja, Tanja wohnt beim Park.

Wohnen Sie hier in der Stadt?

WB Activities 15-16

WA Activities 10-12

Tag!

S Activity 2

19. Wie viel ist...?

◆ zwei plus vier
◆ Zwei plus vier ist sechs.

1. sieben plus drei
2. zwölf minus fünf
3. acht minus vier
4. zehn plus neun
5. zwanzig minus vierzehn
6. sechs plus elf

20. State each problem and then answer it. *Auf Deutsch, bitte!* **(In German, please.)**

◆ 4 + 1 = _____
◆ Vier plus eins ist fünf.

1. 5 + 8 = _____
2. 1 + 6 = _____
3. 12 - 3 = _____
4. 20 - 11 = _____
5. 4 + 10 = _____
6. 17 - 15 = _____

Das stimmt.

Ich heiße Stefan.

21. *Richtig oder falsch?* (Correct or incorrect?) Decide whether or not the response to each question or statement is appropriate. If it is inappropriate, give a response in German that makes sense.

1. Wie geht's?
   Nein.

2. Wo wohnst du?
   Da drüben.

3. Wie heißt er?
   Sie heißt Maria.

4. Guten Tag, Frau Meier.
   Gut.

5. Wohnen Sie in der Stadt?
   Ja.

6. Kennst du Rainer?
   Ja, er ist mein Freund.

7. Wie viel ist fünf plus vier?
   Nein.

8. Wo ist deine Freundin?
   Hier.

9. Wie geht es Ihnen, Herr Schmidt?
   Nicht schlecht.

10. Heißt du Uwe?
    Ja, gut.

1. falsch/Sehr gut.
2. richtig
3. falsch/Er heißt...(boy's name)
4. falsch/Guten Tag...
5. richtig
6. richtig
7. falsch/Fünf plus vier ist neun.
8. richtig
9. richtig
10. falsch/Nein, ich heiße...

22. **Beantworte diese Fragen!**

1. Wie heißt du?
2. Wie geht's?
3. Wohnst du weit von hier?
4. Wie heißt dein Freund? Deine Freundin?
5. Wo wohnt er? Wo wohnt sie?
6. Wer ist neu hier?

Wie heißt deine Freundin?

Tag!

This optional section is intended as a quick check-up or quiz to help the teacher better determine the students' understanding of the chapter.

1. Hallo!, Tag!, Guten Tag! Grüß Gott!, Grüß dich!; (Auf)Wiedersehen!, Tschüs!, Bis später!
2a. Wie heißt du?
2b. Wie alt bist du?
2c. Wo wohnst du?
2d. Wohnst du weit von hier?
2e. Wer ist das?
2f. Kennst du (name of classmate)?
3. null, eins, zwei, drei, vier, fünf, sechs, sieben, acht, neun, zehn, elf, zwölf, dreizehn, vierzehn, fünfzehn, sechzehn, siebzehn, achtzehn, neunzehn, zwanzig
4a. (Answers will vary.)
4b. Grüß dich!
4c. Tschüs! Auf Wiedersehen!
4d. Servus!

 WB Activities 17-18

 WA Activity 13

 S Activity 5

 OP

 TP

VP

Was weißt du?

This section is intended to check your general understanding of this chapter. Unless indicated *auf Englisch* (in English), all your reponses should be in German.

1. Say hello and good-bye to your classmates and teacher.

2. Ask a classmate these questions and listen to the answers. Then reverse roles:

    a. What is your name?

    b. How old are you?

    c. Where do you live?

    d. Do you live far from here?

    e. Who is that?

    f. Do you know (name of classmate)?

3. Count from 0 to 20.

4. What are the answers to these questions?

    a. Explain the difference of du and Sie. (*Auf Englisch.*)

    b. How do young people greet each other in southern Germany?

    c. What are the casual and more formal forms of saying good-bye?

    d. What do Austrians say when they greet each other?

Also, los!

Vokabeln

aus from
bei at, near; *beim Park* near the park
bist: du bist you are
da there; *da drüben* over there
dein(e) your
denn used for emphasis
die **Ecke,-n** corner
es it
der **Freund,-e** boyfriend
die **Freundin,-nen** girlfriend
ganz quite
gehen to go; *Wie geht's?, Wie geht es Ihnen?* How are you?
gleich immediately, right away; *gleich um die Ecke* right around the corner
gut good
hier here
ihr you (familiar plural)
in in
ja yes
kennen to know (person, place)
kommen to come

mein(e) my
die **Minute,-n** minute
nein no
neu new
nicht not
nur only
der **Park,-s** park
schlecht bad
sehr very
sie they
Sie you (formal)
die **Stadt,-̈e** city
stimmen to be correct; *Das stimmt.* That's correct.
um around; *um die Ecke* around the corner
von from
wahr: nicht wahr? Isn't it true? Isn't that so?
weit far
wir we
wo where
woher where from
wohnen to live

The vocabulary section is intended for reference only. Words have been arranged in alphabetical sequence for easy reference. Although the definite article is not introduced until Chapter 2, nouns and articles are listed along with their respective plural forms. Point out to students that it is important to learn the article with each noun. Some teachers have their students prepare flashcards, using colored 3 x 5 notecards: blue = *der*-words; pink/red = *die*-words; yellow = *das*-words, and white = other parts of speech as well as expressions. The color coding supports students' memory as to the somewhat unpredictable articles of nouns.

Nürnberg, eine Stadt

Meine Familie

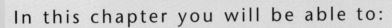

In this chapter you will be able to:

- describe people
- answer a telephone call
- ask what time it is
- point out family members
- ask for and give information
- introduce someone else

Wie findest du die da drüben?

Kennst du sie?

Michael: Wie findest du die da drüben?

Goran: Ganz toll! Ich kenne sie sehr gut.

Michael: Wirklich? Wie alt ist sie denn?

Goran: Fünfzehn. Ivana, komm mal her!

Ivana: Hallo, Goran. Was gibt's?

Goran: Das ist Michael, mein Freund.

Michael: Tag, Ivana. Bist du Gorans Freundin?

Ivana: Aber nein. Goran ist mein Bruder.

1. ***Falsch!*** **The following statements are incorrect. Provide the correct statements in German.**

    1. Goran kennt das Mädchen nicht gut.
    2. Ivana ist sechzehn.
    3. Gorans Freund heißt Mark.
    4. Goran ist Ivanas Freund.

Tag, Ivana.

AC/CD

Hallo, Goran.
Was gibt's?

WB Activity 1

WA Activity 1

AC/CD

1. Er kennt das Mädchen sehr gut.
2. Sie ist fünfzehn.
3. Er heißt Michael.
4. Er ist Ivanas Bruder.

2. Was sagt man? Tell your classmate that...

1. you know a certain person well.
2. you think (name a person) is terrific.
3. your friend is sixteen.
4. (name a person) is your friend.

Sample answers:
1. Ich kenne Petra gut.
2. Robert ist toll.
3. Meine Freundin ist sechzehn.
4. Heiko ist mein Freund.

Ist deine Schwester zu Hause?

Hast du Zeit?

(am Telefon)

Sabine: Sabine Bayer.

Rainer: Hier ist Rainer Kühne. Ist deine Schwester zu Hause?

Sabine: Einen Moment, bitte. Sie ist im Wohnzimmer.

Petra: Hast du Zeit? Kommst du rüber?

Rainer: Ja. Um wie viel Uhr?

Petra: Na, so gegen vier.

Rainer: Das ist zu früh.

Petra: Ist halb sieben zu spät?

Rainer: Nein, das geht. Bis später.

Kommst du rüber?

WB   Activity 2

WA   Activity 2

OT   Activity 13

Meine Familie

3. **Beantworte diese Fragen!**

   1. Wie heißt Petras Schwester?
   2. Ist Petra zu Hause?
   3. Wo ist sie?
   4. Kommt Rainer rüber?
   5. Um wie viel Uhr?

4. ***Wer ist das?*** **Identify each person.** *Diese Person...*

   1. ist im Wohnzimmer.
   2. kommt rüber.
   3. ist Sabines Schwester.
   4. sagt: „Um vier Uhr ist zu früh."

Sprichwort

Freu dich nicht zu früh.

(Don't count your chickens before
they are hatched!)

Für dich

When answering the phone, whether at home or in the office, it is customary in Germany to give one's family name (*Weber!* or *Hier Weber!*). Young people usually answer the phone with their first and last name.

When calling someone you know, you would say *Hier ist...* If you don't know the person, you should start out with *Mein Name ist...*

Rollenspiel

You call your friend and find out if he or she wants to come over. Your friend asks you at what time. You suggest a time, but your friend thinks it's too late. Therefore, you suggest an earlier time to which he or she agrees.

5. *Etwas Persönliches.* (Something personal.)

   1. Wie alt bist du?
   2. Wie heißt dein Freund oder deine Freundin?
   3. Wer ist zu Hause?
   4. Um wie viel Uhr bist du zu Hause?

AC/CD

Aktuelles

The Telephone

The official word for telephone is *Fernsprecher*, but everyone says *Telefon*. The word for phone booth is *die Telefonzelle*. These public phone booths are easily recognized by their bright yellow color. There are always public phones in local post offices and railroad stations and nowadays even in trains and planes.

Most public phones found in phone booths require a *Telefonkarte* which can be purchased at the local post office for 12 or 50 marks. The phone card is inserted into a slot with the magnetic tape side down. The digital display will inform the caller how much credit is left on the card before, during and after the call is made.

Hallo! Ist Christian zu Hause?

Telefonzellen

Meine Familie

Simon macht ein Ferngespräch.

There are still many public phones that will accept coins when making local or long-distance calls. The dialing instructions are clearly posted. In calling, you should follow these steps: 1) Lift the receiver, 2) Put your coins in the slot (three 10 pfennig coins for local calls), 3) Wait for the dial tone, 4) Dial the number.

Long-distance calls to other German cities or foreign countries can be made from any phone booth, at the post office or hotel or from any private phone. If you place a *Ferngespräch* (long-distance call) you should know the *Vorwahl* or *Vorwahlnummer* (area code). In case you don't know this number, you can either look it up in a telephone directory or call *Auskunft* or *Information*. The number for *Auskunft* is: 0 11 18 (national) or 0 01 18 (international).

When making calls from the United States to Germany, Austria or Switzerland, you must dial first the international code "011," followed by the country codes (Germany = 49, Austria = 43, Switzerland = 41), the city or town code and then the local number.

Long-distance calls are measured by pay units (*1 Einheit = 23 Pfennig*) and time. For instance, a person from Munich may call her mother in Hamburg for l mark, but she can talk to her only for a very short time. If she calls someone in Stuttgart, she can talk longer because Stuttgart is not as far from Munich as Hamburg. The caller must feed the coin-operated phone with additional coins in the slots marked *10 Pfennig, 1 Mark, 5 Mark*, whenever there is little money left as indicated by lit-up numbers on the telephone coin box; otherwise the caller will be disconnected immediately.

Die Auskunft, bitte.

Have students determine similarities and differences between the German and the U.S. telephone system. Which one do they prefer?

WB Activity 3

1. *Pfennig*
2. *Vorwahlnummer*
3. *Fernsprecher*
4. *Einheit*
5. *Telefonkarte*
6. *Auskunft (Information)*
7. *Mark*
8. *Telefonzelle*

Was weißt du? **Identify the German words described.**

1. The smallest German monetary unit is called ____.
2. The country code "49" is the ____ for Germany.
3. Another word for *Telefon* is ____.
4. A telephone pay unit is called ____.
5. If the public phone won't accept coins, you'll need a ____.
6. When a phone number is not known, the caller can either look it up in a phone book or call ____.
7. One *Pfennig* is one hundredth of one ____.
8. A ____ is bright yellow and is usually located outside of buildings.

Ergänzung

Die Familie

Albert Brenninger
der Großvater (Opa)

Martha Brenninger
die Großmutter (Oma)

Martina Kemmer
die Tante

Michael Kemmer
der Onkel

Andreas Kemmer
der Vater (Vati)

Silke Kemmer
die Mutter (Mutti)

Christian Kemmer
der Sohn

Nina Kemmer
die Tochter

Andreas Kemmer ist Ninas Vater.

Silke Kemmer ist Christians und Ninas Mutter.

Andreas und Silke Kemmer sind Christians und Ninas Eltern.

Christian ist Ninas Bruder.

Nina ist Christians Schwester.

Christian ist der Sohn von Andreas und Silke Kemmer.

Nina ist die Tochter von Andreas und Silke Kemmer.

Albert Brenninger ist Christians und Ninas Großvater (Opa).

Martha Brenninger ist Christians und Ninas Großmutter (Oma).

Albert und Martha Brenninger sind Christians und Ninas Großeltern.

Michael Kemmer, der Bruder von Andreas Kemmer, ist Christians und Ninas Onkel.

Martina Kemmer ist Christians und Ninas Tante.

Include some additional family members so that all students can participate according to their situation. Additional family members could include: *der Cousin (die Cousine), der Neffe (die Nichte), der Enkel (die Enkelin), der Stiefvater (die Stiefmutter), der Stiefbruder (die Stiefschwester), der Halbbruder (die Halbschwester)*. See also the list in the *Übung macht den Meister* section of this chapter.

 WB Activity 4

 WA Activity 3

 OT Activities 14-15

 S Activity 3

Meine Familie

1. Nina
2. Martina Kemmer
3. Albert Brenninger
4. Martha Brenninger
5. Andreas Kemmer
6. Christian

6. Beantworte diese Fragen!

1. Wer ist Christians Schwester?
2. Wie heißt Ninas Tante?
3. Wie heißt Silke Kemmers Vater?
4. Wer ist Christians Großmutter?
5. Wer ist Michael Kemmers Bruder?
6. Wie heißt Andreas Kemmers Sohn?

7. *Deine Familie.* Talk with a classmate about his or her family members. Then, reverse roles and talk about your family.

Sag's mal! Wie findest du Michael oder Ivana? Er/Sie ist...

intelligent* toll O.K.* arrogant* spitze* altmodisch* super lässig* sympathisch* nett* langweilig gemein* ganz eingebildet* interessant* charmant* gutaussehend* klasse* cool* klug* lustig*

Sprache

Formation of Questions

To form a question you must use the so-called inverted word order. The subject and the verb of the sentence are interchanged.

Statement: *Du kommst früh.* You are coming early.
Question: *Kommst du früh?* Are you coming early?

◆ *Wohnt Herr Riebe in Hamburg?* Does Mr. Riebe live in Hamburg?

◆ *Haben wir Zeit?* Do we have time?

◆ *Kennst du Tina?* Do you know Tina?

Wohnt Herr Riebe in Hamburg?

You can readily see that the formation of questions in German is simpler than in English where most questions use the form of "to do" (do you?, does he?, etc.).

The inverted word order is also used with such question words as those listed below:

◆ *Wie?* How? What? *Wie spät ist es?* How late is it? What time is it?

◆ *Wo?* Where? *Wo wohnst du?* Where do you live?

◆ *Was?* What? *Was hast du?* What do you have?

◆ *Wer?* Who? *Wer ist das?* Who is that?

◆ *Wie viel?* How much? *Wie viel ist drei plus vier?* How much is three plus four?

Wie viel Uhr ist es?

Point out the difference in intonation between a statement and a question.

 Activities 5-6

 Activity 4

 Activity 5

8. **Hartmut is quite inquisitive. He asks you lots of questions. Answer affirmatively.**

   1. Ist Monika vierzehn?
   2. Kommst du rüber?
   3. Kennst du Rainer?
   4. Ist Petra zu Hause?
   5. Wohnst du weit von hier?
   6. Ist es zehn Uhr?

   1. Ja, sie ist vierzehn.
   2. Ja, ich komme rüber.
   3. Ja, ich kenne Rainer.
   4. Ja, sie ist zu Hause.
   5. Ja, ich wohne weit von hier.
   6. Ja, es ist zehn Uhr.

Have students work in groups to come up with additional questions. Have other groups answer them. Then have students reverse roles so that everyone can ask and answer some questions.

Meine Familie

1. Wer kennt Ali sehr gut?
2. Wer ist das?
3. Wo wohnt Herr Tielmann?
4. Wie viel ist vier plus neun?
5. Wo ist Tina?
6. Was haben Petra und Rainer?

1. Wie
2. Wo
3. Wie
4. Wer
5. Wo
6. Wie
7. Wie
8. Wer

9. Ask questions about the italicized items.

◆ Sie heißt *Beate*.
◆ Wie heißt sie?

1. *Dieter* kennt Ali sehr gut.
2. Das ist *Anne*.
3. Herr Tielmann wohnt *in München*.
4. Vier plus neun ist *dreizehn*.
5. Tina ist *im Wohnzimmer*.
6. Petra und Rainer haben *Zeit*.

Wo wohnt Herr Tielmann?

10. *Wie? Wo?* oder *Wer?*

1. ____ alt bist du?
2. ____ wohnt dein Freund?
3. ____ viel Uhr ist es?
4. ____ kommt später?
5. ____ ist Bensheim?
6. ____ heißen Sie?
7. ____ viel ist achtzehn minus neun?
8. ____ ist Ivanas Bruder?

11. Kombiniere...

Kennt	Roland	deine Freundin
Ist	Frau Riebe	sechzehn
Bist	Heidi	toll
Kommt	dein Freund	gegen sieben
	du	zu Hause
		rüber

Ergänzung

10	20	30	40	50
zehn	zwanzig	dreißig	vierzig	fünfzig
60	70	80	90	100
sechzig	siebzig	achtzig	neunzig	hundert einhundert

1000
tausend
eintausend

21
einundzwanzig

22
zweiundzwanzig

Es ist ein Uhr.

Es ist acht Uhr.

Wie viel Uhr ist es?
(Wie spät ist es?)

Es ist halb zehn.

Es ist halb drei.

Es ist elf Uhr.

WA   Activities 5-6

OT   Activities 16-17

Point out that the *s* in *eins* is dropped when *Uhr* (o'clock) is added. Example: *Es ist eins.* but *Es ist ein Uhr.* Practice the different times with a cardboard clock so that students get additional reinforcement.

WB   Activities 7-9

WA   Activity 7

OT   Activities 18-19

S   Activity 4

Meine Familie

12. *Wie viel Uhr ist es?* **Look at the different clocks and indicate in words what time it is.**

1. Es ist neun (Uhr).
2. Es ist halb zwei.
3. Es ist halb fünf.
4. Es ist zwölf (Uhr).
5. Es ist halb elf.
6. Es ist fünf (Uhr).

1.

2.

3.

4.

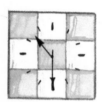

5.

6.

WB Activity 10

13. *Wie ist die Telefonnummer von...?* **You have been asked to look up several phone numbers. Say each name and corresponding phone number as listed.**

Naomi Saber	87 02 18
Josef Sähler	22 71 39
Petra Sawatski	93 24 20
Elfriede Schelle	75 10 54
Markus Schenker	37 19 03
Maria Schiller	68 21 49
Harald Schiermann	83 60 47
Claudia Schlafer	31 02 48
Barbara Schlosser	58 84 01
Arthur Schlotrich	95 26 75
Marianne Schnorre	80 39 63
Iwan Schölkl	61 94 08
Rosa Scholtes	29 77 53
Toni Schreiber	48 39 81
Hannelore Schuster	12 34 60
Andrea Siebert	73 88 93
Hanno Sieger	13 87 59
Konstantin Siewanus	52 06 69
Rita Skaboski	97 49 33
Veronika Sollner	48 53 67
Andrea Sölke	26 09 27

◆ You see: *Hannelore Schuster 12 34 60*
◆ You say: *Hannelore Schuster, zwölf - vierunddreißig - sechzig*

1. Toni Schreiber
2. Maria Schiller
3. Andrea Siebert
4. Rita Skaboski
5. Barbara Schlosser
6. Naomi Saber
7. Veronika Sollner
8. Markus Schenker

Cooperative Learning Activities: Divide the class into groups and have the group members ask each other about their phone numbers *(Wie ist deine Telefonnummer?)*. One person could be the recorder and write down each number.

14. *Um wie viel Uhr...?* **Imagine that you are in charge of a social activity. Various members of your club ask you questions pertaining to time. Give them the appropriate information.**

◆ Um wieviel Uhr kommt Tanja? (sieben Uhr)
◆ Sie kommt um sieben Uhr.

1. Um wie viel Uhr kommt Günter rüber? (halb vier)
2. Um wie viel Uhr hat Gabi Zeit? (drei Uhr)
3. Um wie viel Uhr ist deine Freundin zu Hause? (halb zwei)
4. Um wie viel Uhr kommen Gisela und Tina? (halb neun)
5. Um wie viel Uhr ist dein Freund hier? (sechs Uhr)

1. Er kommt um halb vier rüber.
2. Sie hat um drei Uhr Zeit.
3. Sie ist um halb zwei zu Hause.
4. Sie kommen um halb neun.
5. Er ist um sechs Uhr hier.

Um wie viel Uhr kommen Sie?

Meine Familie

Sprache

The Definite Article
(Nominative Singular): der, die, das (the)

In German there are three variations of the definite article in the nominative singular, *der*, *die* and *das*. The nominative is used to identify the subject.

◆ *Der Junge ist siebzehn.* The boy is seventeen.

◆ *Die Stadt ist toll.* The city is great.

◆ *Das Telefon ist da drüben.* The telephone is over there.

Note that all nouns in German (including names and places) are capitalized. It is extremely important to learn the articles that accompany the individual nouns. We refer to these as masculine *(der)*, feminine *(die)* and neuter *(das)*. Be aware, however, that the nouns associated with either of the three articles are not necessarily "masculine" or "feminine" or "neuter" by context—the article for a man's tie *(die Krawatte)* is feminine, while a woman's scarf *(der Schal)* is masculine.

Singular		
masculine	feminine	neuter
nominative		
der	die	das

15. ***der, die* oder *das*?**

◆ Uhr
◆ die Uhr

1. Mädchen
2. Junge
3. Frau
4. Ecke
5. Tag
6. Telefon
7. Freund
8. Schwester
9. Tante
10. Wohnzimmer
11. Zeit
12. Freundin

die Kuckucksuhr

Lesestück

Zu Hause

Cornelia wohnt mit ihrer Mutter° in Leipzig. Leipzig ist eine Stadt im Osten von Deutschland°. Heute, am Sonntag°, hat sie viel Zeit. Cornelias Freundin heißt Nicole. Was macht° Nicole heute? Cornelia ist am Telefon.

Cornelia und ihre Mutter

Nicole:	Nicole Nitschke!
Cornelia:	Hallo, Nicole! Hier ist Cornelia.
Nicole:	Na, was gibt's?

Was machst du denn?

Cornelia:	Was machst du denn?
Nicole:	Ich lese ein Buch°.
Cornelia:	Wie langweilig°! Ich bin auch zu Hause.
Nicole:	Kommst du rüber?
Cornelia:	Um wie viel Uhr?
Nicole:	Es ist jetzt° drei Uhr. Um halb fünf?

 WB Activities 12-13

 LA Activities 1-3

 WA Activity 8

Cornelia:	Ja, gut. Was machen wir dann°?
Nicole:	Ich habe zwei CDs von den Pilos Puntos°. Ganz toll! Wie findest du die?
Cornelia:	Ist das die Rockgruppe°?
Nicole:	Ja, kennst du die nicht?
Cornelia:	Nicht sehr gut.
Nicole:	Die sind wirklich super!
Cornelia:	Bis später.
Nicole:	Tschüs!

mit ihrer Mutter with her mother; *im Osten von Deutschland* in the east of Germany; *Heute, am Sonntag...* Today, on Sunday...; *Was macht...?* What is... doing?; *Ich lese ein Buch.* I'm reading a book.; *langweilig* boring; *jetzt* now; *dann* then; *Pilos Puntos* name of teenage rock group; *die Rockgruppe* rock group

Personalize the *Lesestück* by having students act out a scene from their own experience. The new words are listed following the *Lesestück* for easy reference, as well as in the vocabulary of this lesson and at the end of this book.

Die sind wirklich super!

Meine Familie

Für dich

You already know that the word *denn* is used primarily for emphasis and has no meaning. The word *dann* means "then" and is used in reference to an earlier statement which carries the meaning "after that" or "next."

16. *Was passt hier?* **Complete these sentences by using the appropriate words listed.**

1. Cornelia kommt	a. Pilos Puntos
2. Es ist jetzt	b. am Telefon
3. Die Rockgruppe ist	c. mit ihrer Mutter
4. Nicole hat	d. um halb fünf
5. Cornelia kennt	e. die Rockgruppe nicht sehr gut
6. Cornelia wohnt	f. wirklich super
7. Die Rockgruppe heißt	g. zwei CDs
8. Cornelia ist	h. drei Uhr

17. **Beantworte diese Fragen!**

1. Wo wohnen Cornelia und ihre Mutter?
2. Wie heißt Cornelias Freundin?
3. Um wie viel Uhr kommt Cornelia rüber?
4. Was hat Nicole?
5. Wie heißt die Rockgruppe?
6. Wie findet Nicole die Rockgruppe?
7. Kennt Cornelia die Rockgruppe?

Cornelia wohnt in Leipzig.

Ergänzung

Point out that there are two words for "Saturday." *Samstag* is used primarily in southern Germany, whereas *Sonnabend* is more frequently heard in northern Germany.

AC/CD

Activities

WB 14-16

WA Activity 9

OT Activities 20-21

S Activity 2

Meine Familie

18. *Welcher Tag ist morgen?* Beantworte diese Fragen!

◆ Heute ist Freitag. Und morgen?
◆ Morgen ist Sonnabend.

1. Morgen ist Freitag.
2. Morgen ist Mittwoch.
3. Morgen ist Sonntag.
4. Morgen ist Donnerstag.
5. Morgen ist Montag.

1. Heute ist Donnerstag. Und morgen?
2. Heute ist Dienstag. Und morgen?
3. Heute ist Samstag. Und morgen?
4. Heute ist Mittwoch. Und morgen?
5. Heute ist Sonntag. Und morgen?

Hast du die CDs von dieser Rockgruppe?

Übung macht den Meister!

PA

1. Pretend you are calling your friend. Ask if your friend has CDs. Your friend tells you that he or she has some from a well-known rock group. Your friend asks if you know this rock group. You answer the question and tell your friend that you'll be over at a certain time.

2. Count from 1 to 50, first counting the odd numbers only and then the even numbers. Try it backward, too.

3. *Meine Familie.* Develop a short family tree using the vocabulary from this chapter. Some additional names for relatives you may wish to use are: *der Urgroßvater* (great-grandfather), *die Urgroßmutter* (great-grandmother), *der Cousin* or *der Vetter* (male cousin), *die Cousine* (female cousin), *der Neffe* (nephew), *die Nichte* (niece), *der Stiefvater* (stepfather), *die Stiefmutter* (stepmother), *der Stiefbruder* (stepbrother), *die Stiefschwester* (stepsister), *der Halbbruder* (half brother), *die Halbschwester* (half sister).

Aktuelles

What Time Is It?

One of the most important phrases to know in any language is "What time is it?" In Germany, you will find many clocks that will answer your question immediately. However, sometimes you will need to ask someone for the time. The most common ways to ask the time are *Wie viel Uhr ist es?* or *Wie spät ist es?* Here are some examples of expressing time in German:

In Meersburg ist es Viertel nach zwei.

Wie spät ist es in München?

10:00 = Es ist zehn Uhr.

8:00 = Es ist acht.

3:30 = Es ist drei Uhr dreißig. (Es ist halb vier.)

12:30 = Es ist zwölf Uhr dreißig. (Es ist halb eins.)

8:15 = Es ist acht Uhr fünfzehn. (Es ist Viertel nach acht. *or:* Es ist ein Viertel neun.)

12:45 = Es ist zwölf Uhr fünfundvierzig. (Es ist Viertel vor eins. *or:* Es ist drei Viertel eins.)

7:10 = Es ist sieben Uhr zehn. (Es ist zehn Minuten nach sieben Uhr. *or:* Es ist zehn nach sieben.)

11:55 = Es ist elf Uhr fünfundfünfzig. (Es ist fünf vor zwölf.)

4:40 = Es ist vier Uhr vierzig. (Es ist zwanzig vor fünf.)

10:20 = Es ist zehn Uhr zwanzig. (Es ist zwanzig Minuten nach zehn. *or:* Es ist zehn Minuten vor halb elf.)

9:35 = Es ist neun Uhr fünfunddreißig. *or:* Es ist fünf Minuten nach halb zehn.

Und wie viel Uhr ist es hier?

Meine Familie

Germans do not use the A.M./P.M. system. The traveler will have to become familiar with the 24-hour system in a hurry, particularly when dealing with the official language used on radio and TV or at train stations and airports. The 24-hour system is used primarily to avoid

Um wie viel Uhr ist die nächste Abfahrt?

Um wie viel Uhr ist die letzte Abfahrt (last departure)?

misunderstandings. There is no problem with the numbers 1 to 12, as they designate the A.M. period of time. Numbers 13 to 24 indicate the hours that we call P.M. A train leaving at 2:21 P.M., for instance, would be announced as *14.21 (vierzehn Uhr einundzwanzig)*.

In everyday conversation, Germans often use the time expressions *morgens*, *nachmittags* and *abends* to avoid misunderstanding. For example, Germans might tell their friends that they are coming to visit them at 8 P.M. by saying, *Wir kommen um acht Uhr abends*.

Wie viel Uhr ist es? **Complete each time expression by providing the missing words.**

1. 12:38 = Es ist zwölf Uhr _____.
2. 6:30 = Es ist _____ sieben.
3. 2:52 = Es ist _____ Minuten vor drei.
4. 9:00 = Es ist _____ Uhr.
5. 10:45 = Es ist _____ vor elf.
6. 4:10 = Es ist _____ nach vier.
7. 1:18 = Es ist ein Uhr _____.
8. 7:35 = Es ist _____ Minuten nach halb acht.

Wie viel Uhr ist es?
(Kirchheim/Teck)

1. achtunddreißig
2. halb
3. acht
4. neun
5. Viertel
6. zehn
7. achtzehn
8. fünf

 WB Activity 17

Praktische Situation

Um wie viel Uhr kommt...? Your teacher is organizing an all-day outing to an amusement park nearby. Not everyone can come at the same time. Form groups of three to five. Write your name and the time that you can come on a piece of paper. Then pass your paper to another student in the group. One student in each group is the recorder and asks each group member, *Um wie viel Uhr kommt* (name of person)? The person holding the paper with that name responds (name of person) *kommt um...Uhr.* The recorder makes a complete list of names and times and reports the information to the class spokesperson, who writes all the names and times in chronological order on the board or on a transparency.

WA Activity 10

Erweiterung

19. *Was ist deine Telefonnummer?* **You are meeting several young people from Germany and would like to have their phone numbers. They give you their numbers. Can you say them in German?**

    1. 7 13 05
    2. 60 24 19
    3. 9 03 31 82
    4. 12 52 77
    5. 3 22 38
    6. 5 09 83 11

    1. sieben / dreizehn / null fünf
    2. sechzig / vierundzwanzig / neunzehn
    3. neun / null drei / einunddreißig / zweiundachtzig
    4. zwölf / zweiundfünfzig / siebenundsiebzig
    5. drei / zweiundzwanzig / achtunddreißig
    6. fünf / null neun / dreiundachtzig / elf

20. *Was fehlt hier?* **(What's missing here?)**

    1. elf, ____, dreizehn, vierzehn, ____ , sechzehn, ____, achtzehn, neunzehn, ____
    2. Montag, ____, Mittwoch, ____, Freitag, Sonnabend, ____
    3. vier, ____, zwölf, sechzehn, ____, ____ achtundzwanzig, zweiunddreißig, ____, vierzig

WB Activity 18

Have students ask each other *Was ist deine Telefonnummer?* to give them more practice with numbers. Point out that Germans usually say phone numbers in clusters (5 78 14 = *fünf, achtundsiebzig, vierzehn*), in comparison to our way of saying the individual digits. In Germany, phone numbers can have four digits in rural areas and up to seven digits in big towns or cities.

WB Activity 19

1. zwölf, fünfzehn, siebzehn, zwanzig
2. Dienstag, Donnerstag, Sonntag
3. acht, zwanzig, vierundzwanzig, sechsunddreißig

21. *Wie viel Uhr ist es?* A number of people don't have a watch. They are asking you for the time. Respond to them by using the cues given.

◆ Wieviel Uhr ist es? (10)
◆ Es ist zehn.

1. Wie viel Uhr ist es? (8)
2. Wie viel Uhr ist es? (12)
3. Wie viel Uhr ist es? (5)
4. Wie viel Uhr ist es? (2)
5. Wie viel Uhr ist es? (9)

1. Es ist acht.
2. Es ist zwölf.
3. Es ist fünf.
4. Es ist zwei.
5. Es ist neun.

22. You are meeting Silke, an acquaintance of yours, in the school cafeteria after school. Respond to Silke based on the information given.

Silke: Grüß Gott!
Du: ____
Silke: Was machst du hier?
Du: ____
Silke: Wie spät ist es?
Du: ____
Silke: Kommst du später rüber?
Du: ____
Silke: So gegen acht.
Du: ____

Sample answers:
Grüß Gott, Silke!
Ich lese ein Buch.
Es ist vier (Uhr).
Um wie viel Uhr?
Ja. Das geht.

Hallo! Grüß Gott!

Kapitel 2

23. *Was fehlt hier?* Use one of the words from the list below to complete each sentence and the conversation.

macht	Zeit	kommt	Wo	Freundin
Stadt	weit	sechzehn	ist	wohnt

1. Wo ____ Rainer?
2. In der ____.
3. Was ____ er heute?
4. Er ____ zu Hause.
5. Hat Rainer eine ____?
6. Ja, Bianca. Sie ist ____.
7. ____ wohnt Bianca?
8. Nicht ____ von Rainer.
9. Hat Rainer heute ____?
10. Ja. Bianca ____ rüber.

1. wohnt
2. Stadt
3. macht
4. ist
5. Freundin
6. sechzehn
7. Wo
8. weit
9. Zeit
10. kommt

24. *Das ist falsch.* Your cousin's younger brother has difficulty with simple addition and subtraction problems. You help him solve each problem.

◆ Drei plus vier ist sechs.
◆ Falsch. Drei plus vier ist sieben.

1. Neun plus drei ist fünf.
2. Zehn minus acht ist null.
3. Zwanzig minus neun ist zehn.
4. Vierzehn plus drei ist dreizehn.
5. Elf plus zwei ist fünfzehn.

1. Falsch. Neun plus drei ist zwölf.
2. Falsch. Zehn minus acht ist zwei.
3. Falsch. Zwanzig minus neun ist elf.
4. Falsch. Vierzehn plus drei ist siebzehn.
5. Falsch. Elf plus zwei ist dreizehn.

Welche Nummern (numbers) haben sie?

Meine Familie

Was weißt du?

1. Tell your classmates about four family members or relatives and indicate their names and ages and where they live.

2. Write down four times during the day and what happens at that time. Working in pairs, ask your classmate to do the same. Take turns pointing to each item on one another's list and identify the time. Reverse roles until all times have been said aloud. Sample items could be: getting up (6:30), breakfast (7:00), beginning of school (8:00), etc. Use only full or half hours on your list.

3. Write down several names and their respective phone numbers. The names and phone numbers can be your own, your relatives', your friends', etc. Exchange your list with a classmate. Ask each other such questions as: *Wer ist das? Was ist Onkel Herberts Telefonnummer?* Your classmate will respond accordingly.

4. Describe where you live, who else lives there and what time you are usually at home.

5. Describe some of the differences in making phone calls on a public telephone in this country and in Germany. (*Auf Englisch.*)

6. Count in fives from 0 to 100.

7. Say in German

   a. how old your friend is

   b. where he or she lives

   c. that your friend's brother or sister is terrific

   d. that you will come over at a certain time

Das Hotel ist nicht weit von hier.

 WB — Activity 20

 WA — Activity 11

S — Activity 6

 OP

 TP VP

---

1. Sample answers:
   Mein Bruder heißt Robert. Er ist zehn.
   Meine Mutter heißt Elisabeth Brown. Sie ist vierzig.
   Meine Tante heißt Veronica Johnson. Sie ist vierunddreißig.
   Mein Großvater heißt Daniel Taylor. Er ist siebzig.

2. Sample answers:
   (pointing to "getting up")
   Wie viel Uhr ist es? Es ist halb sieben.
   (pointing to "breakfast") Es ist sieben (Uhr).

3. Answers will vary.

4. Sample answers:
   Ich wohne in (name of town or city).
   Mein Vater, meine Mutter und mein Bruder wohnen auch da.
   Ich bin um halb vier zu Hause.

5. Answers will vary.

6. null, fünf, zehn, fünfzehn, zwanzig, fünfundzwanzig, dreißig, fünfunddreißig, vierzig, fünfundvierzig, fünfzig, fünfundfünfzig, sechzig, fünfundsechzig, siebzig, fünfundsiebzig, achtzig, fünfundachtzig, neunzig, fünfundneunzig, (ein)hundert

7. Sample answers:
   a. Peter ist vierzehn.
   b. Er wohnt nicht weit von hier.
   c. Peters Bruder (Schwester) ist toll.
   d. Ich komme um halb sechs rüber.

Vokabeln

aber but; *aber nein* of course not

achtzig eighty

an at, on; *am Sonntag* on Sunday

auch also, too

bis until; *Bis später.* See you later.

bitte please

der **Bruder,-** brother

das **Buch,-er** book

die **CD,-s** CD, compact disk

dann then

das the

der the

Deutschland Germany

die the

der **Dienstag,-e** Tuesday

der **Donnerstag,-e** Thursday

dreißig thirty

die **Eltern** (pl.) parents

finden to find; *Wie findest du...?* What do you think of...?

der **Freitag,-e** Friday

früh early

fünfzig fifty

gegen about, around; *gegen vier Uhr* about four o'clock

gehen to go; *das geht* that's possible, that's OK

gibt's: Was gibt's? What's up?

die **Großeltern** (pl.) grandparents

die **Großmutter,-** grandmother

der **Großvater,-** grandfather

habe: ich habe I have

halb half

hast: Hast du...? Do you have...?; *sie hat...* she has...

hat: er/sie hat he/she has

Hause: zu Hause at home

herkommen to come here

heute today

hundert hundred

ihr(e,er) her

in in; *im Osten* in the east

jetzt now

kommen to come; *rüberkommen* to come over; *Kommst du rüber?* Are you coming over?; *herkommen* to come here; *Komm mal her!* Come here!

langweilig boring

lesen to read

machen to do, make; *Was machst du?* What are you doing?

mit with

der **Mittwoch,-e** Wednesday

der **Moment,-e** moment; *Einen Moment, bitte.* Just a moment, please.

der **Montag,-e** Monday

morgen tomorrow

die **Mutter,-** mother

die **Mutti,-s** mom

na well

neunzig ninety

oder or

die **Oma,-s** grandma

der **Onkel,-** uncle

der **Opa,-s** grandpa

der **Osten** east

die **Rockgruppe,-n** rock group, rock band

rüberkommen to come over

der **Samstag,-e** Saturday

die **Schwester,-n** sister

sechzig sixty

siebzig seventy

sind: sie sind they are

so so; *so gegen vier* at about four (o'clock)

der **Sohn,-e** son

der **Sonnabend,-e** Saturday

der **Sonntag,-e** Sunday

spät late; *später* later; *Bis später.* See you later.

super super, great

die **Tante,-n** aunt

tausend thousand

das **Telefon,-e** telephone; *am Telefon* on the telephone

die **Tochter,-** daughter

toll great, terrific; *ganz toll* just great (terrific)

die **Uhr,-en** clock, watch; *Um wie viel Uhr?* At what time?

um at; *Um wie viel Uhr?* At what time?

der **Vater,-** father

der **Vati,-s** dad

viel much

vierzig forty

was what

welcher which

wie how, what; *Wie findest du...?* What do you think of...?

wirklich really

das **Wohnzimmer,-** livingroom

die **Zeit,-en** time

zu at, to, too; *zu Hause* at home

Ein Telefon ist in der Telefonzelle.

das Telefon

Meine Familie

Kapitel **3**

Was machst du?

In this chapter you will be able to:

- ask and tell what someone is doing
- talk about what interests you
- express likes and dislikes
- give opinions
- report information

Was machst du heute?

Heike möchte zum Rockkonzert

Natascha: Was machst du heute?

Heike: Ich spiele Tennis.

Natascha: Und morgen?

Heike: Ich möchte zum Rockkonzert. Kommst du mit?

Natascha: Wie viel kostet die Karte?

Heike: Sie ist sehr preiswert. Nur zwanzig Mark.

Natascha: Prima. Wann geht's los?

Heike: Um acht. Gut, ich kaufe zwei Karten.

Explain that *möchte* can be used without an infinitive and if the verb is understood. If it's not clear, the infinitive will appear at the end of the sentence. (*Ich möchte zum Rockkonzert [gehen]. Ich möchte das kaufen.*)

Natascha

Heike

1. *Richtig oder falsch?* **Determine whether the following statements are correct or incorrect. If they are incorrect, provide a correct statement in German.**

   1. Heike spielt morgen Tennis.
   2. Natascha kommt zum Rockkonzert mit.
   3. Zwei Karten kosten zwanzig Mark.
   4. Das Rockkonzert ist um zwei Uhr.

2. *Wie fragt man?* **(How do you ask?) Read the following questions in English. Then ask the same questions in German. Your classmate will respond in German.**

   1. What are you doing tomorrow?
   2. And today?
   3. Are you coming along?
   4. When does it start?
   5. What are you buying?
   6. Is the ticket reasonable?

Sie hören CDs und Kassetten

Ali: Wohin gehst du denn?

Torsten: Nach Hause. Und du?

Ali: Zu Sarah. Wir hören CDs und Kassetten.

Torsten: Ich sehe fern. Um zehn nach sieben gibt's einen Krimi.

Ali: Musik ist mir lieber. Du, Torsten, ich habe jetzt auch einen Computer. Möchtest du morgen rüberkommen?

Torsten: Ja, gern.

Ich sehe fern.

Musik ist mir lieber.

Was machst du?

AC/CD

1. falsch / Heike spielt heute Tennis.
2. richtig
3. falsch / Zwei Karten kosten vierzig Mark. (Eine Karte kostet zwanzig Mark.)
4. falsch / Das Rockkonzert ist um acht Uhr.

1. Was machst du morgen? Ich spiele Tennis.
2. Und heute? Ich lese ein Buch.
3. Kommst du mit? Ja, ich komme mit.
4. Wann geht's los? Um sieben Uhr.
5. Was kaufst du? Ich kaufe zwei Karten.
6. Ist die Karte preiswert? Ja, sie ist preiswert.

AC/CD

WB Activities 1-2

WA Activity 1

OT Activity 22

3. Beantworte diese Fragen!

1. Wohin geht Torsten?
2. Und wohin geht Ali?
3. Was hören Sarah und Ali?
4. Um wie viel Uhr gibt's einen Krimi?
5. Was hat Ali jetzt?
6. Kommt Torsten heute zu Ali rüber?

4. Was passt hier?

auch   machst   Computer   sehe   CDs   du   sieben   später

- Was hörst ____ jetzt?
- Kassetten und ____. Und was ____ du?
- Ich ____ fern. Und ____?
- Um ____ kommt Anne rüber. Ich habe einen ____. Möchtest du ____ kommen?
- Nein.

Sprichwort

Morgen, morgen, nur nicht heute, sagen alle faulen Leute.

(Don't put off until tomorrow what you can do today.)

Für dich

The German television system is considerably different from the American. The two major networks (*ARD* and *ZDF*) carry a high proportion of documentaries, news magazines, talk shows, cultural programs and commentaries. On

the other hand, the new private channels allow a relatively broad latitude in programming compared with *ARD* and *ZDF*, although the television market is more restricted by regulations in comparison to our television.

Even though there is some advertising on German TV, generally packed into several short broadcasts at the beginning of the evening programs, the main source of income is the monthly operating license fee which each radio and television owner pays. In recent years, several commercial TV channels (cable and satellite) have been introduced in Germany to offer viewers more diverse programs. It is also noteworthy that TV programs do not necessarily start at half past the hour or on the hour. The commercial stations do not share in the license fee and, therefore, show more commercials than public stations.

Rollenspiel

You and your friend discuss what you would like to do today. In your conversation include such items as (1) what activity it is, (2) where it will take place, (3) what time you'll get together and (4) what the cost will be, if any.

5. Etwas Persönliches.

1. Was möchtest du morgen machen?
2. Wann geht's los?
3. Wer kommt mit?
4. Hast du einen Computer zu Hause?
5. Um wie viel Uhr möchtest du fernsehen?
6. Kommt dein Freund oder deine Freundin rüber?

Jochen hat einen Computer zu Hause.

Was machst du?

Aktuelles

Youth Activities

Young people in Germany today have more leisure time *(Freizeit)* than their parents a generation ago. Leisure time plays a big part in the lives of young people. What do they like to do? Their interests are not much different from those of young people in other countries.

Almost half of all young people participate in sports *(Sport)*, ranging from organized sports sponsored by local clubs to neighborhood get-togethers. Soccer clubs *(Fußballklubs)* are the most popular.

Two out of five young people enjoy hanging around town and talking to friends about such things as which

Sportverein Borussia

fashion designers are "in" and all the things you can't afford on an average monthly allowance *(Taschengeld)* of about 60 marks.

Television *(Fernsehen)* occupies a tremendous amount of their time as do videocassette recorders *(Videorekorder)* and CD players *(CD-Spieler)*. Almost half of the Germans have a computer *(Computer)* at home which is used not only for family business transactions but also for playing the many computer games *(Computerspiele)* now available for young and old alike.

im Jugendklub

Ist das ein neues Fahrrad?

Sie spielen gern Billard.

Going to the movies is still a favorite pastime *(Zeitvertreib)* as well as cruising around by bike *(Fahrrad)*, *Mofa (Motorfahrrad)* or motorized bicycle and *Moped*. On weekends, many young people head for the local discos *(Diskos* or *Diskotheken)* that can be found in every German city and town.

There is no lack of leisure-time activities available to young people by the local communities *(Gemeinschaften)*, churches *(Kirchen)*, social clubs *(Gesellschaftsklubs)* and youth organizations *(Jugendorganisationen)*. Many other countries envy the numerous sports facilities, hobby centers, libraries, continuing education courses, trips and youth exchanges offered young people in Germany.

Was machen sie gern?

Was passt hier?

1. Many young people like to join ____.
2. When showing a video, you'll need a ____.
3. The most popular clubs are called ____.
4. Close to 50 percent of all Germans own a ____.
5. A bike with an attached motor is called a ____.
6. Just as in this country, many Germans like to watch ____.
7. Young Germans enjoy more ____ than their parents.
8. Young Germans like to go to their local ____ on weekends.
9. A two-wheel vehicle without a motor is called ____.
10. Most parents give their children ____ for spending money.

1g, 2f, 3j, 4i, 5c, 6a, 7e, 8b, 9h, 10d

a. *Fernsehen*
b. *Diskos*
c. *Mofa*
d. *Taschengeld*
e. *Freizeit*
f. *Videorekorder*
g. *Jugendorganisationen*
h. *Fahrrad*
i. *Computer*
j. *Fußballklubs*

Activity 2

Was machst du?

Ergänzung

The verb forms of *sehen* and *lesen* are covered in later chapters along with other verbs that have stem vowel changes. You may want to avoid the *du, er, sie, es* personal pronouns at this point.

 WB Activities 3-4

 LA Activity 1

 WA Activity 3

OT Activities 23-24

Was spielt er?

6. **Was machen diese Personen?**

1. Bianca

2. Rolf und Jürgen

3. meine Freundin und ich

4. Dieter

5. Herr und Frau Köhler

6. Herr Pigini

1. Bianca spielt Gitarre.
2. Rolf und Jürgen spielen Fußball.
3. Meine Freundin und ich sehen fern.
4. Dieter hört Rockmusik.
5. Herr und Frau Köhler tanzen.
6. Herr Pigini spielt Klavier.

Was machst du?

7. **Was machst du diese Woche? (What are you doing this week?)**
   Your friend wants to get together with you this week.
   Unfortunately, you are busy with various activities. Tell your
   friend what you are doing each day.

You may want to explain
inverted word order here.
See *Sprache* section,
page 81

◆ Montag
◆ Am Montag spiele ich Fußball.

1. Dienstag
2. Mittwoch
3. Donnerstag
4. Freitag
5. Samstag
6. Sonntag

1. Am Dienstag lese ich
   ein Buch.
2. Am Mittwoch
   schwimme ich.
3. Am Donnerstag spiele
   ich Gitarre.
4. Am Freitag sehe ich
   fern.
5. Am Samstag tanze ich.
6. Am Sonntag höre ich
   Musik.

8. **Was machst du gern?** You and your classmate make a list of
   various activities. Then ask each other whether or not you like
   to do each activity. Write *ja* if the response is positive and *nein*
   if it is negative.

Kapitel 3

Sag's mal!

Wie ist die Rockmusik?

super

phantastisch*

total in Ordnung*

echt gut*

toll

gut zum Anhören*

abscheulich*

nicht so gut

zu laut*

ausgezeichnet*

schlecht

es geht so*

nicht besonders gut*

soso*

geil*

erstklassig*

Praktische Situation

Was machst du gern? Was machst du nicht gern? Form groups of three to find out what each of you likes or doesn't like to do.

- Student 1 makes a list under the heading *Was ich gern mache.*
- Student 2 makes a list under the heading *Was ich nicht gern mache.*
- Student 3 makes two lists: one under the heading *Was ich gern mache*; the other under the heading *Was ich nicht gern mache.*

Student 3 also serves as the group's recorder. To begin, Student 3 asks Student 1 what activities he or she likes. If Student 1 likes the same activity as Student 3, Student 3 makes a check beside the name of that activity on the appropriate sheet. Then Student 3 asks Student 2 the same questions. If Student 3 finds that Student 2 dislikes the same activity, Student 3 makes a check beside the name of that activity on the appropriate sheet. After Students 1 and 2 have reported all their likes and dislikes to Student 3, Student 3 may tell the entire class what likes and dislikes all the group members share.

Was machst du?

Sprache

Present Tense of *haben*

Although most verbs show the regular pattern of conjugation (stem + ending), there are several verbs that do not follow this pattern, as in the case with *haben* (to have).

Singular		
	ich habe	I have
	du hast	you have
	er ⎱	he has
	sie ⎬ hat	she has
	es ⎰	it has
Plural		
	wir haben	we have
	ihr habt	you have
	sie haben	they have
	Sie haben	you have
	(sg. & pl.)	

◆ *Hast du Zeit?* Do you have time?
◆ *Ja, ich habe Zeit.* Yes, I have time.
◆ *Habt ihr einen Videorekorder zu Hause?* Do you have a VCR at home?
◆ *Ja, wir haben einen Videorekorder.* Yes, we have a VCR.

9. You are agreeing with your friend on several issues.

◆ Ich habe einen Computer? Und du?
◆ Ich habe auch einen Computer.

1. Ich habe Zeit. Und du?
2. Ich habe CDs. Und du?
3. Ich habe eine Freundin. Und du?
4. Ich habe ein Computerspiel. Und du?
5. Ich habe einen Krimi. Und du?
6. Ich habe eine Karte. Und du?

Even though some of the following sentences contain forms of the direct object, to be introduced in Chapter 4, they should be treated here only in context.

 WB Activity 5

 WA Activity 4

 S Activity 2

AC/CD

1. Ich habe auch Zeit.
2. Ich habe auch CDs.
3. Ich habe auch eine Freundin.
4. Ich habe auch ein Computerspiel.
5. Ich habe auch einen Krimi.
6. Ich habe auch eine Karte.

10. **Wer hat heute Zeit?** You are asking who has some time today. Luckily, everyone does.

◆ Hat Natascha heute Zeit?
◆ Ja, sie hat heute Zeit.

1. Hast du heute Zeit?
2. Habt ihr heute Zeit?
3. Haben Herr und Frau Bilski heute Zeit?
4. Hat Frau Wiedemann heute Zeit?
5. Haben Sabine und Udo heute Zeit?
6. Hat Bruno heute Zeit?

1. Ja, ich habe heute Zeit.
2. Ja, wir haben heute Zeit.
3. Ja, sie haben heute Zeit.
4. Ja, sie hat heute Zeit.
5. Ja, sie haben heute Zeit.
6. Ja, er hat heute Zeit.

Simon und Tina haben heute Zeit.

11. **Kombiniere...**

Daniel	haben	drei Karten
Katarina	spiele	Kassetten
Claudia und Renate	hört	Zeit
Ich	hat	einen Computer
	kaufen	Tennis

Was machst du?

Ergänzung

Note to your students:
The following new rule
applies. *Es ist Viertel drei.*
Wir kommen um viertel
drei nach Hause.

vor   nach

Wie viel
Uhr ist es?

(Wie spät
ist es?)

WA   Activity 5

Es ist Viertel nach eins.

Es ist Viertel vor zehn.

OT   Activities 25-26

Es ist fünf Minuten
nach zwölf.

Es ist acht Minuten
vor vier.

Write various times on the
board or hand out some
flashcards. Ask students
Wie viel Uhr ist es?

Was gibt's
heute im
Fernsehen?

Um 15.10 Uhr
(Um fünfzehn
Uhr zehn)
gibt es...

Wann beginnt das
Fernsehprogramm...?

Es beginnt um
19 Uhr 35
(neunzehn Uhr
fünfunddreißig).

WB   Activities 6-7

heute Morgen   *heute Mittag*   *heute Nachmittag*   *heute Abend*

Sprache

Word Order

As you have seen so far, you can form a sentence in German by starting with the subject followed by the verb and then adding additional information.

◆ *Ich wohne in der Stadt.* I live downtown.

◆ *Heike hört gern Rockmusik.* Heike likes to listen to rock music.

As discussed in the previous chapter, you must use the inverted word order to form questions.

◆ *Gehst du nach Hause?* Are you going home?

◆ *Was machst du heute?* What are you doing today?

The inverted word order is also used when you start a sentence with a word other than the subject of the sentence.

◆ *Später sehe ich fern.* Later I'll watch TV.

◆ *Um halb vier spielen wir Fußball.* At half past three we'll play soccer.

WB Activity 8

S Activity 4

Was spielen die Jungen?

Was machst du?

12. **Tell what everyone is doing at the time indicated. Start your sentence with the time.**

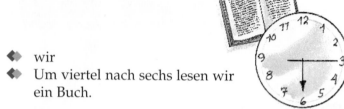

◆ wir
◆ Um viertel nach sechs lesen wir ein Buch.

1. Barbara

2. Herr und Frau Taube

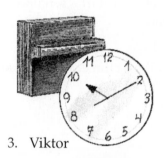

3. Viktor

4. Rainer und Maria

5. Petra und Julia

1. Um viertel vor acht spielt Barbara Basketball.
2. Um sechs Minuten nach fünf sehen Herr und Frau Taube fern.
3. Um zehn Minuten nach zehn spielt Viktor Klavier.
4. Um zwanzig Minuten vor neun tanzen Rainer und Maria.
5. Um fünf Minuten vor drei spielen Petra und Julia Computerspiele.

13. *Was gibt's im Fernsehen?* **Look at the TV schedule and tell what is being shown at the time indicated.**

Sendungen am Samstag

ARD

7.35 Babar
8.00 Floris Zapp Zarapp
8.30 Prinz Eisenherz
9.00 heute
9.03 Käpt'n Blaubär Club
10.00 heute
10.03 Jagd um die Welt
10.30 Metro
11.00 heute
11.03 König der Spaßmacher Komödie, USA 1958
12.40 Umschau
12.55 Presseschau
13.00 heute
13.05 Europamagazin
13.30 Preisgekrönte Industriefilme
14.00 Royalty
15.00 Kinderquatsch
15.30 Ratgeber Auto & Verkehr
16.00 Tagesschau
16.05 Disney Club
17.30 Sportschau
18.04 Wetterschau
18.10 Air Albatros, Serie
19.10 Sportschau/Lottozahlen
20.00 Tagesschau
20.15 Fröhlich eingeschenkt Show mit Heinz Schenk
21.45 Tagesthemen
22.08 Das Wort zum Sonntag
22.13 Schmidteinander
23.13 Long Riders (Vorschau)
0.50 Tagesschau
1.00 Der stählerne Vorhang Film (Vorschau)
2.55 Z.E.N.

ZDF

8.00 Nachbarn in Europa
9.00 heute
9.03 Euro
9.45 Tele-Gym
10.00 heute
10.03 Crack, Drogenreportage
10.45 Kurzratgeber: Reise
11.03 Pingu
11.10 Spreepiraten
11.55 Öko Aktiv
12.00 Sport extra: Tennis-Damen-Turnier in Leipzig, Halbfinale; Golf: German Masters aus Motzen
16.35 heute
16.40 Länderspiegel
17.10 Die große Hilfe
17.15 Die Schwarzwaldklinik
19.00 heute, Wetter
19.25 Vorsicht, Falle!
20.15 Aber bitte mit Sahne Geburtagsshow mit Udo Jürgens und der Ersten Allgemeinen Verunsicherung, Gotthard, PUR, Sepp Maier, Alfred Biolek u. a. (Übertragung aus Innsbruck)
22.00 heute-journal
22.20 Das aktuelle Sport-Studio
23.40 Die MondSchein-Show
0.40 Das Beste aus „Disco '79" u.a. mit Bonnie Tyler; Mod.: Ilja Richter
1.40 heute
1.45 Incident . . ., Film (Vorschau)

◆◆ 17.30
◆◆ Im ARD gibt es um siebzehn Uhr dreißig ein Fernsehprogramm. Es heißt „Sportschau".

1. 9.45
2. 16.00
3. 22.08
4. 19.25
5. 9.03
6. 15.30
7. 23.13
8. 11.10

Was gibt's im Fernsehen?

1. Im ZDF gibt es um neun Uhr fünfundvierzig ein Fernsehprogramm. Es heißt „Tele-Gym".
2. Im ARD gibt es um sechzehn Uhr ein Fernsehprogramm. Es heißt „Tagesschau".
3. Im ARD gibt es um zweiundzwanzig Uhr acht ein Fernsehprogramm. Es heißt „Das Wort zum Sonntag".
4. Im ZDF gibt es um neunzehn Uhr fünfundzwanzig ein Fernsehprogramm. Es heißt „Vorsicht, Falle!"
5. Im ZDF gibt es um neun Uhr drei ein Fernsehprogramm. Es heißt „Euro".
6. Im ARD gibt es um fünfzehn Uhr dreißig ein Fernsehprogramm. Es heißt „Ratgeber Auto & Verkehr".
7. Im ARD gibt es um dreiundzwanzig Uhr dreizehn ein Fernsehprogramm. Es heißt „Long Riders (Vorschau)".
8. Im ZDF gibt es um elf Uhr zehn ein Fernsehprogramm. Es heißt „Spreepiraten".

Was machst du?

14. *Heute Morgen? Heute Mittag? Heute Nachmittag? Heute Abend?*
Indicate when these various activities take place. The times are
given using the 24-hour system.

◆ Der Krimi beginnt um 21.30 Uhr.
◆ Heute Abend.

1. Christine kommt um 19.30 Uhr rüber.
2. Ich bin um 7.30 zu Hause.
3. Meine Tante kommt um 12.00 Uhr.
4. Um 9.30 Uhr spielen wir Tennis.
5. Wir gehen um 20.00 Uhr zur Disko.
6. Das Rockkonzert beginnt Uhr um 15.30 Uhr.
7. Das Fernsehprogramm beginnt sehr spät, um 22.10 Uhr.

1. Heute Abend.
2. Heute Morgen.
3. Heute Mittag.
4. Heute Morgen.
5. Heute Abend.
6. Heute Nachmittag.
7. Heute Abend.

Sprache

zu Hause and *nach Hause*

There is a distinct difference in using these two phrases. *Zu Hause*
means "at home" (location), whereas *nach Hause* implies "(going)
home" (motion).

◆ *Wo ist Heidi?* Where is Heidi?
◆ *Sie ist zu Hause.* She is at home.
◆ *Wohin geht Uwe?* Where is Uwe going to?
◆ *Er geht nach Hause.* He is going home.

WB Activity 9

S Activity 5

15. "*Zu Hause*" oder "*nach Hause*"? Are the various people at
home (*zu Hause*) or are they going home (*nach Hause*)?

1. Um wie viel Uhr gehen Tanja und Silke____?
2. Werner ist nicht ____.
3. Hast du Kassetten ____?
4. Maria kommt spät ____.
5. Herr Braun ist schon früh ____.
6. Ich möchte jetzt ____ gehen.

1. nach Hause
2. zu Hause
3. zu Hause
4. nach Hause
5. zu Hause
6. nach Hause

Was machen sie gern zu Hause?

84

Kapitel 3

Lesestück

Bastian und Uli gehen nach Hause

Bastian und Uli wohnen in Füssen. Das ist eine Stadt in Süddeutschland°. Heute ist Samstag. Es ist halb zwölf. Bastian und Uli haben viel Zeit. Sie gehen jetzt nach Hause. Da kommen Steffie und Anke. Steffie ist Bastians Freundin.

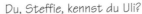

Du, Steffie, kennst du Uli?

Bastian: Hallo! Was macht ihr denn hier?

Steffie: Wir gehen zum Kaufhaus°. Anke kauft eine CD von einer Rockgruppe aus Amerika.

Bastian: Du°, Steffie, kennst du Uli?

Steffie: Ja, er wohnt gleich um die Ecke.

Uli: Aber ich kenne deine Freundin nicht.

Steffie: Oh, Entschuldigung°! Das ist Anke Rühmann. Sie kommt aus Göttingen. Sie ist neu hier.

Uli: Tag, Anke. Wo wohnst du denn?

Anke: In der Steinstraße, nicht weit von der Schule°.

Steffie

Was machst du?

85

Anke

Explain that similar to *möchte* without an infinitive, *muss* also can be without an infinitive as long as the main verb is understood within the context.

Bastian: Hast du später Zeit?

Steffie: Ja, warum°?

Bastian: Mein Vater hat einen neuen Computer. Wir spielen heute Nachmittag Computerspiele.

Steffie: Wirklich? Das mache ich auch gern. Kommst du mit, Anke?

Anke: Klar°. Um wie viel Uhr?

Bastian: Um drei?

Anke: Sagen wir° halb vier. Ich muß zuerst° nach Hause. Meine Tante ist heute aus Augsburg hier. Sie muss um Viertel nach drei zum Bahnhof°.

Uli: Prima. Bring doch deine neue CD mit°.

Bastian: Dann spielen wir Computerspiele und hören Rockmusik.

Bring doch deine neue CD mit.

Dann spielen wir Computers
und hören Rockmusik.

Süddeutschland southern Germany; *zum Kaufhaus* to the department store; *Du...* Say...; *Entschuldigung!* Excuse me!; *die Schule* school; *warum* why; *Klar.* Of course.; *Sagen wir...* Let's say...; *zuerst* first; *der Bahnhof* (railroad) station; *Bring doch...mit.* Why don't you bring...along.

Bis später!

WB Activities 10-12

LA Activity 2

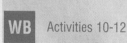
WA Activity 6

16. *Was fehlt hier?* Complete each sentence with an appropriate word.

1. Füssen ist eine ____ in Süddeutschland.
2. Uli und Bastian haben heute viel ____.
3. Sie gehen um halb zwölf ____ Hause.
4. Steffie und Anke gehen zum ____.
5. Anke möchte eine ____ kaufen.
6. Die Rockgruppe kommt aus ____.
7. Uli wohnt gleich um die ____ von Steffie.
8. Anke kommt aus ____.
9. Die Steinstraße ist nicht weit von der ____.
10. Bastians ____ hat einen Computer zu Hause.
11. Ankes Tante ist aus ____.
12. Bastian, Uli, Steffi und Anke hören später ____.

1. Stadt
2. Zeit
3. nach
4. Kaufhaus
5. CD
6. Amerika
7. Ecke
8. Göttingen
9. Schule
10. Vater
11. Augsburg
12. Rockmusik

Füssen ist eine Stadt in Süddeutschland.

17. **Beantworte diese Fragen!**

1. Wohin gehen Uli und Bastian?
2. Ist Anke Bastians Freundin?
3. Woher kommt die Rockgruppe?
4. Kennt Uli Anke?
5. Wo wohnt Anke?
6. Wer hat einen neuen Computer?
7. Was spielt Bastian später?
8. Wohin muss Anke zuerst?
9. Warum?
10. Um wie viel Uhr geht Anke zu Bastian?

AC/CD

1. Sie gehen nach Hause.
2. Nein, Steffie ist Bastians Freundin.
3. Sie kommt aus Amerika.
4. Nein, er kennt sie nicht.
5. Sie wohnt in der Steinstraße (Sie wohnt nicht weit von der Schule.)
6. Bastians Vater hat einen neuen Computer.
7. Er spielt später Computerspiele.
8. Sie muss zuerst nach Hause.
9. Ankes Tante ist da.
10. Sie geht um halb vier.

Was machst du?

Ergänzung

WB — Activities 13-14

LA — Activity 3

WA — Activity 7

S — Activity 3

AC/CD
1. Marcus kommt aus Meißen. Meißen liegt bei Dresden.
2. Volker kommt aus Celle. Celle liegt bei Hannover.
3. Armin kommt aus Bad Homburg. Bad Homburg liegt bei Frankfurt.
4. Sonja kommt aus Burgstadt. Burgstadt liegt bei Chemnitz.
5. Nina kommt aus Ratingen. Ratingen liegt bei Düsseldorf.
6. Simon kommt aus Fürth. Fürth liegt bei Nürnberg.

18. *Woher kommt...?* All the German exchange students in your area have gathered for a welcome reception at your school. You have a list of the students' names and where they are from. As your classmates inquire about each student, you tell them their names, and the town they are from, and the major city nearby.

◆ Woher kommt Anneliese? (Wörth / Regensburg)
◆ Anneliese kommt aus Wörth. Wörth liegt bei Regensburg.

1. Woher kommt Marcus? (Meißen / Dresden)
2. Woher kommt Volker? (Celle / Hannover)
3. Woher kommt Armin? (Bad Homburg / Frankfurt)
4. Woher kommt Sonja? (Burgstadt / Chemnitz)
5. Woher kommt Nina? (Ratingen / Düsseldorf)
6. Woher kommt Simon? (Fürth / Nürnberg)

19. *Wo liegt...?* Look at a German map and locate the following cities.

◆ Hamburg
◆ Hamburg liegt im Norden.

1. Stuttgart
2. Kiel
3. Dresden
4. Leipzig
5. Düsseldorf
6. Bremen
7. Rostock
8. Augsburg

Have students look at a map and ask each other to locate various cities.

1. Stuttgart liegt im Süden.
2. Kiel liegt im Norden.
3. Dresden liegt im Osten.
4. Leipzig liegt im Osten.
5. Düsseldorf liegt im Westen.
6. Bremen liegt im Norden.
7. Rostock liegt im Norden.
8. Augsburg liegt im Süden.

Übung macht den Meister!

1. You and your classmate are planning the activities for the next week. Make a weekly calendar including the days and various times. Then write down all the activities for each one of you with your names next to the activity. Discuss the weekly activities, asking and answering questions.

2. *Um wie viel Uhr...?* Write down three to five questions dealing with time and pass them to another classmate who will answer them. Your questions could include topics such as asking the time for going home, meeting with other friends, participating in activities, watching TV, reading a book, listening to music, etc.

3. Ask your classmates what kind of music they like to listen to and what the music is like. *Was hörst du gern? Warum hörst du das gern? Wie ist die Musik?*

4. Pick a German city and ask one of your classmates a question like *Wo liegt Köln?* Your classmate should provide an answer such as *Köln liegt im Westen.*

Was machst du?

PA

Ask each pair of students to write their names on their proposed schedule. Then have them exchange schedules with their partner and ask what their partner's activity will be. This is good practice of *er/sie* (singular) and *sie* (plural) forms.

WB Activity 15

Aktuelles

Leisure-Time Activities

The German people—young and old—enjoy many leisure-time activities. From September through May, millions of German fans watch the major and minor soccer matches throughout the country every week. During the summer, many Germans head for the water for swimming, sailing or fishing. Some rent boats of various types and explore the rivers and lakes on their own. Every city has one or more outdoor swimming pools that offer many modern facilities to the public.

Segeln in Kiel

Snowboarding in den Alpen

The winter months offer other entertainment opportunities. Ice-skating, for example, has become very popular, particularly among the young. Furthermore, Germans head south to the Alps to go skiing—downhill or cross-country.

Every eighth German is a hiker. Major parks and forests have numerous marked hiking paths that are usually outlined on large boards at the entrance to the park or forest. Bicycling is another popular diversion among all age groups. There are many well-marked bicycle paths in the cities and towns and throughout the countryside.

People who don't care to exert themselves in active sports can stroll around the beautifully landscaped parks found throughout Germany. After a long walk, it is no problem to find a place to sit down. Ample benches are provided for people to relax and watch the world go by.

Outdoor cafés have long been traditional German gathering places. Here, people order a cup of coffee or a glass of cola and sit for an hour or two without an obligation to order anything else.

Die Deutschen fahren gern Fahrrad.

Er hat viel Spaß.

Outdoor chess games are quite popular. Chess figures two or three feet high are moved on one-foot squares. Minigolf courses can be found throughout Germany as well. Unusual to Americans are the concrete putting areas. Also surprising to many Americans is the fact that Germans consider yard work a leisure-time activity. Those who are not fortunate enough to have their own yard may have a *Kleingarten* (sometimes called *Schrebergarten*) on the edge of town. On this rented plot, they spend hours and hours tending flowers, trees, fruits and vegetables.

Germans enjoy reading in their spare time. There are newspaper stands scattered all over. Many Germans, regardless of age, can be seen reading in outdoor restaurants, on benches or, as a matter of fact, anyplace they can find a spot to sit down.

Viele fahren gern mit dem Boot.

Another common leisure-time activity in Germany is watching television. Although most Germans have a wide range of interests, more than one-fourth consider television viewing as their only pastime. Similar to American teenagers, many young people in Germany enjoy listening to popular music on the radio, or on cassettes or CDs. Others practice playing their own instruments. Of course, the larger cities offer international music events, ranging from Broadway musicals and rock concerts to operas.

Tischtennis

The most popular leisure-time activity today is the computer. Germans enjoy the variety of challenging games and the educational opportunities which the computer has to offer.

Sie spielen Schach im Park.

Was machst du?

Was passt hier?

1. watching TV
2. 12.5
3. nine
4. town
5. bicycle paths
6. café
7. squares
8. concrete
9. computer
10. cities

1. More than 25 percent of Germans consider ____ as their leisure-time activity.
2. ____ percent of Germans are hikers.
3. The soccer season in Germany lasts ____ months.
4. The *Kleingarten* is usually found right outside of ____.
5. Many bikers in German towns and cities ride on ____.
6. Germans can sit for a long time in a ____ drinking a cup of coffee.
7. Big chess figures are moved on one-foot ____.
8. Many German minigolf courses are ____.
9. The ____ is the most popular leisure-time activity among Germans.
10. Internationally known rock stars are scheduled throughout the year in larger ____.

Sie fahren auf dem Fahrradweg.

Praktische Situation

Form groups of three. Student 1 prepares a list of leisure-time activities in Germany; Student 2 prepares a list of leisure-time activities in the United States. Student 3 is the discussion leader and begins by asking Student 1 to read the first activity on his or her list. All three students decide if this activity is uniquely German, uniquely American or takes place in both countries. After all activities have been categorized, Student 3 makes a diagram of two intersecting circles and writes each activity in the appropriate place.

20. *Beantworte diese Fragen!* **A new student has moved into your neighborhood. He or she would like to get to know you better and, therefore, is asking you several personal questions. Provide the appropriate information.**

  1. Wie heißt du?
  2. Wo wohnst du?
  3. Wo ist deine Schule?
  4. Was machst du gern?
  5. Hast du am Samstag Zeit?
  6. Hörst du gern Rockmusik?
  7. Hast du Kassetten oder CDs?
  8. Um wie viel Uhr kommst du rüber?

WB Activities 16-18

WA Activities 8-10

21. *Wie sagt man's?* **From the list below, select the appropriate words to complete the various conversational exchanges.**

meine	viel	aus	ganz
ist	zwei	sechzehn	nach

  1. Woher kommst du?

      Ich komme ____ Düsseldorf.
  2. Wie alt bist du?

      Ich bin ____.
  3. Kennst du Uwe?

      Ja, er ____ Petras Freund.
  4. Kommst du am Mittwoch rüber?

      Nein, am Mittwoch habe ich nicht ____ Zeit.
  5. Was machst du jetzt?

      Ich gehe ____ Hause. Und du?
  6. Ich kaufe Julia ____ CDs.

      Wer ist denn Julia?
  7. Das ist ____ Freundin. Kennst du sie?

      Nein.
  8. Sie ist ____ toll.

      Na dann, bis später.

1. aus
2. sechzehn
3. ist
4. viel
5. nach
6. zwei
7. meine
8. ganz

Was machst du?

Hat sie Kassetten?

22. *Was passt hier?* **Find the correct response to each question.**

1. Wie viel Uhr ist es denn?
2. Hast du CDs?
3. Was kosten die Karten?
4. Was gibt's heute Abend im Fernsehen?
5. Spielst du Computerspiele?
6. Wohnst du in Süddeutschland?
7. Hat dein Bruder einen Computer?
8. Warum gehst du so früh nach Hause?
9. Woher kommt Diana?
10. Wann beginnt das Fernsehprogramm?

a. Ja, in Füssen.
b. Einen Krimi.
c. Aus Leipzig.
d. Dreißig Mark.
e. Um 20 Uhr 15.
f. Mein Onkel aus Köln ist da.
g. Es ist jetzt Viertel vor drei.
h. Nein, heute nicht.
i. Ja, zehn oder zwanzig.
j. Nein, aber meine Schwester.

23. Gerd meets Silvia after school. Take Silvia's part and respond to Gerd appropriately.

Gerd: Grüß dich, Silvia!

Silvia: ____

Gerd: Wie viel Uhr ist es jetzt?

Silvia: ____

Gerd: Was machst du denn?

Silvia: ____

Gerd: Nach Hause? So früh?

Silvia: ____

Gerd: Wie heißt denn deine Freundin?

Silvia: ____

Gerd: Und wo wohnt Renate?

Silvia: ____

24. *Was gibt's im Fernsehen?* **List five different television programs that you like to watch, including their respective times. Use the 24-hour system.**

◆ 6:15 P.M. / Sunday / Sports
◆ Um 18 Uhr 15 gibt's „Sports" am Sonntag.

Rückblick

1. **Complete the paragraph choosing the appropriate forms from these verbs:** *kommen, haben, heißen, kosten, wohnen, tanzen, spielen, liegen, hören, sein.*

Susanne ____ in Halle. Halle ____ im Osten von Deutschland. Susanne ____ einen Bruder. Er ____ Rainer. Rainer und Susanne ____ gern Klavier. Susanne ____ aber nicht so gut. Heute ____ Susannes Freundin Monika rüber. Susanne und Monika ____ gern CDs. Am Freitag abend ____ sie gern in einer Disko. Zwei Karten ____ nur zwölf Mark.

2. **Wann? Was? Wie? Wo? Woher? Wohin?**

   1. ____ kommt Dieter? Aus Heidelberg.
   2. ____ machst du jetzt?
   3. ____ geht ihr denn? Nach Hause.
   4. ____ findest du Katarina? Ganz toll.
   5. ____ spielen wir Fußball? Um halb drei.
   6. ____ liegt Füssen?

If students have difficulties with any of these review exercises, you may want to go back to the chapter in which the structural item is practiced.

wohnt, liegt, hat, heißt, spielen, ist, kommt, hören, tanzen, kosten

1. Woher
2. Was
3. Wohin
4. Wie
5. Wann
6. Wo

Activity 1

Wohin gehen sie?

Was machst du?

3. Holger and Uwe are busy this weekend. Tell what they are doing.

◆ Holger / schwimmen
◆ Holger schwimmt.

1. Uwe / Computerspiele spielen
2. Uwe und Holger / ein Buch lesen
3. Holger / Rockmusik hören
4. Holger / CDs kaufen
5. Uwe und Holger / Basketball spielen
6. Holger und Uwe / zum Kaufhaus gehen

Das Mädchen spielt Klavier.

1. Uwe spielt Computerspiele.
2. Uwe und Holger lesen ein Buch.
3. Holger hört Rockmusik.
4. Holger kauft CDs.
5. Uwe und Holger spielen Basketball.
6. Holger und Uwe gehen zum Kaufhaus.

4. *Wie viel Uhr ist es?* **Give the complete answer. Use the 24-hour system.**

◆ 6:10 P.M.
◆ Es ist achtzehn Uhr zehn.

1. 8:12 A.M.
2. 10:40 P.M.
3. 1:30 P.M.
4. 11:23 A.M.
5. 5:52 A.M.
6. 7:06 P.M.
7. 9:00 P.M.
8. 2:38 P.M.
9. 6:48 A.M.
10. 3:15 A.M.

1. Es ist acht Uhr zwölf.
2. Es ist zweiundzwanzig Uhr vierzig.
3. Es ist dreizehn Uhr dreißig.
4. Es ist elf Uhr dreiundzwanzig.
5. Es ist fünf Uhr zweiundfünfzig.
6. Es ist neunzehn Uhr sechs.
7. Es ist einundzwanzig Uhr.
8. Es ist vierzehn Uhr achtunddreißig.
9. Es ist sechs Uhr achtundvierzig.
10. Es ist drei Uhr fünfzehn.

Wie viel Uhr ist es in Binz?

5. *Wer ist...?* Look at the family tree and determine who is described.

Großvater
Herbert Köhler

Großmutter
Ingrid Köhler

Mutter
Marion Stainer

Vater
Helmut Stainer

Onkel
Dieter Stainer

Tante
Petra Stainer

Sven

Ralf

Susanne

1. Er ist Svens Bruder.
2. Sie sind Ralfs Eltern.
3. Sie ist Herbert Köhlers Tochter.
4. Sie ist Ralfs Schwester.
5. Sie sind Susannes Großeltern.
6. Er ist Helmuts Bruder.
7. Sie ist Susannes Tante.
8. Er ist Marions Vater.

1. Ralf
2. Marion und Helmut Stainer
3. Marion Stainer
4. Susanne
5. Herbert und Ingrid Köhler
6. Dieter
7. Petra Stainer
8. Herbert Köhler

Was machst du?

6. ***Kennst du das Mädchen?*** **You are talking to your friend and are trying to find out more about a girl in your class. Using the verbs provided, complete the following dialog.**

Du: Wie (heißen) ____ sie?

Freund: Karin. Sie (wohnen) ____ gleich um die Ecke.

Du: (Kennen) ____ du sie?

Freund: Nicht sehr gut. Sie (haben) ____ einen Bruder und eine Schwester.

Du: Wie (heißen) ____ sie?

Freund: Heiko und Maria. Heiko (spielen) ____ Tennis und Maria (tanzen) ____ gern. Karin, komm bitte her!

Karin: Hallo! Was (machen) ____ du jetzt?

Freund: Wir (gehen) ____ nach Hause. Oh, das ist mein Freund.

Karin: Tag! Ich (haben) ____ heute viel Zeit. Ich (möchten) ____ in die Stadt. (Kommen) ____ du mit?

Freund: Nein.

Du: Ich (gehen) ____ auch in die Stadt, zum Kaufhaus. Ich (kaufen) ____ ein Buch.

Karin: Dann (gehen) ____ wir zwei.

Du: Klar.

Ich kaufe ein Buch.

Kapitel 3

7. **Gisela has moved from Lübeck to Regensburg. She is writing her friend Natascha.**

Have students write a short letter to a friend or relative. Point out to students that Germans no longer capitalize *du*-forms in letters and other correspondence.

26. November

Grüß Gott, Natascha!

Das sagen sie hier und nicht „Tag!" Die Stadt Regensburg ist super. Meine Eltern, mein Bruder Peter und ich wohnen hier in der Stadt nicht weit vom Bahnhof. Zur Schule muss ich fünfzehn Minuten gehen. Meine Freundin Sarah wohnt gleich um die Ecke. Heute am Samstagnachmittag (hier sagen sie nicht „Sonnabend") kommt Sarah rüber. Dann hören wir CDs, spielen Karten und gehen um acht zur Disko. Und wie geht's dir? Wie geht's deinem Freund Michael? Spielt er jetzt nicht Gitarre in einer Rockgruppe? Es ist jetzt halb elf. Ich muss zum Kaufhaus. Ich kaufe da ein Computerspiel. Tschüs!

Deine

Gisela

Beantworte diese Fragen!

1. Sagen sie „Tag!" in Regensburg?
2. Wie findet Gisela Regensburg?
3. Wo wohnt Gisela in Regensburg?
4. Wie weit ist es zur Schule?
5. Wer ist Giselas Freundin?
6. Was machen Gisela und ihre Freundin am Samstag?
7. Wie heißt Nataschas Freund?
8. Wohin geht Gisela?

1. Nein, sie sagen „Grüß Gott!"
2. Sie findet Regensburg super.
3. Sie wohnt in der Stadt nicht weit vom Bahnhof.
4. Fünfzehn Minuten.
5. Sarah ist Giselas Freundin.
6. Sie hören CDs, spielen Karten und gehen zur Disko.
7. Er heißt Michael.
8. Sie geht zum Kaufhaus.

Was machst du?

Was weißt du?

1. *Am Sonnabend gehen wir zum Rockkonzert.* Develop a conversation with a classmate in which you discuss a rock concert that both of you would like to attend. Your conversation may include such items as the time and place of the concert, where you can buy tickets, the cost for the tickets, the names of others who might come along and at what time you have to be home.

2. *Was gibt's im Fernsehen?* Everyone in your class will write down five TV programs (including the days and times) that they would like to watch during the week. Ask one of your classmates at least two questions about each TV program and then reverse roles. You might ask such questions as: *Was gibt's am Sonntag im Fernsehen? Um wie viel Uhr beginnt das Fernsehprogramm? Wie ist es?*

3. Describe what you like to do after school or on the weekend.

4. Point out three activities that you do which Germans your age do not. *Auf Englisch!*

5. Make up a calendar for the week indicating at least four different activities you will be doing.

6. Identify and describe the following words (*auf Englisch*): *Freizeit, Taschengeld, Mofa, Kleingarten.*

Gisela wohnt nicht mehr in Lübeck.

Activities 1-5 (Answers will vary.)

6. *Freizeit* = leisure time, *Taschengeld* = allowance, *Mofa* = motorized bike, *Kleingarten* = rented plot of land

 WB Activity 19

 WA Activity 11

 S Activity 6

 OP **TP**

 VP **CD-ROM**

Vokabeln

Amerika America
der **Bahnhof,-̈e** train station
der **Basketball,-̈e** basketball
beginnen to begin
bringen to bring
der **Computer,-** computer
das **Computerspiel,-e** computer game
doch used for emphasis
du: Du, Steffie... Say, Steffie...
Entschuldigung! Excuse me!
fernsehen to watch television
das **Fernsehen** television; *im Fernsehen* on television
das **Fernsehprogramm,-e** television program
der **Fußball,-̈e** soccer, soccer ball
gehen to go; *Wann geht's los?* When does it start?
gern gladly, with pleasure; *gern haben* to like
gibt's: es gibt there is (are)
die **Gitarre,-n** guitar
haben to have
Hause: nach Hause gehen to go home
heute: heute Morgen this morning; *heute Mittag* this noon; *heute Nachmittag* this afternoon; *heute Abend* this evening

hören to hear, listen to
die **Karte,-n** ticket, card
die **Kassette,-n** cassette
kaufen to buy
das **Kaufhaus,-̈er** department store
klar clear; *Klar.* Of course.
das **Klavier,-e** piano
kosten to cost
der **Krimi,-s** detective story, thriller
lieber: Das ist mir lieber. I prefer that.
liegen to be located, lie
losgehen to start; *Wann geht's los?* When does it start?
die **Mark** mark (German monetary unit)
mitbringen to bring along
mitkommen to come along; *Kommst du mit?* Are you coming along?
möchten would like to; *Ich möchte zum Rockkonzert (gehen).* I would like to go to the rock concert.
muss: ich muss nach Hause (gehen) I have to go home.
die **Musik** music
nach to, after; *nach Hause gehen* to go home
der **Norden** north

preiswert reasonable
prima great
das **Rockkonzert,-e** rock concert
die **Rockmusik** rock music
sagen to say; *Sagen wir...* Let's say...
die **Schule,-n** school
schwimmen to swim
spielen to play
Süddeutschland southern Germany
der **Süden** south
tanzen to dance
das **Tennis** tennis
das **Viertel,-** quarter; *Viertel nach* a quarter after
vor before, in front of; *Viertel vor* a quarter before
wann when
warum why
der **Westen** west
wohin where (to)
zuerst first
zum: zu dem to the

Die Jungen spielen Tennis.

Torsten hat Fußball sehr gern.

Wo ist der Bahnhof?

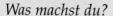

Was machst du?

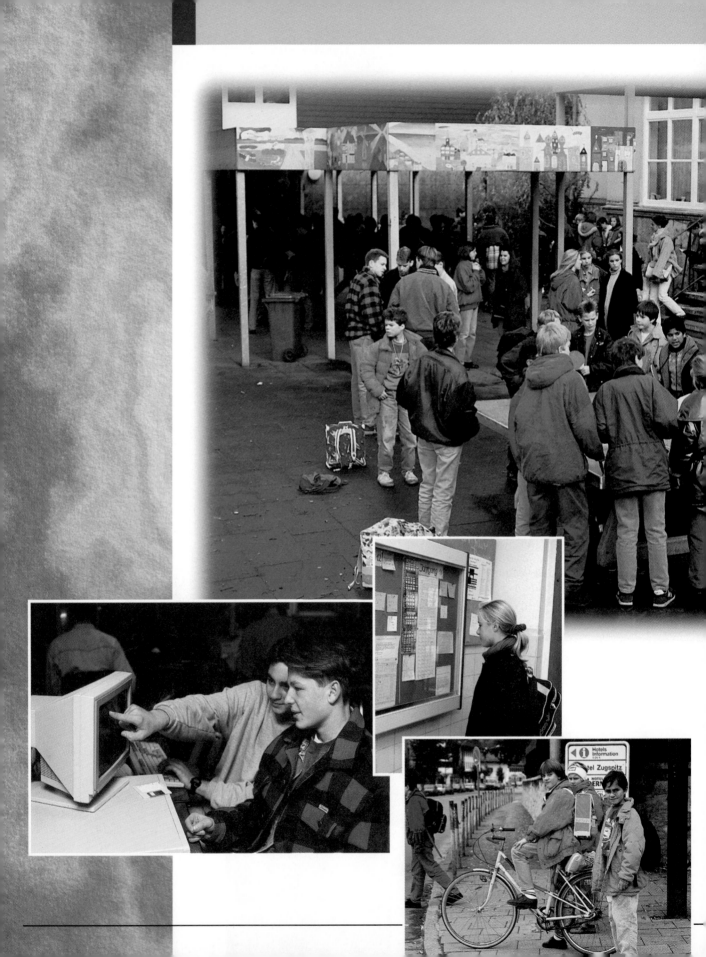

Kapitel **4**

Schule

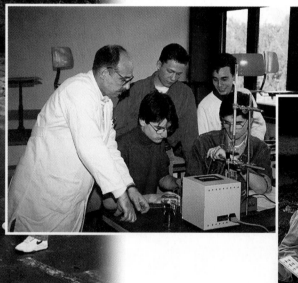

In this chapter you will be able to:

- talk about school
- inquire about details
- identify objects
- describe daily routines
- sequence events
- agree and disagree

Wer ist klug?

Katja:	Mach schnell!
Simone:	Langsam! Langsam! Die Schule beginnt doch erst um acht.
Sofie:	Wir haben gleich Englisch. Die Klasse ist so schwer.
Katja:	Nicht für Simone. So ein Genie! Sie bekommt immer eine Eins.
Simone:	Na ja, ich mache auch meine Hausaufgaben. Und ihr?
Sofie:	Das brauchen wir nicht. Du hast ja alle Antworten.
Simone:	Und wer ist wirklich klug?

Ist Englisch schwer?

Und wer ist wirklich klug?

1. Sie bekommt immer eine Eins.
2. Simone hat alle Antworten.
3. Sie beginnt um acht.
4. Sie kommt langsam.
5. Simone macht die Hausaufgaben für Englisch.

1. *Falsch!* **The following statements are incorrect. Provide the correct statements in German.**

   1. Simone bekommt in Englisch eine Zwei.
   2. Katja und Sofie haben alle Antworten für Englisch.
   3. Die Englischklasse beginnt um halb acht.
   4. Simone kommt schnell.
   5. Sofie macht die Hausaufgaben für Englisch.

Katja

Simone

Sofie

2. *Auf Deutsch, bitte!* **A German exchange student in your school insists on speaking English as he wants to learn the language. You have the opposite goal: you want to learn German. Answer all his questions affirmatively in German.**

1. Do you have all the answers?
2. Does English start at 9:30?
3. Is the class difficult?
4. Are you doing your homework?
5. Is Robert smart?
6. Does he always get a two?

AC/CD

1. Ja, ich habe alle Antworten.
2. Ja, Englisch beginnt um halb zehn.
3. Ja, die Klasse ist schwer.
4. Ja, ich mache meine Hausaufgaben.
5. Ja, Robert ist klug.
6. Ja, er bekommt immer eine Zwei.

AC/CD

Was ist zu Hause?

WB

Activities 1-2

LA

Activity 1

WA

Activity 1

OT

Activity 27

Jan: Hast du dein Mathebuch?

Marco: Ja, in der Schultasche. Wir brauchen den Rechner.

Jan: Oh, der ist zu Hause.

Marco: Du hast doch ein Heft und einen Kopf.

Jan: Das Heft habe ich, aber mein Kopf ist leer.

Marco: Na, das ist ein Problem.

Jan: Du hast recht. In Mathe gibt's immer Probleme!

Hast du dein Mathebuch?

Ja, in der Schultasche.

3. Beantworte diese Fragen!

1. Wo ist Marcos Mathebuch?
2. Wer braucht den Rechner?
3. Wo ist Jans Rechner?
4. Hat Jan ein Heft?
5. Was gibt's immer in Mathe?

Was brauchen Jan und Marco?

AC/CD

1. Es ist in der Schultasche.
2. Marco und Jan brauchen den Rechner.
3. Er ist zu Hause.
4. Ja, er hat ein Heft.
5. In Mathe gibt's immer Probleme.

Schule

4. **Complete each sentence by using the visual cues in your answers.**

1. Was ist in der ____?

   1. Schultasche

2. Maria hat ein ____.

   2. Mathebuch

3. Wo ist mein ____?

   3. Heft

4. Jans ____ ist leer.

   4. Kopf

5. In Mathe gibt's viele ____.

   5. Probleme

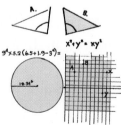

6. Für die Matheklasse brauchen wir den ____.

   6. Rechner

Sprichwort

Er ist nicht auf den Kopf gefallen.

(He wasn't born yesterday.)

AC/CD

Für dich

Grades in German schools are assigned by numbers (1-6) rather than letters (A,B,C,D,F) as we know them. The following grading system is commonly used:

1 = *sehr gut/ausgezeichnet* (very good/excellent)

2 = *gut* (good)

3 = *befriedigend* (satisfactory)

4 = *ausreichend* (adequate)

5 = *mangelhaft* (inadequate)

6 = *ungenügend* (unsatisfactory)

Zeit:	STD	Montag	Dienstag	Mittwoch	Donnerstag	Freitag
8.00-8.45	1	Englisch	Sport	Englisch	Religion	Mathe
8.50-9.35	2	Französisch	Sport	Französisch	Sport	Biologie
9.55-10.40	3	Religion	Erdkunde	Informatik	Chemie	Informatik
10.45-11.30	4	Deutsch	Geschichte	Mathe	Erdkunde	Informatik
11.50-12.35	5	Mathe	Kunst	Deutsch	Deutsch	Geschichte
12.40-13.20	6	Physik	Kunst	Chemie	Französisch	Englisch
	7	P	A	U	S	E
14.35-15.10	8		Klassenstd.		Physik	
15.15-16.00	9		Biologie			
Name:		Julia Danoci	Klasse: 9A			

It is difficult to receive a "1" *(eine Eins)* in a German high school *(Gymnasium)*. Getting a "1" is similar to receiving an "A+" in our high schools. Both grades "5" and "6" are considered failing grades. Generally, tests and quizzes in German schools are more subjective and contain less objective type answers (multiple choice, true and false).

Rollenspiel

Imagine that you have been invited to Germany for a few months. During that time you are going to a *Gymnasium*. It is your first day and you are inquisitive about school matters which you discuss with your host family's son or daughter (your classmate), who will provide all the answers. Your conversation should cover at least the following items: the time school starts, if he or she has English class, what grades he or she gets, if the class is difficult, who the teacher is, what he or she has in the school bag and the time you will go to school.

Aktuelles

School Life

School life in Germany is considerably different from our own. There is practically no social life at German schools. Although schools offer physical education classes—and many have modern facilities—students wishing to participate in various sports activities usually join local sports clubs.

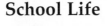
Schule hat begonnen

Achtung Schulweg

More than 80 percent of three- to six-year olds attend the *Kindergarten* which is not part of the school system. The kindergarten is a German institution adopted by many countries; the very word, in fact, has been assimilated into many languages.

Formal education begins at age six when children are required to attend elementary school *(Grundschule)* for a period of four years. It has been a tradition for parents to give their first-grader a *Schultüte* on the first day of school, which is a huge cone filled with candies and cookies. The younger children

Wo sind diese Schulen?

usually carry briefcases or satchels strapped to their backs when going to and coming from school. During their years in the *Grundschule*, children are already accustomed to a sizeable stack of homework.

After the fourth grade in the *Grundschule*, students attend one of the other schools available to them according to their ability. Here the fifth and sixth grades are known as an orientation phase *(Orientierungsstufe)* during which parents, teachers and children can decide which of the other schools is most suitable.

Almost one-half of the students go to the junior secondary school *(Hauptschule)* where they receive a basic education for the next five to six years. Upon completion of the *Hauptschule* most students enter the work force as apprentices while continuing their education at a vocational school *(Berufsschule)* until the age of 18.

A second choice after fourth grade is the intermediate secondary school *(Realschule)*. Less than one-fourth of the remaining students will stay at the *Realschule* for the next six years after which they receive a graduation certificate that qualifies them to attend a technical school *(Fachschule* or *Fachoberschule)*. At the technical schools, students receive training for higher level but nonacademic occupations of all kinds.

The rest of the students, slightly more than one fourth, will continue from grades 5 through 13 at the senior secondary school *(Gymnasium)*. Upon successfully passing oral and written examinations during their last year, students receive the final certificate *(Abitur)* which is a prerequisite for attending a university *(Universität)*. In recent years, considerable changes have been made to accommodate students' interests. A so-called reformed upper phase *(reformierte Oberstufe)* has replaced conventional classes. Students now choose the courses they are most interested in.

Students going to the *Gymnasium* have a very concentrated curriculum. It is not uncommon for these students to take at least 10 or more different subjects a week. A typical schedule readily shows the emphasis on academic subjects.

Schule

A comprehensive school called *Gesamtschule* is common in some parts of Germany for students in grades 5 to 10. Depending on their ability, parents and students decide which courses to take—ranging from basic to more advanced courses. Many of the courses offered in these schools center around vocational education.

Physically or mentally disabled students or those who have other special needs that are not adequately met at the other schools have the option of attending special schools *(Sonderschulen)*.

A particular concern has been created by the numerous children of foreigners living in Germany, many of whom have made Germany their adopted country. These children have become immersed in the German language and culture at a rapid pace. Some schools offer special classes for these children so that they can be better integrated into the German educational system.

Was passt hier?

g
d
i
f
a
c
e
j
h
b

1. Berufsschule
2. Grundschule
3. Fachschule
4. Hauptschule
5. Gymnasium
6. Sonderschule
7. Gesamtschule
8. Kindergarten
9. Universität
10. Realschule

a. a school attended by students for nine years beyond the *Grundschule*

b. a school (for students in grades 5-10) that leads to the *Fachschule*

c. a school attended by those who have special needs

d. an educational institution that all students attend

e. an educational institution (for students in grades 5-10) that offers many vocational courses

f. a school that provides basic education in preparation for a vocational school

g. a vocational school that students attend after they have finished the *Hauptschule*

h. an educational institution for which the *Abitur* is required

i. a technical school

j. a school for early childhood education which is not mandatory

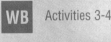
WB Activities 3-4

WA Activity 2

Ergänzung

You may want to add these words for items found in your classroom: *der Lehrertisch* teacher's table/desk; *der Projektor* projector; *die Projektionsfläche* projection screen/area; *die Videokassette* videocassette; *der Videorekorder* videocassette recorder (VCR); *das Übungsheft* exercise book, workbook; *die Heftmaschine* stapler; *der Spitzer* (pencil) sharpener.

AC/CD

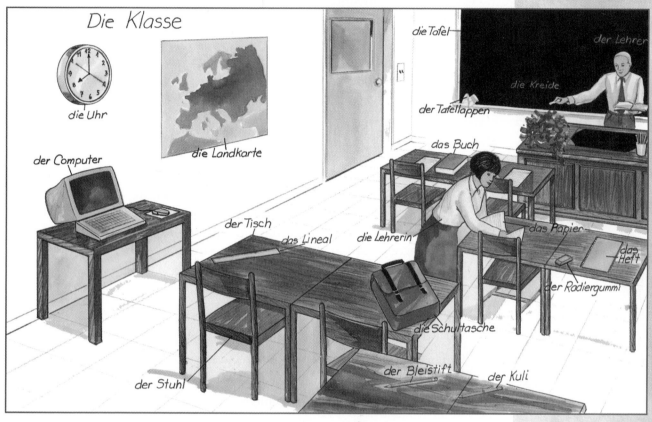

Die Klasse

die Uhr
der Computer
die Landkarte
die Tafel
der Lehrer
die Kreide
der Tafellappen
das Buch
der Tisch
das Lineal
die Lehrerin
das Papier
das Heft
der Radiergummi
die Schultasche
der Stuhl
der Bleistift
der Kuli

◆ Wo ist dein Buch? In der Schultasche.
◆ Wo ist deine Schultasche? Hier.
◆ Wer ist dein Deutschlehrer? Herr Eberhard.
◆ Und deine Mathelehrerin? Frau Grabowski.

 WA Activity 3

 WB Activities 5-6

LA Activity 2

 OT Activities 28-29

TPR Activity: Ask students to show the rest of the class various classroom objects. Example: *Stefan, zeig Renate, wo der Bleistift ist!* Stefan looks around, gets up and goes to a student's desk where a pencil is found and says *Hier ist der Bleistift* while picking it up and showing it to the rest of the class. Before students understand what they are supposed to do, you may want to demonstrate it first yourself.

Schule

5. *Rate mal!* (Guess!) Guess each object in German, including its article. This object is used to...

1. erase a word that was incorrectly penciled in.
2. point out the location of a city.
3. learn some information as you page through it.
4. write the answers on several pages that are bound together.
5. write some information on the chalkboard.
6. indicate that the class period is over.
7. retrieve information on software.
8. sit on.
9. write with and use as an eraser.
10. measure line length and draw straight lines.

6. *Wer oder was ist das?* Identify the missing words. The beginning letters of each word, when read in sequence, will give you the topic of this chapter. Although you haven't had the words *sitzen* and *Geometrie,* can you guess what they mean?

1. Silke sitzt auf einem ____.
2. Petra und Elisabeth spielen Computerspiele auf dem ____.
3. Die Hausaufgaben sind im ____.
4. Wie viel ____ ist es? Es ist halb drei.
5. Für Geometrie brauchen wir ein ____.
6. Herr ____ ist der Deutschlehrer.

Ich habe heute viele Hausaufgaben.

Sag's mal! Wie ist die Klasse?

kameradschaftlich*

interessant*

sehr laut*

ruhig*

leicht

witzig*

kameradschaftlich*

super

nicht so gut

spitze*

langweilig

schwer

einfach toll*

klasse*

zu groß*

aufgedreht*

es geht

die Allerbeste*

AC/CD

You may want to find out what your students think about your class. Use the known expressions as well as the new ones for additional opinions: *interessant* (interesting); *klasse* (great); *spitze* (super); *einfach toll* (just great); *ruhig* (quiet); *sehr laut* (quite noisy); *witzig* (funny); *kameradschaftlich* (friendly); *zu groß* (too big); *die Allerbeste* (the very best); *aufgedreht* (in high spirits, full of energy).

Die Englischklasse ist einfach toll.

Schule

Sprache

The Definite Article (Accusative Singular)

In the sentence *Andrea kauft die Karte* (Andrea buys the ticket) *Andrea* is called the subject (nominative), *kauft* the verb, and *die Karte* the direct object (accusative) of the sentence.

◆ *Kennst du den Onkel?* Do you know the uncle?

◆ *Ich höre die Musik.* I am listening to the music.

◆ *Wir lesen das Buch.* We are reading the book.

Singular			
	masculine	**feminine**	**neuter**
nominative	der	die	das
accusative	den	die	das

From the chart, you can see that the *die* and *das* articles do not change in the accusative and that *der* changes to *den*. In informal conversations, names are often preceded by a form of *der* or *die*.

◆ *Kennst du den Peter?* Do you know Peter?

◆ *Ich finde die Heike toll.* I think Heike is terrific.

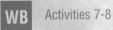

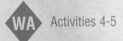

Kennt ihr den Stefan?

Jochen findet die Matheklasse leicht.

7. You always seem to misplace things. Ask where each item is.

◆ Wo ist das Buch?

AC/CD

1.  2.

3. 4.

5. 6.

1. Wo ist der Kuli?
2. Wo ist das Papier?
3. Wo ist das Heft?
4. Wo ist der Bleistift?
5. Wo ist der Radiergummi?
6. Wo ist das Lineal?

8. Tell where you'll find the various objects or places.

AC/CD

◆ Computer / da drüben
Der Computer ist da drüben.

1. Bahnhof / in der Stadt
2. Schultasche / zu Hause
3. Tafel / in der Klasse
4. Schule / in der Schillerstraße
5. Kreide / hier
6. Tisch / im Wohnzimmer
7. Kaufhaus / um die Ecke

1. Der Bahnhof ist in der Stadt.
2. Die Schultasche ist zu Hause.
3. Die Tafel ist in der Klasse.
4. Die Schule ist in der Schillerstraße.
5. Die Kreide ist hier.
6. Der Tisch ist im Wohnzimmer.
7. Das Kaufhaus ist um die Ecke.

Schule

9. **Möchtest du das?** Your father or mother is inquiring what you would like for your birthday. As they point to certain items, you indicate that you would like each one.

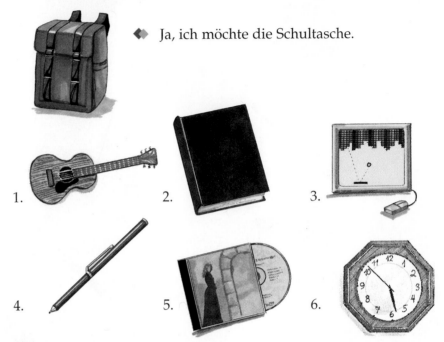

◆ Ja, ich möchte die Schultasche.

1.   2.   3.

4.   5.   6.

1. Ja, ich möchte die Gitarre.
2. Ja, ich möchte das Buch.
3. Ja, ich möchte das Computerspiel.
4. Ja, ich möchte den Kuli.
5. Ja, ich möchte die CD.
6. Ja, ich möchte die Uhr.

10. **Ich kaufe die Kassette. Und du?** You and your friends are going shopping. Everyone seems to be buying something different. Your friends tell you what they are buying, but they also want to know what you plan to purchase.

◆ Ich kaufe die Kassette. Und du?
   Ich kaufe das Buch hier.

1. Ich kaufe die CD hier.

1. Ich kaufe den Fußball. Und du?

2. Ich kaufe den Kuli hier.

2. Ich kaufe die Karte. Und du?

3. Ich kaufe den Rechner. Und du?

3. Ich kaufe das Papier hier.

4. Ich kaufe das Lineal. Und du?

4. Ich kaufe die Schultasche hier.

5. Ich kaufe die Uhr. Und du?

5. Ich kaufe den Bleistift hier.

6. Ich kaufe den Krimi. Und du?

6. Ich kaufe den Computer hier.

11. der, die, das oder den?

1. Kennst du ____ Lehrer?
2. Kaufen Sie ____ Klavier?
3. Wir lesen ____ Buch.
4. Wie findest du ____ Schultasche?
5. Wann beginnt ____ Schule?
6. Ich brauche ____ Kuli.
7. Habt ihr ____ Bleistift?
8. Renate spielt ____ Computerspiel.

1. den
2. das
3. das
4. die
5. die
6. den
7. den
8. das

Da kommt Herr Kauls, der Lehrer.

12. Kombiniere...

Wir	kommt	immer	den Rechner
Britta und Tina	haben	heute	Zeit
Herr Schuber	brauchen	jetzt	recht
			Probleme
			spät

Ergänzung

AC/CD

Most German schools no longer have classes on Saturday.

Personalize your questions. (*Was für Fächer hast du?, Wie oft hast du Deutsch?*—*Englisch, Geschichte...?*, etc.)

You may want to add these subjects, which are commonly taught in American schools: *Informatik* (Computer Science), *Kunst* (Art), *Handarbeit* handicraft; *Werken* (Shop), *Chor* (Choir), *Fahrunterricht* (Driver's Training), *Sozialkunde* (Social Studies).

Stundenplan

Zeit	Montag	Dienstag	Mittwoch	Donnerstag	Freitag
7.55–8.40	Deutsch	Englisch	Deutsch	Mathematik	Englisch
8.45–9.30	Biologie	Geschichte	Biologie	Musik	Französisch
9.30–9.50	Große Pause				
9.50–10.35	Chemie	Erdkunde	Natur-wissen-schaften	Deutsch	Mathematik
10.40–11.25	Mathematik	Französisch	Chemie	Englisch	Physik
11.25–11.45	Große Pause				
11.45–12.30	Physik	Religion	Sport	Religion	Musik
12.35–1.20	Französisch	Mathematik	Sport	Geschichte	Natur-wissen-schaften
1.25–2.10	Latein	Musik			

WB Activity 9 **WA** Activities 6-7 **OT** Activities 30-31 **S** Activity 3

- Was für Fächer hat er? Er hat...
- Was für ein Fach hat sie um viertel zwölf? Um viertel zwölf hat sie Englisch.
- Was lernt sie? Sie lernt...
- Was ist dein Lieblingsfach? Mein Lieblingsfach ist...
- Ist Physik leicht? Nein, Physik ist schwer.
- Wann hat er Englisch? Er hat am Dienstag, Donnerstag und Freitag Englisch.
- Wie viele Mathestunden hast du in der Woche? Ich habe vier Mathestunden in der Woche.
- Was für eine Note bekommt Sofie? Sie bekommt eine Drei.

 Activity 3

13. ***Was für Fächer hat Bettina am Mittwoch?*** **Can you figure out the seven subjects that Bettina has every Wednesday?**

RELIGION
FRANZÖSISCH
ERDKUNDE
MUSIK
MATHEMATIK
BIOLOGIE
LATEIN

14. ***Eine Umfrage*** **(A Survey). Imagine that you are enrolled in a German** *Gymnasium*. **Your host family inquires about your new schedule. You have the same schedule as presented in the** *Ergänzung* **section.** *Beantworte die Fragen!*

   1. Um wie viel Uhr beginnt die Erdkundeklasse?
   2. Was hast du um viertel vor zwölf am Montag?
   3. Wie viele Französischstunden hast du in der Woche?
   4. Um wie viel Uhr ist die Große Pause?
   5. Wann hast du Biologie?
   6. Wann kommst du am Freitag aus der Schule?
   7. Um wie viel Uhr beginnt die Schule?
   8. Was hast du um zwanzig vor elf am Donnerstag?

1. Um 9 Uhr 50.
2. Physik.
3. Drei.
4. Um 9 Uhr 30 und um 11 Uhr 25.
5. Am Montag und am Mittwoch.
6. Um 1 Uhr 20.
7. Um 7 Uhr 55.
8. Englisch.

Praktische Situation

Wann hast du (haben Sie) Zeit? Form groups of three. One student plays the role of a teacher; the other two play the roles of students. The two students must agree on a time when they are both free to see the teacher for additional help. (The teacher, too, must be free at the same time.) Each group member (students and teacher) begins by creating a weekly school schedule. It includes what class meets at what time each day. Be sure to include 7 to 10 free periods during the week.

First, the two students must find at least one mutual free period. For example:

Student 1: *Hast du am Montag um acht Uhr Zeit?*

Student 2: *Nein, dann habe ich Mathe. Hast du am Freitag um neun Uhr Zeit?*

Student 1: *Ja.*

Then, after two students have agreed on a time, they need to ask if the teacher is available also. For example:

Student 1: *Haben Sie am Mittwoch um elf Uhr Zeit?*

Teacher: *Nein, aber ich habe um ein Uhr Zeit.*

Student 1: *Das geht nicht.*

Student 2: *Haben Sie heute um elf Uhr Zeit?*

Teacher: *Ja, das geht.*

(You may or may not find a mutually convenient hour to meet.)

Am Mittwoch habe ich meine Informatikklasse.

Am Montag habe ich keine Zeit.

Kapitel 4

Sprache

Question Words: *Wer? Wen? Was?*

Both question words *wer* (who) and *wen* (whom) ask about a person. *Wer* inquires about the subject of the sentence, whereas *wen* asks about the direct object of the sentence. You can use either word whether masculine, feminine or neuter. To inquire about objects, you must use the question word *was* (what).

◆ *Heike wohnt in der Stadt.* Heike lives in the city.

◆ *Wer wohnt in der Stadt?* Who lives in the city?

◆ *Ich kenne die Lehrerin.* I know the teacher.

◆ *Wen kennst du?* Whom do you know?

◆ *Wir kaufen die Gitarre.* We are buying the guitar.

◆ *Was kauft ihr?* What are you buying?

15. **Wer wohnt dort? Pretend it's noisy and you can't hear what is being said about where various people live. So you ask whom they are talking about.**

   ◆ Frau Schiller wohnt in der Stadt.
     Wer wohnt in der Stadt?

   1. Susanne wohnt beim Park.
   2. Der Lehrer wohnt hier.
   3. Petra wohnt beim Kaufhaus.
   4. Karin und Petra wohnen in Hamburg.
   5. Frau Tobler wohnt in Deutschland.
   6. Wir wohnen da.

16. **Wen bringen wir mit? You have invited several friends to your birthday party. You ask whom everyone is bringing along.**

   ◆ Wen bringst du mit, Angelika? (Holger)
     Ich bringe den Holger mit.

   1. Wen bringst du mit, Anne? (Doris)
   2. Wen bringst du mit, Bernhard? (Sabine)
   3. Wen bringst du mit, Klaus? (Rainer)
   4. Wen bringst du mit, Veronica? (Heiko)
   5. Wen bringst du mit, Tanja? (Susi)

WB Activities 10-11

S Activity 4

AC/CD

1. Wer wohnt beim Park?
2. Wer wohnt hier?
3. Wer wohnt beim Kaufhaus?
4. Wer wohnt in Hamburg?
5. Wer wohnt in Deutschland?
6. Wer wohnt da?

AC/CD

1. Ich bringe die Doris mit.
2. Ich bringe die Sabine mit.
3. Ich bringe den Rainer mit.
4. Ich bringe den Heiko mit.
5. Ich bringe die Susi mit.

17. *Was/Wen kennst du?* Imagine you haven't visited your uncle for years. He doesn't know how much you still remember from the time you saw him last.

◆ Was kennst du? (Park)
  Ich kenne den Park.
◆ Wen kennst du? (Christine)
  Ich kenne die Christine.

1. Was kennst du ? (Stadt)

2. Wen kennst du? (Dieter)

3. Wen kennst du? (Heidi)

4. Was kennst du? (Rockmusik)

5. Wen kennst du? (Onkel)

6. Was kennst du? (Schule)

Kennt ihr den Andreas?

1. Ich kenne die Stadt.
2. Ich kenne den Dieter.
3. Ich kenne die Heidi.
4. Ich kenne die Rockmusik.
5. Ich kenne den Onkel.
6. Ich kenne die Schule.

18. *Wer? Wen? oder Was?*

1. _____ ist das? Das ist Herr Schmidt.

2. _____ bringst du mit? Meine Freundin.

3. _____ kaufen Sie? Einen Krimi.

4. _____ macht ihr heute? Wir spielen Tennis.

5. _____ kommt um sieben? Peter und Angelika.

6. _____ kennt er? Frau Meier.

7. _____ hörst du? Rockmusik.

8. _____ hat Hausaufgaben? Alle.

1. Wer
2. Wen
3. Was
4. Was
5. Wer
6. Wen
7. Was
8. Wer

Sample answers:
1. Ich kenne Heidi.
2. Ich kaufe zwei CDs.
3. Er heißt Joachim. (Sie heißt Monika.)
4. Nein, er (sie) ist nicht klug.
5. Ich komme aus...
6. Ja, ich habe Deutsch.
7. Der Lehrer kommt zu spät.
8. Ja, ich habe viel Zeit.
9. Ich brauche das Buch.

19. Beantworte diese Fragen!

1. Wen kennst du?

2. Was kaufst du?

3. Wie heißt dein Freund (deine Freundin)?

4. Ist er (sie) klug?

5. Woher kommst du?

6. Hast du Deutsch?

7. Wer kommt zu spät?

8. Hast du Zeit?

9. Was brauchst du?

Habt ihr jetzt Zeit?

Lesestück

Ein Tag bei Jochen

Jochen Biedermann wohnt in Bad Homburg. Diese Stadt liegt im Norden von Frankfurt. Jochen ist fünfzehn. Sein Bruder Mark ist erst zwölf. Frau Biedermann, Jochens und Marks Mutter, muss schon° früh ins Büro°. Jochens Schule beginnt fünf Minuten vor acht Uhr. Um viertel acht geht er aus dem Haus. Der Bus kommt zehn Minuten später. Zwanzig vor acht ist er bei der Schule. Wolf und Frank, Jochens Freunde, sind schon da.

After your students are familiar with this text, have them write a short description about their typical school day.

Jochen: Hallo! Hast du dein Englischbuch?

Wolf: Das brauchen wir heute nicht. Wir haben kein° Englisch.

Frank: Da bin ich froh°. Die Hausaufgaben sind viel zu schwer.

Jochen: Nicht für Wolf. Kommt doch nach der Schule rüber. Dann machen wir drei die Hausaufgaben.

Frank: Gute Idee! Geht das, Wolf?

Wolf: Warum nicht? Kommt aber zu meinem Haus. Jochen, bring deine Computerspiele mit.

Jochen: Das mach' ich gern°.

Wolf: Oh, es ist schon fünf vor acht. Wir haben heute Deutsch.

Jochen mit seinen Freunden

Frank

Wolf

Schule

123

Jochen, Wolf und Frank gehen jetzt in die Klasse. Frau Lieberoth ist die Deutschlehrerin. Sie kommt immer pünktlich°. Jochen hat heute Deutsch, Biologie, Chemie, Mathe, Physik und Französisch. Jochen findet Mathe und Physik leicht. In Mathe und Physik bekommt er oft eine Eins. In Deutsch, Biologie und Chemie ist er auch ganz gut, aber in Französisch bekommt er oft eine Vier.

Viele Jungen und Mädchen kommen mit dem Bus.

Gegen zwei Uhr kommt Jochen aus der Schule, und um halb drei Uhr ist er zu Hause. Zuerst macht er die Hausaufgaben für Deutsch. Es dauert° nur eine Stunde. Dann hört er Rockmusik und spielt Computerspiele. Um halb fünf geht er zu Wolf. Er bringt Computerspiele und das Englischbuch mit. Frank kommt auch. Zuerst machen sie die Hausaufgaben. Dann haben sie viel Spaß° mit den Computerspielen. Wie sagt man? „Erst die Arbeit, dann das Vergnügen!"°

schon already; *das Büro* office; *kein* no; *froh* glad; *Das mach' ich gern.* I like to do that.; *pünktlich* on time; *es dauert* it takes; *der Spaß* fun; *Wie sagt man? „Erst die Arbeit, dann das Vergnügen!"* How do they say it? "Business before pleasure!"

Wie lange dauern Jochens Hausaufgaben?

Zuerst macht Jochen die Hausaufgaben für Deutsch.

Später hört er Rockmusik.

 WB Activity 12

 WA Activity 8

Kapitel 4

20. **Was ist die richtige Reihenfolge? (What is the correct sequence?) Place the following sentences in the proper sequence according to what happened in the** *Lesestück.*

1. Jochen macht die Hausaufgaben für Frau Lieberoth.
2. Wolf, Frank und Jochen haben zuerst Deutsch.
3. Jochen geht aus dem Haus.
4. Jochen, Wolf und Frank machen die Hausaufgaben für Englisch.
5. Jochen ist um 7 Uhr 40 bei der Schule.
6. Jochen kommt aus der Schule.
7. Jochen hört Rockmusik.
8. Frau Biedermann geht ins Büro.
9. Jochen geht zu Wolf.
10. Der Bus kommt.
11. Jochen kommt nach Hause.

8
3
10
5

2
6
11
1
7
9
4

21. **Beantworte diese Fragen!**

1. Wo wohnt Jochen?
2. Wie alt sind Jochen und Mark?
3. Wohin muss Frau Biedermann schon so früh?
4. Um wie viel Uhr kommt der Bus?
5. Wer ist schon bei der Schule?
6. Warum brauchen Wolf, Frank und Jochen heute kein Englischbuch?
7. Was haben sie heute zuerst?
8. Wie findet Jochen Physik?
9. Was bekommt er oft in Französisch?
10. Wann ist Jochen zu Hause?
11. Was macht er gleich nach der Schule?
12. Wohin geht er um halb fünf?

1. Jochen wohnt in Bad Homburg.
2. Jochen ist fünfzehn und Mark ist zwölf.
3. Sie muss schon so früh ins Büro.
4. Er kommt 7 Uhr 25.
5. Frank und Wolf sind schon da.
6. Sie haben heute kein Englisch.
7. Sie haben heute zuerst Deutsch.
8. Er findet Physik leicht.
9. Er bekommt oft in Französisch eine Vier.
10. Er ist um halb drei zu Hause.
11. Zuerst macht er die Hausaufgaben.
12. Um halb fünf geht er zu Wolf.

Wie alt sind Jochen und Mark?

in der Chemieklasse

Sprache

Present Tense of *sein*

The forms of *sein* (to be) are irregular; they do not follow the same pattern as regular verb forms.

Singular			
	ich	bin	I am
	du	bist	you are
	er		he is
	sie	ist	she is
	es		it is
Plural			
	wir	sind	we are
	ihr	seid	you are
	sie	sind	they are
	Sie (sg. & pl.)	sind	you are

◆ *Wie alt bist du?* How old are you?

◆ *Wolf und Frank sind schon da.* Wolf and Frank are already there.

 Activity 13

 Activity 9

S Activity 2

22. **Pretend you are interested in learning about several people at a party. Ask some questions using the cues.**

   ◆ Rudi und Peter / neu hier
      Sind Rudi und Peter neu hier?

   1. Andrea und Willi / klug
   2. Uwe / ein Genie
   3. du / Katharinas Freundin
   4. ihr / in Mathe gut
   5. Anne / langweilig

1. Sind Andrea und Willi klug?
2. Ist Uwe ein Genie?
3. Bist du Katharinas Freundin?
4. Seid ihr in Mathe gut?
5. Ist Anne langweilig?

AC/CD

23. *Wo sind alle?* **Your classmates are meeting in front of your school to go on a field trip. A few minutes before departure, your teachers ask where several of your classmates are. Using the cues, tell your teacher where the missing students are.**

   ◆ Uwe / zu Hause
      Uwe ist zu Hause.

   1. Rudi und Toni / da
   2. Heidi / an der Ecke
   3. Sven / in der Schule
   4. Dieter und Ralf / hier
   5. Bettina / am Telefon
   6. Kerstin und Doris / vor dem Kaufhaus

1. Rudi und Toni sind da.
2. Heidi ist an der Ecke.
3. Sven ist in der Schule.
4. Dieter und Ralf sind hier.
5. Bettina ist am Telefon.
6. Kerstin und Doris sind vor dem Kaufhaus.

24. **Supply the correct forms of** *sein.*

   1. Wie viel Uhr ____ es jetzt?
   2. Melanie und Sonja ____ in der Stadt.
   3. ____ du um acht Uhr zu Hause?
   4. Ihr ____ immer so spät.
   5. Ich ____ morgen nicht da.
   6. Deutschland ____ weit von hier.
   7. ____ Sie Herr Krüger?
   8. ____ ihr um sieben hier?
   9. Wer ____ das Mädchen?
   10. Die Hausaufgaben ____ leicht.

1. ist
2. sind
3. Bist
4. seid
5. bin
6. ist
7. Sind
8. Seid
9. ist
10. sind

Schule

Übung macht den Meister!

1. Make up a weekly class schedule including days, subjects, class periods. Exchange your schedule with another person and then ask each other such questions as: *Um wie viel Uhr hast du am Montag Mathe? Was für ein Fach hast du um acht Uhr am Dienstag? Um wie viel Uhr kommst du aus der Schule?*

2. With a classmate, identify eight objects in your classroom. For example, one of you should ask the question *Was ist das da?*, and the other person should answer *Das ist die Uhr.*

3. Compare a German class schedule with yours by making a list with the headings "similarities" and "differences." *Auf Deutsch, bitte!* Here are some samples: *Wir haben auch Englisch und Deutsch. Die Schule ist von Montag bis Freitag. Meine Deutschklasse ist auch 45 Minuten. Ich habe nicht Latein. Ich habe am Dienstag sechs Fächer. Eine Große Pause haben wir nicht. Religion gibt es nicht.*

Aktuelles

A Visit to a *Gymnasium*

The *Kaiserin-Friedrich-Schule* is a *Gymnasium*, located in Bad Homburg, a city north of Frankfurt. The school has undergone many changes since its original structure dating back to 1550. As is typical for a *Gymnasium*, classes are provided for fifth through thirteenth graders Monday through Friday. How do students get to school? Most students walk or ride bikes; others use public or school buses. Classes start at 7:55 A.M. and are over either at 1:20 P.M. or 2:10 P.M., depending on the students' schedules.

Die Kaiserin-Friedrich-Schule in Bad Homburg

Sie lernen Latein.

Let's visit the school and find out more about it. Besides the administrative offices and classrooms, there is a cafeteria which offers sandwiches, pizza, hot dogs, cookies, fruits and beverages. The cafeteria is operated by several mothers who volunteer their time from 9:30 to 1:30. Students are also allowed to leave the school building and have a warm meal in the cafeteria of a local government building across the street.

During the 20-minute break (*Große Pause*), most students congregate in the school yard to eat snacks, chat with friends, read books or do some last-minute homework. A school library (*Schulbücherei*) is available to students who want to spend some time reading during their free period or check out books overnight. Working with computers is also quite popular at this school. Students can request the use of the school's computers according to their needs.

There is a multimedia room which is supervised by an audio-visual technician. The art department has a drawing room, photo lab and a printing and ceramics workshop at its disposal. Physical Education is taught in the two gyms or on an athletic field nearby.

The school places major emphasis on foreign language instruction. Students are required to take either English or Latin at the beginning of fifth grade. The school offers five additional foreign languages: French, Russian, Italian, Spanish and Ancient Greek.

Die Große Pause dauert 20 Minuten.

Was für ein Fach haben sie?

Drei Stunden pro Woche haben sie English.

Once the decision has been made whether to take English or Latin as the first foreign language in the fifth grade, all students stay with the same language group and also remain with their classmates for the other required subjects. In the seventh grade, students who started with Latin must take English as their second language. Those who started with English can choose between Latin or French. The other foreign languages are electives which students can choose at the ninth grade level. However, all ninth graders are required to either take a third foreign language or natural science.

Students continue their study of these languages in the tenth grade. Notice that German students do not have the same subjects every day. The thirteen subjects are scattered throughout the weekly school schedule.

Wie viele Jungen und Mädchen haben die Antwort?

Fächer	Stunden pro Woche
Deutsch	3
1. Latein, Englisch	3
2. Englisch, Latein, Französisch	3
Musik	2
Religion/Ethik	2
Geschichte	2
Erdkunde	1
Mathematik	4
Physik	2
Chemie	2
Biologie	2
Sport	2
3. Latein, Französisch, Russisch	3
Griechisch	6
Naturwissenschaften	2

Students who select Greek rather than Latin, French or Russian as their third foreign language have six hours of Greek instruction. Since they are not taking two hours of natural sciences (*Naturwissenschaften*) and the other three languages offered, these students are also exempt from one hour of either math or biology.

Particularly noteworthy is the fact that students in grades 8 through 11 must take either religion or ethics. Religion is offered as protestant or catholic religious instruction and exposes students primarily to the history and philosophy of Protestantism and Catholicism as well as other world religions. Students who don't want to attend these classes can take ethics instead.

At the end of their final year at this *Gymnasium*, students receive their *Abitur* certificate after passing three comprehensive written examinations and one oral examination. The final grade is a combination of the scores on these examinations, as well as a calculated average of various basic and selected courses.

The *Kaiserin-Friedrich-Schule* sponsors extensive student exchange programs with England, Belgium, Russia and the United States. For example, students who are at least in the eleventh grade are eligible to travel with their classmates to the United States for about three to four weeks during Easter vacation. This exchange program takes place every two years—one year the group comes to the United States, the next year a group of American students goes to Bad Homburg to stay with German families and visit their school. Furthermore, about 20 or more eleventh graders regularly spend a year at different schools in the United States, an unusually high number compared to other schools.

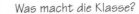
Was macht die Klasse?

Sie machen ihre Klassenarbeit am Computer.

Warum sind sie nicht in der Schule?

 Activities 14-15

Schule

Was weißt du?

1. How many subjects do tenth graders have?
2. What do students receive after passing three written and one oral examinations?
3. What are the two ancient languages offered?
4. How many years do students go to a *Gymnasium*?
5. What subject area is emphasized at this school?
6. How long is the cafeteria open?
7. What class can students take instead of *Religion*?
8. How do most students get to school?
9. Where can students get a warm lunch?
10. Where do students learn how to develop film?

1. 13
2. The *Abitur.*
3. Latin and Greek.
4. 9 years
5. Foreign Languages
6. 4 hours
7. Ethics.
8. They walk or ride their bikes.
9. In the cafeteria of a local government building across the street.
10. In the photo lab (art department).

WB Activity 16

WA Activities 10-11

S Activity 5

Erweiterung

25. Etwas Persönliches.

1. Wie viele Fächer hast du?
2. Um wie viel Uhr hast du Deutsch?
3. Ist Deutsch leicht?
4. Wie heißt dein Deutschlehrer (deine Deutschlehrerin)?
5. Um wie viel Uhr beginnt deine Schule?
6. Was ist dein Lieblingsfach? Warum?

Was machen wir heute nach der Schule?

Zwei Jungen mit ihren Schultaschen.

26. You run into your friend in the hallway during the first week of school. Respond to your friend.

> Du: ____
>
> Freund(in): Na, wie geht's?
>
> Du: ____
>
> Freund(in): Was für Fächer hast du heute?
>
> Du: ____
>
> Freund(in): Was machst du nach der Schule?
>
> Du: ____
>
> Freund(in): Nach Hause? Warum?
>
> Du: ____
>
> Freund(in): Ich habe auch Hausaufgaben. Wir machen sie später.
>
> Du: ____
>
> Freund(in): Ich gehe in die Stadt.
>
> Du: ____

Sample Answers:
Tag!

Ganz gut.

Ich habe Englisch, Geschichte, Mathe, Deutsch und Biologie.
Ich gehe nach Hause.

Ich habe viele Hausaufgaben.

Wohin gehst du?

Gut. Ich komme mit.

WB Activity 17

27. Imagine your German is fluent enough that you can help others who are having difficulties. They start a statement or question, but don't know the German words to finish it. Help them out.

1. Um wie viel Uhr *(begins)* ____ die Schule?
2. Um *(half)* ____ acht.
3. Haben wir am Mittwoch *(chemistry)* ____?
4. Nein, am *(Thursday)* ____.
5. Ich *(have)* ____ heute viele Hausaufgaben.
6. Für *(German)* ____?
7. Ja, und auch für *(history)* ____.
8. Dann hast du heute *(afternoon)* ____ keine Zeit?
9. Nein, aber *(tomorrow)* ____.
10. Gut. Ich *(come)* ____ morgen rüber.

1. beginnt
2. halb
3. Chemie
4. Donnerstag
5. habe
6. Deutsch
7. Geschichte
8. Nachmittag
9. morgen
10. komme

28. **Meine Klasse.** Complete Julia's observations about her class by using the words provided. You will not need all the words.

schwer	beginnt	braucht	Klasse	bekomme
Herr	Uhr	ist	Jungen	immer

1. Frau Novak ist um viertel nach sieben in der ____.
2. Die Mädchen und ____ kommen um fünf vor acht.
3. Die Matheklasse ____ pünktlich.
4. Die Klasse ____ von 7 Uhr 55 bis 8 Uhr 35.
5. Nach der Matheklasse kommt ____ Hoffmann.
6. Die Klasse ist nicht ____.
7. Es gibt aber ____ viele Hausaufgaben.
8. Ich ____ in Mathe gute Noten.

1. Klasse
2. Jungen
3. beginnt
4. ist
5. Herr
6. schwer
7. immer
8. bekomme

29. **Wir gehen zur Schule.** Describe (in narrative and/or dialog style) the following sequence, using the cues merely as a guideline.

You are walking to school... picking up your friend on the way... waiting several minutes before he or she comes out of the house... greeting him or her... talking about several items concerning school... arriving at school... hurrying because the first class begins soon.

Mark hat heute keine Hausaufgaben.

Was macht Spaß?

Land und Leute (Country and People)

Deutschland

Deutschland hat ungefähr° 80 Millionen Einwohner°. Deutschland passt 22 mal° in die USA (Vereinigten Staaten von Amerika), ohne° Alaska und Hawaii. Das Land ist ungefähr halb so groß wie° der Staat Texas. Die weiteste Entfernung° von Norden nach Süden ist 830 Kilometer, von Osten nach Westen 630 km.

Berlin ist die Hauptstadt° von Deutschland. Berlin liegt im Osten. Berlin ist auch die größte° Stadt. Andere° große Städte sind Hamburg, München, Köln, Düsseldorf, Frankfurt, Leipzig, Stuttgart, Hannover, Chemnitz und Dresden. Wo liegen die Städte? Im Norden, Süden, Osten oder Westen?

ungefähr approximately; *die Einwohner* inhabitants; *passt 22 mal* fits 22 times; *ohne* without; *halb so groß wie* half as big as; *die weiteste Entfernung* the farthest distance; *die Hauptstadt* capital; *größte* biggest; *andere* other

Was passt hier? **Complete each statement by matching it with the appropriate item. You will not need all the items listed.**

i 1. Berlin ist

e 2. Deutschland ist

b 3. In Deutschland wohnen

g 4. Deutschland passt 22 mal in die

d 5. Die weiteste Entfernung von Norden nach Süden ist

c 6. Berlin liegt

f 7. Die weiteste Entfernung von Westen nach Osten ist

a. eine alte Stadt

b. 80 Millionen Einwohner

c. im Osten

d. 830 Kilometer

e. halb so groß wie Texas

f. 630 Kilometer

g. USA (ohne Alaska und Hawaii)

h. im Westen

i. die Hauptstadt von Deutschland

This reading selection provides opportunities for students to find out additional information about German-speaking countries. The new vocabulary is considered passive and is used primarily for reading comprehension and cultural understanding.

You may want to introduce the words *nördlich, östlich, südlich* and *westlich* so that students can use them in conjunction with this reading selection.

If students are not familiar with metric measurements, you might point out that 1 mile is approximately 1.6 kilometers.

WB Activity 18

WB Activity 19

 WA Activity 12

 S Activity 6

 OP

 TP

VP

Was weißt du?

1. *Zur Schule.* On your way to school with your friend, you ask about several things. Write five questions that you would like to have answered.

2. Discuss in English some of the differences between your school and a German school.

3. Point to at least seven classroom objects and identify them including the articles *(der, die, das).*

4. Prepare a class schedule of the subjects that you are taking including days of the week and times.

5. *Ein Interview.* Talk to a classmate, asking questions and using the question words *wer, wen, was.*

6. Describe your daily school routine, starting with the time you leave home until you return home.

Dresden

Leipzig

Berlin

Vokabeln

alle all
die **Antwort,-en** answer
die **Arbeit** work
bekommen to get, receive
die **Biologie** biology
der **Bleistift,-e** pencil
brauchen to need
das **Büro,-s** office
der **Bus,-se** bus
die **Chemie** chemistry
dauern to take, last
das **Deutsch** German
diese (form of *dieser*) this
das **Englisch** English
die **Erdkunde** geography
erst just
das **Fach,-̈er** (school) subject
das **Französisch** French
froh glad, happy
für for
das **Genie,-s** genius; *So ein Genie!* Such a genius!
gern machen to like (to do)
die **Geschichte** history
das **Haus,-̈er** house
die **Hausaufgabe,-n** homework
das **Heft,-e** notebook
die **Idee,-n** idea; *Gute Idee!* Good idea!
immer always
kein no
die **Klasse,-n** class

klug smart, intelligent
der **Kopf,-̈e** head
die **Kreide** chalk
der **Kuli,-s** (ballpoint) pen
die **Landkarte,-n** map
langsam slow
das **Latein** Latin
leer empty
der **Lehrer,-** teacher
die **Lehrerin,-nen**
leicht easy
lernen to learn
das **Lieblingsfach,-̈er** favorite (school) subject
das **Lineal,-e** ruler
machen to do, make; *Mach schnell!* Hurry!
die **Mathematik (Mathe)** mathematics (math); *das Mathebuch* math book; *die Mathestunde* math class, lesson
Na ja. Oh well.
die **Naturwissenschaften** (pl.) natural sciences
die **Note,-n** grade
oft often
das **Papier** paper
die **Physik** physics
das **Problem,-e** problem
pünktlich punctual, on time
der **Radiergummi,-s** eraser

der **Rechner,-** calculator
recht right; *Du hast recht.* You're right.
die **Religion** religion
sagen to say; *Wie sagt man...?* How do you/they say...?
schnell fast
schon already
die **Schultasche,-n** school bag, satchel
schwer hard, difficult
sein his
sein to be
der **Spaß** fun; *Sie haben viel Spaß.* They have lots of fun.
der **Sport** sport
der **Stuhl,-̈e** chair
die **Stunde,-n** hour
der **Stundenplan,-̈e** class schedule
die **Tafel,-n** (chalk)board
der **Tafellappen,-** rag (to wipe off chalkboard)
der **Tisch,-e** table
das **Vergnügen** pleasure, enjoyment; *Erst die Arbeit, dann das Vergnügen.* Business before pleasure.
viele many
was für what kind of
wie viele how many
die **Woche,-n** week

Wir haben ein Problem.

Was haben sie in der Schultasche?

Zu Besuch

In this chapter you will be able to:

- talk about the weather
- write a letter
- identify countries and languages spoken there
- ask where someone is from
- give information

Monika kommt zu Besuch

Kai: Was schreibst du denn?

Petra: Einen Brief. Monika, meine Cousine, kommt im März zu Besuch.

Kai: Bleibt sie lange?

Petra: Zwei Wochen. Dann fahren meine Eltern, Monika und ich ein paar Tage nach Österreich.

Kai: Im März ist es so kalt.

Petra: Das ist doch schön. Wir laufen dort Ski.

WB Activity 1

Was schreibt Petra?

Bleibt Monika lange?

1. Wochen
2. Cousine
3. fahren
4. schreibt
5. Österreich
6. kalt

1. *Was fehlt hier?* **(What's missing here?) Complete each statement based on the conversation between Kai and Petra.**

    1. Monika kommt zwei ____ zu Besuch.
    2. Petra ist Monikas ____.
    3. Petra, ihre Eltern und Monika ____ nach Österreich.
    4. Petra ____ einen Brief.
    5. Sie laufen in ____ Ski.
    6. Im März ist es in Österreich ____.

2. Beantworte diese Fragen!

1. Was machen Petra und Monika in Österreich?
2. Wie heißt Petras Cousine?
3. Wie viele Wochen ist Petras Cousine zu Besuch?
4. Wie viele Tage sind alle in Österreich?
5. Wann ist es in Österreich kalt?
6. Was schreibt Petra?

1. Sie laufen Ski.
2. Monika.
3. Zwei Wochen.
4. Ein paar Tage.
5. Im März.
6. Einen Brief.

Wohin fahren alle?

Gülten: Im Sommer besuche ich meine Tante in Bern.

Tanja: Oh, wirklich? Meine Mutter und ich fahren dann auch in die Schweiz. Ihr Bruder wohnt in Zürich.

Gülten: Im Juli und August ist es da warm.

Tanja: Ich schicke Peter eine Karte. Er kommt in drei Wochen zu Besuch.

Gülten: Wer ist Peter?

Tanja: Mein Cousin. Er ist sechzehn. Ganz charmant!

Gülten: Sag mir, wann er hier ist.

Tanja: Klar.

Im Sommer besuche ich meine Tante in Bern.

 WB Activity 2

WA Activity 1

OT Activity 32

Mein Cousin.

Wer ist Peter?

3. *Richtig oder falsch?* Determine whether the following statements are correct or incorrect. If they are incorrect, provide a correct statement in German.

1. Tanjas Bruder wohnt in Zürich.
2. Gülten besucht im Sommer ihre Tante.
3. Peter ist Gültens Cousin.
4. Tanja schickt Peter einen Brief.
5. Im Juli ist es in Zürich warm.
6. Peter kommt im August.

Zürich

4. **Was passt hier?**

muß	besuchen	hast	fahre
beginnt	kommst	macht	bleibst

– Am Donnerstag ____ ich mit meinen Eltern nach München.
– Was ____ ihr da?
– Wir ____ meinen Onkel und meine Tante.
– Wie viele Tage ____ du denn in München?
– Nur drei Tage. Ich ____ am Sonntag schon zu Hause sein.
– Warum ____ du so früh nach Hause?
– Die Schule ____ doch am Montag.
– Ja, du ____ recht.

Sprichwort

Sie bleibt nicht bei der Sache.

(She doesn't stick to the point.)

Für dich

Although school vacation varies slightly among the 16 federal states *(Bundesländer)*, it's common for students to have two or three weeks vacation around Easter *(Osterferien)* which is either in March or April. Students get at least another week off during Pentecost *(Pfingstferien)* in the month of May or June. To avoid congestion on the German highways and freeways during the summer, the federal states stagger the six-week summer vacation period *(Sommerferien)* from the middle of June through the middle of September. Students have another one to two weeks of school vacation during October *(Herbstferien)*. Finally, students have two weeks off at Christmas time *(Weihnachtsferien)*.

Die Schulferien

	HERBST
Baden-Württemberg	2. 11. – 4. 11.
Bayern	31. 10. – 4. 11.
Berlin	22. 10. – 29. 10.
Brandenburg	4. 10. – 8. 10.
Bremen	24. 10. – 31. 10.
Hamburg	24. 10. – 29. 10.
Hessen	17. 10. – 28. 10.
Meckl.-Vorpommern	17. 10. – 22. 10.
Niedersachsen	20. 10. – 1. 11.
Nordrhein-Westfalen	4. 10. – 7. 10.
Rheinland-Pfalz	17. 10. – 22. 10.
Saarland	17. 10. – 22. 10.
Sachsen	13. 10. – 22. 10.
Sachsen-Anhalt	17. 10. – 22. 10.
Schleswig-Holstein	17. 10. – 29. 10.
Thüringen	24. 10. – 29. 10.

WB Activity 3

Rollenspiel

You and your classmate pretend to be related to each other. You call your proposed relative and invite him or her to come and visit you in July or August. Your conversation should include the following: proposed day of visit, length of stay, what you plan to do during the relative's visit and the expected weather. Reverse roles after you have discussed your relative's visit. Be as creative as possible.

5. **Etwas Persönliches.**

   Write a short letter to a friend, inviting him or her to visit you during your summer vacation. Start your letter with either *Liebe...* (name of girl) or *Lieber...* (name of boy) which means "Dear..." and finish your letter with *Dein...* (if you are a boy) or *Deine...* (if you are a girl) which means "Your..."

Aktuelles

Visiting Germans

Most Germans live in a rather small, close network of social relationships that are determined by tradition and custom as well as by education and job status. Home life is of greatest significance, both as a shelter from the turmoils and stress of the outside world and as an expression of one's own private standing. Most German homemakers take great pride in the way their home is furnished and maintained, sometimes even at the cost of cultivating social contacts.

All of this means, of course, that not only foreigners but also Germans who have to move to another location may find it difficult to make new friends.

Der Herr gibt der Dame Blumen.

When it comes to visiting each other, Germans tend to be somewhat more formal than Americans. Casual visits are not common. Therefore, if you have been invited to a German home, you may consider it a special gesture of friendship. You may well expect that your

Zwei Kuchen stehen auf dem Tisch.

visit has been carefully prepared for: the house will be very clean, at least one cake will be served with coffee or soft drinks, a good dinner may have been prepared and the family will be dressed up for the occasion.

If you have been invited for coffee and cake *(Kaffee und Kuchen)* or a meal *(Mahlzeit)*, you are expected to be there right on time. Do not come earlier, or more than 10 or 15 minutes later. It is customary to bring a bouquet of cut flowers *(Blumen)* to the hostess, usually an uneven number of five or seven flowers. When presenting the flowers, do not forget to take off the wrapping before handing them to the hostess. You may want to bring a small gift of candy *(Bonbons)* or other sweets *(Süßigkeiten)* for the children.

Americans coming to Germany will also notice that Germans build more fences than Americans. There are exceptions in modern housing developments, but usually every house has hedges or a fenced-in front yard. If there is a back yard, this will be enclosed with a fence or hedge as well.

Süßigkeiten

ein deutsches Haus

Praktische Situation

Form groups of three. Student 1 prepares a list of social behaviors for when friends or relatives visit in Germany. Student 2 prepares a similar list for the United States. Student 3 is the discussion leader and begins by asking Student 1 to read the first item on his or her list. All three students decide if this behavior is uniquely German, uniquely American or takes place in both countries. After all activities have been categorized, Student 3 makes a diagram of two intersecting circles and writes each behavior in the appropriate place.

Zu Besuch

You may want to use a calendar to practice further the words for the twelve months.

OT   Activities 33-34

Ask students to check the weather report for tomorrow. *(Wie ist das Wetter morgen?)* Expand this section by asking students to check the weather listed in newspapers for other cities. *(Wie ist das Wetter in New York, Chicago, Los Angeles?*, etc.) Finally, use the names of the months and seasons in questions such as *Wie ist das Wetter im Herbst, Frühling (Januar, Mai, Juni)?* and so on.

WB   Activities 4-6

WA   Activities 2-3

OT   Activities 35-36

S   Activity 6

Ergänzung

Die Monate und Jahreszeiten

Januar	Februar	März
Winter	Winter	Frühling
April	Mai	Juni
Frühling	Frühling	Sommer
Juli	August	September
Sommer	Sommer	Herbst
Oktober	November	Dezember
Herbst	Herbst	Winter

Wie ist das Wetter heute?

Die Sonne scheint.

Es regnet.

Es schneit.

Es ist schön.

Es ist schlecht.

Es ist kalt.

Es ist kühl.

Es ist warm.

Es ist heiß.

6. *Im Frühling, Sommer, Herbst oder Winter?* **Relate the months to the seasons.**

◆ Januar
◆ Januar ist im Winter.

1. Juli
2. März
3. Dezember
4. September
5. Mai
6. August

1. Juli ist im Sommer.
2. März ist im Frühling.
3. Dezember ist im Winter.
4. September ist im Herbst.
5. Mai ist im Frühling.
6. August ist im Sommer.

7. *Wie ist das Wetter?* **Look at the photos and determine what the weather is like. Use a different expression for each photo.**

1.

2.

3.

4.

5.

6.

Samples answers:
1. Es ist kalt.
2. Es regnet.
3. Die Sonne scheint.
4. Es ist kühl.
5. Es ist schlecht.
6. Es ist nicht warm.

Zu Besuch

8. **Welcher Monat ist das?** Determine the month in which each even takes place.

1. Thanksgiving
2. Valentine's Day
3. Independence Day
4. Halloween

5. Memorial Day
6. New Year's Day
7. first day of school
8. your birthday

In welchem Monat ist Weihnachten?

Sag's mal! Wie ist das Wetter?

feucht* sonnig* Die Sonne scheint.

schön Es nieselt.* kühl

trocken* kalt

bedeckt* Es regnet. miserabel*

heiter* bewölkt*

schwül*

Es schneit. warm

Nicht so toll. heiß schlecht

9. *Wie ist das Wetter in...?* **Look at the weather report and give an answer to this question for the various cities listed.**

- Dresden
- In Dresden ist es wolkig

- Kiel
- In Kiel ist es heiter. Es gibt auch Schauer.

1. München
2. Berlin
3. Freiburg
4. Rostock
5. Stuttgart
6. Frankfurt

Sample answers:
1. In München gibt es Gewitter.
2. In Berlin ist es wolkig.
3. In Freiburg regnet es.
4. In Rostock gibt es Nieselregen.
5. In Stuttgart gibt es Schauer.
6. In Frankfurt ist es wolkig.

WB Activity 7

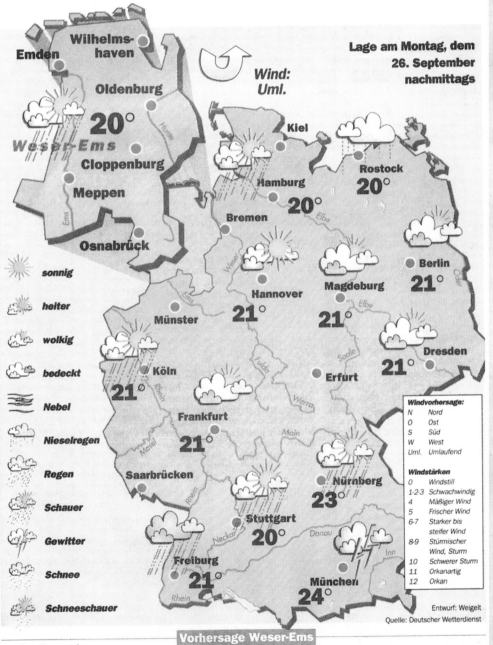

sonnig	
heiter	
wolkig	
bedeckt	
Nebel	
Nieselregen	
Regen	
Schauer	
Gewitter	
Schnee	
Schneeschauer	

Lage am Montag, dem 26. September nachmittags

Wind: Uml.

Emden — Wilhelmshaven — Oldenburg 20° — Weser-Ems — Cloppenburg — Meppen — Osnabrück — Kiel — Hamburg 20° — Bremen — Rostock 20° — Hannover 21° — Magdeburg 21° — Berlin 21° — Münster — Köln 21° — Erfurt — Dresden 21° — Frankfurt 21° — Saarbrücken — Nürnberg 23° — Stuttgart 20° — Freiburg 21° — München 24°

Windvorhersage:

N	Nord
O	Ost
S	Süd
W	West
Uml.	Umlaufend

Windstärken

0	Windstill
1-2-3	Schwachwindig
4	Mäßiger Wind
5	Frischer Wind
6-7	Starker bis steifer Wind
8-9	Stürmischer Wind, Sturm
10	Schwerer Sturm
11	Orkanartig
12	Orkan

Entwurf: Weigelt
Quelle: Deutscher Wetterdienst

Vorhersage Weser-Ems

Zu Besuch

Sprache

Indefinite Article
(Nominative and Accusative Singular)

Singular			
	masculine	**feminine**	**neuter**
nominative	ein	eine	ein
accusative	einen	eine	ein

The articles in the *ein*-group are called indefinite because they do not specifically identify the noun they are associated with. All articles you have learned so far, i.e., *der, die, das*, are *der*-words (definite articles). In English the indefinite article is either "a" or "an."

◆ *ein Junge (der)*

◆ *eine Karte (die)*

◆ *ein Buch (das)*

From the above you can see that only the accusative of the masculine article differs from the nominative *(ein, einen)*. This is also true of the definite article *(der, den)*.

◆ *Ich schreibe den Brief.* I am writing the letter.

◆ *Ich schreibe einen Brief.* I am writing a letter.

The forms of *mein* (my) and *dein* (your) are similar to *ein*-words as they take the same endings. You have already seen some examples in the various dialogs and reading selections.

◆ *Ein Heft ist in der Schultasche?* A notebook is in the school bag?

◆ *Wo ist mein Englischbuch?* Where is my English book?

◆ *Hast du einen Bleistift?* Do you have a pencil?

◆ *Ich finde deinen Freund toll.* I think your friend is great.

 Activities 8-9

 Activities 4

Activity 5

Hast du einen Bleistift?

10. *Was ist das?* **Your friends want to learn some German words. They point to different items. Help them identify each item.**

◆ Das ist eine CD.

1.

2.

3.

4.

1. Das ist eine Gitarre.
2. Das ist ein Brief.
3. Das ist ein Rechner.
4. Das ist ein Telefon.
5. Das ist ein Kuli.
6. Das ist ein Buch.
7. Das ist eine Karte.
8. Das ist eine Kassette.

5.

6.

TPR Activity: You may want to have students get up and point to (touch, pick up) specific objects, to which they respond *Das ist ein(e)...*

7.

8.

Zu Besuch

AC/CD

1. Ein Lehrer ist am Telefon.
2. Ein Stuhl ist im Wohnzimmer.
3. Ein Klavier ist zu Hause.
4. Eine Stadt ist im Norden.
5. Eine CD ist hier.
6. Ein Tisch ist da drüben.

AC/CD

11. *Wo ist...?* **Several people are asking your help in locating specific objects, places or people. Can you help them?**

◆ Bahnhof / in der Stadt
◆ Ein Bahnhof ist in der Stadt.

1. Lehrer / am Telefon
2. Stuhl / im Wohnzimmer
3. Klavier / zu Hause
4. Stadt / im Norden
5. CD / hier
6. Tisch / da drüben

Ist der Bahnhof weit von hier?

12. *Was brauchst du?* **Tell your classmates that various people need the following items. Use the cues provided.**

◆ ich
◆ Ich brauche einen Bleistift.

1. Christa
2. wir

1. Christa braucht ein Heft.
2. Wir brauchen einen Kuli.
3. Mein Bruder braucht ein Lineal.
4. Herr Schmidt braucht einen Radiergummi.
5. Meine Mutter braucht ein Telefon.
6. Der Mathelehrer braucht einen Rechner.

3. mein Bruder
4. Herr Schmidt

5. meine Mutter
6. der Mathelehrer

13. Kombiniere...

Brauchst	wir	einen Brief
Schreiben	Rudi und Dieter	nach Österreich
Besucht	du	eine Karte
Fahren	ihr	den Deutschlehrer
		in die Stadt
		Renate

Ergänzung

Länder und Sprachen

AC/CD

Sie kommt aus Frankreich.

Sie spricht französisch.

Er kommt aus Italien.

Er spricht italienisch.

Er kommt aus Amerika.

Er spricht englisch.

Er kommt aus Österreich.

Er spricht deutsch.

Sie kommt aus Spanien.

Sie spricht spanisch.

 WB Activities 10-11

 LA Activity 1

 WA Activity 5

OT Activities 37-38

 S Activity 3

Zu Besuch

Wie heißen die Nachbarländer von Deutschland?

14. *Wo liegt...?* **Answer this question by locating cities within Germany. You may want to use the map in the front of this book.**

◆ Hamburg
◆ Hamburg liegt im Norden.

1. Dresden
2. Halle
3. Köln
4. München
5. Hamburg
6. Bonn
7. Chemnitz
8. Regensburg

15. *Welche Sprache spricht man in diesen Städten oder Ländern?* **Indicate the language spoken in these international cities or countries. You haven't seen the German names for some of these cities and countries, but you should be able to recognize them.**

◆ Boston
◆ In Boston spricht man englisch.

1. Madrid
2. Berlin
3. Costa Rica
4. Paris
5. Rom
6. München
7. Mexiko
8. London
9. Florenz
10. Kolumbien
11. Chicago
12. Quebec

Praktische Situation

You and your partner each select a European country, city or area of Germany that you would like to visit. Then, taking turns with your partner, ask and answer questions about why you selected the place you would like to visit, what time of year you would go there and what the weather would be like during your visit.

Example:

Student 1: *Ich möchte nach Österreich fahren.*

Student 2: *Warum nach Österreich?*

Student 1: *Das Land ist sehr schön.*

Student 2: *Wann möchtest du dorthin fahren?*

Student 1: *Im Frühling.*

Student 2: *Wie ist das Wetter da im Frühling?*

Student 1: *Es ist etwas kühl.*

Sprache

Plural Forms of Nouns

For singular nouns you must know the gender; that is, you must know whether the noun is a *der-, die-,* or *das*-word. You will have to learn these, of course. In the plural, however, all nouns are *die* in the nominative and accusative, regardless of their gender.

	Singular			Plural
	masculine	feminine	neuter	
nominative	der	die	das	die
accusative	den	die	das	die

When you look up nouns at the end of each chapter and in the end vocabulary section of this book, you will notice that each noun is followed by a comma and an indication of its plural form. Here are some examples of how nouns are listed in this book and in most dictionaries and reference books.

*die **Antwort,-en*** answer
Singular = *die Antwort*; Plural = *die Antworten* (*en* is added)

*der **Lehrer,-*** teacher
Singular = *der Lehrer*; Plural = *die Lehrer* (no change)

*das **Buch,-̈er*** book
Singular = *das Buch*; Plural = *die Bücher* (*u* changes to *ü* and *er* is added)

Zu Besuch

As you can see from the list below, most nouns undergo certain changes from the singular to the plural. There is no definite rule for the formation of plural nouns. You must learn the plural form when you learn a new noun. For simplification, all important nouns that you have learned up to this chapter, have been placed into groups whenever the change from the singular to the plural follows certain patterns.

Hier gibt es viele Karten.

Er hat Hefte und Bücher in seiner Schultasche.

Plural of Nouns

no change			
der Computer	die Computer	der Onkel	die Onkel
der Lehrer	die Lehrer	der Rechner	die Rechner
das Mädchen	die Mädchen		

add -*n*, -*en*, -*nen*			
die Gitarre	die Gitarren	die Schwester	die Schwestern
die Hausaufgabe	die Hausaufgaben	die Stunde	die Stunden
die Idee	die Ideen	die Tante	die Tanten
der Junge	die Jungen	die Woche	die Wochen
die Karte	die Karten	die Antwort	die Antworten
die Kassette	die Kassetten	die Frau	die Frauen
die Klasse	die Klassen	der Herr	die Herren
die Minute	die Minuten	die Uhr	die Uhren
die Note	die Noten	die Freundin	die Freundinnen
die Schule	die Schulen	die Lehrerin	die Lehrerinnen
die Schultasche	die Schultaschen		

add -*e* or ¨*e*			
der Bleistift	die Bleistifte	das Telefon	die Telefone
das Computerspiel	die Computerspiele	der Tisch	die Tische
der Freund	die Freunde	der Bahnhof	die Bahnhöfe
das Heft	die Hefte	der Basketball	die Basketbälle
das Klavier	die Klaviere	der Fußball	die Fußbälle
das Lineal	die Lineale	der Sohn	die Söhne
das Problem	die Probleme	die Stadt	die Städte
der Tag	die Tage	der Stuhl	die Stühle

add ¨ or ¨*er*			
der Bruder	die Brüder	das Buch	die Bücher
die Mutter	die Mütter	das Fach	die Fächer
die Tochter	die Töchter	das Haus	die Häuser
der Vater	die Väter		

add -s			
das Büro	die Büros	der Krimi	die Krimis
die CD	die CDs	der Kuli	die Kulis
der Cousin	die Cousins	der Radiergummi	die Radiergummis

16. *Wie viele bringen sie mit?* You and your friends are planning a fun party and need more than just one of each item for some of the games planned.

◆ Klaus / viele / CD
◆ Klaus bringt viele CDs mit.

1. Renate / acht / Kuli
2. Rolf und Sabine / zwei / Computer
3. Petra / zehn / Buch
4. Aki / fünf / Karte
5. Ralf / ein paar / Computerspiel
6. Heike und Monika / acht / Kassette
7. Günter / drei / Stuhl

17. *Marko hat eine große Familie.* Marko's parents are planning a family reunion with their relatives who live in different parts of Germany. Marko asks his father about various relatives.

◆ Hat Tante Anna eine Schwester? (vier)
◆ Sie hat vier Schwestern.

1. Hat Onkel Bruno einen Bruder? (zwei)
2. Hat Mutti eine Cousine? (fünf)
3. Hat deine Schwester eine Tochter? (drei)
4. Hat Tante Elisabeth einen Sohn? (zwei)
5. Hat Opa einen Cousin? (vier)
6. Hat Muttis Bruder eine Tante? (drei)

Expansion: Ask these questions: *Bringt Klaus viele CDs mit?, Ja (Nein) er bringt (nicht) viele CDs mit. Was bringt er mit? Wie viele CDs bringt er mit?*

AC/CD

1. Renate bringt acht Kulis mit.
2. Rolf und Sabine bringen zwei Computer mit.
3. Petra bringt zehn Bücher mit.
4. Aki bringt fünf Karten mit.
5. Ralf bringt ein paar Computerspiele mit.
6. Heike und Monika bringen acht Kassetten mit.
7. Günter bringt drei Stühle mit.

AC/CD

1. Er hat zwei Brüder.
2. Sie hat fünf Cousinen.
3. Sie hat drei Töchter.
4. Sie hat zwei Söhne.
5. Er hat vier Cousins.
6. Er hat drei Tanten.

Wir beide sind Schwestern.

Sprache

Wie viel? or *Wie viele?*

Generally speaking, *wie viel?* (how much?) is used when expressing a mass or a sum.

◆ *Wie viel Uhr ist es?* What time is it?

◆ *Wie viel kostet das Klavier?* How much does the piano cost?

On the other hand, *wie viele?* (how many?) is used when referring to items that can be counted.

◆ *Wie viele Karten kaufen wir?* How many tickets do we buy?

◆ *Wie viele Freunde hat Tina?* How many friends does Tina have?

WB Activity 14

18. *Wie viel?* oder *Wie viele?*

1. ____ Zeit hast du morgen?
2. ____ Wochen bleibt ihr in Deutschland?
3. ____ CDs hast du zu Hause?
4. ____ kostet der Computer?
5. ____ Arbeit hast du heute?
6. ____ Städte besuchen sie?
7. ____ Tage besucht ihr Onkel Walter?

1. Wie viel
2. Wie viele
3. Wie viele
4. Wie viel
5. Wie viel
6. Wie viele
7. Wie viele

19. **The music at a party is quite noisy. As you listen, you can't hear everything that is being said. Ask the appropriate questions using *wieviel* or *wie viele*.**

◆ Morgen kaufen wir *vier* Karten zum Rockkonzert.
◆ Wie viele Karten kauft ihr morgen?

1. Die Matheklasse beginnt heute um *elf* Uhr.
2. Wir kaufen *vier* Computerspiele im Kaufhaus.
3. Familie Rückert wohnt erst *ein paar* Monate hier.
4. Die Gitarre kostet nur *achtzig* Mark.
5. Mein Onkel hat *drei* Söhne.
6. Ich habe am Sonntag *keine* Zeit.
7. Rainer bringt *sieben* Bücher zur Schule.
8. Dieter hat *zwei* Freundinnen.

AC/CD

1. Um wieviel Uhr beginnt die Matheklasse heute?
2. Wie viele Computerspiele kauft ihr im Kaufhaus?
3. Wie viele Monate wohnt Familie Rückert erst hier?
4. Wieviel kostet die Gitarre nur?
5. Wie viele Söhne hat dein Onkel?
6. Wieviel Zeit hast du am Sonntag?
7. Wie viele Bücher bringt Rainer zur Schule?
8. Wie viele Freundinnen hat Dieter?

AC/CD

Tina besucht ihren Cousin

Simons Cousine Tina wohnt nicht mehr° in Berlin. Seit fünf Monaten° wohnen Tina und ihre Eltern in Magdeburg. Im Sommer hat Tina viel Zeit. Sie möchte dann Simon besuchen. Beide sprechen oft am Telefon.

Wie gefällt es dir in Magdeburg?

Simon: Wie gefällt es dir° in Magdeburg?

Tina: Sehr gut. Die Stadt ist nicht so groß wie° Berlin. Meine Schule ist auch sehr alt, aber meine Lehrer sind alle nett°.

Simon: Du kennst doch Herrn Reuter, den Englischlehrer.

Tina: Na klar.

Simon: Er geht jetzt ein Jahr° nach England. Frau Dietrich ist die neue Lehrerin. Sie ist ganz toll. Meine Noten sind auch viel besser°.

Sehr gut.

Tina: Meine nicht. Du bist in Englisch immer so gut.

Simon: Da hast du recht. Ich mache auch immer meine Hausaufgaben.

Tina: Ja, du bist aber auch ein Genie.

Simon: Du, Tina, komm doch im Juli zu uns zu Besuch°.

Have students write a short paragraph about a person (friend or relative) they plan to or would like to visit. Students should indicate where that person lives, when they would go and what you will do there.

Zu Besuch

159

Simon schreibt Tina eine Karte.

Tina:	Wirklich? Wie viele Tage denn?
Simon:	Möchtest du eine Woche bleiben?
Tina:	Prima. Aber meine Englischbücher bringe ich nicht mit.
Simon:	Das brauchst du auch nicht. Meine Schwester ist ein paar° Monate in Amerika. Wir sprechen dann mit ihr englisch. Sagt man° nicht „Übung macht den Meister"?
Tina:	Ja, da hast du wirklich recht. Schreib mir bitte, wann du Zeit hast.
Simon:	Ich spreche gleich mit meinen Eltern. Morgen nach der Schule schicke ich eine Karte.

In ein paar Tagen bekommt Tina Simons Karte. Zwei Monate später reist° Tina mit einem Zug° von Magdeburg nach Berlin. Es dauert zwei Stunden, bis sie da ist. Simon und seine Eltern warten auf dem Bahnhof auf° Tina. Der Zug kommt auch pünktlich an°. Alle sagen „Hallo!" und „Wie geht's?" und fahren dann gleich vom Bahnhof zu Simons Haus.

Tina liest Simons Karte.

nicht mehr no longer; *seit fünf Monaten* for five months; *Wie gefällt es dir?* How do you like it?; *nicht so groß wie* not as big as; *nett* nice; *das Jahr* year; *besser* better; *Komm doch zu uns zu Besuch.* Why don't you come visit us.; *ein paar* a few; *man sagt* they say; *sie reist* she travels; *der Zug* train; *sie warten auf dem Bahnhof auf* they are waiting at the station for; *kommt...an* arrives

WB Activity 15

LA Activities 2-3

WA Activity 8

GRUSS AUS MAGDEBURG

20. *Was fehlt hier?* Complete each sentence by selecting the appropriate verb and changing it to the correct verb form where necessary. Use each verb only once.

reisen   machen   bekommen   wohnen
sprechen   warten   sein   haben
bringen   besuchen   sagen   schreiben

1. Tina _____ jetzt in Magdeburg.
2. Simon _____ eine Schwester.
3. Simon und Tina _____ am Telefon.
4. Berlin _____ eine große Stadt.
5. Simon _____ immer seine Hausaufgaben.
6. Tina _____ Simon im Juli.
7. Tina _____ keine Englischbücher mit.
8. Man _____: „Übung macht den Meister."
9. Simon _____ Tina morgen.
10. Später _____ Tina auch Simons Karte.
11. Im Juli _____ Tina zu ihrem Cousin.
12. Alle _____ auf dem Bahnhof.

1. wohnt
2. hat
3. sprechen
4. ist
5. macht
6. besucht
7. bringt
8. sagt
9. schreibt
10. bekommt
11. reist
12. warten

21. **Beantworte diese Fragen!**

1. Wo wohnt Tina jetzt?
2. Wann möchte Tina Simon besuchen?
3. Ist Tinas Schule neu?
4. Wer ist Frau Dietrich?
5. Wie ist Simon in Englisch?
6. Wie viele Tage besucht Tina Simon?
7. Wo ist Simons Schwester ein paar Wochen?
8. Was schickt Simon mor
9. Wie kommt Tina von Magdeburg nach Berlin?
10. Wie viele Stunden reist sie?
11. Wer wartet auf dem Bahnhof?
12. Wohin fahren alle?

AC/CD

1. In Magdeburg.
2. Im Sommer.
3. Nein, sie ist alt.
4. Sie ist die neue Lehrerin.
5. Er ist immer gut.
6. Sieben Tage.
7. In Amerika.
8. Eine Karte.
9. Mit einem Zug.
10. Zwei Stunden.
11. Simon und seine Eltern.
12. Zu Simons Haus.

Speech bubbles:
- Was machst du denn hier?
- Ich warte auf Milli.
- Milli ist nicht hier. Sie besucht ihren Opa.
- Was??? Ihr Opa soll sie doch besuchen.
- Ja, du hast recht. Aber Milli besucht ihn lieber in seinem Haus.
- Warum denn?
- Ihr Opa sagt immer: „Komm zu mir. Mein Haus ist auch dein Haus."
- Na ja, Millis Eltern wohnen in keinem Haus und sie können nicht dasselbe sagen.

PA

Übung macht den Meister!

1. You are telling your classmate that a friend of yours has moved to another town or city. Create a dialog in which you discuss the following: your friend's name, his or her current residence, where your friend likes to go to school and the subjects he or she is taking, how your friend likes the school. Add any additional comments you would like.

2. You don't want one of your relatives to come (cousin, aunt, uncle, etc.) and visit you during a certain time of the year. Write a short letter in which you give at least five reasons why he or she should not come at that time. For example, your reasons may include: bad weather, busy schedule, too much work, won't be home, others are already visiting you. Begin your letter with *Lieber/Liebe* and end it with *Dein/Deine*.

3. Discuss the weather in your area during the different seasons and/or months of the year.

4. Cut the national weather report out of a newspaper and use it to ask such questions as *Wie ist das Wetter in...?* (New York, Los Angeles, Miami, Atlanta, Milwaukee, etc.).

Wie ist das Wetter heute?

Es regnet.

Aktuelles

The Weather

The weather is much less extreme in Central Europe than in most parts of the United States. The moderating influence of the western winds from the Atlantic Ocean is stronger than the hot and cold air streams coming from the east. Intense heat is as rare as extreme cold or blizzards. There are heavy storms on the coasts sometimes, but nothing comparable to hurricanes. Earthquakes are practically unknown in Central Europe.

Geographically, Germany lies approximately at the same latitude as southern Canada. Summer days in Germany are longer than in the United States, winter days are shorter. In winter the average daily temperature is between 35°F in central and northern Germany and 21°F in southern Germany. In July, the warmest month of the year, average temperatures in these regions vary between 64° and 68°F. Exceptions are the Upper Rhine Valley in the southwest with its extremely mild climate, northern Bavaria with its warm alpine wind *(Föhn)* from the south, and the Harz Mountains, a climatic zone of its own with cold winds, cool summers and heavy snow in winter.

In den Alpen ist es sehr schön.

Sie haben viel Spaß im Schnee.

Generally, German weather can be compared to the weather in the north-central United States. There is plenty of rain, particularly in the northwestern parts of Germany, but the following tips can be valid for other German regions as well:

1. Accept the fact that it often rains in Hamburg (a drizzly, damp and continuous rain), particularly during the fall and spring.

2. Don't plan an outdoor event where success depends completely upon good weather. Always have an alternate plan in case of rain.

3. Don't cancel plans because of rain or wait until a drizzle stops because you may find yourself postponing for days.

4. Arm yourself with a raincoat (including hood) and an umbrella and forge ahead. You'll notice Germans don't seem to mind being in the rain.

5. Dress warmly.

6. Don't consider putting winter clothes into storage before May.

7. Even sunny days can be cool because of the wind. It's a good idea to have a windbreaker with a hood (and zip-out warm lining for year-round use).

Sommer in Goslar (Harz)

Vergleiche das Wetter in deiner Gegend mit dem Wetter in Deutschland. **(Compare the weather in your area with the weather in Germany.) Point out at least three differences or similarities. Which climate do your prefer and why?**

Erweiterung

Do this exercise as a group competition. Find out who gets the answers the fastest.

1. Musik
2. Mittwoch
3. Uhr
4. Juni
5. Magdeburg
6. Lehrerin
7. Zwei
8. Physik
9. Wetter
10. Fußball
11. Zug
12. Herbst

Activity 4

22. *Was passt hier?* **Which words from both lists match?**

Fußball	Lehrerin	Musik	Uhr
Wetter	Magdeburg	Zug	Mittwoch
Juni	Zwei	Physik	Herbst

1. das Rockkonzert
2. der Tag
3. die Zeit
4. der Monat
5. die Stadt
6. die Schule
7. die Note
8. das Fach
9. die Sonne
10. der Sport
11. der Bahnhof
12. die Jahreszeit

Husum, eine Stadt in Norddeutschland

23. **Etwas Persönliches.**

1. Wie ist das Wetter, wo du wohnst?

2. Wen besuchst du gern?

3. Was machst du gern im Sommer?

4. Hast du Cousinen, Cousins, Brüder oder Schwestern? Wie heißen sie und wie alt sind sie?

5. Hast du nach der Schule viele Hausaufgaben? Wann machst du deine Hausaufgaben?

WB Activity 16

24. **On your way to your aunt's house you meet a friend and talk about various things. Complete your conversation based on what your friend is saying.**

Freund(in): Wohin gehst du denn?

Du: ____

Freun(in): Wo wohnt deine Tante denn?

Du: ____

Freund(in): Kommst du später rüber?

Du: ____

Freund(in): Und morgen?

Du: ____

Freund(in): Um wie viel Uhr kommst du morgen?

Du: ____

Freund(in): Gut, bis morgen.

Du: ____

Sample answers:
Ich besuche meine Tante.
In der Stadt.
Ich habe heute nicht viel Zeit.
Ja, das geht.
So gegen vier.
Tschüs.

25. ***Was fehlt hier?* Complete each word by adding another noun. Make sure that the given article is the same as that of the added noun.**

◆ die Haus____

◆ die Hausaufgabe

1. das Computer____
2. das Fernseh____
3. das Kauf____
4. die Land____
5. das Lieblings____
6. die Mathe____
7. die Rock____
8. die Schul____
9. der Stunden____
10. das Wohn____

As an additional activity, have students form sentences using each newly formed noun.

1. das Computerspiel
2. das Fernsehprogramm
3. das Kaufhaus
4. die Landkarte
5. das Lieblingsfach
6. die Mathestunde
7. die Rockmusik, die Rockgruppe
8. die Schultasche
9. der Stundenplan
10. das Wohnzimmer

 Activity 17

Zu Besuch

26. **With a classmate develop a dialog, using the information strictly as a guideline. Be as creative as possible!**

You suggest to your friend that both of you should visit a former classmate who has moved away. You discuss the month, day and time when you would like to go. You agree to write a letter or postcard informing your classmate when you would like to come. Your conversation should include some additional information such as where your classmate lives now, how many brothers and/or sisters he or she has, what you should bring along and anything else you can think of.

 Activity 18

Was weißt du?

1. Indicate that you would like to visit a relative in the near future and tell why. Your answer should have at least six sentences.

2. Describe the weather in your area throughout the year. Say something about each month.

3. Indicate two cultural differences found when people in Germany and in the United States visit (*Auf Englisch*).

4. Name the nine countries that border on Germany.

5. Select eight international cities and indicate the language spoken in each one.

6. Tell your classmate that you have more than one of each of these: book, (school) subject, friend, computer game, teacher, notebook, cassette, detective story, telephone. Start your sentence with *Ich habe...*

 Activity 19

 Activity 9

 Activity 7

Innsbruck, Österreich

Vokabeln

ankommen to arrive
der **April** April
auf on, at
der **August** August
Belgien Belgium
besser better
der **Besuch,-e** visit; *Sie kommt zu Besuch.* She comes to visit.
besuchen to visit
bleiben to stay, remain
der **Brief,-e** letter
charmant charming
der **Cousin,-s** cousin (male)
die **Cousine,-n** cousin (female)
Dänemark Denmark
deutsch German; *Sie spricht deutsch.* She speaks German.
der **Dezember** December
englisch English; *Er spricht englisch.* He speaks English.
fahren to drive, go
der **Februar** February
Frankreich France
französisch French; *Sie spricht französisch.* She speaks French.
der **Frühling,-e** spring
gefallen to like; *Wie gefällt es dir...?* How do you like it...?
groß big, large; *so groß wie* as big as
heiß hot
der **Herbst,-e** fall, autumn
Holland Holland
Italien Italy

italienisch Italian; *Er spricht italienisch.* He speaks Italian.
das **Jahr,-e** year
die **Jahreszeit,-en** season
der **Januar** January
der **Juli** July
der **Juni** June
kalt cold
kommen to come; *zu Besuch kommen* to come to visit
kommen: *Komm doch zu uns.* Why don't you come to us? *Der Zug kommt pünktlich an.* The train arrives on time.
kühl cool
das **Land,-̈er** country
lange long, long time
laufen to run, go; *Ski laufen* to ski
Luxemburg Luxembourg
der **Mai** May
man one, they, people
der **März** March
mehr more; *nicht mehr* no more, no longer
der **Monat,-e** month
das **Nachbarland,-̈er** neighboring country
nett nice
die **Niederlande** Netherlands
der **November** November
der **Oktober** October
Österreich Austria
paar: ein paar a few
Polen Poland

regnen to rain
reisen to travel
sagen to say; *Sag mir...* Tell me...
scheinen to shine
schicken to send
schneien to snow
schön beautiful, nice
schreiben to write
die **Schweiz** Switzerland
seit since; *seit fünf Monaten* for five months
der **September** September
Ski laufen to ski
der **Sommer,-** summer
die **Sonne** sun
Spanien Spain
spanisch Spanish; *Er spricht spanisch.* He speaks Spanish.
die **Sprache,-n** language
sprechen to speak; *Sie spricht deutsch.* She speaks German.
die **Tschechische Republik** Czech Republic
die **Übung,-en** exercise, practice; *Übung macht den Meister!* Practice makes perfect!
warm warm
warten auf to wait for
das **Wetter** weather
der **Winter,-** winter
der **Zug,-̈e** train

ein heißer Tag an der Nordsee

ein kalter Tag in den Alpen

Zu Besuch

Wie schmeckt's?

In this chapter you will be able to:

- choose from a menu and order at a café
- offer something to eat and drink
- express likes and dislikes
- make requests
- give advice
- talk about what to do today

AC/CD

Matthias hat Hunger

Matthias: Ich habe Hunger.

Falko: Na dann essen wir etwas. Was möchtet ihr gern?

Birgit: Für mich nur Pommes frites.

Falko: Ich möchte eine Fischsemmel.

Matthias: Das schmeckt mir nicht. Bring mir bitte einen Hamburger.

Birgit: Etwas zu trinken? Ich trinke später eine Cola.

Falko: Ich auch, aber eine Fanta.

Matthias: Für mich nichts. Ich habe keinen Durst.

1. *Wer möchte was?* **Look at the illustrations and tell what Matthias, Falko and Birgit are eating now and drinking later by saying either** *Matthias (Birgit, Falko) möchte...essen* **or** *Matthias (Birgit, Falko) möchte...trinken.*

1. Falko möchte eine Fischsemmel essen.
2. Matthias möchte nichts trinken.
3. Falko möchte eine Fanta trinken.
4. Birgit möchte Pommes frites essen.
5. Birgit möchte eine Cola trinken.
6. Matthias möchte einen Hamburger essen.

2. Was fehlt hier?

- Möchtest du etwas ____?
- Nein, ich ____ keinen Hunger.
- Und du? Hast du ____?
- Ja, ich ____ einen Hamburger.
- Und etwas zu ____?
- Oh ja, ___ habe Durst.
- Eine ____ oder eine Cola?
- Bring mir ____ eine Cola.

essen
habe
Hunger
möchte
trinken
ich
Fanta
bitte

Was bringt die Kellnerin?

Kellnerin:	Ja, bitte?
Bettina:	Ich möchte ein Vanilleeis.
Maria:	Bringen Sie mir bitte ein Schokoeis.
Steffie:	Für mich ein gemischtes Eis.
Kellnerin:	Sonst noch etwas?
Bettina:	Nein, danke.
Maria:	Seht mal, wer da kommt!
Steffie:	Wer denn?
Maria:	Petra und Anne. Kommt her!
Bettina:	Hier sind zwei Stühle.

WB
Activity 1

WA
Activity 1

OT
Activity 39

Ja, bitte?

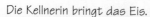
Die Kellnerin bringt das Eis.

Petra und Anne. Kommt her!

1. Kellnerin
2. Steffie
3. Petra und Anne
4. Maria
5. Bettina

Ja, ich möchte einen
Hamburger. Und du?

Nicht für mich, aber ich
esse gern Pommes frites.

Ein Eis schmeckt auch gut.

Da hast du recht. Bring mir
ein Schokoeis.

Gut, ein Schokoeis und für
mich ein gemischtes Eis.

3. **Wer sind diese Personen? Sie...**

    1. bringt das Eis.
    2. möchte gemischtes Eis.
    3. bekommen zwei Stühle.
    4. möchte Schokoeis.
    5. möchte Vanilleeis.

4. *Die logische Reihenfolge, bitte.* (The logical sequence, please.) Rearrange the sentences so that the conversation between the two people makes sense. Here is a clue how the conversation starts: *Hast du Hunger?*

    Gut, ein Schokoeis und für mich ein gemischtes Eis.

    Ein Eis schmeckt auch gut.

    Ja, ich möchte einen Hamburger. Und du?

    Da hast du recht. Bring mir ein Schokoeis.

    Nicht für mich, aber ich esse gern Pommes frites.

Sprichwort

Ich habe Hunger
wie ein Bär.

(I'm so hungry I could eat a horse.)

Für dich

Open-air snack bars in cities and, particularly, at festivals are quite common. At a typical snack bar *(Schnellimbiss)* you will be able to get sausages with bread or a roll and mustard *(Würstchen mit Brot oder Semmel und Senf)* and a soft drink at a reasonable price. A roll is called *Semmel* in southern Germany and *Brötchen* in the northern region. Germany offers more than 30 kinds of rolls.

Brot und Brötchen

The café *(Café* or *Konditorei)* is a German institution that dates back centuries. It's quite common for Germans to sit in a café with friends for an hour or two, order a cup of coffee *(Tasse Kaffee)* and a piece of delicious cake *(Torte)* or just some ice cream *(Eis)*. Depending on weather, people can be seen sitting in outdoor cafés from early May through September.

Was bekommt man in einem Café oder in einer Konditorei?

Hier kann man schnell essen.

Rollenspiel

You and a classmate decide to go to a café and order something to eat and drink. While waiting for the food server (a third classmate), you talk about what you would like to have. The server takes your order. Be as creative as possible.

Wie schmeckt's?

Aktuelles

From the *Ratskeller* to the *Schnellimbiss*

The variety of eating and drinking places in Germany is enormous. The *Ratskeller*, located in the basement of the city hall *(Rathaus)*, can still be found in large and medium-sized cities. The city politicians used to dine here and spend hours discussing city affairs. Today, the *Ratskeller* is still considered to be an upscale restaurant that is often reserved for special occasions.

In the smaller towns, the best places to eat are usually the hotels that include restaurants. When traveling through these smaller towns, you will often see hotels with such names as *Gasthof, Gasthaus, Gaststube* and *Gastwirtschaft.*

Wo findet man einen Ratskeller?

In diesem Hotel gibt's ein Restaurant.

In the afternoon, Germans like to go to a *Café* or *Konditorei* (pastry shop) which serves a wide assortment of cakes and pastries *(Kuchen*

Sie möchten eine Bratwurst essen.

Viele Deutsche gehen gern in ein Café.

und Torten) as well as ice cream, coffee and other beverages.

In Germany you will also find a large variety of foreign restaurants such as Chinese, Greek, Turkish, Italian, American, as well as steak houses, pizzerias, and others. A *Schnellimbiss, Schnellgaststätte, Imbissstube* or simply an *Imbiss* is a snack bar. There you can get a quick bite to eat and something to drink for a reasonable price. You usually eat standing at a counter or at a small round table.

Most of these snack bars offer a variety of sausages. The *Bratwurst* is fat, white and spicy; the *Currywurst* is similar, but served with a curry sauce; *Bockwurst* is longer and reddish, something like a thick American hot dog. The *Frankfurter* is thinner and usually sold in pairs. At an *Imbiss* sausages are eaten using the fingers. You don't get a bun, but often a slice of bread *(eine Scheibe Brot)* or a small roll *(Brötchen* or *Semmel)* that comes with the sausages.

Other fast-food places sell pizza and American-style hamburgers and hot dogs as well as grilled chicken *(Brathähnchen)*.

Was passt hier?

1. When you are in a hurry and don't have time to sit down, you would eat in a ____.
2. A slice of bread is called *eine* ____.
3. A ____ is located in the city hall.
4. Sausages that are thin and often sold in twos are called ____.
5. A *Semmel* is also known as ____.
6. The name of a sausage that is not white and is a bigger version of our hot dog is called ____.
7. Germans like to go to a ____ and have a piece of delicious pastry.
8. Cakes are called ____.

Was kann man in diesem Imbiss essen?

1. *Schnellimbiss, Schnellgaststätte, Imbissstube, Imbiss*
2. *Scheibe Brot*
3. *Ratskeller*
4. *Frankfurter*
5. *Brötchen*
6. *Bockwurst*
7. *Café, Konditorei*
8. *Kuchen*

 WB   Activity 2

Wie schmeckt's?

You may want to introduce some additional ice cream flavors such as *Himbeereis* (raspberry ice cream), *Blaubeereis/Heidelbeereis* (blueberry), *Orangeneis* (orange), *Bananeneis* (banana).

Ergänzung

Was für Eis möchtest du essen?

Ich möchte gern Schokoeis mit Schlagsahne essen.

Vanilleeis

Zitroneneis

Erdbeereis

Was trinkst du gern?

ein Glas Milch

eine Tasse Kaffee

Ich trinke gern Apfelsaft.

eine Tasse Kakao

eine Cola

ein Glas Eistee

Wohin gehen wir jetzt?

Ins Eiscafé.   In die Pizzeria.   Ins Restaurant.

5. *Wir sind in einem Imbiss.* **You are joining several friends for lunch. You tell the food server what everyone wants to order.**

◆ Tobias
◆ Tobias möchte Vanilleeis.

1. Sandra

2. Michael

3. Silke und Angelika

4. Katrin

5. Bruno

6. Holger und Karsten

1. Sandra möchte ein Glas Eistee.
2. Michael möchte einen Hamburger.
3. Silke und Angelika möchten Schokoeis.
4. Katrin möchte eine Fischsemmel.
5. Bruno möchte eine Cola.
6. Holger und Karsten möchten Pommes frites.

6. *Möchtest du ins Café gehen?* **You and your friend want to eat or drink something. One of you gives reasons why you don't want to go to a particular café, while the other gives reasons why you *do* want to go there. Come up with at least four reasons either for or against. Here are some reasons that you may wish to use.**

Ich möchte ins Café gehen.

Ich habe Hunger (Durst).

Martina und Renate kommen auch.

Sie haben da Erdbeereis mit Schlagsahne.

Ich kenne das Café sehr gut.

Da spielen sie oft Musik.

Im Café haben wir immer Spaß.

Ich möchte nicht ins Café gehen.

Ich habe keine Zeit.

Rolf geht doch auch nicht.

Das Café ist zu weit.

Es kostet zu viel.

Es schmeckt mir da nicht.

Im Café ist es nicht preiswert.

The forms of *möchten* are introduced at the beginning of the *Sprache* section of this chapter. You may want to go over that section first and explain that the endings of *möchten* are the same as those of regular verbs except the *er, sie, es* forms which do not have a *-t*. You may want to introduce some other beverages and foods like *Orangensaft* (orange juice), *ein Glas Wasser/Mineralwasser* (a glass of water/mineral water), *ein Würstchen* (hot dog).

Wie schmeckt's?

Sag's mal! Wie schmeckt's?

geht so*
hervorragend*
phantastisch*
gut
super
trocken*
schlecht
ganz gut
bestens*
echt gut*
köstlich*
lecker*
delikat*
ekelhaft*
absolut spitze*
schmackhaft*
nicht besonders*

Sprache

The Modal Auxiliaries: *mögen (möchten), müssen, wollen*

Modal auxiliaries (sometimes called helping verbs) help to set the mood of the particular sentence in which they occur. Look at the English sentence and see how each modal auxiliary changes the meaning.

◆ Anne **likes** to read a book.　　*Anne **mag** ein Buch lesen.*
◆ Rainer **would like** to read a book.　*Rainer **möchte** ein Buch lesen.*
◆ Boris **must (has to)** read a book.　*Boris **muss** ein Buch lesen.*
◆ Julia **wants to** read a book.　　*Julia **will** ein Buch lesen.*

As you can see, the meaning or "mood" in each of these sentences is different. The same is true in German. You will notice, however, that the word order remains constant in these sentences.

Mögen is most commonly used to express liking or preference in the sense of *gern haben* (like to have), *gern essen* or *trinken* (like to eat or drink). Today it is frequently used in the negative, often without the main verb: *Er mag das Buch nicht.* (He doesn't like the book.). A more common form derived from *mögen* is *möchten* (would like to). *Sie möchte nach Deutschland fahren.* (She would like to go to Germany.). You have already learned some of the *möchte*-forms in earlier chapters.

When using a modal auxiliary, it is very important to remember that the infinitive of the main verb is placed at the end of the sentence. The modal auxiliary appears in the position normally held by the verb.

	modal auxiliary			infinitive	
statement	Tina	will	in die Stadt	gehen.	
question	Will	Tina	in die Stadt	gehen?	

Sometimes the main verb can be eliminated, provided that the meaning is clear by using only the modal auxiliary.

◆ *Ich muss schon um sieben Uhr in die Schule.* I have to go to school already at seven o'clock.

◆ *Möchtest du ein Glas Milch?* Would you like (to have) a glass of milk?

	mögen to like	**möchten** would like (to do)	**müssen** must, to have to	**wollen** to want to
ich	mag	möchte	muss	will
du	magst	möchtest	musst	willst
er **sie** } **es**	mag	möchte	muss	will
wir	mögen	möchten	müssen	wollen
ihr	mögt	möchtet	müsst	wollt
sie	mögen	möchten	müssen	wollen
Sie	mögen	möchten	müssen	wollen

Point out that modal auxiliaries *mögen, möchten, müssen, wollen* have no ending when using them with *ich, er, sie, es*. Mention that *mögen* is mostly used in the negative *(Ich mag das nicht)*.

 WB Activities 6-7

 WA Activity 3

 S Activity 1

Wie schmeckt's?

1. Uli und Stefan möchten Frau Riedel besuchen.
2. Heidi möchte zu Petra rüberkommen.
3. Wir möchten Schokoeis essen.
4. Rudi möchte einen Krimi lesen.
5. Mein Freund möchte Rockmusik hören.
6. Deine Schwester möchte einen Brief schreiben.

1. Ja, wir wollen nach Hause fahren.
2. Ja, sie will jetzt essen.
3. Ja, sie wollen Ski laufen.
4. Ja, ich will Tennis spielen.
5. Ja, sie will fernsehen.
6. Ja, wir wollen in die Stadt gehen.
7. Ja, sie will die Karte schicken.

1. Ich muss ein Buch lesen.
2. Ich muss etwas Deutsch lernen.
3. Ich muss eine halbe Stunde Gitarre spielen.
4. Ich muss zum Kaufhaus gehen.
5. Ich muss einen Rechner kaufen.
6. Ich muss etwas essen und trinken.

7. **Was möchten alle nach der Schule machen?** Tell what everyone would like to do after school.

◆ Christa / nach Hause gehen
◆ Christa möchte nach Hause gehen.

1. Uli und Stefan / Frau Riedel besuchen
2. Heidi / zu Petra rüberkommen
3. wir / Schokoeis essen
4. Rudi / einen Krimi lesen
5. mein Freund / Rockmusik hören
6. deine Schwester / einen Brief schreiben

Was möchten die Leute trinken?

8. **Sie wollen das.** Everyone wants to do the things suggested.

◆ Willst du deinen Onkel besuchen?
◆ Ja, ich will meinen Onkel besuchen.

1. Wollt ihr nach Hause fahren?
2. Will Gisela jetzt essen?
3. Wollen Ralf und Ali Ski laufen?
4. Willst du Tennis spielen?
5. Will Gabriele fernsehen?
6. Wollt ihr in die Stadt gehen?
7. Will Frau Schulz die Karte schicken?

9. **Was musst du heute Nachmittag machen?** Before going to a party, you have to take care of several things.

◆ meine Hausaufgaben machen
◆ Ich muss meine Hausaufgaben machen.

1. ein Buch lesen
2. etwas Deutsch lernen
3. eine halbe Stunde Gitarre spielen
4. zum Kaufhaus gehen
5. einen Rechner kaufen
6. etwas essen und trinken

Have students do the same activity using the negative (*Ich muss meine Hausaufgaben nicht machen.*)

10. *Warum mögen sie das nicht?* **You've heard that several people you know don't like certain things. You are asking them why not.**

◆ Dieter / Krimi
◆ Warum mag Dieter den Krimi nicht?

1. Ursula und Sabine / Musik
2. Frau Lehmann / Buch
3. Rainer / Fach
4. Elisabeth / Fernsehprogramm
5. ihr / Kaufhaus
6. du / Sport

1. Warum mögen Ursula und Sabine die Musik nicht?
2. Warum mag Frau Lehmann das Buch nicht?
3. Warum mag Rainer das Fach nicht?
4. Warum mag Elisabeth das Fernsehprogramm nicht?
5. Warum mögt ihr das Kaufhaus nicht?
6. Warum magst du Sport nicht?

11. **Kombiniere...**

Meine Freundin
Herr Tobler
Ihr
Björn und Christian
Du

wollt
müssen
möchte
musst
will

morgen
heute Abend
am Sonntag

in die Stadt fahren
deine Arbeit machen
Klavier spielen
einen Hamburger essen

Wie schmeckt's?

Ergänzung

Und was isst Richard gern zum Mittagessen?

Und Selina?

Und du?

Eine Pizza.

Wiener Schnitzel mit Pommes frites oder Bratwurst mit Kartoffeln und Salat.

Sauerbraten mit Gemüse und Spätzle.

Was isst du zum Frühstück?

Ich esse Brötchen, eine Scheibe Brot, Butter und Marmelade.

Was möchtest du zum Abendessen?

Schmeckt dir der Fisch?

Ein Wurstbrot und ein Käsebrot.

Kalte Platte. (Wurst und Käse)

Nein, nicht besonders.

12. *Was essen wir diese Woche?* **Your mother or father is planning the menu for the week and would like your advice.**

◆ Sonntag / Sauerbraten
◆ Am Sonntag möchte ich Sauerbraten.

1. Montag / eine Pizza
2. Dienstag / Fisch mit Kartoffeln
3. Mittwoch / einen Hamburger mit Pommes frites
4. Donnerstag / Kalte Platte
5. Freitag / Bratwurst mit Brötchen
6. Sonnabend / Wiener Schnitzel mit Gemüse

Paired Activity: Have students prepare a we lunch or dinner menu. While one student list to the other talk about various meals, he or s will jot down what the partner will eat. Ask students to reverse ro Before starting this ac you may want to list a additional words need

13. *Ich esse gern...* Tell one of your classmates what you usually eat for breakfast, lunch and dinner. Reverse roles by asking your classmate what he or she likes to eat. *Was isst du gern zum Frühstück, Mittagessen und Abendessen?*

Praktische Situation

Was gibt es zum Frühstück, Mittagessen und Abendessen? To find out what your partner likes to eat and drink for each meal, begin by making three columns on a piece of paper with the headings *Frühstück*, *Mittagessen* and *Abendessen*. In each column write your favorite foods and beverages. Then with your partner, take turns asking and answering questions about what you like to eat and drink for each meal.

Example:

Student 1: *Was möchtest du zum Frühstück?*

Student 2: *Zum Frühstück möchte ich eine Scheibe Brot, Butter und Marmelade.*

Student 2: *Was möchtest du trinken?*

Student 1: *Zum Frühstück möchte ich ein Glas Milch trinken.*

Write your partner's responses next to yours. After you have finished asking and answering questions, each of you writes a summary stating what foods and beverages you both like (if any) for each meal.

Sprache

Negation

The word *kein* means "no" or "not any" and negates nouns.

◆ *Ich habe kein Buch.* I have no book.

◆ *Tanja hat keine Zeit.* Tanja doesn't have time. (Tanja has no time.)

The endings of *kein* are identical to those of *ein*-words.

◆ *Peter kauft eine Gitarre.* Peter is buying a guitar.

◆ *Angelika kauft keine Gitarre.* Angelika doesn't buy a guitar. (Angelika buys no guitar.)

◆ *Hast du einen Bleistift?* Do you have a pencil?

◆ *Nein, ich habe keinen Bleistift.* No, I don't have a pencil. (No, I have no pencil.)

Wie schmeckt's?

The word *nicht* means "not" and negates verbs, adjectives and adverbs.

◆ *David schreibt nicht.* David is not writing.

◆ *Carola will die Arbeit nicht machen.* Carola doesn't want to do the work.

Although there is no specific rule as to the position of *nicht* within a sentence—its position depends upon what is being negated in the sentence—*nicht* always appears after the subject and verb and usually after the object.

◆ *Wir essen nicht.* (We aren't eating.)

◆ *Wir essen die Pizza nicht.* (We aren't eating the pizza.)

◆ *Wir essen die Pizza jetzt nicht.* (We aren't eating the pizza now.)

WB Activities 9-10

WA Activity 5

S Activity 3

AC/CD

Paired Activity: Divide the class into pairs. Have students write down as many objects as they can think of. Have one student ask the question, *Was bringst du zur Party mit?* while he or she points to the word.

Ich bringe...
1. keine CD mit.
2. kein Buch mit.
3. keine Gitarre mit.
4. keinen Computer mit.
5. keine Schultasche mit.
6. keinen Fußball mit.

14. *Was bringst du nicht mit?* **Your friends want to know what you are bringing to a party this weekend. Tell them that you aren't bringing the following things.**

◆ Ich bringe keine Kassette mit.

1.

2.

3.

4.

5.

6.

15. There is a mix-up in the school cafeteria. Many students are missing part of their lunch. Tell what each person doesn't have.

◆ Christa
◆ Christa hat kein Wurstbrot.

Beispiel:

1. Susanne	5. Tobias
2. Ralf	6. Karsten
3. Bettina	7. Tanja
4. Melanie	8. Sven

AC/CD

1. Susanne hat kein Käsebrot.
2. Ralf hat keine Pizza.
3. Bettina hat kein Schokoeis.
4. Melanie hat keinen Hamburger.
5. Tobias hat keine Bratwurst.
6. Karsten hat keine Milch.
7. Tanja hat kein Brötchen.
8. Sven hat keinen Salat.

16. Beantworte diese Fragen mit „nein"!

◆ Macht Tina die Arbeit?
◆ Nein, sie macht keine Arbeit.

1. Haben Renate und Ingrid Zeit?
2. Bekommt Hans in Englisch eine Zwei?
3. Besucht Gabriele einen Onkel?
4. Schickt Herr Meier einen Brief?
5. Schreibst du heute eine Karte?
6. Kauft ihr ein Buch?
7. Lernst du jetzt Englisch?

As an alternate activity, have students come up with different answers to the question *Macht Tina die Arbeit? Nein, sie spielt Gitarre.*

AC/CD

1. Nein, sie haben keine Zeit.
2. Nein, er bekommt in Englisch keine Zwei.
3. Nein, sie besucht keinen Onkel.
4. Nein, er schickt keinen Brief.
5. Nein, ich schreibe heute keine Karte.
6. Nein, wir kaufen kein Buch.
7. Nein, ich lerne jetzt kein Englisch.

Wie schmeckt's?

AC/CD

1. Nein, die Musik ist nicht toll.
2. Nein, das Fernsehprogramm beginnt nicht um halb sieben.
3. Nein, die Pommes frites schmecken nicht gut.
4. Nein, Günter geht nicht in die Stadt.
5. Nein, es ist nicht sehr kalt.
6. Nein, Heiko kennt den Lehrer nicht gut.
7. Nein, der Zug kommt nicht pünktlich.
8. Nein, die Karte kostet nicht zwölf Mark.

AC/CD

Nein, ich...
1. lerne nicht viel.
2. bin nicht um eins zu Hause.
3. habe keinen Bruder.
4. möchte kein Wurstbrot.
5. will nicht zum Kaufhaus gehen.
6. trinke keine Cola.
7. komme nicht um drei nach Hause.
8. esse keine Pizza.

17. **You don't seem to be in a good mood today and you contradict everything your friend tells you.**

◆ Herr Hoffmann sagt das.
◆ Nein, Herr Hoffmann sagt das nicht.

1. Die Musik ist toll.
2. Das Fernsehprogramm beginnt um halb sieben.
3. Die Pommes frites schmecken gut.
4. Günter geht in die Stadt.
5. Es ist sehr kalt.
6. Heiko kennt den Lehrer gut.
7. Der Zug kommt pünktlich.
8. Die Karte kostet zwölf Mark.

18. **Your classmates ask you some questions, all of which you answer negatively.**

◆ Hast du heute Zeit?
◆ Nein, ich habe heute keine Zeit.

◆ Kommst du um vier?
◆ Nein, ich komme nicht um vier.

1. Lernst du viel?
2. Bist du um eins zu Hause?
3. Hast du einen Bruder?
4. Möchtest du ein Wurstbrot?
5. Willst du zum Kaufhaus gehen?
6. Trinkst du eine Cola?
7. Kommst du um drei nach Hause?
8. Isst du eine Pizza?

Hmm, das Eis schmeckt aber gut.

Lesestück

Gehen wir in die Pizzeria!

Torsten hat heute Nachmittag viel Zeit. Er weiß nicht°, was er machen will. Sein Freund Ali hat eine gute Idee. Er will in die Pizzeria gehen. Da sind immer viele Schulfreunde. Um halb sechs kommt Torsten zu Ali rüber.

AC/CD

Role-Playing Activity: Have students write about their own experience going to a pizza place or other restaurant. One or two students could play the part of the customer(s), the other the food server. Select individual groups for class presentations.

Torsten: Grüß dich, Ali! Gehen wir doch gleich!°

Ali: Einen Moment. Ich brauche noch etwas Geld°. Hast du zehn Mark? Ich bekomme mein Taschengeld° erst morgen.

Torsten: Klar, bis morgen gebe ich dir° gern das Geld.

Ali: Ich muss um sieben schon zu Hause sein.

Grüß dich, Ali!

Torsten: Kein Problem. Ich will auch so gegen sieben nach Hause. Im Fernsehen gibt's heute einen tollen Krimi. Den muss ich sehen.

Ali: Mein Onkel und meine Tante kommen zu Besuch. Sie bleiben nicht lange. Mutti sagt, ich muss wenigstens° „Guten Tag" sagen.

Torsten: Komm! Gehen wir!

Im Fernsehen gibt's heute einen tollen Krimi.

Wie schmeckt's?

Vor der Pizzeria ist eine Speisekarte°. Torsten und Ali lesen sie nicht. Sie wissen, was sie essen möchten. Sie gehen in die Pizzeria und finden auch gleich einen Tisch.

Lesen Torsten und Ali die Speisekarte?

Kellner: Bitte schön?°

Torsten: Ich möchte gern eine Limo° und Tortellini mit Käse und Tomaten.

Ali: Bringen Sie mir bitte eine Pizza mit Salami, Käse und Tomaten. Ich möchte ein Spezi°.

Kellner: Danke. Möchtet ihr auch ein Pizza-Brot?

Ali: Ja, bitte.

Kellner: Die Limo und das Spezi bringe ich gleich.

(*später*)

Torsten: Na, wie schmeckt's?

Ali: Gut, wie immer°.

Torsten: Du, Ali, kennst du noch Veronika Kramer?

Ali: Die wohnt doch jetzt in Lübeck. Aber ich sehe sie da mit Roland an dem Tisch.

Torsten: Sie wohnt mit ihrer Mutter in Lübeck; ihr Vater wohnt noch hier in der Stadt. Sie besucht ihren Vater oft und dann auch Roland. Er ist jetzt ihr Freund.

Ali: Du weißt aber viel.

Torsten: Nicht nur ich, alle in der Schule wissen das, nur du nicht.

Bitte schön?

Ali und Torsten essen und gehen dann nach Hause. Torsten will seinen Krimi im Fernsehen sehen, und Ali will zu Hause sein, wenn seine Tante und sein Onkel zu Besuch kommen.

 WB Activity 11

 **LA** Activity 3

WA Activities 6-7

er weiß nicht he doesn't know; *Gehen wir doch gleich!* Let's go right away!; *das Geld* money; *das Taschengeld* allowance; *ich gebe dir* I'll give you; *wenigstens* at least; *die Speisekarte* menu; *Bitte schön?* May I help you?; *die Limo* lemonade, soft drink; *das Spezi* cola and lemon soda; *wie immer* as always

Aber ich sehe sie da mit Roland an dem Tisch.

19. Weißt du, wer das ist?

1. _____ trinkt eine Limo.
2. _____ wohnt mit ihrer Mutter in Lübeck.
3. _____ will wissen, was Ali und Torsten essen und trinken möchten.
4. _____ kommt um halb sechs zu Ali rüber.
5. _____ kommen zu Besuch.
6. _____ will später einen Krimi im Fernsehen sehen.
7. _____ bringt Tortellini, Pizza-Brot und eine Pizza.
8. _____ wohnt noch in der Stadt.
9. _____ wollen um sieben Uhr zu Hause sein.
10. _____ möchte eine Pizza mit Salami, Käse und Tomaten.
11. _____ gibt seinem Freund zehn Mark.
12. _____ gehen in eine Pizzeria.
13. _____ ist Veronikas Freund.
14. _____ trinkt ein Spezi.

20. Beantworte diese Fragen!

1. Was bekommt Ali morgen von seinen Eltern?
2. Wo wohnen Veronika Kramers Vater und Mutter?
3. Wo ist eine Speisekarte?
4. Was braucht Ali?
5. Warum muss Ali um sieben nach Hause?
6. Wo wohnt Veronika?
7. Was finden Ali und Torsten in der Pizzeria gleich?
8. Was trinkt Ali?
9. Wie viel Geld bekommt Ali von Torsten?
10. Was ist auf der Pizza?

AC/CD

Torstens Tortellini schmeckt sehr gut.

Wie schmeckt's?

Sprache

wissen

The verb *wissen* (to know) has irregular forms when it is used with *ich*, *du* and *er, sie, es*. The plural forms are regular.

ich	weiß		wir	wissen
du	weißt		ihr	wisst
er			sie	wissen
sie	weiß		Sie	wissen
es				

Note that both words, *kennen* and *wissen*, mean "to know." However, *kennen* means "to know a person, a place or a thing," whereas *wissen* means "to know something" (as a fact).

◆ *Kennst du Sabine?* Do you know Sabine?

◆ *Weißt du, wer Sabine ist?* Do you know who Sabine is?

◆ *Wir kennen Hamburg.* We know Hamburg.

◆ *Wir wissen, wo Hamburg ist.* We know where Hamburg is.

◆ *Kennen Sie dieses Buch?* Do you know this book?

◆ *Wissen Sie, wo dieses Buch ist?* Do you know where this book is?

Wer's weiß ißt ⊛Haller EIS

WB Activity 12

WA Activity 8

S Activity 2

Kapitel 6

21. **Wer weiß die Antwort?** Your teacher is asking several questions to which your classmates have the answers.

◆ Gloria
◆ Gloria weiß die Antwort.

Wer weiß die Antwort?

1. Robert und Doris
2. Ich
3. Uwe
4. Alex und David
5. Sonja und Peter
6. Heidi

1. Robert und Doris wissen die Antwort.
2. Ich weiß die Antwort.
3. Uwe weiß die Antwort.
4. Alex und David wissen die Antwort.
5. Sonja und Peter wissen die Antwort.
6. Heidi weiß die Antwort.

22. **Kennen oder wissen?** Provide the correct form of the appropriate verb.

1. ____ Sie, um wie viel Uhr Ali kommt?
2. Ich ____ Tina. Sie ist ein Genie.
3. ____ du Frau Kowalski?
4. ____ ihr, was Günter und Ralf heute Nachmittag machen?
5. ____ Christine die Antwort?
6. Wir ____, wo Herr Böhme wohnt.
7. ____ ihr Frau Thielmanns Tochter?
8. Beate ____ Susanne gut.

1. Wissen
2. kenne
3. Kennst
4. Wisst
5. Weiß
6. wissen
7. Kennt
8. kennt

This activity is ideal for role-playing. Some of the activities can be done in smaller or larger groups. For additional activities and/or games, see the front section of this teacher's edition.

PA

Übung macht den Meister!

1. *Was gibt's heute?* Imagine that you and one of your classmates own a restaurant. Make up a daily menu that lists various beverages, meals and prices. While making up your menu, ask such questions as *Was gibt's zu essen/trinken? (Was haben wir zu essen/trinken?), Wie viel soll das kosten?*

2. *Ich möchte...* Tell one of your classmates that you would like to go and have some ice cream and ask if he or she would like to come along. Determine when and where you should meet.

3. Make up a list of your favorite ice cream flavors and include the price for each in German marks (DM). Pretend that you are the food server. Your customers (classmates) ask what flavors you have today. You tell the flavors and the cost. Some additional flavors you may wish to know are: *Ananaseis* (pineapple), *Pfirsicheis* (peach), *Nusseis* (nut).

WB Activity 13

Wie schmeckt's?

191

Aktuelles

Eating Out

Almost all German restaurants display their menu (*Speisekarte*) outside, next to the entrance. When entering a German restaurant, men generally precede women. This is clearly a remainder from times when the man was the one to decide whether the locality was fit for the woman to enter. In entering first, he could screen her from curious stares and relieve her of the task of choosing a table.

Hier ist kein Platz mehr frei.

Contrary to American custom, there are no hostesses in typical German restaurants to greet and seat you. Normally, you look for a table yourself. If you can't find an empty table, it's customary to join people you don't know if there is room at their table. When joining others at a table, you should ask *Ist hier noch frei?* The usual response will be *Ja, bitte* or *Bitte sehr*. In above-average restaurants, a food server will approach you and suggest a table, or lead you to the table that has been reserved for you.

Was möchten Sie?

When asking for the menu, just say *Die Speisekarte, bitte*. Never ask for *das Menü* as you would be ordering a complete meal. Many restaurants offer a complete dinner with soup (*die Suppe*) and dessert (*der Nachtisch*) called *das Gedeck* or *das Menü*. The male server (*der Kellner*) is addressed as *Herr Ober*, the female server (*die Kellnerin*) as *Fräulein*. In recent years, the more commonly used address for both the male and the female server is simply *Bedienung*. In small towns and villages, the local restaurant is often a family enterprise, where the proprietor and his wife wait on their guests. In such a place, you would call the proprietor *Herr Wirt* and his wife *Frau Wirtin*.

German table manners are somewhat different from ours. Whenever Germans eat something that requires cutting, they hold the fork in the left hand and the knife in the right, keeping them this

So essen die Deutschen.

way throughout the meal. The knife is also used to push the food onto the fork. If a knife is not needed, the left hand is placed on the table beside the plate, not in the lap.

Most Germans do not cut potatoes with a knife, but use the fork instead. This dates back to the times when blades were not yet made of stainless steel. Fish is not cut with a regular knife either; instead, a special fish knife or a fork is used. Rarely will you see a German drink plain water with the meal; mostly beer, wine, fruit juice or soft drinks are ordered. If you would like to drink regular water, you need to ask for *Leitungswasser* (tap water); otherwise, the server may bring you carbonated water.

beim Mittagessen

How do you ask for the check? *Bedienung, ich möchte zahlen!* or *Die Rechnung, bitte!* or very short, *Zahlen, bitte!* Normally you pay the server at your table; rarely do you pay at the counter or cash register. A 10 to 15 percent service charge *(Bedienung)* and a 15% value-added tax *(Mehrwertsteuer)* are included in the total amount. Since a tip is already part of the bill, an extra tip is not necessary. However, most people do round off the bill to the nearest mark or more, according to the amount to be paid and the service rendered. For instance, if the check amounts to DM 15,10 you may say *Sechzehn Mark, bitte!* to the server, thus indicating that you expect change for only sixteen marks and that the rest can be kept. The small additional tip is given to the food server upon paying and is not left on the table when leaving the restaurant.

Although paying by check or credit card is still not as customary in Germany as it is in the United States, particularly in smaller local eating establishments, these methods of payment have become more popular in recent years.

Ich möchte Wiener Schnitzel.

Wie schmeckt's?

Was passt hier?

1. The ____ is an added service charge.
2. The ____ is usually served before the main meal.
3. The menu is called the ____.
4. After eating the main meal, you might order a ____.
5. The female server is called ____.
6. The value-added tax is called the ____.
7. A male server is referred to as ____ when you want to get his attention and pay your bill.
8. When you are ready to pay your bill, you will ask the server for the ____.
9. A ____ is a complete meal.
10. The ____ is the owner of a small restaurant in a town.

a. *Kellnerin*
b. *Speisekarte*
c. *Gedeck*
d. *Herr Ober*
e. *Wirt*
f. *Nachtisch*
g. *Suppe*
h. *Rechnung*
i. *Bedienung*
j. *Mehrwertsteuer*

Erweiterung

23. *Ergänze die Sätze im Dialog!* (Complete the sentences in the dialog.) Be sure that each sentence is meaningful.

 – Hast du ____?
 – Ja, ich ____ etwas essen.
 – Möchtest ____ einen Hamburger?
 – Ja, bitte, mit ____.
 – Willst du auch etwas ____?
 – Nein, danke. Ich habe keinen ____.
 – Da drüben ____ ein Eiscafé.
 – ____ kenne es.
 – Was für ____ schmeckt da besonders gut?
 – Das Schokoeis ____ mir immer.
 – Na gut. ____ wir zum Eiscafé!

WB Activities 14-16

 WA Activities 9-10

 S Activity 5

24. **Was passt hier?** Use the items below to complete each sentence of the conversation.

Bratwurst	eine	viel	Glas	Freundin
ein	etwas	Hunger	für	Stunde

1. Bringen Sie mir ____ gemischtes Eis.
2. Und ____ dich?
3. Ein ____ Apfelsaft.
4. Sonst noch ____?
5. Ja, wir haben ____.
6. Möchtet ihr ____ mit Brötchen?
7. Ja, das ist ____ gute Idee.
8. Bringen Sie für meine ____ eine Pizza.
9. Die Pizza dauert eine halbe ____.
10. Das geht. Wir haben ____ Zeit.

1. ein
2. für
3. Glas
4. etwas
5. Hunger
6. Bratwurst
7. eine
8. Freundin
9. Stunde
10. viel

25. **Gehen wir ins Restaurant!** Describe (in narrative and/or dialog style) the following sequence, using the cues merely as guidelines.

You call your friend and ask him or her to go to a restaurant near your home. After both of you agree, you discuss the time and place you should meet. As soon as you meet your friend, you realize that you don't have enough money for the restaurant. Your friend tells you that he or she can lend you some money until tomorrow. Both of you look at the menu posted outside and discuss what you would like to order. Once you have decided, you and your friend go inside.

Torsten und Ali lesen die Speisekarte vor dem Restaurant.

Wie schmeckt's?

26. *Was passt hier?* Find the reponses that answer the questions.

1g, 2h, 3c, 4e, 5i, 6a, 7f, 8j, 9b, 10d

1. Wie schmeckt's?
2. Was möchten Sie essen?
3. Etwas zu trinken?
4. Wann musst du zu Hause sein?
5. Weißt du, wo Monika wohnt?
6. Kennst du Achim?
7. Willst du später rüberkommen?
8. Was wollen wir heute Nachmittag machen?
9. Was gibt's heute Abend im Fernsehen?
10. Wie viel Taschengeld bekommst du denn?

a. Nein, aber seine Schwester.
b. Einen tollen Krimi.
c. Ein Glas Milch, bitte.
d. Zwanzig Mark die Woche.
e. So gegen halb neun.
f. Nein, ich habe heute keine Zeit.
g. Gut, danke.
h. Wiener Schnitzel mit Kartoffeln, bitte.
i. In Bremen.
j. Gehen wir doch ins Eiscafé.

Was gibt's heute in diesem Café?

27. *Bitte schön?* Pretend that you are in a German restaurant. When the food server comes, you discuss the menu, meals and beverages.

Samples answers:
Ich möchte etwas trinken.
Eine Limo, bitte.
Was haben Sie?
Ist die Bratwurst gut?
Ich möchte lieber einen Hamburger.
Ja, bitte.

Kellner: Bitte schön?

   Du: ____

Kellner: Möchtest du Cola oder Limo?

   Du: ____

Kellner: Gut, das bringe ich gleich. Etwas zu essen?

   Du: ____

Kellner: Hier ist die Speisekarte.

   Du: ____

Kellner: Oh ja. Die Bratwurst schmeckt sehr gut.

   Du: ____

Kellner: Möchtest du den Hamburger mit Pommes frites?

   Du: ____

Kapitel 6

Rückblick

1. *Was fehlt hier?* **Complete the dialog using the proper forms of the verbs listed.**

bekommen brauchen wollen sein machen
müssen haben gehen kommen geben

– ＿＿＿ du heute Nachmittag rüberkommen?
– Ja, gut. Ich ＿＿＿ viel Zeit. Was ＿＿＿ wir dann?
– Anne und ich ＿＿＿ zuerst ins Eiscafé.
– Ich ＿＿＿ gern mit. Ich ＿＿＿ aber etwas Geld.
– Warum? ＿＿＿ du kein Geld von deinen Eltern?
– Nur zwanzig Mark. Ich ＿＿＿ aber noch ein Buch kaufen.
– Na gut. Ich ＿＿＿ dir das Geld. Komm schon um drei. Im Eiscafé ＿＿＿ dann immer viele Schulfreunde.

2. **Wer? Was? Wo? Wohin? Wie viel? Wie viele?**

1. ＿＿＿ weißt du? Wer morgen ins Kino gehen möchte.
2. ＿＿＿ spielt die Rockgruppe? In München.
3. ＿＿＿ Schwestern hast du? Nur die eine.
4. ＿＿＿ ist das? Sie heißt Erika.
5. ＿＿＿ fahren wir alle? Nach Deutschland.
6. ＿＿＿ Uhr ist es jetzt? Viertel vor acht.
7. ＿＿＿ kommt morgen zu Besuch? Meine Tante aus Dortmund.
8. ＿＿＿ ist Jürgen? Zu Hause.
9. ＿＿＿ machst du am Sonntag? Wir besuchen meinen Opa in Halle.
10. ＿＿＿ Zeit hast du heute? Ein paar Stunden.

If students have problems completing any of these activities, you may want to go back to the chapter in which the structural item or topic was covered.

Willst
habe, machen
gehen
komme, brauche
Bekommst
muss
gebe, sind

1. Was
2. Wo
3. Wie viele
4. Wer
5. Wohin
6. Wie viel
7. Wer
8. Wo
9. Was
10. Wie viel

das Zentrum der Stadt Halle

1. Hast
2. sind
3. weiß
4. Kennt
5. wissen
6. bin
7. Kennen
8. hat

1. schlecht
2. leicht
3. viel
4. früh
5. kalt
6. kein
7. plus
8. alt
9. nach
10. da (dort)

ist, möchte, hat, muss,
geht, dauert, heißen,
kennt, essen, schmeckt,
kommen, bringt

3. *Kennen, wissen, sein oder haben?* **Complete each sentence by providing the correct form of one of these verbs.**

   1. ____ du einen Bruder? Ja, Jürgen ist mein Bruder.

   2. Die Bücher ____ nicht sehr preiswert.

   3. Ich ____ nicht, wo meine Tante wohnt.

   4. ____ ihr Frau Kaufmann, die Deutschlehrerin? Nein, wir wissen nicht, wer das ist.

   5. Sabine und Udo ____, wo die Antwort im Buch ist.

   6. Ich ____ am Sonnabend zu Hause.

   7. ____ Sie die Stadt Hamburg?

   8. Maria ____ Hunger.

4. *Was ist das Gegenteil von diesen Wörtern?* **(What are the opposites of these words?)**

1. gut		6. ein
2. schwer		7. minus
3. etwas		8. neu
4. spät		9. vor
5. heiß		10. hier

5. *Christine hat viel Zeit.* **Complete the following paragraph by providing the proper verb forms from the list below.**

schmecken	dauern	bringen	sein
müssen	kennen	gehen	möchten
kommen	essen	heißen	haben

Christine ____ heute Nachmittag zu Hause. Es ist langweilig. Sie ____ mit ihrer Freundin Karin zur Pizzeria in die Stadt fahren. Karin ____ aber heute keine Zeit. Sie ____ ihre Hausaufgaben machen. Christine ____ zum Eiscafé Rialto, gleich um die Ecke. Sind Schulfreunde da? Es ____ nicht lange, bis zwei Schulfreundinnen kommen. Christines Schulfreundinnen ____ Carmen und Julia. Sie ____ Carmen und Julia schon viele Jahre. Alle drei ____ Eis. Das Erdbeereis ____ besonders gut. Später ____ Carmen und Julia zu Christine rüber. Julia ____ ein paar CDs mit. Sie haben alle viel Spaß.

6. **Was brauchen wir?** You and your classmates are planning a party. Indicate what you need or don't need.

◆ kein / Kalte Platte
◆ Wir brauchen keine Kalte Platte.

◆ drei / Bleistift
◆ Wir brauchen drei Bleistifte.

1. ein paar / Tasse
2. viele / Glas
3. zwanzig / Kuli
4. kein / Tisch
5. kein / Eistee
6. zwölf / Brötchen
7. drei / Tomate
8. ein / Käse

Was brauchen wir zum Picknick?

Wir brauchen...
1. ein paar Tassen.
2. viele Gläser.
3. zwanzig Kulis.
4. keinen Tisch.
5. keinen Eistee.
6. zwölf Brötchen.
7. drei Tomaten.
8. einen Käse.

7. **Nein, das stimmt nicht.** You don't agree with what is being said.

◆ Tobias hat eine Freundin.
◆ Tobias hat keine Freundin.

◆ Wir schreiben das.
◆ Wir schreiben das nicht.

1. Wir trinken gern Cola.
2. Das Wiener Schnitzel schmeckt gut.
3. Der Kellner hat eine Mark.
4. Tina möchte mit Frau Tucholski sprechen.
5. Wir haben Zeit.
6. Peter geht oft ins Eiscafé.
7. Christa kommt morgen zu Besuch.
8. Herr Werner kauft einen Computer.

1. Wir trinken nicht gern Cola.
2. Das Wiener Schnitzel schmeckt nicht gut.
3. Der Kellner hat keine Mark.
4. Tina möchte nicht mit Frau Tucholski sprechen.
5. Wir haben keine Zeit.
6. Peter geht nicht oft ins Eiscafé.
7. Christa kommt morgen nicht zu Besuch.
8. Herr Werner kauft keinen Computer.

Das Frühstück schmeckt gut.

Wie schmeckt's?

WB Activities 16-17

 WA Activity 11

 S Activity 6

OP

VP

TP

CD-ROM

Answers:
a. Bitte schön? (Bitte sehr?, Ja, bitte?)
b. Hast du (Haben Sie) Hunger?
c. Möchtest du (Möchten Sie) eine Bratwurst mit Pommes frites?
d. Wie schmeckt's?
e. Möchtest du (Möchten Sie) eine Cola?
f. Die Pizza kostet 18 Mark.

Was weißt du?

1. *Was isst und trinkst du zum Frühstück, Mittagessen und Abendessen?* Name at least one item that you eat and drink at breakfast, lunch and dinner.

2. *Was möchtest du oder musst du machen?* Indicate three activities that you would **like to do** and three activities that you **have to do** during the week. Start the sentences with either *Ich möchte...* or with *Ich muß...*

3. Respond to each of these questions:

   a. *Was trinkst du gern?*

   b. *Was für Eis möchtest du essen?*

   c. *Was willst du am Sonnabend oder am Sonntag machen?*

   d. *Gehst du gern in eine Pizzeria? Warum? Warum nicht?*

   e. *Was für Pizza isst du gern?*

4. Describe some differences you might experience when going to a German restaurant versus an American restaurant (types of restaurants, service, eating, foods, etc.). *Auf Englisch, bitte!*

5. Pretend that you are a food server in a German restaurant. How would you say the following:

   a. May I help you?

   b. Are you hungry?

   c. Would you like a bratwurst with french fries?

   d. How do you like it?

   e. Would you like a cola?

   f. The pizza costs 18 marks.

6. Complete each of the following sentences:

   a. *Heute Nachmittag möchte ich...*

   b. *Ich will...*

   c. *Weißt du, wann...*

   d. *Morgen muß ich...*

   e. *Ich esse gern...*

   f. *Zum Abendessen trinke ich...*

Vokabeln

das **Abendessen** supper, dinner
der **Apfelsaft** apple juice
besonders special, specially; *nicht besonders* not especially
bitte please; *Ja, bitte?*, *Bitte schön?* May I help you?
die **Bratwurst,-e** bratwurst
bringen to bring; *Bringen Sie mir...* Bring me...
das **Brot,-e** bread
das **Brötchen,-** hard roll
die **Butter** butter
die **Cola,-s** cola
danke thanks
dir (to) you
der **Durst** thirst; *Durst haben* to be thirsty
das **Eis** ice cream
das **Eiscafé,-s** ice cream parlor, café
der **Eistee** ice tea
das **Erdbeereis** strawberry ice cream
erst just, *erst morgen* not until tomorrow
essen to eat
etwas some, a little, something
die **Fanta** brand name of soda (orange-flavored)
der **Fisch,-e** fish
die **Fischsemmel,-n** fish sandwich
das **Frühstück** breakfast
geben to give
gehen to go; *Gehen wir doch gleich!* Let's go right away!
das **Geld** money

gemischt: ein gemischtes Eis assorted ice cream
das **Gemüse** vegetable(s)
das **Glas,-̈er** glass
der **Hamburger,-** hamburger
der **Hunger** hunger; *Hunger haben* to be hungry
der **Kaffee** coffee
der **Kakao** hot chocolate
die **Kalte Platte** cold-cut platter
die **Kartoffel,-n** potato
der **Käse** cheese
das **Käsebrot,-e** cheese sandwich
der **Kellner,-** waiter
die **Kellnerin,-nen** waitress
die **Limo,-s** lemonade, soft drink
die **Marmelade,-n** jam, marmalade
mich me
die **Milch** milk
mir (to) me
mögen to like
müssen to have to, must
nichts nothing
noch still, yet
die **Pizza,-s** pizza
das **Pizza-Brot,-e** pizza bread
die **Pizzeria,-s** pizza restaurant
die **Platte,-n** plate; *Kalte Platte* cold-cut platter
die **Pommes frites** (pl.) french fries
das **Restaurant,-s** restaurant
die **Salami** salami
der **Salat,-e** salad
der **Sauerbraten** sauerbraten (marinated beef)
die **Scheibe,-n** slice; *eine Scheibe Brot* a slice of bread

die **Schlagsahne** whipped cream
schmecken to taste; *Das schmeckt mir nicht.* I don't like it.; *Wie schmeckt's?* How do you like it?
das **Schokoeis** chocolate ice cream
der **Schulfreund,-e** schoolmate
sehen to see; *ein Fernsehprogramm sehen* to watch a TV program; *Seht mal!* Look!
sonst besides, otherwise; *Sonst nocht etwas?* Anything else?
die **Spätzle** spaetzle (kind of homemade pasta)
die **Speisekarte,-n** menu
das **Spezi,-s** cola and lemon soda
das **Taschengeld** allowance
die **Tasse,-n** cup
die **Tomate,-n** tomato
Tortellini tortellini (filled pasta)
trinken to drink
das **Vanilleeis** vanilla ice cream
wenigstens at least
wenn when
wie as, how
das **Wiener Schnitzel** breaded veal cutlet
wissen to know
wollen to want to
die **Wurst,-̈e** sausage
das **Wurstbrot,-e** sausage sandwich
das **Zitroneneis** lemon ice cream

Hier gibt's viel Eis.

Was kauft man hier?

Wie gefällt dir das?

In this chapter you will be able to:

- make suggestions
- ask about prices
- describe and choose clothing items
- write a letter and a card
- talk about a department store

Der weiße Pulli ist zu eintönig.

Kaufen Christine und Anne etwas?

1. Das T-Shirt
2. Der rote Pulli
3. Der weiße Pulli
4. Das T-Shirt
5. Der rote Pulli

Der Pulli steht Christine gut

Christine: Wie gefällt dir der Pulli hier?

Anne: Weiß? Der ist zu eintönig. Du brauchst etwas Farbe. Das T-Shirt ist sehr bunt.

Christine: Ja, das steht dir gut. Es hat viele Farben — blau, beige, rosa und rot.

Anne: Es gefällt mir auch. Ich kaufe es später. Ja, und du?

Christine: Ich glaube, du hast recht. Der rote Pulli steht mir besser. Er kostet auch nur 60 Mark.

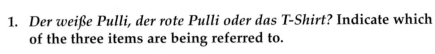
Das T-Shirt ist sehr bunt.

1. **Der weiße Pulli, der rote Pulli oder das T-Shirt? Indicate which of the three items are being referred to.**

   1. _____ hat vier Farben.
   2. _____ kostet sechzig Mark.
   3. _____ ist für Anne zu eintönig.
   4. _____ ist bunt.
   5. _____ steht Christine besser.

2. Beantworte diese Fragen!

1. Was kauft Anne später?
2. Was braucht Christine?
3. Welche Farben hat das T-Shirt?
4. Wie viel kostet der rote Pulli?
5. Wie steht Anne das T-Shirt?

AC/CD

1. Das T-Shirt.
2. Etwas Farbe.
3. Blau, beige, rosa und rot.
4. Er kostet 60 Mark.
5. Es steht Anne gut.

Alex will Jeans kaufen

Boris: Hallo, Alex! Was machst du denn hier?

Alex: Ich will Jeans kaufen. Sie sind heute sehr preiswert.

Boris: Hm, die Auswahl hier ist gut. Soll ich vielleicht eine Jacke kaufen?

Alex: Warum nicht? Deine Jacke ist schon so alt. Du kannst bestimmt eine finden.

Hallo, Alex!

Boris: Diese Jeans passen dir gut. Wie findest du diese Jacke für mich?

Alex: Dunkelblau? Nicht schlecht. Auch nicht teuer.

Boris: Gut, dann haben wir beide Glück!

Wie passen Alex die Jeans?

WB Activity 2   **WA** Activity 1

Was soll Boris kaufen?

3. *Richtig oder falsch?* Determine whether the following statements are correct or incorrect. If they are incorrect, provide a correct statement in German.

1. Die Jeans passen Alex gut.
2. Die Auswahl ist schlecht.
3. Alex will eine Jacke kaufen.
4. Die Jeans sind nicht teuer.
5. Die Jacke ist rot.
6. Die Jacke von Boris ist neu.

AC/CD

1. richtig
2. falsch / Die Auswahl ist gut.
3. falsch / Alex will Jeans kaufen. (Boris will eine Jacke kaufen.)
4. richtig
5. falsch / Die Jacke ist dunkelblau.
6. falsch / Die Jacke von Boris ist alt.

Wie gefällt dir das?

4. Was passt hier?

sind	bekommst	weiß	gefällt
hast	kostet	sehen	finde

- Die Auswahl _____ mir gut.
- Ja, und alle T-Shirts _____ sehr bunt.
- Wie viel _____ denn ein T-Shirt?
- Ich _____ nicht.
- Oh, hier kann ich es _____, dreißig Mark.
- Das _____ ich teuer.
- Da _____ du nicht recht.
- Na ja, du _____ ja auch immer Geld von deinem Vater.

AC/CD

Sprichwort

Kleider machen Leute.

(Clothes make the person.)

Für dich

A pullover, called *Pullover*, is often referred to as *Pulli* for short. When buying clothing items in Germany, you should be aware that sizes are different. For example, a U.S. size 8 dress would be size 36 in Germany, and a U.S. size 8 pair of shoes is size 39 in Germany.

Running sales throughout the year, which is quite common in this country, is not done in Germany. Generally, there are two sales during the year, each lasting two weeks. One is called *Sommerschlussverkauf* (end-of-summer sale) and the other *Winterschlussverkauf* (end-of-winter sale). Each sale starts officially on the last Monday in July and the last Monday in January, respectively. Many shops have started to run an *Ausverkauf* (seasonal sale, bargain sale) much earlier than on the fixed dates, offering certain items at reduced prices as *Sonderangebote* (special offers).

Sind die Schuhe teuer?

Wie viel kostet der Pullover?

During the warmer season, major department stores as well as smaller shops display some of their reduced merchandise outside to entice shoppers to come inside.

Rollenspiel

You and one of your classmates play the roles of the shopper and the salesperson in a department store (*Kaufhaus*). In your conversation you should cover such details as: what clothing item you are looking for (including colors), how much you want to spend, whether or not you consider the item expensive, asking the salesperson's opinion and expressing what you like and dislike about the item. Have your classmate act as a salesperson and assist you in your shopping effort. Then, reverse roles.

 Activity 44

5. **Etwas Persönliches.**

   Write a paragraph in which you discuss what you are planning to do this weekend, including purchase of a certain clothing item that you need due to the changing seasons. Use your creativity as much as possible.

Wie gefällt dir das?

Aktuelles

The Ins and Outs of Shopping

When shopping in Germany, you should become familiar with the German monetary system. As you have already learned, the German monetary unit is called the *Mark*. Often, you will see a *DM (Deutsche Mark)* in front of the price. The smallest monetary denomination is the *Pfennig*. In recent years, there has been a trend to discontinue the one- and two-pfennig coins. Sales items are usually priced to avoid the use of pfennigs. There are seven different mark bills: 5, 10, 20, 50, 100, 200, 500 and 1,000. There are eight different coins: 1 pfennig, 2 pfennigs, 5 pfennigs, 10 pfennigs, 50 pfennigs, 1 mark, 2 marks and 5 marks.

Until late 1996, all stores were required to close Monday through Friday at 6:00 P.M. except on Thursdays when stores could stay open until 8:30 P.M. On Saturdays, stores had to close at 2:00 P.M. except on the first Saturday of the month when stores could close by 6:00 P.M.

Wie viel Geld ist das?

German shops are not open as many hours as American stores. Although stores are open Monday through Friday from about 8:00 or 9:00 A.M. until 8:00 P.M., they close on Saturday at 4:00 P.M. Banks, post offices and small stores usually close for a two-hour break at noon. Banks are not open on Saturdays and Sundays and close at different times between 4:00 P.M. and 6:00 P.M. during the week.

Emine möchte das Kleid anprobieren.

When entering a small shop, a customer (*Kunde* or *Kundin*) will say *Guten Tag* (northern Germany) or *Grüß Gott* (southern Germany). When leaving, you often hear *Auf Wiedersehen* (northern Germany) or *Auf Wiederschauen* (southern Germany). In smaller shops you are usually approached by a salesperson (*Verkäufer* or *Verkäuferin*). If you're not ready to buy something, you can say *Ich möchte mich nur umsehen* (I just want to look around). You can never go wrong by using *bitte* and *danke*.

You should always try on (*anprobieren*) footwear and clothing as not only the sizes vary, but also the cuts. Also there are many variations among products from

Hier gibt's Sonderangebo

various countries—France, Italy, Greece, Spain, eastern Europe or the Far East. When trying on a clothing item, look for the dressing room *(Umkleidekabine)*. Exchanging items bought is called *Umtausch*. You'll always need the receipt to exchange or return merchandise.

When looking for *Sonderangebote* (special offers), be aware of the large signs that show the word *ab* before the price: *Hemden ab 15,-* (shirts 15 marks and up), as there will only be a few shirts available at that price.

In comparison to Americans, Germans usually pay for everything in cash, although credit cards are used more and more today. When you see a price tag in a German store you can be sure that it shows the total price.

Was kauft man in dieser Boutique?

Was passt hier? You will not need all the phrases listed.

1. When entering a shop in Augsburg, customers would say ____.
2. If you want to try on some slacks, you'll look for the ____.
3. One hundredth of a mark is a ____.
4. Stores stay open until 4:00 P.M. on ____.
5. The currency of Germany is the ____.
6. A shopper exchanging items would use the word ____.
7. Ties are usually worn with ____.
8. The people in Hamburg would say ____ when leaving a store.
9. When shopping for reduced merchandise, you would not want to ignore items marked ____.
10. Mr. Schulz is a frequent ____ at the local supermarket where he buys his groceries.

1k, 2g, 3o, 4b, 5n, 6c, 7a, 8i, 9f, 10l

a. *Hemden*
b. *Sonnabend*
c. *Umtausch*
d. *Verkäuferin*
e. *Verkäufer*
f. *Sonderangebot*
g. *Umkleidekabine*
h. *Guten Tag*
i. *Auf Wiedersehen*
j. *Kundin*
k. *Grüß Gott*
l. *Kunde*
m. *Auf Wiederschauen*
n. *Mark*
o. *Pfennig*

WB Activity 3

Wie gefällt dir das?

Die Farben

WB Activities 4-5

WA Activity 2

OT Activities 45-46

S Activity 1

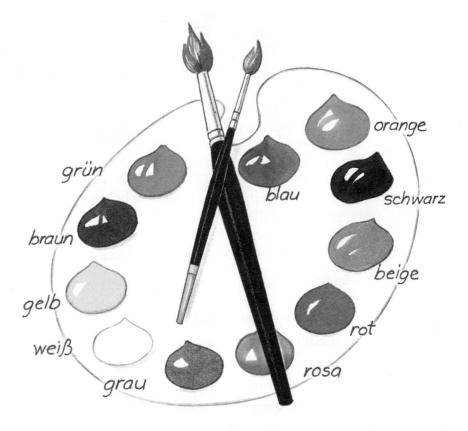

grün

orange

blau

schwarz

braun

beige

gelb

rot

weiß

grau

rosa

hell

dunkel

bunt

◆ Welche Farbe hat der Pulli? Er ist rot.
◆ Und das T-Shirt? Es ist bunt.

6. Welche Farbe hat...? Describe the various items shown.

- Jeans
- Die Jeans sind blau.

1. Der Pulli ist braun.
2. Die Tasse ist weiß.
3. Das Haus ist beige.
4. Die Kassette ist rot.
5. Die Jacke ist grau.
6. Der Stuhl ist schwarz.

1.

2.

3.

4.

5.

6.

7. Beschreibe dein Klassenzimmer! (Describe your classroom.) Look around your classroom and identify at least five objects, including their colors.

- Da drüben ist ein Tisch. Er ist braun.
- Hier ist ein Heft. Es ist blau.

Hier ist ein Lineal. Es ist weiß.

Die Landkarte ist bunt.

Sag's mal!

Wie gefällt dir dieses T-Shirt?
Es ist...

nett
mein Stil*
elegant
nicht schlecht
toll
schrecklich*
schön
zu klein*
zu kurz*
cool
modisch*
eintönig
scharf *
schick
zu bunt
zu grell*
nicht mein Geschmack*
nicht so gut
kitschig*
hässlich*

Sprache

The Modal Auxiliaries: *dürfen, können, sollen*

You have already learned the forms of these modal auxiliaries: *mögen* (*möchten*), *müssen* and *wollen*. The three new modal auxiliaries (*dürfen, können, sollen*) follow the same word order as the others. Notice that the forms of *dürfen* and *können* have a stem vowel change when using *ich, du, er, sie, es*, whereas the forms of *sollen* follow a regular pattern.

◆ *Darfst du in die Stadt gehen?* Are you allowed to go downtown?

◆ *Wir können die Arbeit machen.* We can do the work.

◆ *Meine Schwester soll den Brief schreiben.* My sister is supposed to write the letter.

Zehra und Emine sollen Obst kaufen.

Kapitel 7

	dürfen	können	sollen
	may, to be allowed to	can, to be able to	should, to be supposed to
ich	darf	kann	soll
du	darfst	kannst	sollst
er sie } es	darf	kann	soll
wir	dürfen	können	sollen
ihr	dürft	könnt	sollt
sie	dürfen	können	sollen
Sie	dürfen	können	sollen

 WB Activities 6-7

 WA Activity 3

S Activities 3-4

Similar to the previous chapter, point out again that these new modal auxiliaries *dürfen, können, sollen* have no ending when using them with *ich, er, sie, es* and that *dürfen* and *können* have irregular forms with the *ich, er, sie, es* pronouns.

AC/CD 8. *Was könnt ihr alles?* **Tell what the various people can do.**

◆ Gisela / deutsch sprechen
◆ Gisela kann deutsch sprechen.

1. Paul / Gitarre spielen
2. Christine und Karin / gut Ski laufen
3. meine Freundin / die Hausaufgaben machen
4. Dieters Schulfreunde / den Brief nach Deutschland schicken
5. dein Bruder / schon früh nach Hause kommen
6. wir / erst morgen Onkel Walter besuchen

AC/CD 9. *Das dürfen sie.* **Mr. and Mrs. Hoffmann often limit the leisure-time activities of their three children, Julia, Angelika and Jochen. They are describing to their visiting relatives what their children are allowed to do during the week.**

◆ Julia / nach vier Uhr zu ihren Freundinnen gehen
◆ Julia darf nach vier Uhr zu ihren Freundinnen gehen.

1. Jochen / nach der Schule ins Eiscafé gehen
2. Angelika und Julia / am Sonntag Rockmusik hören
3. Jochen / heute Abend fernsehen
4. Angelika / nur zehn Minuten am Telefon sprechen
5. alle drei / nach der Arbeit Basketball spielen
6. Julia und Angelika / am Sonnabend ihre Freundinnen besuchen

Wohin darf Jochen nach der Schule gehen?

1. Paul kann Gitarre spielen.
2. Christine und Karin können gut Ski laufen.
3. Meine Freundin kann die Hausaufgaben machen.
4. Dieters Schulfreunde können den Brief nach Deutschland schicken.
5. Dein Bruder kann schon früh nach Hause kommen.
6. Wir können erst morgen Onkel Walter besuchen.

1. Jochen darf nach der Schule ins Eiscafé gehen.
2. Angelika und Julia dürfen am Sonntag Rockmusik hören.
3. Jochen darf heute Abend fernsehen.
4. Angelika darf nur zehn Minuten am Telefon sprechen.
5. Alle drei dürfen nach der Arbeit Basketball spielen.
6. Julia und Angelika dürfen am Sonnabend ihre Freundinnen besuchen.

10. *Was sollen sie bis morgen machen?* Your German teacher is telling students what their responsibilities are. Indicate what everyone is supposed to do.

◆ ein Buch lesen (Maria)
◆ Maria soll ein Buch lesen.

1. nach der Klasse die Kassette hören (Tina und Peter)
2. die Hausaufgaben besser machen (ich)
3. deutsch sprechen (wir)
4. sein Deutschbuch in die Schule bringen (Roland)
5. pünktlich in der Klasse sein (Susi und Anke)
6. einen Brief auf Deutsch schreiben (Wolf und Günter)

11. **Etwas Persönliches.**

1. Was sollst du nicht machen?
2. Wohin darfst du am Sonnabend oder Sonntag gehen?
3. Wie kannst du in die Stadt kommen?
4. Was kannst du nicht lesen?
5. Um wie viel Uhr sollst du zu Hause sein?
6. Wann kannst du fahren?

12. **Kombiniere...**

ich
mein Freund
Frau Tobler
wir
Jürgen und Tobias

sollen
können
darf
muss
möchten

einen Brief
die Arbeit
ein Buch
Musik
eine CD

machen
kaufen
hören
lesen
schreiben

---

1. Tina und Peter sollen nach der Klasse die Kassette hören.
2. Ich soll die Hausaufgaben besser machen.
3. Wir sollen deutsch sprechen.
4. Roland soll sein Deutschbuch in die Schule bringen.
5. Susi und Anke sollen pünktlich in der Klasse sein.
6. Wolf und Günter sollen einen Brief auf Deutsch schreiben.

Ergänzung

AC/CD

Was hat Bernhard an?

Er hat einen Pulli an.

das Hemd
die Krawatte
der Anzug
der Pullover (Pulli)
die Jeans
der Handschuh (das Paar Handschuhe)
das T-Shirt
das Sweatshirt
die Hose

Was hat Anne an?

Sie hat einen Rock an.

der Mantel
die Jacke
die Bluse
die Socke
(das Paar Socken)
das Kleid
der Rock
der Strumpf
der Schuh (das Paar Schuhe)
(das Paar Strümpfe)

Wie ist die Hose?
Und wie sind die Jeans?
Sie ist zu kurz.
Sie sind zu lang.

Passt die Bluse?
Ja, sehr gut.

Ist die Jacke zu groß?
Nein, die ist zu eng.

WB	**LA**	**WA**	**OT**	**S**
Activities 8-10	Activities 1-2	Activities 4-6	Activities 47-48	Activity 5

Was machst du?

13. *Was haben sie an?* **Describe what everyone is wearing.**

◆ Gisela
◆ Gisela hat ein T-Shirt an.

1. Herr Holzke hat einen Mantel an.
2. Andreas hat ein Hemd an.
3. Tanja hat eine Bluse an.
4. Heike hat eine Jacke an.
5. Meine Lehrerin hat ein Kleid an.
6. Holger hat einen Anzug an.

1. Herr Holzke

2. Andreas

3. Tanja

4. Heike

5. meine Lehrerin

6. Holger

14. *Wie gefällt dir...?* **With a classmate discuss what others in the class are wearing. Your conversation should include such questions as:** *Wie gefällt dir...? Was hat...an? Welche Farbe hat...?* **Be as creative as possible.**

Welche Farben haben die T-Shirts?

Wie gefällt dir dieses Hemd?

15. *Was passt oder was passt nicht? Und warum?* Describe the clothing items worn by the people in the illustration and indicate what does or doesn't fit.

Praktische Situation

In groups of three, play the roles of a department store manager (*Manager*) with a 10,000 mark budget, a salesperson in the men's department (*Verkäufer/Verkäuferin*) and a salesperson in the women's department. The salespeople are going to inventory their present stock and then submit to the manager a list of clothing items needed in each department. First, the two salespeople present the manager with a list of items they have in stock and the prices for their respective departments. Then they present the manager with a second list of items they would like to add to their inventory, and their prices. The manager and salespeople, working together, must agree on the items to be purchased, making sure that they stay within the budget. The manager should write the final list and submit it to the corporate purchasing department (your teacher). Some useful words and expressions that you have learned are: *Was für/Wie viele Kleidungsstücke brauchen wir (nicht)? Wir haben 5000 Mark. Wir müssen (sollen, können)...kaufen. Wie viel kostet...? Das ist zu teuer/preiswert.*

WB   Activity 11

Wie gefällt dir das?

Sprache

Future Tense

Explain that (in German) the future can be expressed using either the present tense plus an adverb of time or *werden +* infinitive. (*Wir fahren am Montag nach Köln,* or *Wir werden am Montag nach Köln fahren.*

In expressing events that will take place at any time after the present, we may use the future tense.

◆   *Ich werde eine Jacke kaufen.* I will buy a jacket.

Similar to the modal auxiliaries, *werden* acts as a helping (auxiliary) verb and requires a second verb in the infinitive form. This verb is usually found at the end of a clause or sentence.

werden		
ich	werde	I will
du	wirst	you will
er		he will
sie }	wird	she will
es		it will
wir	werden	we will
ihr	werdet	you will
sie	werden	they will
Sie	werden	you will

Should the content of the conversation or description imply future events, the present tense often with an adverb of time *(morgen, heute)* is used.

◆   *Wir spielen morgen Fußball.* We'll play soccer tomorrow.

◆   *Im Herbst fahren wir nach Frankreich.* In the fall we'll be going to France.

WB   Activity 12

WA   Activity 7

S   Activity 2

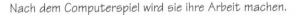
Nach dem Computerspiel wird sie ihre Arbeit machen.

16. *Was wird Sabine nach der Schule machen?* Describe what Sabine will be doing after school.

◆ Gitarre spielen
◆ Sabine wird Gitarre spielen.

1. Rockmusik hören
2. Hausaufgaben machen
3. mit Dieter am Telefon sprechen
4. einen Brief schreiben
5. etwas essen und trinken
6. ein Buch lesen

Wird Boris die Jacke kaufen?

Nicole wird später ihren Freund besuchen.

17. *Wann wird das sein?* Indicate when the various events take place.

◆ Wir gehen in die Pizzeria. (heute Abend)
◆ Wir werden heute Abend in die Pizzeria gehen.

1. Anke besucht ihre Freundin. (am Sonntag)
2. Eine Rockgruppe spielt in der Stadt. (in zwei Tagen)
3. Wir gehen ins Eiscafé. (heute Nachmittag)
4. Jürgen und Tina fahren nach Österreich. (im Winter)
5. Mein Lehrer kommt eine Stunde später. (morgen)
6. Ich kaufe Jeans. (am Dienstag)

Viele Touristen werden im Winter nach Süddeutschland fahren.

Lesestück

Heike und Natascha werden nach Österreich fahren

Heike und Natascha sind gute Freundinnen. In einer Woche werden
beide nach Lienz reisen. Lienz liegt
in Südösterreich. In Lienz wohnt
Katrin, Heikes Cousine. Heike und
Natascha wollen zwei Wochen lang
bei Katrin bleiben. Natascha kommt
heute zu Heike rüber. Heike will
mit Natascha sprechen, was sie
beide nach Österreich mitbringen
sollen. Auf einem Tisch liegt ein
Brief von Katrin. Natascha sagt
Heike, sie soll den Brief lesen.

Heike und Natascha sprechen,
was sie mitbringen sollen.

Heike hat einen
Brief von Katrin.

Liebe° Heike,

jetzt sind es nur noch zehn Tage, bis du mit deiner
Freundin Natascha hier bist. Meine Mutti sagt, der
Zug wird um 18 Uhr 32 im Bahnhof ankommen.
Wir werden schon ein paar Minuten früher da
sein. Ihr wollt bestimmt wissen, welche
Kleidungsstücke° ihr mitbringen sollt.

Wie du weißt, ist es hier im Juni sehr schön. Am
Tag° ist es warm, aber am Abend° ist es oft kühl.
Du weißt ja, wir wohnen in den Bergen°. Da kann
es oft kühl oder kalt sein. Ihr braucht also°
T-Shirts, Sweatshirts, Pullis und Jacken. Kleider,
Röcke und Blusen könnt ihr zu Hause lassen°. Die
braucht ihr nicht. Ihr sollt aber Jeans und
Tennisschuhe mitbringen.

Viele Grüße, auch an° deine Eltern.

Deine° Katrin

Natascha: Wir brauchen also Kleidungsstücke für warmes und kühles Wetter.

Heike: Ja. Findest du diese Jacke hier zu kurz?

Natascha: Nein, die passt dir gut.

Heike: Die Farbe gefällt mir aber nicht. Ist die Jacke nicht zu dunkel?

Natascha: Mir gefällt sie. Sie wird auch warm sein.

Wie steht Heike der Pulli?

Heike: Und der Pulli? Ist der zu groß?

Natascha: Aber nein. Der steht dir sehr gut. Mir gefällt auch die Farbe. Wenn du den Pulli nicht mitbringen willst, dann kannst du mir bestimmt den Pulli geben.

Heike: Na ja, ich glaube, du hast recht. Ich brauche vielleicht noch ein Paar Tennisschuhe. Die hier sind zu alt.

Wie sind Heikes Tennisschuhe?

Natascha: Prima. Gehen wir doch in die Stadt. Ich muss ein Sweatshirt und Jeans kaufen. Können wir heute Nachmittag gehen?

Heike: So gegen vier?

Natascha: Ja, das geht.

Liebe... (female) Dear...; *das Kleidungsstück* clothing item; *am Tag* during the day; *am Abend* in the evening; *der Berg* mountain; *also* then, so; *lassen* to leave; *Viele Grüße...an*; Best regards to...; *Deine...* (female) Your...

Have students write a short letter to a real or fictitious person. You may want to select the best ones to be read to the class and/or be displayed on a bulletin board.

 WB Activities 13-14

 LA Activity 3

 WA Activity 8

Wie gefällt dir das?

18. Was fehlt hier?

wollen	ist	schreibt	sind
braucht	kaufen	findet	steht
wird	wohnen	sagt	mitbringen

1. Heike _____ mit Natascha nach Lienz fahren.
2. Katrins Mutter _____, wann der Zug in Lienz ankommt.
3. Natascha _____ Heikes Jacke nicht zu kurz.
4. Im Juni _____ es in Österreich sehr schön.
5. Der Pulli _____ Heike gut.
6. Natascha muss Jeans _____.
7. Heike und Natascha _____ zwei Wochen lang bei Katrin bleiben.
8. Heike _____ Tennisschuhe.
9. Natascha und Heike _____ gute Freundinnen.
10. Katrin _____ Heike einen Brief.
11. Katrin und ihre Eltern _____ in den Bergen.
12. Katrin schreibt ihrer Cousine, sie und Natascha sollen Jeans und Tennisschuhe _____.

AC/CD

19. Beantworte diese Fragen!

1. Wohin werden Heike und Natascha fahren?
2. Wie lange bleiben sie da?
3. Warum kommt Natascha zu Heike rüber?
4. Wann werden beide nach Österreich fahren?
5. Wie wird das Wetter in Lienz am Tag sein?
6. Warum kann es am Abend kühl sein?
7. Was für Kleidungsstücke sollen Heike und Natascha für kühles Wetter mitbringen?
8. Findet Natascha Heikes Jacke zu kurz?
9. Wie gefällt Natascha die Farbe von Heikes Pulli?
10. Sind Heikes Tennisschuhe neu?
11. Was will Natascha in der Stadt kaufen?
12. Um wie viel Uhr werden beide in die Stadt gehen?

Katrin wohnt in den Bergen.

Sprache

Words Used for Emphasis

A number of German words are used strictly for emphasis. Such words are *aber, denn, doch* and *ja*. These words cannot be translated literally, but are particularly important in conversational usage.

- *Du bist klug.* You're smart.
- *Du bist **aber** klug!* **Aren't** you smart!

- *Was machst du hier?* What are you doing here?
- *Was machst du **denn** hier?* What are **you** doing here? or: Tell me, what you are doing here.

- *Bring deine neue CD mit.* Bring the new CD along.
- *Bring **doch** deine neue CD mit.* Why **don't** you bring your new CD along?

- *Du weißt, wir wohnen in den Bergen.* You know, we live in the mountains.
- *Du weißt **ja**, wir wohnen in den Bergen.* You know **very well**, we live in the mountains.

Wie gefällt dir das?

20. *Was ist der Unterschied?* (What's the difference?) Read the dialog between Katja and Lars. Then read it again, including the words used for emphasis. Do you notice a difference in meaning and in mood?

> *Katja:* Tag, Lars! Wohin gehst du (denn)?
>
> *Lars:* Ins Kaufhaus. Ich will die neue CD von den *Pilos Puntos* kaufen.
>
> *Katja:* Du hast (doch) schon eine.
>
> *Lars:* Na klar. Ich höre (aber) immer nur die eine CD. Willst du mitkommen? Du hast (doch) bestimmt Zeit?
>
> *Katja:* Wann bist du (denn) wieder zu Hause? Um fünf?
>
> *Lars:* Du weißt (ja), ich habe nicht viel Zeit. In einer Stunde kommt mein Klavierlehrer. Dann muss ich wieder zu Hause sein.
>
> *Katja:* Wie viel kostet (denn) die CD?
>
> *Lars:* Zwanzig Mark. Warum fragst du (denn)?
>
> *Katja:* Ich möchte (doch) auch eine kaufen.

Übung macht den Meister!

Paired Activity: Divide the class into several groups and have them practice this activity.

 Activity 15

Role-playing activity: Have students act out this scene to make it a more meaningful learning experience.

1. *Wir gehen ins Kaufhaus.* You are planning to go shopping. Make a list of clothing or other items you intend to buy. Ask one of your classmates to do the same. After both of you have finished your shopping list, ask each other questions. You may want to ask such questions as: *Wo kaufst du deine Kleidungsstücke?*, *Was kannst du da alles kaufen?*, *Für wen?*, *Wie viel (Geld) kostet...?*, and so forth.

2. *Bitte?* Pretend you are standing in front of a counter in a big department store and the salesperson is ready to help you. You are looking for a specific clothing item. Ask him or her about the cost, the color you want and any suggestions for purchasing your desired item. Be as creative as possible. Some useful expressions might be: *Wie viel kostet...?*, *Welche Farbe?*, *Möchten Sie...?* Either create a complete conversation or have one of your classmates play the part of the salesperson (*Verkäufer* or *Verkäuferin*).

3. *Was hat er/sie heute an?* Select three of your classmates and describe what they are wearing, including the colors.

4. *Was sollst du mitbringen?* Develop a short narrative of what you should take along when visiting a friend or relative during the summer. Indicate the items, their colors and how appropriate they will be for normal weather in the area of your visit.

Aktuelles

Das Kaufhaus

For the person who doesn't speak German or has a limited knowledge of the language, a visit to a department store offers easier shopping opportunities than the smaller shops. Many Germans also like to frequent the larger department stores.

As you enter most department stores on the ground floor *(Erdgeschoss)*, you will usually see a list of the departments posted next to the escalator *(Rolltreppe)* or the elevator *(Fahrstuhl)*. Let's take a tour through a department store, starting downstairs *(Untergeschoss)*. What will you find there?

Sie kauft ein Brot.

In almost all major department stores, you'll find a supermarket *(Supermarkt)*. As in this country, Germans take a shopping cart *(Einkaufswagen)* and then select their groceries. Few shoppers will pass by the bread and pastry counter without stopping; Germans are great bread and pastry eaters. The selection there is overwhelming. Don't be surprised if you find a line of people waiting patiently at a counter to order from the wide assortment of sausages and cold cuts *(Wurst)* or cheeses *(Käse)*. You can order chunks or slices that are weighed according to your request. If you prefer to buy prepackaged cold cuts and meats, you can go directly to the packaged meat display and help yourself.

Hier gibt's Wurst.

The fresh fruits and vegetables are found in the *Obst und Gemüse* section. The fruit display closely resembles that found in American supermarkets; however, the unit of

Was kann man hier kaufen?

Wie gefällt dir das?

measurement is different. The metric pound *(Pfund)* used in Germany weighs about 10 percent more than the U.S. pound. It's easy to weigh the different kinds of fruit. Just place them on a scale which has all the various items graphically displayed on buttons. Push the button which displays the selected fruit or vegetable and the scale will print out the exact weight and price.

Although some Germans still believe that frozen foods are *ungesund* (unhealthy), you will nevertheless find a large selection in the frozen food section. If you need assistance, look for sales personnel dressed in white smocks.

After you have finished your grocery shopping, you can go directly to any of the cash registers *(Kasse)*. If you haven't brought your own shopping bag *(Einkaufstasche)*, the clerk will sell you a plastic bag and expect you to bag your own groceries while he or she is ringing up the various items. There is the usual charge of at least 20 pfennigs for each bag.

You'll find the greatest selection of goods on the ground floor. Shoppers usually will spend more time here than on any other floor, thus most of the specials *(Sonderangebote)* are located on that floor for the shopper who doesn't want to spend a lot of time roaming around in the entire store. All of the specials are clearly marked and arranged on various tables. Other items you may find on this floor are jewelry *(Schmuck)*, leather goods *(Lederwaren)*, books and stationery *(Bücher und Schreibwaren-artikel)*, greeting cards *(Glückwunschkarten)* and even a travel agency *(Reisebüro)*.

In welcher Abteilung ist man hier?

Standing in the music department *(Musikabteilung)*, you may have the feeling you're back in the United States. Much of the music on cassettes and CDs *(Kassetten und CDs)* comes from here. You'll find hits by American artists along with recordings by German rock groups that have become popular in Germany and beyond its borders.

Although small clothing items, such as stockings, ties, scarfs and other special accessories, are found on the ground floor, major items of clothing for children, women and men are normally located on the

ein Sonderangebot
für Hemden

Explain that the first floor in a U.S. building is considered the ground floor *(Erdgeschoss)* in a German building. When talking about specific floors in Germany, students should add one floor. Example: The fourth floor in Germany *(4. Obergeschoss)* is the fifth floor here.

das Fotostudio im Zweiten Obergeschoss

second floor *(Erstes Obergeschoss.* Remember that all sizes are in metric measurements. On the third floor *(Zweites Obergeschoss)*, you'll find a beauty shop *(Friseursalon)* and a photography studio *(Fotostudio)* that specializes in family portraits.

Continuing your tour through the department store, you'll come to the fourth floor *(Drittes Obergeschoss)*. Here you'll find household articles *(Haushaltsartikel)*, such as electric coffeepots and cooking utensils. If you want to buy a gift, look for the department called *Geschenkartikel.*

Eventually, you'll get to the fifth floor *(Viertes Obergeschoss)*. Here you'll come across a popular department, the *Computer-Center,* which displays the most technologically advanced computers and software. If you are ready to sit down and have a beverage and a snack or meal, you'll also find a *Restaurant* on the top floor of the department store.

im Computer-Center

Was passt hier?

1. a place where you pay for your purchases
2. a measurement for weighing fruits and vegetables
3. a department where you can buy earrings
4. a movable device when buying groceries
5. a sign that announces reduced prices or special offers
6. a means of transportation that will take people from one floor to the next
7. a word that refers to a floor of a building
8. a department where you would buy pots and pans
9. a card that you would like to send to your friend for his or her birthday
10. a place where you would go to find out about vacation specials
11. an item for carrying groceries
12. a word that categorizes items such as apples and oranges

1k, 2f, 3j, 4b, 5l, 6c, 7i, 8a, 9h, 10d, 11g, 12e

 Activity 16

a. *Haushaltsartikel*
b. *Einkaufswagen*
c. *Fahrstuhl*
d. *Reisebüro*
e. *Obst*
f. *Pfund*
g. *Einkaufstasche*
h. *Glückwunschkarte*
i. *Obergeschoss*
j. *Schmuck*
k. *Kasse*
l. *Sonderangebote*

Wie gefällt dir das?

WB Activities 17-19

WA Activity 9

Sample answers:
Bitte schön?
Welche Farbe?
Nein, es passt sehr gut.
Vierzig Mark.

Da drüben.
Ja, wir haben im Mai viele
Blusen.
Und diese Bluse hier?
Nein, sie ist sehr preiswert.

TPR Activity: Have
students bring various
clothing items to class to
act out this completed
dialog using the items to
demonstrate. Make sure
that they use colors, along
with the names of the
individual clothing items.

1. essen
2. anhaben
3. kosten
4. bleiben
5. trinken
6. gehen
7. haben
8. schreiben

Erweiterung

21. *Bitte schön?* Imagine you are employed in a department store and have to assist customers (*Kunde/Kundin*). Complete the following two dialogs with meaningful sentences.

    Du: ____
  Kunde: Ich möchte ein Hemd.
    Du: ____
  Kunde: Blau oder grau. Finden Sie dieses Hemd zu lang?
    Du: ____
  Kunde: Wie viel kostet es?
    Du: ____
  Kunde: Das ist preiswert. Ich kaufe es.

  Kundin: Wo sind die Blusen?
    Du: ____
  Kundin: Oh, die Auswahl ist groß.
    Du: ____
  Kundin: Diese Bluse ist etwas zu kurz.
    Du: ____
  Kundin: Prima. Die passt. Ist die Bluse teuer?
    Du: ____

22. *Was ist logisch?* (What is logical?) From the list below, find the words that best complete the phrases.

trinken   gehen   haben   bleiben
schreiben   essen   kosten   anhaben

1. eine Bratwurst
2. einen Mantel
3. etwas Geld
4. zwei Wochen
5. ein Glas Milch
6. nach Hause
7. viel Glück
8. einen Brief

Wir essen Bratwurst gern.

23. Etwas Persönliches.

1. Du hast 200 Mark. Was möchtest du kaufen?
2. Was hast du heute an? Welche Farben haben deine Kleidungsstücke?
3. Wo kannst du in deiner Stadt Kleidungsstücke kaufen?
4. Wohin reist du im Sommer? Wen besuchst du dann?

24. *Kannst du den Brief nicht lesen?* You received a letter from a pen pal in Germany but, unfortunately, you have difficulty reading it as the letter was dropped and got dirty. Rewrite the letter including the missing details.

> *17. März 19[99]*
>
> Lieb**er** [Robert]!
>
> Wie [geht] es dir? Mir geht es ganz [gut].
> Mein Vater, meine, [Mutter] und ich werden im
> August nach [Italien] reisen. Wie du weißt,
> kann [ich] italienisch sprechen. Wir werden
> viel Spaß [haben]. Von Stuttgart [müssen] wir
> zuerst nach Österreich fahren; dann kommen
> die Berge, wo es etwas langsamer gehen wird.
> Wir [werden] eine Woche in Rom und eine [Woche]
> in Florenz bleiben. Im September geht's los mit
> der [Schule]. Die Schule beginnt schon um [halb]
> acht. Das ist sehr früh.
>
> Viele [Grüße] auch an deine Eltern!

AC/CD

Possible letter:
17. März 19*99*

Lieb*er Robert*!

Wie *geht* es dir? Mir geht es ganz *gut*. Mein Vater, meine *Mutter* und ich werden im August nach *Italien* reisen. Wie du weißt, kann *ich* italienisch sprechen. Wir werden viel Spaß *haben*. Von Stuttgart *müssen* wir zuerst nach Österreich fahren; dann kommen die Berge, wo es etwas langsamer gehen wird. Wir *werden* eine Woche in Rom und eine *Woche* in Florenz bleiben. Im September geht's los mit der *Schule*. Die Schule beginnt schon um *halb* acht. Das *ist* sehr früh.

Viele *Grüße* auch an deine Eltern!

Wie gefällt dir das?

Have students write about
any of their planned future
trips (real or imaginary).

25. *Im Sommer geht's los!* Your classmate has invited you to come along on a camping trip (*eine Campingreise*) during the summer. With your classmate, develop a conversation discussing what you should bring along, expected weather conditions, when you'll leave, how long you'll stay, who is coming along, etc.

Im Sommer machen viele Deutsche eine Campingreise.

Activity 20

Activities 10-11

Activity 6

Was weißt du?

1. *Kleidungsstücke.* Identify three clothing items and indicate their colors, whether or not you like them, and why.

2. Describe some of the differences in shopping in an American vs. a German department store. *Auf Englisch.*

3. *Ich habe...an.* Tell your classmate what you are wearing today. Give as many details as possible.

4. Identify five items in your classroom, including their colors.

5. *Was wirst du machen?* Discuss at least three activities that you will do in the near future. Use *werden.*

6. Write a short letter to your friend or relative in which you inform him or her that you would like to come for a visit during the summer. Ask several questions concerning clothing items, weather, best time to come, and so forth.

Vokabeln

der **Abend,-e** evening; *am Abend* in the evening
also then, so
anhaben to have on, wear
der **Anzug,-̈e** suit
die **Auswahl** selection, choice
beide both
beige beige
der **Berg,-e** mountain
bestimmt definitely, for sure
blau blue
die **Bluse,-n** blouse
braun brown
bunt colorful
Dein(e)... Your...
dunkel dark; *dunkelblau* dark blue
dürfen may, to be permitted to
eintönig monotonous, dull
eng tight
die **Farbe,-n** color
früher earlier
gefallen to like; *Es gefällt mir.* I like it.
gelb yellow

glauben to believe
das **Glück** luck; *Glück haben* to be lucky
grau gray
grün green
der **Gruß,-̈e** greeting; *Viele Grüße an...* Best regards to...
der **Handschuh,-e** glove
hell light
das **Hemd,-en** shirt
die **Hose,-n** pants, slacks
die **Jacke,-n** jacket
die **Jeans** (pl.) jeans
das **Kleid,-er** dress
das **Kleidungsstück,-e** clothing item
können can, to be able to
die **Krawatte,-n** tie
kurz short
lang long
lassen to leave
Liebe(r)... Dear...
der **Mantel,-̈** coat
orange orange
das **Paar,-e** pair

passen to fit
der **Pulli,-s** sweater, pullover
der **Pullover,-** sweater, pullover
der **Rock,-̈e** skirt
rosa pink
rot red
der **Schuh,-e** shoe
schwarz black
die **Socke,-n** sock
sollen should, to be supposed to
stehen to stand, be; *Es steht dir gut.* It looks good on you.
der **Strumpf,-̈e** stocking
das **Sweatshirt,-s** sweatshirt
das **T-Shirt,-s** T-shirt
der **Tag,-e** day; *am Tag* during the day
der **Tennisschuh,-e** tennis (athletic) shoe
teuer expensive
vielleicht perhaps
weiß white
werden will, shall

Wieviel kostet das T-Shirt?

Sind die Blusen preiswert?

Die Hemden und Krawatten sind sehr bunt.

Wie gefällt dir das?

Kapitel **8**

Geburtstag

In this chapter you will be able to:

- talk about birthday presents
- offer and accept gifts
- congratulate someone
- identify rooms and furniture
- describe daily activities
- express intentions
- tell someone to do something

233

Was werden Rainer und Carola Gisela zum Geburtstag kaufen?

Was für ein Geschenk hat Rainer?

Rainer: Am Freitag hat Gisela Geburtstag. Dann wird sie fünfzehn.

Carola: Hast du schon ein Geschenk?

Rainer: Ja, ich schenke ihr ein Fotoalbum. Und du?

Carola: Ich weiß nicht. Vielleicht kaufe ich ihr eine CD, ein Buch oder Ohrringe.

Rainer: Sie liest doch gar nicht so oft. Ohrringe hat sie aber immer gern.

Carola: Eine Glückwunschkarte brauche ich auch noch.

Am Freitag hat Gisela Geburtstag.

Hast du schon ein Geschenk?

 WB Activity 1

1. schenkt
2. Ohrringe
3. Geburtstag
4. vierzehn
5. kaufen
6. liest

1. Was fehlt hier?

1. Rainer ____ Gisela ein Fotoalbum.
2. Gisela hat ____ gern.
3. Am Freitag hat Gisela ____.
4. Gisela ist heute ____ Jahre alt.
5. Carola wird Gisela Ohrringe ____.
6. Gisela ____ nicht oft.

2. Beantworte diese Fragen!

1. Wann hat Gisela Geburtstag?
2. Wie alt wird sie dann?
3. Was schenkt Rainer Gisela?
4. Welche Geschenke will Carola vielleicht kaufen?
5. Warum wird Carola bestimmt kein Buch kaufen?
6. Was für eine Karte braucht Carola noch?

1. Am Freitag.
2. Fünfzehn.
3. Ein Fotoalbum.
4. Eine CD, ein Buch oder Ohrringe.
5. Gisela liest nicht so oft.
6. Eine Glückwunschkarte.

Michael und Goran wollen zu Marcs Party gehen.

Wer geht zur Party?

AC/CD

Kommst du?

Goran:	Wann hat Marc die Party?
Michael:	Samstagnachmittag. Kommst du?
Goran:	Klar. Martina kommt bestimmt auch.
Michael:	Kennst du sie schon lange?
Goran:	Erst seit Juli. Sollen wir Geschenke mitbringen?
Michael:	Jürgen macht das. Er kauft ein Poster und eine Kassette für alle.
Goran:	Wann geht's denn los?
Michael:	So gegen halb vier.

Klar.

 WB Activity 2

 LA Activity 1

 WA Activity 1

3. *Falsch!* These statements are incorrect. Provide the correct statements in German.

   1. Die Party ist am Sonntag.
   2. Goran hat die Party.
   3. Goran kennt Martina seit Juni.
   4. Alle kaufen ein Poster und eine Kassette.
   5. Die Party beginnt um 4 Uhr 30.

4. *Geschenke für Verenas Geburtstag.* **Verena's friends are planning a surprise birthday party. Prior to the party, they all get together and decide what each one should give Verena.**

   ◆ Sven
   ◆ Sven möchte einen Pulli (Pullover) schenken.

   1. Tanja und Angelika   4. Rainer und Uwe
   2. Dieter   5. Ralf
   3. Susanne   6. Heike

Sprichwort

Einem geschenkten Gaul sieht man nicht ins Maul.

(Don't look a gift horse in the mouth.)

WB Activity 3

AC/CD

Für dich

Similar to one of our customs, Germans attach a greeting card (*Glückwunschkarte*) to a gift. *Herzlichen Glückwunsch zum Geburtstag!* is the most accepted and popular form of congratulating a German on his or her birthday. The first two words, *Herzlichen Glückwunsch*, or the plural, *Herzliche Glückwünsche*, will fit almost any occasion if you wish to congratulate someone in German, be it a birthday (*Geburtstag*), a name day or Saint's Day (*Namenstag*), a wedding (*Hochzeit*) or an anniversary (*Jubiläum*).

You may want to introduce *Alles Gute zum Geburtstag!* as another common birthday greeting.

Geburtstag

Rollenspiel

You and a classmate decide how much money you want to spend for one of your classmates whose birthday is coming up. Each of you make a list that includes at least three items and their prices in marks. Then, ask your partner the following: how much money you have, how much you want to spend, the cost for each selected item and, finally, your reasons for purchasing one of these items. If appropriate, you may decide to buy one gift together. Be as creative as possible.

Aktuelles

Have students select three or four special occasions in Germany and compare them to what they are accustomed to. You may also introduce some regional differences in this country.

Special Occasions

There are many special occasions that can mark a family calendar throughout the years. Birthdays in Germany are celebrated not unlike ours. Generally, children's birthdays are celebrated among the immediate family. Teenagers often invite their friends to a birthday party.

der Geburtstagskuchen

Although the presence of many foreign workers and their families has greatly increased the importance of religious communities, which decades ago were hardly represented in Germany, most Germans belong to a Christian church—Protestant or Roman Catholic. About half are Protestant (mostly in northern Germany), the other half Catholic (mostly in southern Germany). A special occasion in the Christian church that usually takes place within the first three months of a child's birth is baptism (*Taufe*), to which the closest relatives are invited.

die Taufe

Even though a birthday (*Geburtstag*) is the common celebration, in southern Germany the Saint's Day or name day (*Namenstag*) is still observed. Children here are often named after a saint whose birthday is observed on that day. Similar to a birthday, gifts are also received on *Namenstag*. At the age of 13 or 14, many Germans go through a religious instruction process which culminates in confirmation (*Konfirmation*), when these young adults become full members of the church.

As you have already learned in an earlier chapter, there are three different schools after the *Grundschule* that students can attend. Upon graduating from the *Hauptschule*, students receive a certificate called *Abschlusszeugnis*. When they graduate from the *Realschule*, they get a certificate called *Mittlere Reifezeugnis*. Finally, students graduating from the *Gymnasium* receive their *Abitur*.

The road to marriage usually starts with the engagement *(Verlobung)*. When the engagement becomes official, couples send out written announcements to their friends and relatives who will respond with cards of congratulations. Many will also send flowers. Bridal showers, a common practice in the United States, are not customary in Germany. Engagement presents are given on the day of the engagement. Most engaged couples exchange matching wedding rings which are worn on the left hand.

die Hochzeit

The engagement eventually leads to the wedding *(Hochzeit)*. Some American customs, such as the big wedding cake, the throwing of confetti or rice, the wedding march are not part of the German tradition. However, the custom of *Polterabend* *(poltern = to make a loud noise)* is very popular in Germany. The evening before the wedding, friends of the couple go to the bride's house and smash piles of old pottery (no glass is allowed) at the door or under the window. It's an old superstition that the loud noise helps to avert bad luck. To ensure future married bliss, the bride is expected to sweep up the broken pieces all by herself.

In Germany, the civil marriage is obligatory. It takes place at the local registrar's office *(Standesamt)* in the presence of two witnesses. A church wedding usually follows the civil marriage.

Wedding presents often are delivered at the house while the family is attending the church ceremony or—if you are invited to the *Polterabend*—on the eve of the wedding. At the wedding ceremony, the wedding rings are changed from the left to the right ring finger.

Similar to our country, an anniversary *(Jubiläum)* is considered a special occasion. A silver wedding anniversary *(silberne Hochzeit* or *Silberhochzeit)* means that a couple has been married for 25 years. After 50 years of marriage it is a golden anniversary *(goldene Hochzeit)*.

Mother's Day (*Muttertag*), which falls on the second Sunday in May, was introduced in the United States in 1914 and in Germany in 1923. Contrary to the United States, however, in Germany, Father's Day (*Vatertag*) is not celebrated on a Sunday but on Ascension Day (*Himmelfahrtstag*), which is on a Thursday, 40 days after Easter (*Ostern*).

When someone dies, the family members of the deceased will place an obituary (*Todesanzeige*) in the local paper that often includes personal and emotional comments from the immediate family. In most cases a black-rimmed announcement is mailed out to relatives and friends of the deceased.

Perhaps one of the quickest ways to learn about special occasions in Germany is by going to a department store or bookstore and browsing through the numerous greeting cards.

Identify the special occasions or events that are described in German. You may not understand every word, but you should be able to figure out what is being described or referred to. These are words that you may need to know: *viel Lärm machen* **to make lots of noise;** *die Geburt* **birth;** *wichtig* **important;** *das Ereignis* **event;** *ist gestorben* **died;** *die Zeitung* **newspaper;** *dorthin* **there;** *die Kirche* **church.**

1. Polterabend
2. Muttertag
3. Taufe
4. Goldene Hochzeit
5. Abitur
6. Geburtstag
7. Verlobung
8. Todesanzeige
9. Standesamt
10. Abschlusszeugnis
11. Vatertag
12. Konfirmation

 WB Activity 4

 WA Activities 2-3

 OT Activity 49

1. Einen Tag vor der Hochzeit machen sie viel Lärm.
2. Ein besonderer Tag im Mai für die Mutti.
3. Ein paar Tage oder Wochen nach der Geburt.
4. Fünfzig Jahre nach der Hochzeit.
5. Ein wichtiges Dokument für die Universität.
6. Renate wird dann sechzehn. Ein Jahr später wird sie siebzehn.
7. Ein besonderes Ereignis für Monika vor der Hochzeit. Rolf und Monika geben dem Partner einen Ring.
8. Annelieses Großmutter ist am Dienstag gestorben. Es steht heute in der Zeitung.
9. Am Hochzeitstag gehen sie vor der Kirche zu diesem Büro.
10. Sie bekommen das nach der Hauptschule.
11. Dieser Tag ist ungefähr sechs Wochen nach Ostern.
12. Ein besonderer Tag in der Kirche, wenn Tina dreizehn oder vierzehn wird.

Ergänzung

Was für ein Geschenk bekommst du?

Ein Fahrrad.

Eine Kamera.

Ein Radio.

Eine Uhr.

Einen Fernseher.

Kleidung.

Schmuck.

Wann hast du Geburtstag?

Ich habe am ersten Oktober Geburtstag.

Am vierzehnten April. Und du?

WB Activity 5

LA Activity 2

WA Activities 4-5

OT Activities 50-51

5. *Wann haben sie Geburtstag?* **You and your classmate each select six people (friends, relatives or famous people). Then alternate by telling your partner the name and birthday of each person. Each one of you record this information on a sheet of paper. When you are finished, compare one another's list to make sure you both have recorded the information correctly.**

> *Du:* Martin Luther Kings Geburtstag ist am sechzehnten Januar.

> *Schulfreund:* Meine Mutter hat am fünften Mai Geburtstag.

6. *Was wirst du...schenken?* **Several birthdays are coming up and you want to buy some presents. Select three people you know, indicate when their birthdays are, what you will buy and how much each item costs.**

Jürgen hat am achtundzwanzigsten Juli Geburtstag. Ich werde Jürgen ein Buch kaufen. Es kostet zwanzig Mark.

Angelika hat am Mittwoch Geburtstag. Ich kaufe Angelika eine Uhr. Sie kostet fünfunddreißig Mark.

Geburtstag

Sag's mal!

Was möchtest du zum Geburtstag?

CDs

Klamotten*

ein Armband*

eine Halskette*

Bücher

ein Paar Schuhe

ein Fahrrad

Geld

einen Anzug

eine Stereoanlage*

einen Tennisschläger*

einen Fernseher

ein Moped*

einen Videorekorder

ein Radio mit Wecker

einen Computer

Sprache

Verbs with Stem Vowel Change

A number of verbs in German do not follow the regular pattern of conjugation, but undergo a change in the *du* and *er, sie, es* forms. You will become familiar with two such groups of verbs, one changing from *a* to *ä*, the other from *e* to *i* (or *ie*).

Stem vowel change *a* to *ä*

Here are the verbs with vowel changes that you already know.

	du	er, sie, es
fahren	fährst	fährt
gefallen	gefällst	gefällt

◆ *Ralf fährt mit dem Fahrrad zu seiner Freundin.* Ralf rides his bike to his girlfriend's.

◆ *Gefällt dir diese Krawatte?* Do you like this tie?

Sie fahren mit ihren Fahrrädern.

Stem vowel change *e* to *i* and *e* to *ie*

Here are the verbs with vowel changes that you already know.

 Activity 6

S Activity 2

	du	er, sie, es
essen	isst	isst
geben	gibst	gibt
lesen	liest	liest
sehen	siehst	sieht
sprechen	sprichst	spricht

◆ *Um wie viel Uhr isst du Mittagessen?* At what time do you eat lunch?

◆ *Frau Meier spricht englisch.* Mrs. Meier speaks English.

Was liest der Herr?

7. ***Wohin fahren alle?* Tell where everyone is going.**

◆ Frau Tobler / Stuttgart
◆ Frau Tobler fährt nach Stuttgart.

1. Tobias und Robert / Deutschland
2. Herr Krüger / Hamburg
3. Petra und Maria / Südösterreich
4. Rudis Freundin / München
5. Meine Schulfreunde / Norddeutschland
6. Anne / Köln

1. Tobias und Robert fahren nach Deutschland.
2. Herr Krüger fährt nach Hamburg.
3. Petra und Maria fahren nach Südösterreich.
4. Rudis Freundin fährt nach München.
5. Meine Schulfreunde fahren nach Norddeutschland.
6. Anne fährt nach Köln.

Wohin fahren Petra und Maria?

Geburtstag

8. Was machen Angelika und Tanja heute Nachmittag? Complete the dialog with the appropriate forms of the verbs listed below. Use each verb only once.

gefallen   sehen   machen   haben   geben
lesen   sprechen   fahren   rüberkommen   sein

Angelika ____ mit ihrer Freundin Tanja am Telefon. Sie will heute Nachmittag mit dem Bus in die Stadt ____.

Angelika: ____ du jetzt Zeit? Kannst du um drei ____?

Tanja: Nein. Vielleicht in zwei Stunden. Wann ____ du dein Buch für die Deutschklasse?

Angelika: Das kann ich heute Abend ____.

Tanja: ____ du dann nicht fern? Um 19 Uhr 30 ____ im Fernsehen ein toller Krimi vom Wilden Westen.

Angelika: Das Fernsehprogramm ____ mir nicht. Kommst du mit in die Stadt?

Tanja: Klar, bis später. Du musst mir aber bis morgen etwas Geld ____.

(margin answers)
spricht
fahren
Hast
rüberkommen
liest
machen
Siehst
ist
gefällt
geben

9. Kombiniere...

Andrea
wir
Günter und Helmut
du

sehen
isst
sprechen
liest

morgen
heute Nachmittag
jetzt

am Telefon
im Fernsehen
einen Krimi
nichts
ein Käsebrot

Ergänzung

Die Wohnung oder das Haus

das Schlafzimmer
der Schrank
der Wecker
der Schreibtisch
das Bett
das Wohnzimmer
das Bücherregal
der CD-Spieler
das Bild
der Fernseher
die Lampe
das Sofa
der Tisch
der Videorekorder
der Sessel
der Stuhl

das Bad
das Waschbecken
die Toilette
die Badewanne
die Küche
der Mikrowellenherd
der Herd
das Spülbecken
der Kühlschrank
die Geschirrspülmaschine

WB Activities 7-8

WA Activity 7

OT Activities 52-53

S Activity 6

10. Identify the German words that are described.

◆ a device that enables you to read when the rest of the room is dark

◆ eine Lampe

1. a piece of furniture that you'll use to rest on during the night
2. a device that includes shelves to hold books
3. an oven in which liquid can be heated at accelerated speed
4. an electronic system of transmitting images and sound over a wire or through space
5. a piece of furniture that has a flat surface and four legs
6. a tub in which you can bathe
7. an electronic device on which you can copy a TV program
8. a device on which you set the time to wake up in the morning
9. a machine that washes and dries dishes
10. a place where you would wash dishes if you didn't have a dishwasher
11. a seat typically having four legs and standing next to a table
12. a piece of furniture with drawers at which you can study

1. *ein Bett*
2. *ein Bücherregal*
3. *ein Mikrowellenherd*
4. *ein Fernseher*
5. *ein Tisch*
6. *eine Badewanne*
7. *ein Videorekorder*
8. *ein Wecker*
9. *eine Geschirrspül-maschine*
10. *ein Spülbecken*
11. *ein Stuhl*
12. *ein Schreibtisch*

Expansion: Have students describe a room in their house or apartment. You may want to introduce some additional words to expand the students' vocabulary such as *das Kinderzimmer* (children's room); *der Flur* (entrance hall); *der Keller* (basement, cellar); *die Garage* (garage); *der Balkon* (balcony); *die Veranda* (porch). *Geburtstag*

245

11. *Was ich alles in meinem Zimmer habe.* **Describe at least five objects that you have in your living room or in your own room.**

Praktische Situation

Divide the class into groups of four to plan a surprise party for a friend. Working on their own, Student 1 prepares an invitation that contains for whom and why the party is being given, the time and date, and the party's location. Student 2 decides whom to invite. Student 3 makes a list of appropriate gifts that guests might bring. Student 4 plans what food and beverages will be served.

Then have all group members meet. Each group member presents his or her ideas. After discussing all the suggestions that have been offered, the group decides on the final invitation, guest list, gift suggestions and refreshments. Groups may turn in the party plans to the teacher, or each group may compare their plan with the other groups to see which party will be the most fun.

Sprache

Personal Pronouns

Nominative (*er, sie, es*)

In German, as you have learned in previous chapters, there are three personal pronouns *er, sie* and *es*, which can replace *der, die* and *das* respectively.

Wie ist der Sommer?

- *Der Sommer ist heiß.* The summer is hot.
- *Er ist heiß.* It is hot.

- *Die Lehrerin steht an der Tafel.* The teacher is standing at the board.
- *Sie steht an der Tafel.* She is standing at the board.

- *Das Land ist groß.* The country is big.
- *Es ist groß.* It is big.

Accusative (*ihn, sie, es*)

The accusative case for the personal pronouns *er, sie* and *es* is *ihn, sie* and *es*. Notice that only the masculine pronoun *er* changes to *ihn*. The other pronouns *sie* and *es* have the same forms in the nominative as well as in the accusative case.

- *Dieter kauft einen Kuli.* Dieter is buying a pen.
- *Dieter kauft ihn.* Dieter is buying it.

◆ *Kennst du **Frau Kuhlmann***? Do you know Mrs. Kuhlmann?

◆ *Ja, ich kenne **sie***. Yes, I know her.

◆ *Gabi sieht **das Fernsehprogramm** heute Abend gern.* Gabi likes to watch the TV program tonight.

◆ *Sieht ihre Freundin **es** auch gern?* Does her girlfriend like to watch it too?

The following table shows these as well as other personal pronouns.

WB   Activity 9

  WA   Activity 8

  S   Activity 4

Singular		Plural	
nominative	accusative	nominative	accusative
ich	mich *(me)*	wir	uns *(us)*
du	dich *(you)*	ihr	euch *(you)*
er	ihn *(him, it)*	sie	sie *(them)*
sie	sie *(her, it)*	Sie (sg. & pl.)	Sie *(you)*
es	es *(it)*		

12. *Wie finden sie die Kleidungsstücke?* **Tina is going shopping with several of her friends. Tell what everyone thinks about the various clothing items.**

◆ Findet Andrea den Pulli schön? Nein,...
◆ Nein, sie findet ihn nicht schön.

1. Findet Thomas die Jeans zu lang? Ja,...
2. Finden Ursula und Renate die Bluse eintönig? Nein,...
3. Findet Julia den Mantel teuer? Ja,...
4. Findet Hans das Paar Schuhe zu groß? Ja,...
5. Finden Peter und Rainer die Jacken preiswert? Nein,...
6. Findet Angelika den Rock zu kurz? Nein,...

13. *Sie macht es nicht.* **Alexandra does not want to do what her sister does, and tells her so.**

◆ Ich mache meine Arbeit.
◆ Ich mache sie nicht.

1. Ich kaufe eine Glückwunschkarte.
2. Ich werde meine Jacke anhaben.
3. Ich trinke den Eistee.
4. Ich höre das Rockkonzert gern.
5. Ich möchte ein Geschenk mitbringen.
6. Ich brauche deinen Stuhl.
7. Ich schicke eine Karte.
8. Ich kann die Hausaufgaben schreiben.

AC/CD

1. Ja, er findet sie zu lang.
2. Nein, sie finden sie nicht eintönig.
3. Ja, sie findet ihn teuer.
4. Ja, er findet es zu groß.
5. Nein, sie finden sie nicht preiswert.
6. Nein, sie findet ihn nicht zu kurz.

AC/CD

1. Ich kaufe sie nicht.
2. Ich werde sie nicht anhaben.
3. Ich trinke ihn nicht.
4. Ich höre es nicht gern.
5. Ich möchte es nicht mitbringen.
6. Ich brauche ihn nicht.
7. Ich schicke sie nicht.
8. Ich kann sie nicht schreiben.

14. *Was fehlt in den Dialogen?* **Complete the short dialogs with meaningful personal pronouns.**

◆◆ Ich gehe in die Stadt.
◆◆ Kann ich *dich* in die Stadt fahren?

1. sie
2. euch
3. Sie
4. ihn
5. es
6. es
7. mich
8. ihn

1. Karin kennt Frau Albers sehr gut.
   Ich kenne ____ auch gut.

2. Es ist so dunkel.
   Das stimmt. Wir können ____ gar nicht sehen, Jens und Johann.

3. Guten Tag!
   Kenne ich ____? Heißen Sie Frau Köhler?

4. Kommst du am Samstag mit Rudi zur Party?
   Klar, ich bringe ____ mit.

5. Steffie hat um halb elf Deutsch.
   Hat sie ____ denn gern?

6. Ich lese das Buch für die Englischklasse am Montag.
   Musst du ____ bis dann schon lesen?

7. Warum könnt ihr ____ nicht besuchen?
   Du hast doch keine Zeit.

8. Schreibst du Christine den Brief?
   Ja, ich schicke ____ heute Nachmittag.

An wen schreibt Petra einen Brief?

Warum lesen sie die Landkarte?

Angelika hat Geburtstag

Sonntag, der vierte Juni, ist für Angelika Heinemann ein besonderer Tag. An diesem Tag hat sie Geburtstag. Sie will ein paar Schulfreunde einladen°. Deshalb° spricht sie mit ihrer Mutter. Hoffentlich° wird sie einen Kuchen backen°.

Angelika: Mutti, ich möchte für meinen Geburtstag ein paar Schulfreunde einladen. Geht das?

Mutter: Wie viele sollen denn kommen?

Angelika: Fünf oder sechs. Ich weiß noch nicht, wer kommen kann.

Mutter: Angelika, bis zu deinem Geburtstag sind es nur noch sechs Tage. Da haben wir nicht viel Zeit. Ruf doch deine Freunde gleich an!°

Angelika: Das mach' ich auch. Kannst du einen Kuchen backen?

Mutter: Gern. Wollt ihr im Wohnzimmer feiern°?

Angelika: Ja, da ist mehr Platz als° in meinem Zimmer.

Mutter: Soll ich noch eine Kalte Platte zubereiten°?

Angelika: Ja, bitte.

Mutter: Hilf mir aber bei der Arbeit°, bitte!

Angelika: Na klar.

Angelika ruft ihre Schulfreunde an. Vier werden kommen — Annemarie, Rolf, Doris und Maria. Sie schickt allen eine Einladung°. Sie weiß, dass° ihre Mutter alles sehr schön zubereiten wird. Deshalb hilft Angelika ihr auch bei der Arbeit.

Endlich° ist der Tag da. Ihre Schulfreunde kommen pünktlich. Angelika, ihr Vater, ihre Mutter und ihr Bruder begrüßen° die Schulfreunde. Angelikas Schulfreunde bringen Geschenke mit und wünschen° ihr einen „Herzlichen Glückwunsch zum Geburtstag"°. Sie gehen alle ins Wohnzimmer. Angelika will gleich ihre Geschenke sehen. Was für Geschenke

It's not uncommon in Germany to write birthday invitations and send them to people you want to invite.

Angelika schickt allen eine Einladung.

Geburtstag

wird sie denn bekommen? Rolf gibt ihr ein Buch über Amerika. Von Maria bekommt sie eine CD und von Doris ein Fotoalbum. Dann bekommt sie noch einen Wecker von Annemarie. Annemarie sagt Angelika: „Das ist ein besonderes Geschenk.

Was machen Angelika und ihr Vater?

Jetzt musst du pünktlich aus dem Bett und darfst nicht mehr zu spät zur Schule kommen." Alle lachen°.

Der Kuchen schmeckt sehr gut.

So gegen vier Uhr bringt Frau Heinemann den Geburtstagskuchen. Er schmeckt sehr gut. Alle sprechen über° Schule, Freunde, Sport und besonders, was sie im Sommer machen werden. Später spielt Herr Heinemann Klavier und Angelika spielt Gitarre. Nach zwei Stunden deckt° Frau Heinemann den Tisch. Aus der Küche bringt sie eine Kalte Platte mit Wurst und Käse, Brot, Salat, Limo und Cola. Nach dem Abendessen sehen sie eine bekannte Quizshow° im Fernsehen. Um halb neun gehen alle nach Hause. Angelika dankt° ihrem Freund und ihren Freundinnen noch einmal° für die schönen Geschenke.

 WB Activity 10

 LA Activity 3

 WA Activity 9

einladen to invite; *deshalb* that's why; *hoffentlich* hopefully; *einen Kuchen backen* to bake a cake; *Ruf doch...an!* Why don't you call...!; *feiern* to celebrate; *mehr Platz als* more space than; *zubereiten* to prepare; *Hilf...bei der Arbeit!* Help with the work!; *die Einladung* invitation; *dass* that; *endlich* finally; *begrüßen* to greet; *wünschen* to wish; *Herzlichen Glückwunsch zum Geburtstag!* Happy birthday!; *lachen* to laugh; *sprechen über* to talk about; *decken* to set (table); *eine bekannte Quizshow* a well-known quiz show; *danken* to thank; *noch einmal* once more

Familie Heinemann und ihre Gäste

15. *Was ist die richtige Reihenfolge?* **Place the sentences in the proper sequence according to what happened in the** *Lesestück.*

1. Frau Heinemann sagt ihrer Tochter, sie soll ihr helfen.
2. Frau Heinemann bringt den Kuchen.
3. Sie essen Kalte Platte.
4. Heinemanns begrüßen Angelikas Schulfreunde.
5. Frau Heinemann deckt den Tisch.
6. Frau Heinemann sagt ihrer Tochter, dass sie einen Kuchen backen wird.
7. Frau Heinemann will wissen, wie viele zum Geburtstag kommen.
8. Maria gibt Angelika eine CD.
9. Um 8 Uhr 30 gehen Angelikas Schulfreunde nach Hause.
10. Angelika will ihre Schulfreunde einladen.
11. Alle gehen ins Wohnzimmer.
12. Angelika und ihr Vater machen Musik.
13. Angelika ruft ihre Schulfreunde an.

10, 7, 6, 1, 13, 4, 11, 8, 2, 12, 5, 3, 9

16. **Beantworte diese Fragen!**

1. Wann hat Angelika Geburtstag?
2. Warum spricht sie mit ihrer Mutter?
3. Was soll Angelika gleich machen?
4. Warum werden sie im Wohnzimmer und nicht in Angelikas Zimmer feiern?
5. Wer kommt zu Angelikas Geburtstag?
6. Was für Geschenke bekommt sie von Maria und Rolf?
7. Warum gibt Annemarie Angelika einen Wecker?
8. Was bringt Angelikas Mutter so gegen vier Uhr?
9. Was essen alle später?
10. Was für ein Fernsehprogramm gibt es im Fernsehen?

AC/CD

1. Am vierten Juni.
2. Sie will ein paar Schulfreunde einladen.
3. Sie soll ihre Schulfreunde anrufen.
4. Da ist mehr Platz.
5. Annemarie, Rolf, Doris und Maria.
6. Von Maria bekommt sie eine CD und von Rolf ein Buch über Amerika.
7. Angelika kommt oft zu spät zur Schule.
8. Sie bringt den Geburtstagskuchen.
9. Kalte Platte.
10. Eine Quizshow.

Wer kommt zu Angelikas Geburtstag?

Sprache

The Command Form

Familiar Command

To form commands in English, the speaker simply takes the infinitive without "to," e.g., "go," "run" or "write." In German, the familiar command form in the singular is constructed by eliminating the *en* from the infinitive, i.e., by maintaining the stem. In German, commands (imperative sentences) are always followed by an exclamation point.

◆ *Geh! geh(en)* Go!

◆ *Schreib! schreib(en)* Write!

When you address more than one person, the familiar (plural) form is as follows:

◆ *Kommt zu Peter rüber!* Come over to Peter!

◆ *Spielt im Park!* Play in the park!

It is helpful to remember that the familiar plural command is the same as the *ihr*-form but without *ihr*.

NOTE: Familiar commands of verbs with stem vowel changes *e* to *ie* (as introduced earlier in this chapter) are formed by eliminating the verb ending from the *du*-form (*essen - Iss!, geben - Gib!, lesen - Lies!, sehen - Sieh!, sprechen - Sprich!, helfen - Hilf!*)

Fahr vorsichtig

Es könnte auch Dein Kind sein

Formal Command

The singular and the plural formal command are formed by inverting subject and verb.

- *Sprechen Sie deutsch, bitte!* Please speak German!
- *Hören Sie die Musik!* Listen to the music!

You will notice right away that this formation is identical to the construction of a question. There is, however, a distinct difference between the intonation of a question and a formal command.

The *wir*-Command Form (Let's...)

The *wir*-command form is used when asking for some action in the sense of **Let's** (do something)...!

- *Gehen wir!* Let's go!
- *Schenken wir Angelika ein Fotoalbum!* Let's give Angelika a photo album!

Command Form Used in Public or Official Language

Besides the common command forms already discussed, you may encounter another command form used mostly in legal documents or on official signs at train stations, airports, etc.

- (sign in front of a house or driveway)
- *Bitte nicht parken!* Please don't park here!

- (sign inside a train or airport)
- *Nicht rauchen!* Don't smoke!

- (announcement of train departure)
- *Türen schließen!* Close doors!

WB
Activity 11

WA
Activities 10-11

 Activity 5

Notice that these commands use the infinitive verb form.

17. **You have invited several of your friends to a birthday party. You instruct each friend what to do before and during the party.**

- den Tisch decken
- Deck bitte den Tisch!

1. einen Kuchen kaufen
2. mit Anke über die Party sprechen
3. eine Glückwunschkarte schreiben
4. mit den Schulfreunden tanzen
5. etwas früher kommen
6. bis neun Uhr bleiben

AC/CD

1. Kauf bitte einen Kuchen!
2. Sprich bitte mit Anke über die Party!
3. Schreib bitte eine Glückwunschkarte!
4. Tanz bitte mit den Schulfreunden!
5. Komm bitte etwas früher!
6. Bleib bitte bis neun Uhr!

Geburtstag

18. *Herr Krüger sagt seiner Klasse, was sie machen soll.* **Mr. Krüger, the German teacher, is telling several of his students what they are supposed to do.**

◆ Heidi und Renate / nach Hause gehen
◆ Heidi und Renate, geht nach Hause!

1. Dieter und Sonja / die Hausaufgaben machen
2. Tina und Anne / Klavier spielen
3. Angelika und Hans / das Deutschbuch lesen
4. Uwe und Lisa / einen Brief schreiben
5. Sascha und Rolf / nicht so laut sprechen
6. Holger und Maria / das Lesestück beginnen
7. Susi und Anja / zwanzig Karten kaufen

TPR Activity: Have students follow your instructions as you use the command form(s). Examples: *Geh an die Tafel!, Schreib das Wort...an die Tafel!! Mach dein Buch auf!*, etc.

1. Dieter und Sonja, macht die Hausaufgaben!
2. Tina und Anne, spielt Klavier!
3. Angelika und Hans, lest das Deutschbuch!
4. Uwe und Lisa, schreibt einen Brief!
5. Sascha und Rolf, sprecht nicht so laut!
6. Holger und Maria, beginnt das Lesestück!
7. Susi und Anja, kauft zwanzig Karten!

19. **Provide the appropriate command forms.**

◆ (rufen) _____ Sie bitte Frau Ehrhard an!
◆ Rufen Sie bitte Frau Ehrhard an!

1. (kommen) _____ her, Helmut!
2. (machen) _____ schnell, Anne und Julia!
3. (besuchen) _____ Sie doch die schöne Stadt!
4. (essen) _____ dein Brot!
5. (schenken) _____ Tante Hilda eine Bluse, Bärbel und Boris!
6. (lesen) _____ das Buch bis Freitag, Steffie!
7. (gehen) _____ wir doch am Samstagnachmittag ins Kino!

1. Komm
2. Macht
3. Besuchen
4. Iss
5. Schenkt
6. Lies
7. Gehen

20. **Can you figure out what these instructions mean?**

1. Langsamer fahren!
2. Etwas lauter sprechen!
3. Parken verboten!
4. Bitte nicht rauchen!
5. Bitte das Wasser nicht trinken!

1. Drive slower!
2. Speak a bit louder!
3. No parking!
4. No smoking! (Please don't smoke!)
5. Please don't drink the water!

Fußgänger
bitte gegenüberliegende
Straßenseite benutzen

Parkschein-automat

Hier
Parkschein
lösen

Radfahrer
bitte
absteigen

Einfahrt
freihalten

Betreten auf
eigene Gefahr

Übung macht den Meister!

1. *Was machen wir zum Geburtstag?* You want to give your friend a surprise birthday party. You discuss this with one of your relatives (father, mother, brother or sister). Your conversation should include such details as: the age of your friend, the day and time you would like to have the party, whom to invite, what to have to eat and drink, what to do at the party, etc. Have one of your classmates be the relative and present the finished conversation to the rest of the class.

2. *Was für ein Geschenk sollen wir kaufen?* You would like to buy a gift for someone who has a special occasion coming up. Describe what and when this occasion is, how much money you want to spend, what and why you want to buy a certain gift. Be as creative as possible.

3. *Beschreib deine Wohnung oder dein Haus!* (Describe your apartment or your house.) Your description may make reference to these questions: *Wie viele Zimmer gibt es?*, *Gefällt dir ein Zimmer besonders? Warum? (Es ist neu, schön, groß.).*

4. *Dort möchte ich wohnen.* Imagine the house or apartment of your dreams! On a separate sheet of paper, draw the floor plan of your ideal residence, labeling all the rooms in German. It may have one or two floors. Then choose any room in this house or apartment and make a larger drawing of it on another piece of paper, adding whatever you would buy to decorate and furnish the room. You may either draw the decorations and furniture or find pictures of them in back issues of magazines to cut out and attach to your drawing.

Role-playing Activity: Your students may want to work in small groups to gather all the information and then present it to the rest of the class.

Aktuelles

Common Courtesies

Germans have a reputation as great handshakers. They used to shake each other's hands not only when being introduced, but also as a part of everyday greetings, meaning little more than saying hello.

This custom has changed in the last ten or twenty years, however, as life has become less formal and more hectic. Today more Germans shake hands only when meeting strangers, when seeing friends or relatives after a prolonged absence, or when congratulating someone. The practice varies so much in all regions and population groups that it is impossible to give a valid rule for all occasions. When in doubt, wait for the German to make the first move.

Geburtstag

At a small German party everybody greets acquaintances with a handshake, beginning with the host. A stranger normally waits until the host makes the introductions. When meeting acquaintances in the street, in shops or elsewhere in public, Germans usually shake hands only if they intend to stop and chat.

Darf ich vorstellen?

It is sometimes funny to watch two couples greet each other: they all stretch out their hands at once and suddenly pull them back before contact, smiling wryly. There is a superstition that one should never shake hands crosswise, as this surely will bring bad luck.

Hallo! Wie geht's?

What do you say when introducing people to one another in Germany? Say *Darf ich bekannt machen?* or *Darf ich vorstellen? Herr Meier, Frau Schmidt*. The two shake hands, smile and say *Guten Tag, Herr/Frau...* to each other. A friendly nod when shaking hands would do too. You may also say *Freut mich sehr* or *sehr angenehm* (corresponding to "Very glad to meet you") on such occasions, but these phrases are regarded as somewhat old-fashioned by many Germans and not used much today. Young people may simply introduce another person with *Das ist...*, to which both could respond *Hallo*.

As a rule, Germans prefer being introduced to a stranger by a third person instead of introducing themselves. However, if the circumstances call for it, it is perfectly all right to introduce oneself. Just say your last name: *Schmidt*. As we are used to saying "How are you?" when being introduced, we may also be tempted to say *Wie geht es Ihnen?* when being introduced to a German. This is not customary, however. *Wie geht es Ihnen?* is a greeting for someone you already know, and when using it be prepared to get a detailed answer. Even the more casual *Wie geht's?* may be understood as an inquiry rather than a polite greeting. *Danke gut!* (thank you, fine) would be the normal response.

Point out some of the similarities and differences between German and U.S. customs in greeting each other, including handshaking and introductions.

TPR Activity: Have students practice introductions using these as well as previously learned expressions.

Erweiterung

21. *Was machst du am Samstag?* **You'll have plenty of time on Saturday. Your friend asks what you're planning to do. Create an appropriate dialog.**

Freund(in): Was machst du am Samstag?

   Du: ____

Freund(in): Komm doch mit zu Tanja.

   Du: ____

Freund(in): Sie hat Geburtstag.

   Du: ____

Freund(in): Peter, Natalie und vielleicht auch Jürgen und Anne.

   Du: ____

Freund(in): So gegen sieben.

   Du: ____

22. *Bianca hat Geburtstag.* **Ergänze diese Sätze!**

1. Biancas ____ ist morgen. Sie wird vierzehn.
2. Sie wird ein paar ____ einladen.
3. Dieter kann nicht kommen. Er schickt Bianca eine ____.
4. Die ____ beginnt um halb fünf.
5. Alle bringen ____ mit.
6. Biancas Schulfreunde wünschen ihr „Herzlichen ____ zum Geburtstag!"
7. Bianca bekommt von Thomas ein ____.
8. Heidi gibt Bianca eine ____.
9. Die Mädchen hören ____; die Jungen sehen fern.
10. Um halb sieben deckt Biancas Mutter den ____.
11. Eine halbe Stunde später bringt ihre Mutter eine Kalte ____ ins Wohnzimmer.
12. Um acht Uhr gehen alle nach Hause. Bianca dankt ihren Freunden und ____ für alle Geschenke.

Zum Geburtstag recht viel Glück, wünsch ich unserm besten Stück. **Angelika** froh und heiter, ersteigt erneut die Lebensleiter. Gings bergauf und manchmal ab, nie machte sie mal schlapp. Mach so weiter voller Schwung, dann bleibst Du auch auf Dauer jung. **Mutti Röschen**

Zum **50.** Geburtstag

Von ganzem Herzen alles Gute wünschen Dir lieber **Manfred** „die Rheingönheimer" Heiko, Claudia, Jürgen, Petra und Phillip

Geburtstag

Sample answers:
 Ich weiß nicht.
 Warum?
 Wer kommt denn?
 Um wie viel Uhr soll ich kommen?
 Gut, bis später.

 WB Activity 12

 WA Activity 12

S Activity 1

WB Activity 13

Sample answers:
 1. Geburtstag
 2. Schulfreunde
 3. Glückwunschkarte
 4. Party

 5. Geschenke
 6. Glückwunsch
 7. T-Shirt
 8. Bluse
 9. Musik
 10. Tisch
 11. Platte
 12. Freundinnen

23. *Was passt hier?* **Group the following words into four categories:** *Familie, Geschenk, Haus, Fach.*

1. Ohrringe	6. Rechner
2. Bruder	7. Eltern
3. Schlafzimmer	8. Küche
4. Geschichte	9. Computerspiel
5. Bad	10. Chemie

24. *Sprich mit einem Schulkameraden!* **Discuss with a classmate the following details: Tell your partner that you have a present and would like to bring it. He or she wants to know why you have a present. Give a reason. Ask your classmate if he or she would like to see it. Your friend does. Finally, you determine a time to get together.**

25. Etwas Persönliches.

1. Wann hast du Geburtstag?
2. Wie alt wirst du?
3. Was für ein Geschenk möchtest du zum Geburtstag bekommen?
4. Wen wirst du einladen?

26. *Wo findet man das alles? Im Wohnzimmer? Im Schlafzimmer? In der Küche? Im Bad?* **Indicate where you may find these items, some of which could be found in more than one room.**

◆ Schreibtisch
◆ Der Schreibtisch steht im Wohnzimmer.

WB

Activity 14

Activity 3

1. das Bücherregal
2. die Badewanne
3. der Schrank
4. das Sofa
5. die Geschirrspülmaschine
6. der Videorekorder
7. das Bett
8. der Sessel
9. der Wecker
10. der Tisch

im Wohnzimmer

in der Küche

Land und Leute

Österreich

Österreich ist eine Republik. Das Land liegt in der Mitte° von Europa. Österreich ist ungefähr so groß wie der Staat Maine.

Es hat mehr als sieben Millionen Einwohner. Ungefähr 99% (Prozent) sprechen deutsch. Österreichs Nationalfahne° ist rot-weiß-rot.

Das Land liegt zum größten Teil° in den Alpen. Der höchste° Berg ist der Großglockner. Die Donau ist der längste Fluss°. Sie fließt° von Westen nach Osten.

Die Hauptstadt von Österreich ist Wien. Mehr als 20% der Österreicher wohnen in der Hauptstadt. Wien liegt im Osten Österreichs. Da ist das Land flach°. Die Donau fließt durch° Wien. Im Süden liegt Graz, auch eine große Stadt. Linz liegt im Nordosten. Die Donau fließt auch durch Linz. Nach Wien, Graz, und Linz kommt Salzburg im Nordwesten. Salzburg ist eine beliebte° Stadt. Viele Touristen kommen im Sommer zum Musikfest° nach Salzburg. Innsbruck ist die fünftgrößte Stadt in Österreich. Diese Stadt liegt im Westen und ist während jeder Jahreszeit° beliebt. Besonders schön ist es da im Winter.

Welche Städte möchtest du in Österreich besuchen? Wien, Graz, Linz, Salzburg oder Innsbruck? Warum möchtest du sie gern sehen?

in der Mitte in the center; *die Nationalfahne* national flag; *zum größten Teil;* for the most part; *höchst-* highest; *der längste Fluss* the longest river; *fließt* flows; *flach* flat; *durch* through; *beliebt-* popular; *das Musikfest* music festival; *während jeder Jahreszeit* during every season

Graz

Salzburg

Wien

Geburtstag

 WB   Activities 15-16

 WA   Activity 13

Was passt hier? Select the most appropriate answer.

1j, 2g, 3h, 4e, 5a, 6i, 7f, 8c, 9b, 10d

1. Österreich liegt
2. Der höchste Berg heißt
3. Die Donau fließt
4. Wien ist
5. Graz liegt
6. Österreich ist
7. Die Hauptstadt liegt
8. Viele Touristen kommen
9. Die Donau ist
10. Zum größten Teil liegt das Land

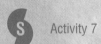

Welcher Fluss fließt durch Linz?

a. im Süden
b. der längste Fluss
c. nach Salzburg
d. in den Alpen
e. die Hauptstadt

f. im Osten
g. der Großglockner
h. durch Linz und Wien
i. eine Republik
j. in der Mitte von Europa

Was weißt du?

1. *Wer hat Geburtstag?* Indicate who among your friends or relatives has a birthday soon. In your description include when the birthday takes place, what you might buy and the cost for that item.

2. Describe two similarities and two differences of special occasions in this country versus Germany. *Auf Englisch!*

3. Ask at least five of your classmates when their birthdays are (including the day and the month). Then put the dates in chronological order, writing out the dates. (Example: *Robert hat am sechsten Mai Geburtstag.*)

4. *Zum Geburtstag möchte ich...* Imagine that you could get any birthday present you wish. Indicate the present you would like to receive, and why.

5. *Was soll ich kaufen?* Pretend you just moved into a house or apartment. Your room is completely empty. List the five most important items that you would like to have in your room.

6. *Darf ich bekannt machen?* With two other classmates, practice introducing each other.

 WB Activity 17

 **WA** Activity 14

 S Activity 7

 OP

TP

VP

 CD-ROM

Vokabeln

anrufen to call up; *Ruf doch...an!* Why don't you call...!

die **Arbeit** work; *bei der Arbeit helfen* to help with the work

backen to bake

das **Bad,-̈er** bathroom

die **Badewanne,-n** bathtub

begrüßen to greet

bekannt well-known

das **Bett,-en** bed

das **Bild,-er** picture

das **Bücherregal,-e** bookshelf

der **CD-Spieler,-** CD player

danken to thank

dass that

decken to cover; *den Tisch decken* to set the table

deshalb therefore, that's why

einladen to invite

die **Einladung,-en** invitation

einmal once; *noch einmal* once more

endlich finally; *Endlich ist der Tag da.* Finally, the day is here.

das **Fahrrad,-̈er** bicycle

feiern to celebrate

der **Fernseher,-** TV, television set

das **Fotoalbum, Fotoalben** photo album

gar nicht not at all, by no means

der **Geburtstag,-e** birthday

der **Geburtstagskuchen,-** birthday cake

das **Geschenk,-e** present, gift

die **Geschirrspülmaschine,-n** dishwasher

die **Glückwunschkarte** greeting card

helfen to help; *bei der Arbeit helfen* to help with the work

der **Herd,-e** stove

herzlich sincere, cordial; *Herzlichen Glückwunsch zum Geburtstag.* Happy birthday!

hoffentlich hopefully

die **Kamera,-s** camera

die **Kleidung** clothes, clothing

der **Kuchen,-** cake

die **Küche,-n** kitchen

der **Kühlschrank,-̈e** refrigerator

lachen to laugh

die **Lampe,-n** lamp

mehr...als more than

der **Mikrowellenherd,-e** microwave oven

noch still, yet; *noch einmal* once more

der **Ohrring,-e** earring

die **Party,-s** party; *eine Party geben* to give a party

der **Platz,-̈e** place; *da ist mehr Platz als...* there is more room than...

das **Poster,-** poster

die **Quizshow,-s** quiz show

das **Radio,-s** radio

schenken to give a present

das **Schlafzimmer,-** bedroom

der **Schmuck** jewelry

der **Schrank,-̈e** cupboard, closet

der **Schreibtisch,-e** desk

der **Sessel,-** armchair, easy chair

das **Sofa,-s** sofa

sprechen über to talk about

das **Spülbecken,-** (kitchen) sink

die **Toilette,-n** toilet, restroom

der **Videorekorder,-** VCR, videocassette recorder

das **Waschbecken,-** (bathroom) sink

der **Wecker,-** alarm clock

die **Wohnung,-en** apartment

wünschen to wish

zubereiten to prepare (a meal)

das Bett

Was kann man hier kaufen?

Geburtstag

Unterhaltung

In this chapter you will be able to:

- talk about a film
- express likes and dislikes
- describe weekend activities and hobbies
- point out tasks and obligations
- make plans

Was läuft denn in der Schaumburg?

Gehen wir ins Kino!

Jürgen: Was läuft denn in der Schaumburg?

Susanne: Ein Film aus Amerika.

Jürgen: Der soll echt gut sein. Gehen wir dahin?

Susanne: Vielleicht kommen Cornelia und Nicole mit?

Jürgen: Ich rufe Cornelia gleich an.

1. *Ergänze diese Sätze!* **Complete each sentence with the appropriate form of the verb. You will not need all the verbs listed.**

wollen   laufen   sein   heißen

haben   sollen   rufen   mitkommen

1. heißt
2. ist
3. soll
4. will
5. mitkommen
6. ruft

1. Das Kino ____ die Schaumburg.
2. Der Film ____ aus Amerika.
3. Er ____ sehr gut sein.
4. Jürgen ____ ins Kino gehen.
5. Werden Cornelia und Nicole ____?
6. Jürgen ____ Cornelia an.

Ich rufe Cornelia gleich an.

(am Telefon)

Jürgen: Was hast du und Nicole heute Nachmittag vor?

Cornelia: Ich muss jetzt für meine Mutti etwas einkaufen.

Wir laden euch beide ein.

Jürgen: Susanne und ich gehen um halb sieben ins Kino. In der Schaumburg gibt's einen tollen Film aus Amerika. Wollt ihr mitkommen?

Na gut. Bis später.

Cornelia: Ich weiß wirklich nicht.

Jürgen: Wir laden euch beide ein.

Cornelia: Na gut. Bis später.

2. Beantworte diese Fragen!

1. Was muss Cornelia heute Nachmittag machen?
2. Wann wollen Jürgen und Susanne ins Kino gehen?
3. Was für einen Film gibt's in der Schaumburg?
4. Warum gehen Cornelia und Nicole doch ins Kino?

AC/CD

1. Sie muss etwas einkaufen.
2. Sie wollen um halb sieben ins Kino gehen.
3. In der Schaumburg gibt's einen tollen Film aus Amerika.
4. Susanne und Jürgen laden sie ein.

Cornelia: Wartet ihr schon lange?

Susanne: Nein, wir sind erst ein paar Minuten hier.

Jürgen: Kommt, der Film geht gleich los.

Cornelia: 48 Mark für vier Karten? Ihr gebt ja wirklich viel aus.

Abgemacht!

Nicole: Das nächste Mal bezahlen wir.

Jürgen: Abgemacht!

Wartet ihr schon lange?

WB Activity 1

LA Activity 1

WA Activity 1

OT Activity 54

Unterhaltung

AC/CD

1. Sie warten erst ein paar Minuten.
2. Er beginnt gleich.
3. Vier Karten kosten 48 Mark.
4. Nicole und Cornelia bezahlen das nächste Mal. (Jürgen und Susanne bezahlen dieses Mal.)

1. mit
2. ein
3. aus
4. vor
5. ein
6. los

AC/CD

3. *Falsch!* **The following statements are incorrect. Provide the correct statements in German.**

1. Susanne und Jürgen warten lange vor dem Kino.
2. Der Film beginnt in zwanzig Minuten.
3. Eine Karte kostet achtundvierzig Mark.
4. Nicole und Cornelia bezahlen dieses Mal.

4. **Was fehlt hier?**

1. Kommt ihr ins Kino ____?
2. Cornelia kauft etwas in der Stadt ____.
3. Jürgen gibt viel Geld für die Kinokarten ____.
4. Was haben Susanne und Cornelia heute Nachmittag ____?
5. Susanne und Jürgen laden Cornelia und Nicole ins Kino ____.
6. Der Film geht gleich ____.

Sprichwort

Bei dir ist wohl der Film gerissen.

(You're probably not playing with a full deck.)

Für dich

About half of all films in Germany come from the United States. Almost all American films are dubbed with a German soundtrack—there are no subtitles; the English has been carefully translated into German to match the lip movements.

Movie theaters are required by law to indicate the age of admittance for each film (similar to our rating system). The standard phrase, for example, is *frei ab 14 Jahren* or *freigegeben ab 14* (admittance 14 years or older).

There are over 3,500 theaters in Germany today. Before the main feature starts, for about 30 minutes numerous commercials are shown advertising local, regional and national companies.

WB Activity 2

WA Activity 2

Rollenspiel

You and your classmate would like to go to see a film. Both of you talk about at least six films that are presently showing in local theaters. You discuss why or why not you would like to see each film, and agree on one which both of you would like to see first. In your conversation, include such items as likes and dislikes and any other reasons for seeing or not seeing a particular film.

Aktuelles

Entertainment

Entertainment in Germany is a national pastime. Put simply—Germans love to be entertained. This is obvious to the visitor who sees numerous billboards *(Reklametafeln)* and round columns *(Litfaßsäulen)* covered with posters announcing the various events taking place in town. Local newspapers *(Zeitungen)* and brochures *(Broschüren)* distributed by the tourist office provide all the information on entertainment and attractions in the area.

Larger cities provide the most opportunities for different types of entertainment. Internationally known stars tour Germany throughout the year. American rock stars have made a long-lasting impact, particularly among the younger generation.

eine Litfaßsäule

Unterhaltung

Neighborhood movie theaters *(Kinos)* feature both German and foreign films. American films are particularly popular. Admission is between performances only. Children are not allowed at adult showings, and certain age groups are excluded from other films under the German Youth Protection Law *(Jugendschutzgesetz)*.

Was läuft im Kino?

Because of its long tradition of cultural diversity, Germany has always been extremely rich in theaters *(Theater)*, operas *(Opern)* and concert halls *(Konzertsäle)*, museums *(Museen)*, and libraries *(Bibliotheken* or *Büchereien)*, most of which are generously supported by state and local subsidies. In Germany there are 300 theaters, 80 symphony orchestras and 1,800 museums. Most Germans buy their theater tickets well in advance or they subscribe to season tickets. If tickets are available, they can be purchased shortly before the start of the performance at the theater ticket office *(Abendkasse)*.

Die Semper-Oper in Dresden

When buying tickets, you have to know the difference in seating. *Parkett* in German means "orchestra," a *Loge* is a box, *1. Rang* means "first balcony," *Balkon* is usually the center part of the first balcony, and *Gallerie* is the gallery. *Reihe 7, Platz 10* would mean "7th row, seat number 10." Germans usually dress up and check their coats at the checkroom *(die Garderobe)* when visiting a theater, opera or concert.

Outdoor theaters present plays during the summer months for local audiences and tourists. Small-time entertainment is provided by various groups, especially university students. To the delight of shoppers, most shopping areas attract musicians who depend on the audience's generosity.

ein Poster vom Berliner Zoo

Every large city has a zoo *(Zoo* or *Tiergarten)*, which caters to all ages. American and European circus troupes *(Zirkus)* tour the country every year. As in the United States, German cities hold fairs *(Jahrmarkt* or *Volksfest)* at least once or twice a year, offering carnival attractions of many types and the traditional rides for thrill-seekers.

There are numerous festivals in Germany throughout the year. Dressed in their folk costumes, various groups provide color and entertainment for the townspeople and visitors alike. The largest bands and crowds can be seen at the annual *Oktoberfest* in *München*, where over a million people congregate in an atmosphere that the Germans call *Gemütlichkeit*. The *Oktoberfest* takes place from late September to early October, but the famous *Karneval* in *Köln* is usually held during the month of February. Hundreds of thousands of people line the streets to watch the parade.

Oktoberfest in München

Was passt hier? **You will not need all the items listed.**

1. a small pamphlet
2. an arena often covered by a tent and used for entertainment shows
3. a place where objects of lasting interest are displayed
4. a specific place to sit at a sporting event
5. a flat surface (panel or wall) designed to carry outdoor advertising
6. a well-known event during the winter
7. a building for dramatic stage performances
8. a paper that contains news, editorials and advertising
9. a cultural or entertainment event held in many cities every year
10. a place where animals can be viewed
11. a place that shows films
12. a place where clothing items are checked

a. *das Volksfest*
b. *die Garderobe*
c. *die Litfaßsäule*
d. *der Platz*
e. *das Oktoberfest*
f. *der Zirkus*
g. *die Bibliothek*
h. *der Karneval*

i. *das Kino*
j. *die Broschüre*
k. *das Theater*
l. *das Museum*
m. *die Zeitung*
n. *das Parkett*
o. *der Zoo, der Tiergarten*
p. *die Reklametafel*

1j, 2f, 3l, 4d, 5p, 6h, 7k, 8m, 9a, 10o, 11i, 12b

 WB Activity 3

 WA Activity 3

Unterhaltung

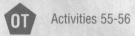

Have students pick an activity or hobby and write a short paragraph answering such questions as *Welches Hobby hast du? Was machst du gern? Mit wem/Wann machst du es? Kannst du beschreiben, was du machst (wie man es macht)?*

WB   Activity 4

LA   Activity 2

WA   Activity 4

OT   Activities 55-56

S   Activity 4

Ergänzung

Was machst du am Wochenende?

Ich gehe ins Kino.

Ich gehe zum Rockkonzert.

Ich gehe in die Disko.

Ich gehe zu Ralf (Gisela).

Ich gehe einkaufen.

Karten

Fußball

Tennis

Schach

Münzen

Poster

Radio

CDs

Kassetten

fernsehen

Klavier

Briefmarken

Bücher

Klarinette

Gitarre

Zeitung

Ski laufen

fotografieren

Welche Hobbys hast du?

Schach (Karten, Fußball, Tennis) spielen
Briefmarken (Poster, Münzen) sammeln)
Rockmusik (CDs, Kassetten, Radio) hören
fernsehen
Bücher (Zeitung) lesen
Klarinette (Klavier, Gitarre) spielen
Ski laufen
fotografieren

5. *Was machen alle am Wochenende?* Indicate what everyone is doing this weekend based on the illustrations.

◆ Timo
◆ Timo sieht fern.

1. Holger und Axel   2. Dieters Freund

3. Petra   4. Annes Vater

5. Lisa und Tanja   6. wir

1. Holger und Axel sammeln Briefmarken.
2. Dieters Freund spielt Schach.
3. Petra hört Radio.
4. Annes Vater liest eine Zeitung.
5. Lisa und Tanja laufen Ski.
6. Wir spielen Basketball.

6. *Und was machst du gern?* Tell your classmates five activities that you would like to do.

Was machen Jochen und sein Freund gern?

Sag's mal!

Was für ein Hobby hast du?

Wandern*

Strand-Volleyball spielen*

Rollschuh laufen*

Freunde besuchen

Fotografieren

alte Filme sehen

Lesen

Skateboarding*

Segeln* Fahrrad fahren*

Reiten*

Computerspiele Zeichnen*

Sprache

Verbs with Separable Prefixes

You can combine verbs with prefixes and thus change their meaning. In most cases such prefixes are prepositions, just as in English (to take — to undertake).

◆ *(ankommen) Der Zug kommt pünktlich an.* The train is arriving on time.

◆ *(einladen) Steffie lädt Rainer zur Party ein.* Steffie is inviting Rainer to the party.

The prefixes, which you can add or eliminate, are called *separable*. The prefixes are separated from their verbs and placed at the end of the sentence.

◆ *(vorhaben) Was **hast** du heute **vor**?* What are you planning (to do) today?

◆ *(fernsehen) Wir **sehen** am Abend **fern**.* We are watching TV tonight.

Der Bus kommt pünktlich an. (Berlin)

These are the verbs with separable prefixes you have learned so far:

anhaben	dahingehen	herkommen	rüberkommen
ankommen	einladen	losgehen	vorhaben
anrufen	einkaufen	mitbringen	ausgeben
fernsehen	mitkommen		

The accent is always on the separable prefix (*an*kommen, **vor**haben).

WB Activity 5

WA Activity 5

S Activity 2

7. *Was ist denn alles bei Joachim los?* **Today is Joachim's birthday. Summarize everything that is going on.**

◆ seine Tante / am Nachmittag aus Hamburg / ankommen
◆ Seine Tante kommt am Nachmittag aus Hamburg an.

1. sein Vater / für die Geburtstagsparty / einkaufen
2. seine Mutter / die Großeltern / einladen
3. seine Freundin / um vier Uhr / rüberkommen
4. sein Freund / am Abend / anrufen
5. seine Eltern / viel Geld / für Joachims Geburtstag / ausgeben

AC/CD

1. Sein Vater kauft für die Geburtstagsparty ein.
2. Seine Mutter lädt die Großeltern ein.
3. Seine Freundin kommt um vier Uhr rüber.
4. Sein Freund ruft am Abend an.
5. Seine Eltern geben viel Geld für Joachims Geburtstag aus.

AC/CD

8. **Beantworte diese Fragen!**

◆ Was bringt Tina mit? (ein Fotoalbum)
◆ Sie bringt ein Fotoalbum mit.

1. Was hat Elisabeth heute an? (ein Pulli)
2. Wer kommmt ins Kino mit? (alle)
3. Was haben Peter und Uwe am Abend vor? (nichts)
4. Um wie viel Uhr kauft Herr Sorge in der Stadt ein? (um drei Uhr)
5. Wie viele Jungen lädt Tanja zur Party ein? (fünf)
6. Wo kommt Onkel Friedrich an? (im Bahnhof)
7. Wo sieht Sarah fern? (im Wohnzimmer)

1. Sie hat heute einen Pulli an.
2. Alle kommen ins Kino mit.
3. Sie haben am Abend nichts vor.
4. Er kauft um drei Uhr in der Stadt ein.
5. Sie lädt fünf Jungen zur Party ein.
6. Er kommt im Bahnhof an.
7. Sie sieht im Wohnzimmer fern.

Was hat Emine an?

Marco und Daniel geben Geld am Imbiss aus.

an, fern, vor, rüber, mit,
ein, los, mit, aus

9. *Ergänze diesen Dialog!* **Complete the following conversation with the appropriate prefixes.**

- Zuerst rufe ich meinen Sohn Bernd ____. Hoffentlich hört er das Telefon.
- Warum soll er es denn nicht hören?
- Ach wissen Sie, er sieht jeden Tag um diese Zeit ____. Das Telefon ist in der Küche. Dann hört er es oft nicht.
- Warum wollen Sie denn mit Bernd sprechen?
- Ich habe viel in der Stadt ____. Später gehe ich noch zu meiner Schwester ____. Er soll nicht auf mich warten.
- Na, dann komme ich in die Stadt ____. Ich muss auch dahin. Ist das OK?
- Klar. Ich kaufe bei Schuhmanns in der Kantstraße ____. Es ist da sehr preiswert.
- Also, gehen wir gleich ____.
- Einen Moment, bitte. Ich bringe noch 200 Mark ____.
- Na, geben Sie nicht so viel Geld ____.
- Bestimmt nicht.

10. **Kombiniere...**

Was
Warum
Wann
Wer
Wo

kaufst
bringt
gibt
habt
ruft

Dieter
Sabine
Herr Sauer
ihr
du

in der Stadt
zu Hause
für den Anzug
heute
für die Party
ein Geschenk
viel Geld

ein
mit
aus
vor
an

Ergänzung

Was musst du oft oder manchmal zu Hause machen?

manchmal:

den Tisch decken (abräumen)

staubsaugen

mein Fahrrad reparieren

zum Markt gehen

oft:

das Bett machen

mein Zimmer aufräumen

die Hausaufgaben machen

das Geschirr spülen

den Rasen mähen

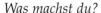

Was machst du?

AC/CD

Have students write a paragraph of a typical weekday during which they have to do several tasks. If necessary, you may want to introduce some additional words such as *Schnee schaufeln* (to shovel snow); *die Garage sauber machen* (to clean the garage), *meiner Mutter/meinem Vater helfen* (to help my mother/father); *den Wagen/das Auto waschen* (to wash the car).

 WB Activity 6

 WA Activity 6

 OT Activities 57-58

S Activity 5

11. *Was müssen sie machen?* Björn and Sara have their own responsibilities and need to help their mother with the daily chores. Indicate what each is doing.

Björn

Sara

1. Björn muss die Hausaufgaben machen.
2. Sara muss den Tisch decken.
3. Björn muss das Geschirr spülen.
4. Sara muss den Rasen mähen.
5. Björn muss das Bett machen.
6. Sara muss zum Markt gehen.
7. Björn muss den Tisch abräumen.
8. Sara muss staubsaugen.

1.

2.

3.

4.

5.

6.

7.

8.

12. *Was musst du zu Hause machen?* Describe six tasks that you
and other members of your family have to do during the week.

◆ Meine Mutter muss in der Stadt einkaufen.

13. *Was machst du gern? Was machst du nicht gern?* Look at the
illustrations and decide which activities you like and which
you don't like. Explain your answers.

◆ Ich spiele Fußball gern. Ich habe viel Spaß.
◆ Ich spiele Fußball nicht gern. Es gefällt mir nicht.

1.

2.

3.

4.

5.

6.

Praktische Situation

Was machst du am Wochenende? In groups of three, students will decide what two activities they would like to do together this weekend. First, each student lists five activities that he or she would like to participate in and gives reasons for each choice (for example, everyone likes this activity, the weather is going to be warm, this is an inexpensive activity, everyone can participate, etc.). Then students share their lists with their group. Student 1 reads his or her list while Students 2 and 3 record the information under the appropriate columns headed *Was ich gern mache* and *Was ich nicht gern mache*. After each student has finished, the group tallies the results to come up with two activities they would like to do, and the reasons for the choices. A spokesperson may present the results to the class.

Sprache

Accusative Prepositions

The accusative case always follows these prepositions:

durch	through
für	for
gegen	against
ohne	without
um	around

◆ *Wir fahren durch die Stadt.* We are driving through the city.

◆ *Hast du ein Geschenk für ihn?* Do you have a present for him?

◆ *Sie spielen gegen uns.* They are playing against us.

◆ *Ich komme ohne das Buch.* I'm coming without the book.

◆ *Gehst du um die Ecke?* Are you going around the corner?

Contractions

These accusative prepositions and articles are contracted as long as there is no special emphasis on the article.

durch	+	**das**	=	**durchs**
für	+	**das**	=	**fürs**
um	+	**das**	=	**ums**

◆ *Wie viel Geld gibst du fürs Rockkonzert aus?* How much money are you spending on the tickets for the rock concert?

◆ *Ich gebe 80 Mark für das Rockkonzert aus.* I'm spending 80 marks on the tickets for the rock concert.

 **WB** Activities 7-8

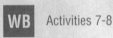 **WA** Activity 7

 **S** Activity 1

14. *Sie kommen immer ohne diese Sachen zur Schule.* Herr Kowalski is annoyed with some of his students because they forget periodically to bring certain items to school.

◆ Renate
◆ Renate, warum kommst du immer ohne ein Buch?

1. Uwe

2. Stefan und Susanne

3. Rainer

4. Natascha

5. Boris und Axel

6. Angelika

1. Uwe, warum kommst du immer ohne einen Bleistift?
2. Stefan und Susanne, warum kommt ihr immer ohne ein Heft?
3. Rainer, warum kommst du immer ohne ein Lineal?
4. Natascha, warum kommst du immer ohne einen Radiergummi?
5. Boris und Axel, warum kommt ihr immer ohne eine Schultasche?
6. Angelika, warum kommst du immer ohne einen Kuli?

15. *Wie viel bezahlst du für...?* Indicate how much you are paying for the different items.

◆ Ich bezahle achthundert Mark
für die Gitarre.

1.

2.

3.

4.

5.

6.

1. Ich bezahle neunzig Mark für den Pullover (Pulli).
2. Ich bezahle fünfunddreißig Mark für die Karte.
3. Ich bezahle vierhundert Mark für das Fahrrad.
4. Ich bezahle fünfzig Mark für das Geschenk.
5. Ich bezahle zweihundertundfünfzig Mark für das Bild.
6. Ich bezahle neunhundertundfünfzig Mark für den Fernseher.

16. Form complete sentences using the information provided.

◆ wir / fahren / durch / Stadt
◆ Wir fahren durch die Stadt.

1. Peter / fahren / um / Bahnhof
2. ich / bezahlen / ein paar Mark / für / Buch
3. Frau Riehmann / kommen / ohne / Mantel
4. meine Freundin / haben / kein Geschenk / für / Onkel
5. Katja und ihre Freundin / gehen / durch / Schule

1. Peter fährt um den Bahnhof.
2. Ich bezahle ein paar Mark für das Buch.
3. Frau Riehmann kommt ohne den Mantel.
4. Meine Freundin hat kein Geschenk für den Onkel.
5. Katja und ihre Freundin gehen durch die Schule.

Lesestück

Die Pilos Puntos Schülerrockband

Pilos Puntos ist eine bekannte deutsche Schülerrockband° Man sagt, dass diese Rockgruppe die erfolgreichste° Schülerrockband der Welt° ist. Man hört sie oft im Fernsehen und im Radio. Die Pilos Puntos sind zwischen° 17 und 20 Jahre alt. Jedes Jahr reisen sie in viele Länder und geben dort Konzerte. Besonders oft reisen sie durch Europa. Deshalb heißt ihr bekanntestes Lied° „Europa". Dieses Lied kann man auf der CD „Türme aus Kristall" hören.

Zu dieser Rockgruppe gehören° sechs Jugendliche° mit viel Talent: Martina Flüs, Marc Heidermann, Marcel Kowalewski, Christian Buddrus, Klaus Laarmann und Axel Sardemann. Hier sprechen die deutschen Stars über sich selbst°:

Martina: Hallo! Mein Name ist Martina Flüs. Ich singe. Ich bin 17 Jahre alt. Meine Hobbys sind in die Schule gehen und Saxophon spielen. Ich spiele bei den Pilos Puntos seit acht Jahren mit und sehr oft denke ich an° unsere vielen Tourneen° innerhalb° von Europa aber auch außerhalb° von Europa.

Marc: Hallo! Mein Name ist Marc Heidermann. Ich spiele Keyboards und ich singe bei Pilos Puntos. Ich bin vor ein paar Tagen 20 Jahre alt geworden° und meine Hobbys sind Segelfliegen°, Fahrrad fahren, mit Leuten° ins Kino gehen, auf Partys und allgemein° Spaß haben.

Martina Flüs

Die Pilos Puntos im Konzert

The interview with the *Pilos Puntos* rock band includes some words that normally would not appear in a first-level textbook.

However, to maintain a high student interest in the German rock scene, many teachers/consultants suggested in keeping the original recorded version and exposing students to a more realistic and authentic setting. **Important:** The recorded material includes the interview as printed in the *Lesestück*, and the well-known hit song by the *Pilos Puntos* titled "*Europa*" one of the selections from their CD "*Türme aus Kristall.*"

Christian Buddrus

Marcel: Hallo! Ich bin der Marcel und ich spiele seit über° zehn Jahren bei den Pilos Puntos Schlagzeug°. Meine Hobbys sind meine Freunde und vor allem° die Musik. Mit meinen Freunden gehe ich gerne auf Partys oder in die Stadt und kauf' mir etwas Schickes zum Anziehen° oder für meine Wohnung. Meine Lieblingslieder° zur Zeit sind bei den Pilos Puntos „Türme aus Kristall" und „Der Seiltänzer" und vor allem esse ich auch gerne Pasta.

Wer spielt Schlagzeug gern?

The correct expression should have been *sich mit Freunden treffen* which is listed properly in the vocabulary section. However, reflexive verbs have not not yet been introduced.

Christian: Mein Name ist Christian Buddrus. Ich spiele Gitarre. Ich bin 18 Jahre alt. Meine Hobbys sind Gitarre spielen, sich mit Freunden treffen° und auf Partys gehen. Ich spiele seit 1992 bei den Pilos Puntos.

Europa

Wunderland vom Schwarzmeer zum Atlantik
Breite Ströme zieh'n mich mit sich fort.
Steile Felsen kratzen an den Wolken.
Dunkle Wälder streicheln sanft das Land.

Polarlicht malt ein Zauberband,
der Südwind streut Saharasand.
Der Golfstrom wärmt den Meeresstrand.
Europa, grenzenloses Land.

Du willst andre nicht besiegen,
Du gibst vielen Völkern Raum.
Europa sanft nach allen Kriegen,
mit dir lebt der Menschen Traum.

Schnelle Züge fliegen mit der Sonne,
tausend Pferde, golden glänzt ihr Haar.
Labyrinthe, Tempel, Kathedralen,
zwischen Türmen der Vernunft.

Polarlicht malt ein Zauberband,
der Südwind streut Saharasand.
Der Golfstrom wärmt den Meeresstrand.
Europa, grenzenloses Land.

Du willst andre nicht besiegen,
Du gibst vielen Völkern Raum.
Europa sanft nach allen Kriegen,
mit dir lebt der Menschen Traum.

Klaus Laarmann

Martina Flüs und Marc Heidermann

Have students select their favorite rock singer or band and write a brief description of what they know about the performer(s). If students are not into rock music, you may want to have them write about a well-known politician, film star or athlete.

Klaus: Mein Name ist Klaus und ich spiele seit elf Jahren Gitarre. Seit acht Jahren bin ich bei Pünktchen, Pünktchen* dabei° und meine Hobbys sind außer° Musik noch Sport. Ich bin 20 Jahre alt.

Axel: Hallo! Mein Name ist Axel Sardemann. Ich spiele Bass und nebenbei noch° etwas Gitarre. Ich bin 21 Jahre alt. Meine Hobbys sind Musik und Sport. Ich spiele seit zehn Jahren bei den Pilos Puntos.

Marcel Kowalewski

Und was möchten die Pilos Puntos in der Zukunft° machen? Martina Flüs sagt es am besten°: „Für die Zukunft wünsche ich mir und den anderen° Pilos Puntos, dass sie jeden Tag ein Schrittchen weiterkommen°."

die Schülerrockband student rock band; *erfolgreichst-* most successful; *die Welt* world; *zwischen* between; *das Lied* song; *gehören...zu* to belong to; *der Jugendliche* teenager; *sprechen...über sich selbst* to talk about themselves; *denken an* to think about; *die Tournee* tour; *innerhalb* inside; *außerhalb* outside; *ich bin vor ein paar Tagen...geworden* I turned...a few days ago; *Segelfliegen* (sail) gliding; *die Leute* people; *allgemein* generally; *seit über* more than; *das Schlagzeug* drums; *vor allem* mainly; *etwas Schickes zum Anziehen* something smart to wear; *das Lieblingslied* favorite song; *sich mit Freunden treffen* to meet with friends; *Ich bin...dabei* I'm taking part; *außer* besides; *nebenbei noch* besides that; *die Zukunft* future; *am besten* the best; *den anderen* the others; *dass sie...ein Schrittchen weiterkommen* that they make headway

* *Pünktchen, Pünktchen* was the name of this rock group before it was changed to *Pilos Puntos.*

 WB Activities 9-10

 LA Activity 3

 WA Activity 8

17. *Welche Hobbys haben die Rockstars?* **Match the names with the hobbies listed. There may be more than one person with the same hobby, and more than one hobby per person.**

1. Klaus Laarmann
2. Axel Sardemann
3. Martina Flüs
4. Christian Buddrus
5. Marcel Kowalewski
6. Marc Heidermann

a.	Sport	g.	mit Freunden zusammenkommen
b.	Fahrrad fahren	h.	Segelfliegen
c.	Musik	i.	ins Kino gehen
d.	in die Schule gehen	j.	Gitarre spielen
e.	auf Partys gehen	k.	etwas Schickes zum Anziehen kaufen
f.	Saxophon spielen		

1. Klaus Laarmann (a, c)
2. Axel Sardemann (a, c)
3. Martina Flüs (d, f)
4. Christian Buddrus (e, g, j)
5. Marcel Kowalewski (c, e, g, k)
6. Marc Heidermann (b, e, h, i)

18. **Beantworte diese Fragen!**

1. Auf welcher CD ist das bekannte Lied „Europa"?
2. Wer ist 18 Jahre alt?
3. Wer spielt Saxophon?
4. Wie viele Jahre spielt Klaus schon Gitarre?
5. Reisen die Pilos Puntos nur in Europa?
6. Wie alt sind die Pilos Puntos?
7. Seit wann spielt Christian in dieser Schülerrockband?
8. Wer spielt Schlagzeug?

AC/CD

1. Es ist auf der CD „Türme aus Kristall".
2. Christian.
3. Martina.
4. Seit elf Jahren.
5. Nein, sie reisen auch außerhalb von Europa.
6. Sie sind zwischen 17 und 21 Jahre alt.
7. Seit 1992.
8. Marcel.

Rock-Export aus Ronsdorf

„Pilos Puntos" auf Frankreich-Tournee gefeiert / Erholung am Mont Blanc

„Rock around the Mont Blanc" - Pilos Puntos bei den Schweizern

Jetzt heißen sie „Pilos Puntos"

Wuppertaler Nachwuchsband im Finale bein „Gibraltor Song Festival"

Sprache

Compound Nouns

The article of a compound noun is determined by the article of the last word in the compound.

◆ der Nachbar, das Land = das Nachbarland

◆ die Geburt, der Tag = der Geburtstag

WB Activity 11

WA Activity 9

S Activity 3

19. *Welche Wörter passen zusammen?* **Form compound nouns by combining the words from the two lists. Be sure to use the correct article for your new compound noun.**

das Fach	der Plan	das Brot	der Tag
die Zeit	das Essen	das Konzert	das Stück
der Schuh	die Tasche	die Karte	das Album
das Café	das Spiel	die Spülmaschine	

1. das Tennis
2. die Stunde
3. das Foto
4. der Liebling
5. der Abend
6. die Geburt
7. die Wurst
8. der Computer
9. die Schule
10. das Land
11. das Eis
12. das Jahr
13. das Geschirr
14. der Rock
15. die Kleidung

1. der Tennisschuh
2. der Stundenplan
3. das Fotoalbum
4. das Lieblingsfach
5. das Abendessen
6. der Geburtstag
7. das Wurstbrot
8. das Computerspiel
9. die Schultasche
10. die Landkarte
11. das Eiscafé
12. die Jahreszeit
13. die Geschirrspülmaschine
14. das Rockkonzert
15. das Kleidungsstück

Have students look for additional compound nouns in German newspapers. They may have to use a dictionary to determine the meaning. The key for forming compound nouns is to find all the individual nouns within the compound noun and use the article of the last noun that is part of the compound noun.
Example: *Die Ferienortinformationsbüro-angestellte (die Ferien, der Ort, die Information, das Büro, die Angestellte)* which means the (female) employee of a resort information office.

Point out that sometimes *-e, -s, -es* may be added to form a compound noun.

Unterhaltung

Übung macht den Meister!

1. Discuss with one of your classmates which film he or she would like to see, what time it starts and when you should leave to be on time.

2. Talk to at least three classmates and find out what hobbies each one has. Make a list and report back to the class.

3. Describe two hobbies you have and give reasons why you like them.

4. Make a list of activities that you would like to do this weekend. Then discuss them with one of your classmates. Your description should include: name of each activity, description, how often/how long you will be involved in each activity and whether or not you will do each activity by yourself or with others.

5. Pretend you are going to a rock concert. Describe such details as preparing to buy tickets, how you will get there, who will be playing.

Aktuelles

Music: Classical to Pop

Few art forms are as internationally known as music. The Beatles and the Rolling Stones, Beethoven and Mozart, to name but a few examples, probably eclipse Michelangelo and Goethe in terms of worldwide fame; their language is more abstract and more universal than the conceptual forms of the fine arts or of literature. The subordinate role of spoken or written language is apparent here from the predominance of English-language pop music. German was long regarded as too stiff and hard a language for the rebellious, critical or

Alle jubeln beim Rockkonzert.

even emotional pop sound. Consequently, German groups produced songs with English lyrics; not until the late seventies did some groups invent a German sound that could be molded to the international pop style. Thus, a growing number of young musicians followed the trend of the "new German wave," in which irony, another hallmark of post-modernist culture, frequently played a decisive role. Not that the Germans have turned their back on the international scene: almost all international stars make regular appearances in Germany.

Little needs to be said about the standing of classical music in Germany. The country, with its numerous orchestras and opera houses, is extremely well endowed, and has long attracted worldwide interest. This preeminence attracts a wealth of musical talent to Germany and, as a result, the majority of members of large orchestras as well as conductors and singers come from abroad.

Between the classical and pop worlds lie the highly successful musicals of recent years, in particular those produced by Andrew Lloyd Webber. These productions demand the utmost in technical skill on the part of the performers, and commercial marketing skills on the part of the promoters.

Herbert Grönemeyer, ein bekannter deutscher Star

High-profile advertising for individual productions whips up interest over several years, drawing huge audiences reluctant to miss the spectacle.

Goethe-Denkmal
(monument) in Leipzig

WB Activities 13-14

20. *Wer sind diese Leute?* Identify each famous person or group with one or two sentences, and say why they are famous. You may have to go to your library to find out more information.

1. The Beatles
2. The Rolling Stones
3. Ludwig van Beethoven
4. Wolfgang Amadeus Mozart
5. Michelangelo
6. Johann Wolfgang von Goethe
7. Andrew Lloyd Webber

21. Was passt hier?

glaube	kosten	hat	gibt
läuft	gehen	bringe	möchte
kommt	weiß	beginnt	sind

WB Activities 15-17

WA Activity 10

S Activity 6

– Möchtest du ins Kino ____?

– Was für ein Film ____ denn heute?

– Im Capitol ____ es einen Film aus Frankreich.

– Wie viel ____ die Karten?

– Alle Karten ____ heute preiswert...nur acht Mark.

– Um wie viel Uhr ____ der Film?

– Ich ____ es nicht. Ich ____, so gegen halb sieben.

– Wer ____ denn mit?

– Renate ____ heute keine Zeit. Ihre Schwester ____ aber mitkommen.

– Gut, ich ____ meinen Bruder mit.

– Abgemacht.

22. *Was fehlt hier?* **Complete each sentence by using the separable prefixes listed. You may be able to use a prefix more than once.**

mit	los	ein	dahin	aus
fern	rüber	an	vor	

Was hat Maria heute Nachmittag ____? Vielleicht kauft sie im Kaufhaus etwas ____. Zuerst ruft sie ihre Freundin Lisa ____.

Maria: Was machst du denn?

Susanne: Ich sehe ____. Im Fernsehprogramm gibt es einen tollen Film. Und du?

Maria: Ich gehe in die Stadt. Komm doch ____!

Susanne: Wann gehst du denn ____?

Maria: Um drei. Warum kommst du nicht zu mir ____? Wir gehen dann von hier ____.

Susanne: Ich habe nicht viel Geld. Deshalb gebe ich auch nichts ____.

Maria: Das ist OK. Ich lade dich zu einem Eis ____.

Susanne: Na gut. Bis später.

23. *Was machen alle gern?* Complete each sentence with the appropriate word.

1. Herr Haller ____ am Morgen gern die Zeitung.
2. Meine Freundin ____ im Winter gern Ski.
3. Die Jugendlichen ____ in der Rockband Gitarre und Keyboard.
4. ____ Sarah gern? Nein, sie hat keine Kamera.
5. Svens Schulfreunde ____ gern Poster.
6. Wir ____ Rockmusik gern.
7. Am Wochenende ____ Claudia und Tanja gern in die Disko.
8. Nach der Schule ____ ich oft fern. Um diese Zeit gibt es immer interessante Fernsehprogramme.

24. **Etwas Persönliches.**

1. Wie oft gehst du ins Kino?
2. Welche Filme hast du gern?
3. Was für ein Hobby hast du?
4. Was machst du am Wochenende?
5. Was musst du jeden Tag zu Hause machen?
6. Welche Rockband hast du gern?

Haben die Leute die Rockband gern?

Unterhaltung

Was spielt er gern?

25. *Wie sagt man's?* From the list below, select appropriate words to complete the conversational exchanges.

Wochenende	kosten	Deutsch	Briefmarken
besonders	laufen	Mark	gehören
Rasen	ist	Stadt	bekannt
geht	gern		

1. Mark
2. Deutsch
3. besonders, kosten
4. geht
5. ist, Stadt
6. bekannt, gern
7. Wochenende, laufen
8. Briefmarken
9. gehören
10. Rasen

1. Hast du Geld für eine Karte?

   Nein, ich habe nur fünf ____.

2. Der Film ist aus München.

   Verstehst du denn ____?

3. Gehst du gern ins Kino?

   Ja, ____ am Sonntagnachmittag.

   Warum nicht am Freitag?

   Dann ____ die Karten nur sieben Mark.

4. Komm, der Film ____ gleich los.

   Einen Moment. Ich muss noch die Karten kaufen.

5. Am Donnerstag gehen wir zum Rockkonzert.

   Wo ____ das denn?

   In der ____.

6. Die Band ist in Amerika ganz ____.

   Ich kenne sie nicht.

   Hörst du denn keine Musik?

   Nein, ich habe diese Rockmusik nicht ____.

7. Was machst du am ____?

   Ich werde in den Bergen Ski ____.

   Viel Spaß!

8. Sammelst du ____?

   Nein, aber mein Bruder sammelt schon lange.

9. Wie viele Jugendliche ____ denn zu dieser Rockband?

   Ich glaube, acht.

10. Warum kannst du nicht früher rüberkommen?

    Ich muss noch den ____ mähen.

Gehst du gern ins Kino?

Rückblick

If any of these activities are difficult to describe in German, you may want to go back to the chapter in which the particular structure or vocabulary was explained.

1. Welche Wörter passen hier zusammen?

Mark	Klarinette	Bett	Geburtstag
Fußball	Anzug	Amerika	Milch
Moment	Juli	Klasse	Mittwoch

1. Land
2. Sport
3. Kleidungsstück
4. Musikinstrument
5. Glückwunschkarte
6. Schule
7. Kühlschrank
8. Geld
9. Tag
10. Minute
11. Monat
12. Schlafzimmer

eine Glückwunschkarte

1. Amerika
2. Fußball
3. Anzug
4. Klarinette
5. Geburtstag
6. Klasse
7. Milch
8. Mark
9. Mittwoch
10. Moment
11. Juli
12. Bett

2. *Ergänze die richtigen Wörter.* Provide the correct forms of the modal auxiliaries and the future tense.

1. Ich (müssen) ＿＿ jetzt mein Zimmer aufräumen.
2. Katja (dürfen) ＿＿ bis elf Uhr in der Disko bleiben.
3. (Werden) ＿＿ du am Wochenende nach Hamburg fahren?
4. Wir (möchten) ＿＿ schon früh ins Kino gehen.
5. Angelika und Sabine (wollen) ＿＿ im Sommer nach Italien reisen.
6. Warum (sollen) ＿＿ du später den Rasen mähen?
7. Ich (werden) ＿＿ dich heute Abend anrufen.
8. (Können) ＿＿ ihr die Hausaufgaben nicht machen?

1. muss
2. darf
3. Wirst
4. möchten
5. wollen
6. sollst
7. werde
8. Könnt

Kommt Rainer mit? **Complete the following conversation using the appropriate forms of the verbs.**

läuft, gibt, gefällt, siehst, fährst, isst

    Rainer: Was (laufen) ____ denn im Kino?

      Axel: Im Palast-Kino (geben) ____ es einen tollen Film aus Amerika.

    Rainer: Der soll nicht besonders gut sein. Ich glaube, der (gefallen) ____ mir nicht.

      Axel: Im Astoria gibt's ein Drama aus Frankreich. Den Film (sehen) ____ du bestimmt nicht gern. Ich gehe lieber ins Palast-Kino.

    Rainer: Um wie viel Uhr (fahren) ____ du denn dahin?

      Axel: Nach dem Abendessen, so gegen halb sieben.

    Rainer: Vielleicht komme ich schon jetzt rüber. Was (essen) ____ du denn zum Abendessen?

      Axel: Kalte Platte mit Wurst und Käse.

    Rainer: Na, dann bin ich bald bei dir. Tschüs.

4. ***Sag deinem Schulfreund oder deiner Schulfreundin, was er oder sie machen soll.*** **Pretend you are your classmate's parent and that you are instructing him or her what to do.**

    ◆ dein Buch lesen
    ◆ Lies dein Buch!

Was macht der Mann?

1. Mach die Hausaufgaben!
2. Deck den Tisch!
3. Spül das Geschirr!
4. Reparier dein Fahrrad!
5. Mäh den Rasen!
6. Mach dein Bett!
7. Geh zum Markt!
8. Sprich lauter!

    1. die Hausaufgaben machen
    2. den Tisch decken
    3. das Geschirr spülen
    4. dein Fahrrad reparieren
    5. den Rasen mähen
    6. dein Bett machen
    7. zum Markt gehen
    8. lauter sprechen

Und was macht Daniel?

5. ***In welchem Zimmer findet man das?*** **Indicate in which of the following rooms you are most likely to find these items:** *im Wohnzimmer, im Schlafzimmer, in der Küche, im Bad. Wo findest du...?*

- ◈ ein Bild
- ◈ Im Wohnzimmer. (Im Schlafzimmer.)

1. ein Bett
2. ein Mikrowellenherd
3. eine Badewanne
4. eine Geschirrspülmaschine
5. einen Fernseher
6. ein Sofa
7. einen Wecker
8. einen Sessel

1. Im Schlafzimmer.
2. In der Küche.
3. Im Bad.
4. In der Küche.
5. Im Wohnzimmer (Im Schlafzimmer.)
6. Im Wohnzimmer.
7. Im Schlafzimmer.
8. Im Wohnzimmer.

6. **Change the italicized words to personal pronouns.**

- ◈ Wo ist *der Bleistift*?
- ◈ Wo ist er?

- ◈ Ich kenne *Anneliese*.
- ◈ Ich kenne sie.

1. Rolf kauft *die Karten*.
2. Wie findest du *das Kleid*?
3. Brauchst du *den Stuhl*?
4. Ich werde *das Fotoalbum* kaufen.
5. Zieh *den Mantel* doch an!
6. Anke muss *den Brief* heute Nachmittag schreiben.
7. Warum machst du nicht *die Hausaufgaben*?
8. Wir hören *die Musik* gern.

1. Rolf kauft *sie*.
2. Wie findest du *es*?
3. Brauchst du *ihn*?
4. Ich werde *es* kaufen.
5. Zieh *ihn* doch an!
6. Anke muss *ihn* heute Nachmittag schreiben.
7. Warum machst du *sie* nicht?
8. Wir hören *sie* gern.

Sie macht ihre Hausaufgaben.

Unterhaltung

7. *Bilde neue Wörter und Sätze!* (Form new words and sentences!) Create compound nouns by adding appropriate nouns. Include the new article as well. Then use each compound noun in a sentence.

◆ Computer____
◆ das Computerspiel. Ich kaufe ein Computerspiel im Kaufhaus.

1. Geburts____
2. Käse____
3. Tennis____
4. Kleidungs____
5. Lieblings____
6. Kauf____
7. Wochen____
8. Fernseh____
9. Apfel____
10. Mittag____

WB   Activity 18

WA   Activity 11

S   Activity 7

OP

TP

VP   (das Taschengeld [pocket money], die Briefmarke [stamp], die Schulfreundin [schoolmate], der Mikrowellenherd [microwave oven])

Was weißt du?

1. *Sprich über einen Film!* Talk to your classmate about the following items:

   - a film you would like to see
   - what time it starts
   - who will come along
   - where the film is showing
   - how much a ticket costs

2. *Was machen sie am Wochenende oder was für Hobbys haben sie?* Identify three people you know, and say what they usually do on weekends or what hobbies they have.

3. *Was musst du zu Hause oft machen?* Describe at least four activities or chores that you are required to do at home.

4. *Diese Rockband oder dieser Rockstar gefällt mir.* Identify a rock band or a rock star you like. In your description include such details as how many are in the band, how old they are, what instruments the various band members play and anything else you know about them.

5. Complete each of the following sentences:

   a. *Am Wochenende lade ich...*
   b. *Gibst du viel Geld für...?*
   c. *Wir fahren durch...*
   d. *Wen bringt ihr...?*
   e. *Am Nachmittag sehe ich...*

6. Can you form four compound nouns from these words? What do these words mean?

der Herd	*die Tasche*	*die Schule*	*die Freundin*
die Marke	*das Geld*	*der Brief*	*die Mikrowelle*

Vokabeln

Abgemacht! Agreed!
abräumen to clear (table)
allem: vor allem mainly
allgemein general(ly)
ander- other; *die anderen* the others
anziehen to wear, put on
aufräumen to clean up
außer besides
außerhalb out of, outside
ausgeben to spend (money)
der **Bass,-̈e** bass
bekannt known
best- best; *am besten* the best
bezahlen to pay
die **Briefmarke,-n** stamp
dabei sein to take part, be a member
dahingehen to go there
denken an to think about/of
die **Disko,-s** disco
echt real(ly)
einkaufen to shop; *einkaufen gehen* to go shopping
erfolgreich successful
der **Film,-e** film, movie
fotografieren to take pictures
gegen against
gehören zu to belong to
das **Geschirr** dishes

das **Hobby,-s** hobby
innerhalb within, inside
der **Jugendliche,-n** teenager, young person
das **Keyboard,-s** keyboard
das **Kino,-s** movie theater, cinema
die **Klarinette,-n** clarinet
das **Konzert,-e** concert
laufen to run
die **Leute** (pl.) people
das **Lieblingslied,-er** favorite song
das **Lied,-er** song
mähen to mow
manchmal sometimes
der **Markt,-̈e** market
die **Münze,-n** coin
nächst- next; *das nächste Mal* the next time
nebenbei besides that
die **Pasta** pasta
der **Rasen** lawn; *den Rasen mähen* to mow the lawn
reparieren to repair
sammeln to collect
das **Saxophon,-e** saxophone
das **Schach** chess
schick chic, smart (looking)
das **Schlagzeug** drums, percussion

das **Schrittchen,-** small step; *ein Schrittchen weiterkommen* to make a little headway
die **Schülerrockband,-s** student rock band
das **Segelfliegen** sail gliding
seit: seit über...Jahren for more than...years
singen to sing
sprechen: sprechen über sich selbst to talk about themselves
spülen to wash
staubsaugen to vacuum
das **Talent,-e** talent
die **Tournee,-n** tour
treffen: sich mit Freunden treffen to meet with friends
die **Unterhaltung,-en** entertainment
vorhaben to plan, intend
warten to wait
weiterkommen to advance, go further
die **Welt,-en** world
das **Wochenende,-n** weekend
die **Zeitung,-en** newspaper
das **Zimmer,-** room
die **Zukunft** future
zwischen between

Wie viele Filme laufen in diesem Kino?

auf dem Markt (Würzburg)

Sport

In this chapter you will be able to:

- talk about sports
- express likes and dislikes
- restate information
- inquire about personal preferences
- identify parts of the body

Bastian

Ramon ist zu langsam und nicht sehr koordiniert.

Sie spielen Tennis

Bastian: Möchtest du mit uns Volleyball spielen?

Steffie: Heute nicht. Um zwei spielen Anke und ich Tennis.

Bastian: Wir brauchen noch zwei.

Steffie: Ruf doch Martina und Ramon an. Die machen immer gern mit.

Bastian: Martina ist schon sportlich. Aber mit dem Ramon geht's oft nicht so gut. Er ist zu langsam und nicht sehr koordiniert.

Steffie

1. Was passt hier?

1e, 2d, 3b, 4f, 5a, 6c

1. Martina ist
2. Steffie und Anke spielen
3. Ramon ist
4. Bastian braucht
5. Bastian soll
6. Steffie möchte

a. Martina und Ramon anrufen
b. zu langsam
c. heute nicht Volleyball spielen
d. Tennis
e. sportlich
f. noch zwei Leute

Steffie: Was hast du denn mit dem Bein?

Anke: Es ist heute ganz steif. Beim Tennisspiel wird es bestimmt locker.

Steffie: Komm, gehen wir!

Anke: Fahren wir doch mit dem Fahrrad! Es dauert sonst zu lange.

Steffie: Siehst du den Tennisschläger hier? Der ist ganz neu.

Anke: Toll! Heute hast du bestimmt eine gute Chance. Mein Schläger ist alt und ich bin auch nicht in guter Form.

Was hast du denn mit dem Bein?

Der Tennisschläger ist ganz toll.

2. **Richtig oder falsch? Determine whether the following statements are correct or incorrect. If they are incorrect, provide a correct statement in German.**

1. Steffies Bein ist ganz steif.
2. Anke will mit dem Fahrrad fahren.
3. Mit dem Fahrrad dauert es zu lange.
4. Steffies Schläger ist nicht alt.
5. Anke wird heute gegen Steffie eine gute Chance haben.

1. falsch / Ankes Bein ist ganz steif.
2. richtig
3. falsch / Mit dem Fahrrad dauert es nicht zu lange.
4. richtig
5. falsch / Steffie wird heute gegen Anke eine gute Chance haben.

Anke: Hoffentlich bekommen wir noch einen Tennisplatz.

Steffie: Um zwei ist meistens nicht viel los.

Anke: Du hast recht. Da spielen nur zwei Leute.

Steffie: Hast du ein paar Bälle?

Anke: Ja, die hier sind alt. Zum Üben sind sie aber gut genug.

Steffie: Das Netz ist etwas zu hoch.

Anke: Das macht nichts. Das ist ein Vorteil für mich.

ese Tennisbälle sind alt.

Sport

Ist das Netz zu hoch?

WB   Activities 1-2

WA   Activities 1-2

OT   Activity 59

3. **Was fehlt hier?**

1. Anke ____ ein paar alte Bälle.
2. Um zwei Uhr ____ meistens nicht viele Leute.
3. Es ____ nichts, dass das Netz zu hoch ist.
4. Steffie und Anke ____ noch einen Tennisplatz.
5. Ankes Bälle ____ alt.
6. Für Anke ____ es ein Vorteil, wenn das Netz zu hoch ist.

4. **Beantworte diese Fragen!**

1. Warum kann Steffie heute nicht Volleyball spielen?
2. Warum wird Steffie heute eine gute Chance gegen Anke haben?
3. Sind viele Leute auf dem Tennisplatz?
4. Warum will Bastian nicht, dass Ramon Volleyball spielt?
5. Warum fahren Steffie und Anke mit dem Rad zum Tennisplatz?
6. Warum soll Bastian Martina und Ramon anrufen?
7. Warum glaubt Anke, dass sie einen Vorteil hat?
8. Was hat Anke mit dem Bein?

Sprichwort

Lass mich aus dem Spiel.

(I want no part of it.)

Für dich

The international success of stars like Steffi Graf, Boris Becker and Michael Stich has made tennis in Germany a national sport. Most tennis courts in Germany are not public but belong to sports clubs. Furthermore, clay tennis courts are more common than hard surface or grass courts. In recent years, volleyball has also become more popular and is played almost exclusively indoors.

Michael Stich

Steffi Graf

Rollenspiel

Your classmate is trying to convince you to come along and participate in a certain sport. You really don't feel like it, and you give several reasons for not wanting to join. Although your classmate will try to be very persuasive, you seem to have an excuse for every possible question, request and enticement. Be as creative as possible.

WB Activity 3

WA Activity 3

Aktuelles

Sport für alle

Sports are an extremely popular form of leisure-time activity in Germany. This is reflected not only in the popularity of sports television broadcasts, but also in the fact that there are more than 75,000 clubs affiliated with the German Sports Federation (*Deutscher Sportbund*). At least 21 million people, over one-fourth of the population, are members of sports clubs, and another 12 million "do their own thing." In Germany, sports clubs and activities are autonomous, the various organizations being self-governing. The state provides only support where sports organizations lack the necessary funds.

Germany is known as the "world champion at building sports facilities." Particularly, the western part of the country has an extensive network of facilities for mass-participation and competitive sports. For instance, there are about 50,000 athletic fields, nearly 30,000 gymnasiums and about 8,000 indoor and outdoor swimming pools.

eine große Sporthalle in Dortmund

Germans are just as conscientious about physical fitness as Americans. There are numerous health and fitness clubs in Germany where members can work out and improve or maintain their physique. Running, jogging, hiking and walking are just some of the sports supported by the German Sports Federation. Throughout Germany, usually in a forest or park area, you can find designated exercise areas marked *Trimm-Dich-Pfad* (literally meaning "Slim Down Path"). And, of course, the numerous hiking paths (*Wanderwege*)

auf einem Trimm-Dich Pfad

found all over Germany further attest to the fact that Germans like to stay fit.

Soccer (*Fußball*) is by far the most popular sport, evidenced by Germany's biggest sports organization (*Deutscher Fußballbund*) which has over 5 million members.

The sport with the longest tradition in Germany is gymnastics (*Turnen*), which became popular in the early nineteenth century and today is the second most popular sport with over 3 million Germans participating. For many decades, tennis (*Tennis*) in Germany was reserved only for the upper class. This is no longer true today. With world-class champions Steffi Graf, Boris Becker and Michael Stich, tennis has skyrocketed in popularity more than any other sport in Germany and now ranks third on the list.

Fußball

Turnen

Over a million Germans belong to rifle and pistol clubs (*Schützenvereine*). Many members enjoy the marksmanship training as well as hunting (*Jagen*) in areas that are leased to trained and licensed hunters. A less expensive sport is fishing (*Angeln*). Germans fish not only in the lakes, but also in the various rivers.

ein Jäger

Table tennis *(Tischtennis)* is among the top ten most popular sports. Besides numerous clubs, many people play this sport in schools, youth hostels or at home. The sport of golf *(Golf)* is very expensive and played by only a few Germans who belong to private clubs. There are not many golf courses in Germany today.

Was spielen die Mädchen?

During the winter months, many Germans head for the mountains in southern Germany, Austria or Switzerland to go skiing *(Ski laufen)*. Those who master the skill after years of hard training can compete in local, national or even international competition.

Segeln macht Spaß.

Water sports, such as sailing *(Segeln)*, enjoy a tremendous popularity among Germans. Sailing particularly is popular on the North Sea and Baltic Sea, as well as in the few sailing lakes that Germany has to offer. During the past 15 years, surfing *(Surfen)* has been enthusiastically received by Germans. There are well over a million people who participate in this sport.

Sie laufen Ski in den Alpen.

Was macht diese Person?

For those who enjoy participating in more challenging sports, Germany offers numerous opportunities. Gliding *(Segelfliegen)* is especially popular in central and southern Germany. There the hills and mountains provide favorable air currents needed to stay in the air for a long time. Recently, hot-air ballooning *(Ballonfahren)* has become very popular in Germany. The challenge is not only to go up and stay in the air, but also to come down in the original spot. Those who are most daring participate in a sport called hang-gliding *(Drachenfliegen)*, in which they jump off cliffs or hills strapped to a kite-like sail and glide high through the air. Finally, the sport of mountaineering *(Bergsteigen)* is practiced in the mountainous regions of Germany. Those who become experts eventually climb the many challenging peaks found in the Alps.

Was passt hier?

1h, 2i, 3b, 4l, 5f, 6g, 7d, 8a, 9e, 10k, 11j, 12c

 WB Activity 4

 WA Activity 4

1. *Angeln*
2. *Ski laufen*
3. *Drachenfliegen*
4. *Tischtennis*
5. *Surfen*
6. *Fußball*
7. *Wandern*
8. *Jagen*
9. *Ballonfahren*
10. *Segelfliegen*
11. *Tennis*
12. *Bergsteigen*

Surfen

a. hunting
b. hang-gliding
c. mountaineering
d. hiking
e. hot-air ballooning
f. surfing
g. soccer
h. fishing
i. skiing
j. tennis
k. gliding
l. table tennis

Ergänze diese Sätze mit dem Namen einer Sportart. Auf Deutsch, bitte!

1. Tischtennis
2. Fußball
3. Ballonfahren
4. Deutscher Fußballbund
5. Jagen
6. Trimm-Dich-Pfad
7. Segelfliegen
8. Deutscher Sportbund
9. Bergsteigen
10. Schützenverein

1. Many people play ____ in schools or at home.
2. The most popular sport in Germany is ____.
3. ____ is a sport where several people at a time go up and travel with the wind.
4. The ____ is Germany's biggest sports organization.
5. Germans who are interested in the sport of ____ have to obtain a license and find a land owner who lets them hunt.
6. A ____ is a designated exercise area, often located in a park or a forest.
7. The mountains and hills of central and southern Germany provide the right conditions for ____.
8. Most German sports clubs belong to the ____.
9. The mountain peaks of the Alps are popular for ____.
10. Germans who want to improve their marksmanship may want to join a ____.

Ergänzung

Welche Sportart treibst du?

Ich spiele Tischtennis.

Ich spiele Tennis.

Ich spiele Basketball.

Ich spiele Fußball.

Ich spiele Golf.

Ich spiele Eishockey.

Ich spiele Volleyball.

Was machst du sonst noch gern?

Ich schwimme gern.   Ich fahre gern Rad.   Ich laufe gern Schlittschuh.

Ich wandere gern.

Ich bastle gern.

Ich laufe gern Ski.

AC/CD

Group Activity: Divide the class into groups of three or four. Have each student list all the sports he or she enjoys watching or participating in. Then, each student will ask the others in the group which sports they like and dislike *(Was machst du gern/nicht gern?)* and why. After each student has answered, the group tallies the results to come up with three sports activities that the group likes best and three that they like least. A spokesperson may present the results to the class.

WB Activities 5-6

LA Activity 1

WA Activity 5

OT Activities 60-61

S Activity 2

Sport

5. Was machen diese Leute gern?

1. Renate wandert gern.
2. Wir spielen gern Basketball.
3. Meine Freunde fahren gern Rad.
4. Dieter und Bastian spielen gern Tischtennis.
5. Katrins Schwester läuft gern Schlittschuh.
6. Ich bastle gern.

1. Renate

2. wir

3. meine Freunde

4. Dieter und Bastian

5. Katrins Schwester

6. ich

Was machen diese Leute gern?

6. Was macht Katrin alles im Juli? Katrin is planning various activities during the month of July. Describe each one. Begin your description with all the Sunday activities for the month followed by all the activities for each of the other six days.

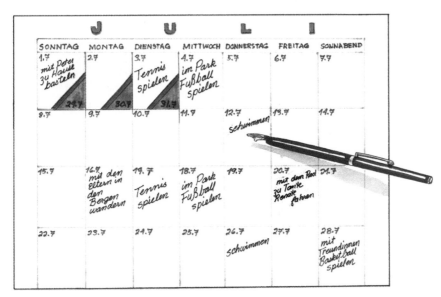

◆ Katrin wird am Sonnabend, den achtundzwanzigsten Juli, mit Freundinnen Basketball spielen.

1. Katrin wird am Sonntag, den ersten Juli, mit Peter zu Hause basteln.
2. Katrin wird am Montag, den sechzehnten Juli, mit den Eltern in den Bergen wandern.
3. Katrin wird am Dienstag, den dritten Juli (und den siebzehnten Juli), Tennis spielen.
4. Katrin wird am Mittwoch, den vierten Juli (und den achtzehnten Juli), im Park Fußball spielen.
5. Katrin wird am Donnerstag, den zwölften Juli (und den sechsundzwanzigsten Juli), schwimmen.
6. Katrin wird am Freitag, den zwanzigsten Juli, mit dem Rad zu Tante Renate fahren.

AC/CD

Some additional words that have not been introduced but might be practical for students to know are: *der Handball*; *das Squash*; *das Turnen* (gymnastics); *das Reiten* (horseback riding); *das Eishockey, die Leichtathletik* (track and field); *Schlittschuh laufen* (skating); *das Badminton*; *Jogging; das Tauchen* (diving); *Fahrrad fahren* (biking); *Rollschuh laufen* (roller skating); *das Surfen* (surfing); *das Segeln* (sailing).

Sag's mal!

Welcher Sport gefällt dir? Mir gefällt...

Tennis

Reiten*

Volleyball

Eishockey*

Schlittschuh laufen*

Handball*

Turnen*

Jogging

Badminton*

Surfen*

Tauchen*

Squash*

Tanzen

Fußball

Schwimmen

Rollschuh laufen*

Ski laufen

Segeln*

Golf

Tischtennis

Fahrrad fahren*

Basketball

Leichtathletik*

Praktische Situation

Wir haben viel Spaß. Conduct a survey on sports and hobbies to see what your classmates are involved in. Begin by making a survey sheet with five columns where you will note the responses of five of your classmates. Ask your classmates the following questions.

1. *Welche Sportart treibst du? Was für ein Hobby hast du?*
2. *Warum hast du diese Sportart oder dieses Hobby gern?*
3. *Wo spielst du oder wo machst du dieses Hobby?*
4. *Wann treibst du diesen Sport oder wann machst du dieses Hobby?*
5. *Wie oft spielst du oder wie oft machst du dein Hobby?*
6. *Wie gut spielst du diesen Sport oder wie gut machst du dein Hobby?*
7. *Wer macht alles mit?*

As each classmate responds to your questions, record his or her responses in the appropriate column.

Example:

> You: *Welche Sportart treibst du gern?*
>
> Classmate 1: *Volleyball.*
>
> You: *Was machst du gern?*
>
> Classmate 2: *Ich lese gern.*

After you have finished, turn in your survey sheet so that the results can be tallied. Your teacher may choose to conduct a survey orally. If so, be ready to respond.

Sprache

Dative (Indirect Object)

In the sentence *Ich kaufe ein Buch*, you know that *Ich* is the subject, *kaufe* is the verb and *ein Buch* is the direct object or accusative.

Now, consider this sentence: *Ich kaufe dem Freund eine Karte.* In this sentence *dem Freund* is called the indirect object or dative. Whereas *eine Karte* is directly connected with the action of the verb, *dem Freund* is indirectly connected with the verb and therefore called the indirect object. The easiest way to identify the indirect object is to determine if "to" or "for" can be put before the noun. In the above example, it would be "I am buying a ticket **for** the friend." (Or: I am buying the friend a ticket.)

	Singular			Plural
	masculine	feminine	neuter	
nominative	der	die	das	die
	ein	eine	ein	
accusative	den	die	das	die
	einen	eine	ein	
dative	dem	der	dem	den
	einem	einer	einem	

In the plural, the dative article is always *den*, regardless of the gender of the noun. To form the dative plural an *-n* or *-en* is added to the plural, unless the plural noun already ends in *-n* or *-s*.

You are already familiar with the question word *wer?* (who?), which refers to the subject (person), and the question word *wen?* (whom?), which refers to the direct object (person). The question word *wem?* (to whom? for whom?) refers to the dative case (person).

◆ *Ich schicke **dem** Lehrer einen Brief.* I'm sending the teacher a letter.

◆ ***Wem** schickst du einen Brief?* To whom are you sending a letter?

You have already learned the meaning of the possessive adjectives (*mein*/my, *dein*/your, *sein*/his, *ihr*/her). These possessive adjectives take the same endings as those of the indefinite article.

◆ *Ich schicke **meinem** Lehrer einen Brief.* I'm sending my teacher a letter.

◆ *Tanja schenkt **ihrer** Freundin eine Bluse zum Geburtstag.* Tanja is giving her girlfriend a blouse for her birthday.

 WB Activity 5

 WA Activity 5

S Activity 3

Der Trainer gibt seinen Spielern Tips.

Sport

7. *Wem soll ich das denn schicken?* You have several items that you are supposed to mail. Can you take care of it?

◆ Onkel
◆ Schick doch dem Onkel ein Fotoalbum!

1. Freund

2. Schwester

3. Lehrerin

4. Frau

5. Großeltern

8. *Wem kaufst du diese Sachen?* Indicate for whom you are buying the various items.

◆ meine Freundin / einen Rechner
◆ Ich kaufe meiner Freundin einen Rechner.

1. sein Bruder / eine Kassette
2. mein Vater / eine Karte
3. ihre Schwester / einen Pulli
4. dein Freund / ein Paar Handschuhe
5. meine Tante / eine Bluse
6. sein Onkel / ein Geschenk

9. Kombiniere...

Klaus und Willi
Herr Reuter
Katarina
Wir

zum Geburtstag
seinem Sohn
seinem Sohn
meinem Onkel

geben
schenkt
brauchen
möchte

zwei Karten
ein Fahrrad
kein Geld
ein Poster

Ergänzung

die Körperteile

der Kopf

das Haar
die Stirn
das Ohr
das Auge
die Nase
der Mund
der Zahn
die Lippe
der Hals
das Kinn

die Schulter
der Arm
die Hand
das Bein
der Fuß

Sport

AC/CD

You may want to introduce some additional words like *das Gesicht* (face); *der Rücken* (back); *das Knie* knee; *der Ellbogen* elbow; *der Bart* (beard); *die Augenbrauen* (eyebrows); *die Zunge* (tongue).

WB Activity 8

WA Activity 7

OT Activities 62-63

S Activity 1

1. Mund
2. Hand
3. Kopf
4. Finger
5. Ohr
6. Nase
7. Haar
8. Auge

10. Kannst du diese Sätze ergänzen?

Fußball spielt man mit dem Fuß.

1. Ich spreche mit dem _____.
2. Ich schreibe mit der _____.
3. Ich denke mit dem _____.
4. Ich zeige (point...to) mit dem _____ auf die Landkarte.
5. Ich höre mit dem _____.
6. Ich rieche (smell) mit der _____.
7. Ich habe _____ auf dem Kopf.
8. Ich kann mit dem _____ sehen.

Sprache

Dative Prepositions

The dative case always follows these prepositions:

aus	out of, from
außer	besides, except
bei	with, near, at
mit	with
nach	after
seit	since
von	from, of
zu	to, at

◆ *Tina kommt um halb zwei aus der Schule.* Tina is getting out of school at two o'clock.

◆ *Außer einem Bruder hat Holger noch eine Schwester.* Besides the one brother, Holger also has a sister.

◆ *Herr Schulz wohnt beim Bahnhof.* Mr. Schulz lives near the train station.

◆ *Kommst du mit deiner Freundin zur Party?* Are you coming to the party with your girlfriend?

◆ *Wohin gehen wir nach dem Film?* Where are we going after the movie?

◆ *Seit einem Jahr wohne ich hier.* I've been living here for one year.

◆ *Ich komme vom Kino.* I'm coming from the movie theater.

◆ *Barbara fährt mit dem Fahrrad zur Schule.* Barbara is riding her bicycle to school.

Contractions

These dative prepositions and articles are contracted as long as there is no special emphasis on the article.

bei	+	dem	=	beim
von	+	dem	=	vom
zu	+	dem	=	zum
zu	+	der	=	zur

WB Activity 9

WA Activity 8

S Activity 5

AC/CD **11.** *Wo warten die Jugendlichen?* **Indicate where these young people are waiting.**

◆ Markt
◆ Sie warten beim Markt.

1. Restaurant
2. Kino
3. Disko

4. Eiscafé
5. Schule
6. Park

1. Sie warten beim Restaurant.
2. Sie warten beim Kino.
3. Sie warten bei der Disko.
4. Sie warten beim Eiscafé.
5. Sie warten bei der Schule.
6. Sie warten beim Park.

AC/CD **12.** *Alle wollen zwei Kleidungsstücke kaufen.* **Ask what else everyone wants to purchase besides what they have selected.**

◆
◆ Was kaufst du außer dem Paar Handschuhe?

oup Activity: Divide ...ss into groups of ...ee or four. Tell ...dents how much ...ney they have to ...end (in marks) to ...rchase clothing ...ms. Have each ...up work together ...make a list of ...rious clothing ...ms, including the ...ce for each. Then ...k each group ...mber to make a ...: of the most ...portant items that ...or she wishes to ...rchase. This a fun ...tivity. (Note: ...ocate enough ...ney—at least 500 ...rks—so that ...dents can ...rchase all clothing ...ms that they need ...wear.

1. Was kaufst du außer dem Pullover (Pulli)?
2. Was kaufst du außer der Krawatte?
3. Was kaufst du außer dem Hemd?
4. Was kaufst du außer dem Anzug?
5. Was kaufst du außer dem Paar Schuhe?
6. Was kaufst du außer der Bluse?
7. Was kaufst du außer der Jacke?
8. Was kaufst du außer dem T-Shirt?

13. *Was wollen wir später machen?* **Find out what your friends want to do after certain activities.**

◆ Was wollen wir nach der Schule machen? (Kaufhaus)
◆ Gehen wir doch zum Kaufhaus!

1. Gehen wir doch zum Park!
2. Gehen wir doch zur Disko!
3. Gehen wir doch zum Eiscafé!
4. Gehen wir doch zum Bahnhof!
5. Gehen wir doch zur Tante!

1. Was wollen wir nach dem Film machen? (Park)
2. Was wollen wir nach dem Konzert machen? (Disko)
3. Was wollen wir nach der Party machen? (Eiscafé)
4. Was wollen wir nach dem Mittagessen machen? (Bahnhof)
5. Was wollen wir nach der Arbeit machen? (Tante)

14. **Provide the proper preposition for each sentence. Use these dative prepositions:** *aus, außer, bei, mit, nach, seit, von, zu.* **There may be more than one possible preposition in some sentences.**

1. bei
2. aus, von
3. von
4. mit
5. seit
6. von
7. Außer
8. bei
9. nach, seit, zu
10. zu

1. Lass dein Fahrrad ____ dem Haus!
2. Warum kommt ihr so spät ____ der Schule?
3. Ich werde eine Karte ____ meiner Kusine bekommen.
4. Monika geht ____ ihrer Freundin ins Kino.
5. Herr Schmidt ist ____ dem Monat Juni nicht mehr zu Hause.
6. Wohnst du weit ____ dem Bahnhof?
7. ____ seiner Mutter kommt auch sein Vater zum Fußballspiel.
8. Sie warten ____ dem Kaufhaus.
9. Was macht ihr ____ dem Geburtstag?
10. Fahren wir schon um acht ____ der Disko?

Außer den Spielern kommen auch viele Zuschauer
(spectators) schon früh vor dem Spiel.

Lesestück

AC/CD

Ein großer Tag

Ibrahim Tanko ist ein bekannter und beliebter Fußballspieler° in
Deutschland. Heute spielt er beim Sportklub Borussia Dortmund in der
Bundesliga°. Seine Karriere hat in der Dortmunder Jugendmannschaft
begonnen°. Gehen wir ein paar Jahre zurück°. Da können wir schon viel
von Ibrahim und seinem großen Tag hören:

Jugendmannschaft von Borussia Dortmund

Ibrahim ist der Star in der Jugendmannschaft von Borussia
Dortmund. Jeden Montag und Donnerstag trainiert er mit
seiner Mannschaft°. Einmal° die Woche spielt Borussia
Dortmund gegen eine andere Mannschaft. Dieses Jahr ist
Ibrahims Mannschaft klasse°. Sie steht in seiner Liga° an
zweiter Stelle°. Morgen wird seine Mannschaft gegen die
beste deutsche Jugendmannschaft in Bremen spielen. Heute
am Donnerstag trainieren er und die anderen Spieler der
Jugendmannschaft zwei Stunden. Der Trainer spricht lange
mit seinen Spielern. Er gibt den Spielern Tips für das Spiel°
am nächsten Tag.

Endlich ist der große Tag da. Der Trainer und seine
Mannschaft fahren mit einem Bus nach Bremen. Im Bus sprechen manche°
über das Spiel, andere spielen Karten oder Backgammon. Nach vier
Stunden kommen sie in Bremen an. Viele Dortmunder Fans sind auch
schon da. Eine halbe Stunde vor dem Spiel laufen alle Spieler auf den
Fußballplatz°. Manche schießen den Ball aufs Tor°, andere laufen mit dem
Ball und geben ihn ab°. In einem Fußballspiel gebraucht° man besonders
die Füße und den Kopf.

Das Spiel beginnt um drei Uhr. Beide Mannschaften spielen heute sehr gut.
Nach 45 Minuten gibt es eine Halbzeit°. Es steht° noch 0:0. Alle
Dortmunder wissen, dass sie in der zweiten Halbzeit besser spielen
müssen. Der Trainer wünscht seinen Spielern viel Glück und schickt sie
wieder auf den Fußballplatz. Das Tempo wird jetzt auch schneller.
Nach 87 Minuten bekommt Ibrahim den Ball und schießt ihn direkt ins
Tor. Alle jubeln und schreien°. Sie müssen noch drei Minuten spielen.
Dann wissen es alle: „Die Jugendmannschaft von Borussia Dortmund
ist Deutscher Meister°." Ibrahim ist der große Held°.

Have students write a
short paragraph about one
of their sports heroes. The
description should include
such items as name, age,
sports activity and
accomplishments.
Newspaper articles may
further enhance this
activity.

Ibrahim Tanko ist der große Held.

der Fußballspieler soccer player; *die Bundesliga* National League; *Seine Karriere hat
in der Dortmunder Jugendmannschaft begonnen.* His career started in the
Dortmund Youth Club.; *zurück* back; *die Mannschaft* team; *einmal* once; *klasse*
super; *die Liga* league; *Sie steht an zweiter Stelle.* It's in second place.; *das Spiel*
game; *manche* a few; *der Fußballplatz* soccer field; *schießen...aufs Tor* to shoot on
goal; *abgeben* to pass; *gebrauchen* to make use of; *die Halbzeit* halftime; *Es steht...*
The score is...; *Alle jubeln und schreien.* They all are cheering and screaming.;
Deutscher Meister National Champion of Germany; *der Held* hero

WB Activity 10   LA Activities 2-3   WA Activity 9   Activity 6

15. *Was fehlt hier?* Provide the correct verb forms from the list below.

fahren	wünschen	schießen	sein
trainieren	geben	laufen	beginnen
gebrauchen	stehen		

1. Ibrahims Mannschaft ____ an zweiter Stelle.
2. Das Fußballspiel ____ um drei Uhr.
3. Beim Fußballspiel ____ die Spieler ihre Füße und Köpfe.
4. Der Trainer ____ seiner Mannschaft ein paar Tips.
5. Vor dem Spiel ____ die Spieler auf den Fußballplatz.
6. Dieses Jahr ____ Ibrahims Mannschaft klasse.
7. Ibrahim ____ jeden Montag und Donnerstag.
8. Der Trainer ____ den Spielern viel Glück.
9. Ibrahim ____ den Ball ins Tor.
10. Alle ____ mit einem Bus nach Bremen.

16. **Beantworte diese Fragen!**

1. Bei welchem Sportklub spielt Ibrahim Tanko heute?
2. Wie oft trainiert Ibrahim mit seiner Mannschaft?
3. Wie gut ist Ibrahims Mannschaft dieses Jahr in seiner Liga?
4. Gegen wen spielen die Dortmunder morgen?
5. Was gibt der Trainer seinen Spielern für das große Spiel?
6. Wie kommen alle von Dortmund nach Bremen?
7. Was machen die Spieler vor dem Fußballspiel?
8. Um wie viel Uhr beginnt das Spiel?
9. Wie steht es vor der Halbzeit?
10. Was macht Ibrahim nach 87 Minuten?

Sprache

Verbs Followed by the Dative Case

There are a number of verbs in German that require the dative case. Some of these verbs are *danken* (to thank), *gefallen* (to like, please), *glauben* (to believe), *helfen* (to help), *passen* (to fit, suit), *stehen* (to suit).

◆ *Das Sweatshirt passt deiner Schwester sehr gut.* The sweatshirt fits your sister very well.

◆ *Kannst du dem Lehrer helfen?* Can you help the teacher?

Remember that *gefallen (gefällst, gefällt)* and *helfen (hilfst, hilft)* have a vowel change with the personal pronouns *du, er, sie, es.*

17. *Glaubst du ihnen?* **Your classmate is asking whether or not you believe these people. Respond to your classmate accordingly.**

   ◆ Glaubst du deiner Freundin? (Ja,...)
   ◆ Ja, ich glaube meiner Freundin.

   ◆ Glaubst du dem Fan. (Nein,...)
   ◆ Nein, ich glaube dem Fan nicht.

   1. Glaubst du der Lehrerin? Nein,...
   2. Glaubst du meinem Onkel? Ja,...
   3. Glaubst du seinem Vater? Ja,...
   4. Glaubst du der Frau? Nein,...
   5. Glaubst du dem Trainer? Ja,...
   6. Glaubst du dem Mädchen? Nein,...

18. *Wem soll Alexander bei der Arbeit helfen?* **Indicate whom Alexander is supposed to help.**

   ◆ sein Bruder
   ◆ Er soll seinem Bruder helfen.

   1. seine Freundin
   2. sein Lehrer
   3. sein Vater
   4. seine Schwester
   5. seine Mutter
   6. sein Trainer

Er soll seiner Familie beim Frühstück helfen.

Sport

The verb *glauben* may take either the dative or accusative case. If used with a person, the dative case follows *(Ich glaube der Lehrerin)*. If used with an object, the accusative is used *(Ich glaube das nicht).*

 WB Activity 11

 WA Activity 10

S Activity 4

AC/CD

1. Nein, ich glaube der Lehrerin nicht.
2. Ja, ich glaube deinem Onkel.
3. Ja, ich glaube seinem Vater.
4. Nein, ich glaube der Frau nicht.
5. Ja, ich glaube dem Trainer.
6. Nein, ich glaube dem Mädchen nicht.

AC/CD

1. Er soll seiner Freundin helfen.
2. Er soll seinem Lehrer helfen.
3. Er soll seinem Vater helfen.
4. Er soll seiner Schwester helfen.
5. Er soll seiner Mutter helfen.
6. Er soll seinem Trainer helfen.

19. **Construct meaningful sentences using the cue words given.**

◆ Kleid / Tante / stehen / nicht schlecht
◆ Das Kleid steht der Tante nicht schlecht.

1. Hose / passen / Freund / sehr gut
2. Katrins Arbeit / gefallen / Lehrer / gar nicht
3. Anzug / stehen / Großvater / ganz toll
4. Ich / können / Schulfreundin / nicht glauben
5. Wir / helfen / Eltern / zu Hause
6. Trainer / danken / Mannschaft / nach dem Spiel

Übung macht den Meister!

1. *Eine Umfrage* (A Survey). Ask at least ten classmates which sports or activities they participate in. Then, summarize your results in a short oral or written report which can be done orally or in writing.

2. *Ich werde in diesem Spiel spielen.* Select a sport you're interested in. Imagine you are participating in a scheduled tournament or contest. Describe the tournament or contest, including some of these details: location, date, number of players or participants (*der Teilnehmer,-; die Teilnehmerin,-nen*), length of game, how often the tournament or contest takes place and any other specific details.

3. *Was machst du gern?* Ask your classmates what they would like to do this weekend. Here are some questions you may wish to use:

   a. *Was machst du dieses Wochenende?*

   b. *Wie viele werden kommen?*

   c. *Was ist da alles los?*

   d. *Wie lange dauert es?*

4. *Was für Körperteile hat ein Mensch? Ein Mensch hat...* In your description, give such answers as *Ein Mensch hat zwei Augen.* Then ask each other the question *Wozu braucht man Augen?* (Answer: *Zum Sehen.*) Here are some additional useful words for your answers: *denken* (to think), *riechen* (to smell). Others that you already know are: *hören, sprechen, essen, schwimmen, Schlittschuh laufen, wandern, schmecken,* etc.

Aktuelles

Fußball

Soccer is the most popular and most widely played sport in Germany. It is not only a team sport, but also is much enjoyed by millions of spectators every week during the soccer season which runs from late August until May or early June. During television broadcasts of international matches the battle for control of the leather ball holds many millions of people spellbound in front of their TV screens; you get the impression that all other forms of social life are nonexistent. The fact that Germany has won the World Cup three times (1954, 1972, 1990) has certainly added considerably to the popularity of the sport.

Deutschland gewinnt das Spiel.

Each of the 18 teams in the national league (*Bundesliga*) plays a total of 34 games (17 at home and 17 away). The team that wins the game receives 3 points. When a game ends in a tie, each team receives 1 point. The team with the most points at the end of the season is the national champion or *Deutscher Fußballmeister*. The two teams at the bottom of the final standings drop out of the national league and are required to participate in the second league (*2. Bundesliga*). On the other hand, the two teams with the best second league record are admitted into the national league for the following year.

Each goal (*Tor*) consists of two posts 8 feet high and 8 yards apart, connected by a crossbar at the top, with nets (*Netze*) attached to the rear. The playing area has a maximum length of 120 yards and a minimum length of 100 yards. The width ranges from 55 to 75 yards. The playing area is outlined by a white line, and flags are placed in each corner; the sidelines are known as touch lines, and the end lines as the goal lines.

Fußball-Bundesliga

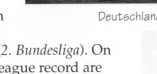

...ussia Dortmund – SC Freiburg	3:2
...ern München – Fortuna Düsseldorf	2:2
...nchengladbach – 1860 München	0:2
...nsa Rostock – 1. FC Schalke 04	0:1
...rder Bremen – FC Schalke 04	1:2
...Stuttgart – Karlsruher SC	3:1
...St. Pauli – KFC 05 Uerdingen	0:2
...yer Leverkusen – 1. FC Kaiserslautern	1:1
...ntracht Frankfurt – Hamburger SV	1:4

1	(1)	Borussia Dortmund	34	19	11	4	76:38	68
2	(2)	Bayern München	34	19	5	10	66:46	62
3	(3)	FC Schalke 04	34	14	14	6	45:36	56
4	(4)	Mönchengladbach	34	15	8	11	52:51	53
5	(7)	Hamburger SV	34	12	14	8	52:47	50
6	(5)	Hansa Rostock	34	13	10	11	47:43	49
7	(6)	Karlsruher SC	34	12	12	10	53:47	48
8	(9)	1860 München	34	11	12	11	52:46	45
9	(8)	Werder Bremen	34	10	14	10	39:42	44
10	(11)	VfB Stuttgart	34	10	13	11	59:62	43
11	(10)	SC Freiburg	34	11	9	14	30:41	42
12	(15)	1. FC Köln	34	9	13	12	33:35	40
13	(12)	Fortuna Düsseldorf	34	8	16	10	40:47	40
14	(14)	Bayer Leverkusen	34	8	14	12	37:38	38
15	(13)	FC St. Pauli	34	9	11	14	43:51	38
16	(16)	1. FC Kaiserslautern	34	6	18	10	31:37	36
17	(17)	Eintracht Frankfurt	34	7	11	16	43:68	32
18	(18)	KFC 05 Uerdingen	34	5	11	18	33:56	26

Heimbilanz

Auswärtsbilanz

1 Bor. Dortmund	17	7	7	3	31:24	2
...m München	17	8	2	7	31:26	2
	17			4	17:20	2

The midfield line goes from one touch line to the other and runs through the center of the field parallel with the goal lines. In the center of the field is a circle, where the ball is placed for the kick-off at the beginning of the game or after a goal has been scored. Near each goal is the goal area; the other is called the penalty-kick area. The spot for a penalty kick *(Elfmeter)* is 12 yards from the center of the goal line. Also, at each corner there is a small marked area to be used for a corner kick.

The soccer ball *(Fußball)* has a circumference of about 27 inches and has a weight of between 14 and 16 ounces, with an inflation pressure of about 12 pounds. Shoes are the most important part of the player's equipment. Regulation shoes are laced shoes with cleats.

Es gibt 11 Spieler in einer Fußballmannschaft.

There are 11 players *(Spieler)* on a soccer team *(Fußballmannschaft)*. Only up to two players are allowed to be substituted during the game. Most professional teams today use various formations. The objective is to put the ball in the opponent's goal. When the ball has been kicked into the goal, the scoring team gets one point. A regulation game lasts 90 minutes (two periods of 45 minutes each) with a half-time of 10 minutes. The time is not controlled by the clock or time keeper but by the referee *(Schiedsrichter)*, who has the option of adding time after regulation for injury or other time-outs.

The referee also controls the game with the help of two linespersons *(Linienrichter)*. He or she whistles for any game infractions such as fouls or other misconduct. For serious fouls, the referee shows a yellow card to caution the player who committed the foul. If a player receives two yellow cards or a red card for a more serious foul, he or she is ejected from the game.

 **WB** Activity 12

WA Activity 11

Ein Fußballspiel dauert 90 Minuten.

Select the appropriate words from the list that best completes each sentence.

Fernseher   Schiedsrichter   Deutscher   Fußballmeister
Linienrichter Fußballsaison   Gelbe Karte   Mannschaft
Bundesliga   Fußballplatz   2. Bundesliga   Rote Karte
Tor   Ecke   Fußball   Schuhe

1. For a serious foul, a player receives a ____.
2. ____ are very important as part of the players' equipment.
3. Only 18 teams can participate in the ____.
4. The ____ is 24 feet long and 8 feet high.
5. The person who whistles when a foul has been committed is called the ____.
6. The object of soccer is to score with the ____.
7. The best team at the end of the German soccer season is pronounced ____.
8. Corner kicks are taken from an area called ____.
9. The ____ lasts for at least nine months.
10. The game of soccer is played on a ____.
11. After a player receives a ____, he or she is ejected from the game.
12. Most Germans watch the weekly soccer games on their ____.
13. The two national teams that have the worst record at the end of the season drop down to the ____.
14. A soccer ____ consists of 11 players.
15. Two ____ assist the referee during a game.

1. Gelbe Karte
2. Schuhe
3. Bundesliga
4. Tor
5. Schiedsrichter
6. Fußball
7. Deutscher Fußballmeister
8. Ecke
9. Fußballsaison
10. Fußballplatz
11. Rote Karte
12. Fernseher
13. 2. Bundesliga
14. Mannschaft
15. Linienrichter

Erweiterung

20. **Welche Wörter gehören zu diesen vier Kategorien: Sport, Schule, Körper oder Kleidung?**

◆ Schwimmen
◆ Sport

WB Activities 13-15

1. Schulter
2. Mantel
3. Schlittschuh laufen
4. Stundenplan
5. Stirn
6. Rock
7. Hals
8. Tafel
9. Bein
10. Basketball
11. Landkarte
12. Tischtennis
13. Krawatte
14. Kopf
15. Hausaufgaben

1. Körper
2. Kleidung
3. Sport
4. Schule
5. Körper
6. Kleidung
7. Körper
8. Schule
9. Körper
10. Sport
11. Schule
12. Sport
13. Kleidung
14. Körper
15. Schule

21. Etwas Persönliches.

1. Welche Sportart treibst du?
2. Welche Sportart siehst du manchmal gern im Fernsehen?
3. Warum gefällt dir dieser Sport?
4. Welche Körperteile gebraucht man bei diesem Sport?
5. Was machst du außer Sport noch gern?
6. Welche Sportarten gibt es bei dir in der Schule?

22. *Alexander spielt gern Basketball.* Complete each sentence with an appropriate verb form from the list.

stehen	machen	werden	liegen
spielen	gehen	beginnen	müssen
sein	trainieren		

Alexander _____ auf ein Gymnasium in Göttingen. Diese Stadt _____ in Norddeutschland. Alexander _____ sehr sportlich. Er _____ zwei oder drei Tage jede Woche. Im Herbst _____ er in einer Jugendmannschaft Basketball. Im Frühling _____ er in einer Tennismannschaft mit. Seine Mannschaft _____ an erster Stelle. Er _____ noch ein Spiel gegen Duderstadt spielen. Hoffentlich _____ seine Mannschaft gewinnen. Das Basketballspiel _____ am Sonnabend um zwei Uhr.

geht, liegt, ist, trainiert, spielt, macht, steht, muss, wird, beginnt

23. *Was ist dein Lieblingssport?* Describe your favorite sport in one or two paragraphs. Your description might include such details as: When do you participate (time of year)? Where and how often do you practice? With whom do you play? How often does your team participate?

Ibrahim spricht mit seinem Tr...

24. Ergänze die folgenden Sätze!

1. Susanne kauft _____ ein Geschenk.
2. Hilfst du _____ bei der Arbeit?
3. Nach _____ muss ich nach Hause.
4. Sprich doch mit _____!
5. Um wie viel Uhr kommst du aus _____?
6. Wir kommen mit _____ zur Disko.
7. Das Kleid steht _____ sehr gut.
8. Wann schickst du _____ einen Brief?

Sample answers:
1. ihrem Freund
2. deinem Vater
3. der Disko
4. deiner Mutter
5. dem Kino
6. den Schulfreunden
7. meiner Freundin
8. der Lehrerin

25. *Wie sagt man's?* From the list below, select appropriate words to complete the conversational exchanges.

muss	schaffe	mähen	brauchen	glaube
gehe	spielen	treibst	trainiert	kaufe
machst	hast	ist	bleibt	

1. Was ____ du im Sommer?
   Wir fahren mit den Rädern nach Österreich.
   Wie lange ____ ihr denn dort?
   Bestimmt zwei Wochen.

2. Welche Sportart ____ du denn?
   Ich spiele gern Golf.
   Ist der Sport nicht teuer?
   Nicht für mich. Ich ____ oft mit meinem Vater. Der bezahlt.

3. Wie weit ____ der Fußballplatz denn von hier?
   Bestimmt noch fünf Kilometer.
   Das ____ ich nicht.
   Na, mit dem Rad ist es doch nicht schwer.

4. Am Sonntag ____ wir gegen die beste Mannschaft.
   Viel Glück!
   Das ____ wir auch. Unsere Mannschaft ist nicht sehr gut.
   Das ____ ich nicht. Du bist doch ein guter Spieler.
   Das schon, aber wir brauchen elf gute Spieler.

5. Um wie viel Uhr ____ ihr heute?
   Wie immer, um vier. Kommst du zum Fußballplatz?
   Nein, ich ____ meinem Vater helfen.
   Was musst du denn machen?
   Ich soll den Rasen ____.

6. Gegen Rainer ____ du bestimmt keine Chance.
   Ist er denn so gut?
   Ja, er spielt schon seit vier Jahren Tennis.
   Ich ____ aber heute einen tollen Tennisschläger.
   Du brauchst mehr als einen guten Tennisschläger.

Gegen Bremen haben sie eine gute Chance.

Sport

26. *Ergänze diesen Dialog!* Complete the following dialog. You may use only one specific word in each space. The last letter for each possible word has been provided. The first letters of the completed words when read in sequence will tell you that you have correctly completed this dialog.

Disko, acht, spät, immer, schon, teuer, rufst, ich, charmant, heute, tanze, ich, gibt (**Das ist richtig**)

– Am Freitag gehen wir alle in die ____o.
– Um wie viel Uhr geht's denn los?
– Die Band spielt um ____t.
– Ist das nicht zu ____t?
– Die Musik beginnt ____r um diese Zeit. Wir werden ____n um halb acht da sein.
– Ist es denn sehr ____r?
– Nein, ganz preiswert, nur vier Mark für eine Karte.
– Gut. Ich komme auch. Wo ist das Telefon?
– Wen ____t du denn an?
– Zuerst möchte ____h mit Katrin sprechen. Sie ist so ____t.
– Ich glaube, ____e Nachmittag ist sie zu Hause.
– Ich ____e gern mit ihr, besonders wenn die Band langsame Musik spielt.
– Und mit wem soll ____h zur Disko kommen?
– Es ____t doch viele nette Schulfreundinnen. Bestimmt kennst du eine.

 **WB** Activity 16

 **WA** Activity 12

 S Activity 7

 OP

TP

VP

Was weißt du?

1. Describe a sport you are participating in or that you like to follow on TV or in a newspaper. Your description should include the name of the sport, some observations on how the sport is played, and when (during the year) the sport is played.

2. *Sport in Deutschland und in den USA.* List at least four differences or similarities between sports in Germany and those commonly played in the United States. *Auf Englisch!*

3. *Was machst du gern?* Write a paragraph about one or two activities that you like. List the activity/activities and give reasons why you like it/them.

4. *Körperteile.* Describe the following parts of the body: *der Mund, der Fuß, das Auge, das Ohr, die Hand.*

5. *Welcher Sport ist an deiner Schule sehr beliebt?* Explain which sport is popular at your school. Give as much information and insight as possible.

Vokabeln

abgeben to pass (ball)
der **Arm,-e** arm
das **Auge,-n** eye
außer except
das **Backgammon** backgammon
der **Ball,̈-e** ball
die **Ballkontrolle** ball control
basteln to do (handi)crafts
bei with, at, near, by
das **Bein,-e** leg
die **Bundesliga** National League
die **Chance,-n** chance
dort there
einmal once; *einmal die Woche* once a week
das **Eishockey** ice hockey
der **Fan,-s** fan
der **Finger,-** finger
die **Form,-en** form, shape
der **Fuß,̈-e** foot
der **Fußballplatz,̈-e** soccer field
der **Fußballspieler,-** soccer player
gebrauchen to use, make use of
genug enough
das **Golf** golf
das **Haar,-e** hair
die **Halbzeit** halftime
der **Hals,̈-e** neck
die **Hand,̈-e** hand
hart hard
der **Held,-en** hero
hoch high
jubeln to cheer
die **Jugendmannschaft,-en** youth team
die **Karriere,-n** career

das **Kinn,-e** chin
klasse super, great, terrific
der **Klub,-s** club
koordiniert coordinated
der **Körperteil,-e** part of body
die **Liga, Ligen** league
die **Lippe,-n** lip
locker loose
los: *Da ist viel los.* There is a lot going on.
machen: *Das macht nichts.* That doesn't matter.
manche some, a few
die **Mannschaft,-en** team
meins mine
meistens mostly
der **Meister,-** champion; *Deutscher Meister* National Champion of Germany
mitmachen to participate
der **Mund,̈-er** mouth
die **Nase,-n** nose
das **Netz,-e** net
das **Ohr,-en** ear
das **Rad,̈-er** bike; *Rad fahren* to bike
reden to talk, speak
schaffen to manage (it), make (it); *Das schaffen wir.* We'll make it.
schießen to shoot
Schlittschuh laufen to ice skate
schreien to scream
die **Schulter,-n** shoulder
sehen to see; *Sieh mal!* Look!

das **Spiel,-e** game
die **Sportart,-en** kind of sport
der **Sportklub,-s** sports club
sportlich athletic, sporty
der **Star,-s** star (athlete)
stehen to stand, be; *Die Mannschaft steht an zweiter Stelle.* The team is in second place. *Es steht...* The score is...
steif stiff
die **Stelle,-n** place, spot; *Die Mannschaft steht an zweiter Stelle.* The team is in second place.
die **Stirn,-en** forehead
das **Tempo** tempo, speed
der **Tennisplatz,̈-e** tennis court
der **Tennisschläger,-** tennis racket
das **Tennisspiel,-e** tennis game
der **Tip,-s** tip, hint, suggestion
das **Tischtennis** table tennis
das **Tor,-e** goal; *aufs Tor schießen* to shoot on goal
der **Trainer,-** trainer, coach
trainieren to train
treiben to do; *Sport treiben* to participate in sports
üben to practice; *zum Üben* for practice
der **Volleyball** volleyball
der **Vorteil,-e** advantage
wandern to hike
der **Zahn,̈-e** tooth
zurück back
zusammenkommen to get together

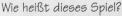

Wie heißt dieses Spiel?

Der Trainer gibt seiner Mannschaft Tips.

Kapitel **11**

Reisen

In this chapter you will be able to:

- talk about traveling
- ask for and give directions
- identify important places in a city
- describe a trip
- ask for information

Wohin geht's denn?

Nach Süddeutschland.

Wohin reisen sie?

Katharina: Was machst du denn hier?

Laura: Ich baue das Zelt auf. Mein Vater hat das Zelt für unsere Reise gekauft.

Katharina: Wohin geht's denn?

Laura: Nach Süddeutschland. Wir haben schon letztes Jahr eine Reise dorthin gemacht.

Katharina: Wie lange bleibt ihr dort?

Laura: Eine Woche auf einem Campingplatz in der Nähe von München. Dann besuchen wir noch eine Woche meine Tante in Regensburg.

Laura wird das Zelt aufbauen.

1. *Die richtige Antwort.* **Select the appropriate response for each question.**

1c, 2f, 3d, 4g, 5a, 6e

1. Wo bleibt ihr denn?
2. Wohin geht's?
3. Wen besuchst du auf deiner Reise?
4. Was baust du da auf?
5. Wie lange bist du auf deiner Reise?
6. Wer hat das Zelt gekauft?

a. Zwei Wochen.
b. Eine Reise nach Regensburg.
c. Auf einem Campingplatz.
d. Meine Tante.

e. Mein Vater.
f. Nach Köln.
g. Unser Zelt.

Vater: Das hat wirklich nicht lange gedauert.

Laura: Ja, Katharina und ich haben beide an dem Zelt gearbeitet.

Vater: Jetzt weißt du wenigstens, wie man das Zelt aufbaut.

Laura: Es ist ja auch ganz einfach. Haben wir für alles im Auto Platz?

Vater: Zu viel Gepäck können wir nicht mitnehmen.

Laura: Das brauchen wir auch gar nicht.

Das hat wirklich nicht lange gedauert.

Jetzt weißt du wenigstens, wie man das Zelt aufbaut.

2. Was fehlt hier?

1. Im Auto ____ für alles Platz.
2. Ich ____, wie viel Uhr es ist.
3. Es ____ lange gedauert.
4. Ihr könnt viel Gepäck ____.
5. Weißt du, wie man das Zelt ____?
6. Habt ihr lange an dem Zelt ____?

1. ist
2. weiß
3. hat
4. mitnehmen
5. aufbaut
6. gearbeitet

Katharina spricht mit ihrer Freundin Laura über die Reise.

Katharina: Hast du schon gepackt?

Laura: Klar. Morgen geht's früh um sieben los.

Katharina: Wir fahren auch in die Ferien — aber erst nächste Woche.

Laura: Fahrt ihr wieder zur Ostsee?

Katharina: Ja, zum Timmendorfer Strand. Dieses Jahr lassen wir unser Auto zu Hause. Wir fahren lieber mit dem Zug.

Laura: Na, dann viel Spaß!

Katharina: Danke, gleichfalls.

AC/CD

WB Activity 1

WA Activity 1

OT Activity 64

Reisen

329

3. *Falsch!* **The following statements are incorrect. Provide the correct statements in German.**

   1. Laura fährt zur Ostsee.
   2. Katharinas Familie wird mit dem Auto fahren.
   3. Katharina hat schon gepackt.
   4. Laura fährt nächstes Jahr in die Ferien.
   5. Lauras Familie fährt spät am Abend los.

4. **Beantworte diese Fragen!**

   1. Was baut Laura auf?
   2. Wohin fahren Laura und ihre Familie?
   3. Wie viele Tage bleiben sie auf einem Campingplatz?
   4. Was machen sie dann?
   5. Wer hat alles an dem Zelt gearbeitet?
   6. Was sollen sie nicht mitnehmen?
   7. Um wie viel Uhr wird Laura mit ihrer Familie in die Ferien fahren?
   8. Wann fährt Katharina in die Ferien?
   9. Wohin wird sie fahren?
   10. Fährt Katharinas Familie mit dem Auto?

Sprichwort

Er guckt wie ein Auto.

(He is flabbergasted.)

Für dich

Camping has been popular in Germany for many years. Millions of people spend their vacation in tents, campers or recreational vehicles (RVs) on the many campgrounds found throughout the country. The *DCC-Campingführer* is the official guide of the *Deutscher Camping-Club*, listing more than 7,000 camping grounds in 33 countries. Highly recommended camping sites are marked with the symbol of the *Deutscher Camping-Club*, a tent that resembles a tepee which is enclosed in a capital "C."

The guide furnishes a wealth of information such as fees, sanitary facilities, food service, swimming and fishing opportunities, special sights, description of the area and directions on how to get there.

WB   Activity 2

Rollenspiel

You have decided to go on a bike or camping tour with a classmate. Try to convince your classmate to come along. Discuss when, where and how long you would be gone, if anyone else is coming along, what clothing and other items to pack and any other matters that need to be taken care of prior to departure. When you are finished, reverse roles and have your classmate invite you to come along on a real or imaginary trip.

Aktuelles

Der Bahnhof

Traveling by train in Germany can be rewarding or frustrating for the foreign traveler. If you're well prepared, however, you won't have any problems going on this new and exciting adventure. When traveling between major cities, look for the main railroad station (*Hauptbahnhof*), usually located in the heart of the city. Should you be in a small town, simply ask for the *Bahnhof*.

Upon entering a train station, become familiar with the facilities. If you need information about a specific train,

Hauptbahnhof in Leipzig

Reisen

Viele Leute sind jeden Tag auf dem Hamburger Hauptbahnhof.

look for the schedules usually posted in a prominent location. There are normally two such schedules. One is marked *Abfahrt* (departure), the other *Ankunft* (arrival). The first schedule gives destinations, times of departure and other valuable information. In case you want to learn about these details in more privacy and at your leisure, you should look for the information office, marked either *Reiseauskunft* or *Information*.

The major stations have installed large overhead departure schedules that indicate the departure time, type of train, destination and other information such as possible transfers. If you are in a hurry or need speedy personal attention, look for an official wearing a uniform. The official usually has a detailed train schedule and will have an answer to your questions at his or her fingertips.

The facilities at train stations are generally well marked. Know the German names and you'll have no difficulty finding your way around. Buy your ticket at any window or counter (*Schalter*) marked *Fahrkarten*. Let's assume you want to travel to Frankfurt. To ask for a ticket simply say to the clerk, *Nach Frankfurt, bitte*. If your ticket is to be one-way, add the word *einfach*, which means literally "simple." If you want a round-trip ticket, say *hin und zurück*, which means "there and back."

Um wie viel Uhr fahren die Züge von München ab?

Man kann bei einem Imbiss schnell etwas essen.

After you have purchased your ticket, you may decide to check your luggage instead of taking it directly to the train. Look for a sign marked *Reisegepäck-Annahme*. Most travelers, however, prefer to take their luggage with them on the train. To check your luggage temporarily until departure, you should look for coin-operated lockers marked *Schließfächer*.

Most stations, large or small, have some eating facilities. In major stations you may find the words *Cafeteria* and *Restaurant*. If you don't want to sit down at a table, try to locate a snack bar (*Imbiss*) that offers hot dogs, cold sandwiches and beverages. Those who would like to take some of the delicious German chocolates or candies on their trip can buy these goodies at specialty stands. Would you like to read some newspapers, magazines or books? Look for a stand marked *Zeitungen-Bücher*. Germans rarely go to visit friends or relatives in other towns without taking along a small gift, such as candies *(Bonbons)* or more typically flowers *(Blumen)*. It is quite common to find flower shops at the train station.

If you have little luggage to carry, you won't have any problems taking it directly to the train. However, if you have more luggage than you can carry easily, look for a luggage cart marked *Koffer-Kuli*. You can place your luggage on the cart and wheel it right to the train. In most cities, there is no charge for the use of these carts. Be sure to give yourself plenty of time to get to the train. The trains of the German Rail *(Deutsche Bahn)*—often marked with the initials *DB*—are punctual and won't wait for you.

Wie viel kannst du verstehen? Auf Deutsch, bitte!

1. Ich weiß nicht, um wie viel Uhr der Zug fährt. Ich frage in der ____.
2. Wenn man zu viel Gepäck hat und es zum Zug mitnehmen will, dann braucht man einen ____.
3. Regina will wissen, wann ihr Freund ankommt. Sie findet diese Information auf einem Plan. Da steht ganz klar das Wort ____.
4. Herr und Frau Wiesmann haben viel Gepäck und möchten es nicht zum Zug mitnehmen. Deshalb gehen sie zur ____.
5. Züge kommen in kleinen Städten auf einem ____ an.
6. Torsten besucht seinen Vater in Magdeburg. Sein Vater wird ihn wieder nach Hause fahren. Torsten sagt am Schalter: „Nach Magdeburg, bitte, ____.“
7. Wenn man mit dem Zug fahren will, braucht man eine ____.
8. Katrina besucht ihre Kusine Sophie in Dresden. Sie bringt ihr ein paar ____ mit. Die schmecken immer gut. Katrina weiß auch, dass Sophie die gern isst.
9. Wenn die Leute ein Wurstbrot im Stehen essen wollen, dann bekommen sie es bei einem ____.
10. Die Züge in Deutschland gehören zur *Deutschen* ____.

1. *Reiseauskunft/Information*
2. *Koffer-Kuli*
3. *Ankunft*
4. *Reisegepäck-Annahme*
5. *Bahnhof*
6. *einfach*
7. *Fahrkarte*
8. *Bonbons*
9. *Imbiss*
10. *Bahn*

WB Activity 3

Ergänzung

Verkehrsmittel — das Schiff — das Flugzeug — das Boot — der Zug — die Straßenbahn — der Bus — das Moped — das Fahrrad — das Auto — das Motorrad

Have students ask each other this question: *Wie kommst du zur Schule?* (mit dem Bus, Auto, Fahrrad, zu Fuß).

Wie kommen sie nach Berlin?	Peter fährt mit dem Auto. Ich fahre mit dem Zug. Heidi fliegt mit dem Flugzeug
Gehst du zu Fuß in die Stadt? Und du?	Nein, ich fahre mit dem Fahrrad. Ich fahre lieber mit meinem Moped.
Fährst du mit dem Schiff nach Europa?	Nein, ich fliege.
Was machst du auf dem See?	Ich fahre mit dem Boot.

 WB Activities 4-5

 LA Activity 1

 WA Activities 2-4

 OT Activities 65-66

 S Activity 2

5. Wie kann Monika nach Bremen kommen?

◆ Fahrrad
◆ Mit dem Fahrrad.

1. Bus

2. Zug

1. Mit dem Bus.
2. Mit dem Zug.
3. Mit dem Motorrad.
4. Mit dem Schiff.
5. Mit dem Auto.
6. Mit dem Moped.

3. Motorrad

4. Schiff

5. Auto

6. Moped

6. *Wie kommt man am besten dorthin?* **Select the most appropriate phrase for each situation described. Use only one of these phrases:** *zu Fuß, mit dem Schiff, mit dem Auto, mit dem Flugzeug.*

1. Lisa wohnt in Washington und will im Sommer nach München reisen.

2. Herr Schmidt geht gern zum Eiscafé Milano. Es ist nur eine Ecke von seiner Wohnung.

3. Heiko und Günter wollen von New York nach England reisen. Die Reise dauert sechs Tage.

4. Tina bekommt zu ihrem Geburtstag nächste Woche bestimmt ein Fahrrad. Jeden Tag geht sie jetzt noch mit ihrer Freundin um halb acht in die Schule.

5. Krämers wollen im Winter mit der ganzen Familie in der Schweiz Ski laufen. Von Augsburg nach Garmisch-Partenkirchen sind es 130 Kilometer.

6. Die meisten Touristen fliegen nach Europa, aber manche wollen lieber eine längere Reise machen.

1. Mit dem Flugzeug.
2. Zu Fuß.
3. Mit dem Schiff.
4. Zu Fuß.
5. Mit dem Auto.
6. Mit dem Schiff.

Praktische Situation

Was nimmst du alles mit? Imagine that you and three other family members are going on a short vacation together this summer by car. Each family member (you, your father, mother, sister, brother, grandmother, etc.) lists 15 essential items to bring along. However, you are all traveling together in a very small car and space is at a premium. Next cut down to five items, write one important reason why each person should be permitted to take that specific item along. Then get together with the other three group members, each reading your list and giving your reasons. The group must reach a consensus on what five items each person is allowed to bring along. Once your final list has been completed, your group leader may want to read your group's list to other classmates to compare it with theirs.

AC/CD

Some additional expressions that your students may find useful in giving directions (not covered before) are: *an der Kreuzung links* (at the intersection to the left); *an der ersten Ampel rechts* (at the first light to the right); *mit dem Bus Nummer 23* (with Bus Number 23); *quer über die Straße* (across the street); *hinter dem Bahnhof links* (behind the station on the left); *direkt an der Hauptstraße* (right on the main street); *einfach diese Straße entlang* (simply down this road); *über die Brücke gehen* (go across the bridge) *in der Innenstadt* (downtown).

 WB Activity 6

 LA Activity 2

 OT Activity 67

Sag's mal!

Wo ist das Kaufhaus? Wie komme ich hin?

in der Innenstadt*

auf der rechten Seite

quer über die Straße*

einfach die Straße entlang*

nach links abbiegen

immer geradeaus

an der Kreuzung links*

an der ersten Ampel rechts*

die nächste Straße rechts

hinter dem Bahnhof links*

mit dem Bus Nummer 23*

direkt an der Hauptstraße*

die Straße geradeaus

zweite Straße rechts

über die Brücke gehen*

Sprache

Present Perfect Tense (Regular Verbs)

The present perfect is used more frequently in German conversation than in English. It is often called the „conversational past."

To simplify matters, weak verbs are labeled "regular verbs" and strong verbs appear as "irregular verbs."

◆ *haben* + (*ge* + *er/sie/es* verb form)

◆ *Er hat es gesagt.* He has said it.

In English, three forms (*He has said, He was saying* or *He said*) may be used. To simplify, only the present perfect form is used throughout.

The form *gesagt* (asked) is called the past participle, which in German is placed at the end of the sentence.

◆ *Ich habe ein Rad gekauft.* I bought a bike.

The regular verbs you have learned so far are:

arbeiten (to work)	**reden** (to talk, speak)
brauchen (to need)	**regnen** (to rain)
danken (to thank)	**reisen** (to travel)*
dauern (to last, take)	**sagen** (to say)
decken (to set [table])	**sammeln** (to collect)
feiern (to celebrate)	**schaffen** (to manage, make [it])
glauben (to believe)	**schenken** (to give a present)
hören (to hear)	**schicken** (to send)
jubeln (to cheer)	**schmecken** (to taste)
kaufen (to buy)	**schneien** (to snow)
kosten (to cost)	**spielen** (to play)
lachen (to laugh)	**spülen** (to wash, rinse)
lernen (to learn)	**tanzen** (to dance)
machen (to do, make)	**wandern** (to hike)*
mähen (to mow)	**warten** (to wait)
packen (to pack)	**wohnen** (to live)
passen (to fit)	**wünschen** (to wish)

* Note that the present perfect tense of *reisen* (*gereist*) and *wandern* (*gewandert*) take the forms of *sein* (*ich bin gereist/gewandert, du bist gereist/gewandert...*). See next chapter for more details about verbs dealing with motion.

The past participle of verbs with inseparable prefixes (like *be-*) is simply the *er, sie, es* form of the present tense. This is also true of verbs ending in *-ieren*.

◆ *Ich habe meine Freundin besucht.* I visited my girlfriend.

◆ *Was hast du denn fotografiert?* What did you take pictures of?

 Activities 7-8

 Activity 5

Activities 1 and 4

7. **Was hat Andrea alles am Wochenende gemacht?**

◆ viel Rockmusik hören
◆ Sie hat viel Rockmusik gehört.

1. in der Disko tanzen
2. ihren Freund besuchen
3. Karten für ein Konzert kaufen
4. den Rasen mähen
5. beim Fußballspiel fotografieren
6. ihrem Vater eine CD schenken
7. Hausaufgaben für Montag machen
8. mit Anna Tennis spielen

Group Activity: *Was hast du am Wochenende gemacht?* Distribute a sheet with about ten activities indicated and have students ask each other questions such as *Hast du die Hausaufgaben gemacht? Bist du auf einer Party gewesen?* When a student answers *ja*, he or she must sign the questioner's sheet. The ten signatures for the ten questions must all be different. The first student to have ten signatures wins.

8. **Kannst du beschreiben, was die Jugendlichen im Sommer gemacht haben?**

◆ Katharina / Laura besuchen
◆ Katharina hat Laura besucht.

1. Uli / zu Hause arbeiten
2. Susanne und Claudia / mit Freunden am Telefon reden
3. Ralf / mit seiner Mannschaft Fußball spielen
4. Maria / viele Briefmarken sammeln
5. Toni / oft den Rasen mähen
6. Herr und Frau Thiel / den Tisch zum Geburtstag decken

9. *Was passt hier?* **Complete the sentences using the proper past participle.**

kaufen	wohnen	spülen	schmecken
regnen	dauern	warten	passen

1. Habt ihr lange in der Schule ____?
2. Heute scheint die Sonne, aber am Wochenende hat es ____.
3. Haben Sie die Jeans ____?
4. Die Arbeit hat drei Stunden ____.
5. Das Kleid hat Monika nicht ____.
6. Ich habe das Geschirr ____.
7. Wie hat das Eis ____?
8. Frau Taukes Wohnung ist in der Schillerstraße. Früher hat sie in der Brandstraße ____.

10. Kombiniere...

Laura
Die Touristen
Kurt
Unsere Klasse
Meine Schulfreunde

haben
hat
ist
sind

heute
am Sonntag
morgen
früh
bis um elf

Augsburg besucht
eine Reise gemacht
in der Disko getanzt
ihr Gepäck gepackt
spät zu Hause

Ergänzung

Wie komme ich zur Stadtmitte?

Zu Fuß.

Zu Fuß oder mit dem Auto? Gehen Sie geradeaus bis zur Post. Dann biegen Sie rechts ab. Nach ungefähr zehn Minuten kommen Sie zum Bahnhof. Dann sind Sie in der Stadtmitte.

Wo ist das Kaufhaus, bitte?

Hier gleich um die Ecke auf der linken Seite.

Entschuldigen Sie! Können Sie mir sagen, wo die Post ist?

Nein, ich bin auch fremd hier. Vielleicht kann Ihnen der Herr Auskunft geben.

Ja, die Post ist ganz in der Nähe. Sehen Sie das Café links an der Ecke? Gehen Sie am Café und auch am Museum vorbei. An der nächsten Ecke sehen Sie ein Kaufhaus und neben dem Kaufhaus ist dann schon die Post.

AC/CD

Divide the class into several groups. Each student within a group will identify three different places (*Schule, Kino, Bahnhof,* etc.) and write his or her name with these places on a card to be distributed to others in the group. Students will ask each other how they get from one place to another. Example: *Robert, wie kommst du von zu Hause zur Schule?/Ich gehe zu Fuß. (Ich gehe geradeaus bis zum Kino, dann biege ich links ab.)* Continue this activity until all places have been discussed.

 WB Activity 9   WA Activities 6-7   S Activity 6

Reisen

11. *Wie komme ich dorthin?* Imagine that you are a tour guide in Germany and that you need to give directions to various people.

◆ Wie komme ich zum Kaufhaus? (hier nach links)
◆ Gehen Sie hier nach links.

1. Wie komme ich zur Post? (geradeaus)
2. Wie komme ich zum Museum? (zwei Ecken, dann nach rechts)
3. Wie komme ich zum Kaufhaus? (auf dieser Straße bis zum Bahnhof)
4. Wie komme ich zum Kino? (eine Ecke, dann links)
5. Wie komme ich zum Café? (immer geradeaus bis zur Kantstraße)

1. Gehen Sie geradeaus.
2. Gehen Sie zwei Ecken, dann nach rechts.
3. Gehen Sie auf dieser Straße bis zum Bahnhof.
4. Gehen Sie eine Ecke, dann links.
5. Gehen Sie immer geradeaus bis zur Kantstraße.

12. *Sprich mit einem Schulfreund, wie ihr beide von zu Hause zur Schule kommt. Dann schreib alles auf.* (Then write everything down.)

Sprache

Dative

Personal Pronouns

As you have already learned, the direct object (accusative) is the result of the action (verb) of the sentence, whereas the indirect object receives the action indirectly through the direct object.

	direct object	
Ich kaufe	eine Karte	
	indirect object	**direct object**
Ich kaufe	dem Freund	eine Karte

Now substitute a personal pronoun for the indirect object in the last sentence.

	indirect object	direct object
Ich kaufe	ihm	eine Karte

Notice that there is no change in word order, but simply a substitution of an indirect object pronoun. For review, the pronouns you have already learned are included in the following table.

♦ *Schenkst du deiner Schwester ein Paar Tennisschuhe?* Are you giving your sister a pair of tennis shoes?

♦ *Schenkst du ihr ein Paar Tennisschuhe?* Are you giving her a pair of tennis shoes?

 WB Activity 10

 WA Activity 8

 S Activity 5

Singular			Plural		
nominative	accusative	dative	nominative	accusative	dative
ich	mich	mir	wir	uns	uns
du	dich	dir	ihr	euch	euch
er	ihn	ihm	sie	sie	ihnen
sie	sie	ihr			
es	es	ihm	Sie (sg. & pl.)	Sie	Ihnen

13. *Was bringen sie alles zur Party?* **Everyone has agreed to bring a present to exchange. Tell what everyone is bringing, using the correct personal pronouns.**

AC/CD

♦ Alexander bringt Günter eine Kassette. Was bringt Alexander Günter?

♦ Er bringt ihm eine Kassette.

1. Natascha bringt Katrin ein Buch. Was bringt Natascha Katrin?
2. Wolfgang bringt Anne ein T-Shirt. Was bringt Wolfgang Anne?
3. Dieter bringt Jürgen einen Fußball. Was bringt Dieter Jürgen?
4. Susanne bringt Hans eine Kamera. Was bringt Susanne Hans?
5. Erika bringt Jens ein Fotoalbum. Was bringt Erika Jens?

1. Sie bringt ihr ein Buch.
2. Er bringt ihr ein T-Shirt.
3. Er bringt ihm einen Fußball.
4. Sie bringt ihm eine Kamera.
5. Sie bringt ihm ein Fotoalbum.

AC/CD

14. *Wem kauft ihr ein Geschenk?* **Indicate for whom you are buying a present.**

♦ deiner Oma
♦ Wir kaufen ihr ein Geschenk.

1. Rainer	4. meinem Freund
2. seiner Freundin	5. Gisela
3. Katrin und Peter	6. Herr und Frau Krause

1. Wir kaufen ihm ein Geschenk.
2. Wir kaufen ihr ein Geschenk.
3. Wir kaufen ihnen ein Geschenk.
4. Wir kaufen ihm ein Geschenk.
5. Wir kaufen ihr ein Geschenk.
6. Wir kaufen ihnen ein Geschenk.

Die Kleidungsstücke gefallen den Mädchen.

Reisen

15. *Wie geht es ihnen?* Ask how the various people are. Use the information provided in your responses.

◆ Wie geht es dem Peter? (sehr gut)
◆ Es geht ihm sehr gut.

1. Wie geht es der Regina? (nicht schlecht)
2. Wie geht es deiner Freundin? (ganz gut)
3. Wie geht es dem Alex? (super)
4. Wie geht es seinem Großvater? (besser)
5. Wie geht es Tina? (schlecht)

16. Change the italicized nouns into pronouns with their corresponding articles.

◆ Der Trainer spricht oft mit *den Spielern*.
◆ Der Trainer spricht oft mit ihnen.

1. Die Kleidungsstücke gefallen *den Mädchen*.
2. Monika kauft *ihrer Freundin* ein Geschenk.
3. Wir gehen mit *unserem Lehrer* ins Museum.
4. Kannst du *deiner Mutter* nicht helfen?
5. Gib *dem Ralf* doch den Fußball!
6. Wann fahren wir wieder zu *deiner Tante*?
7. Außer *den Jungen* kommen noch viele Mädchen.
8. Angelika wohnt im Sommer bei *ihrer Tante*.

Boris fährt mit seinem Freund Alex nach Salzburg.

Auf dem Bahnhof

Boris und Alex haben vor, eine Reise nach Salzburg zu machen. Stefan, ein Cousin von Boris, wohnt da. Stefan hat im letzten Jahr Boris in Bremen besucht. Dieses Jahr sollen Boris und sein Freund den Stefan zehn Tage lang besuchen. Gestern° haben Boris und Alex alles gepackt. Der Zug wird schon um zehn Uhr abfahren°.

Vor dem Bahnhof sehen sie noch schnell auf den Fahrplan°. Da lesen sie, wann und auf welchem Gleis° der Zug abfährt. Da steht auch noch, dass sie in München umsteigen° müssen.

Boris und Alex sprechen über ihre Reise.

Boris: Wir kommen erst um 16 Uhr 20 in München an.

Alex: Ich bin froh, dass wir da nicht lange warten müssen, nur fünfzehn Minuten.

Boris: Die Reise von München nach Salzburg dauert nur eine Stunde und zwanzig Minuten.

Alex: Kommt Stefan zum Bahnhof?

Boris: Bestimmt! Er wohnt nicht in der Stadt und zu seinem Haus ist es mit dem Bus zu weit.

Alex: Komm! Wir müssen noch Fahrkarten° kaufen.

Boris: Da drüben ist ein Schalter° frei°.

Alex und Boris gehen zu dem Schalter. Dort kauft jeder seine Fahrkarte mit der Bahn-Card°. Die Fahrkarte ist dann viel preiswerter. Auf einer großen Tafel steht genau, wann und wo alle Züge abfahren. Da lesen sie auch, dass der Zug nach München von Gleis 4 abfährt.

Alex und Boris gehen zu dem Schalter.

After students are familiar with the text, have them write a description about a future or past trip. If they haven't gone or are not planning to go anywhere, have them describe an imaginary trip. Select some of the narratives to be read by individual students. You may also want to put them up on a board with the heading *Reisepläne*.

The German Railroad (*Deutsche Bahn*) periodically introduces special fares in order to entice Germans to travel by train. The *Bahn-Card* is a personal ID card, purchased for one year, to qualify for half-priced tickets.

Was essen und trinken sie?

Alex: Ich habe Hunger. Willst du etwas essen?

Boris: Nein, danke. Vielleicht trinke ich eine Fanta.

Alex: Da ist ein Imbiss°. Mal sehen°, was die da haben.

Boris: Die Auswahl ist nicht sehr groß.

Alex: Ein Würstchen° schmeckt mir immer.

Boris: Stefan hat mir letzten Monat einen Brief geschickt. Er hat jetzt eine Freundin. Die geht auch in seine Schule.

Alex: Wie alt ist sie denn?

Boris: Sechzehn, genauso alt wie° Stefan.

Alex: Dann wird er bestimmt für uns keine Zeit haben.

Boris: Doch°. Seine Freundin ist diesen Monat mit ihren Eltern in Italien. Sie kommt erst in drei Wochen wieder zurück°.

Alex: Na, dann haben wir kein Problem.

Beide gehen jetzt langsam zum Gleis 4. Der Zug steht schon da. Ihre Fahrkarten sind für Zweite Klasse. Sie gehen von einem Wagen zum anderen°. Viele Leute sind schon im Zug. Boris und Alex finden endlich in einem Abteil° Platz°. Es dauert nur ein paar Minuten, bis der Zug abfährt. Erst jetzt beginnen ihre Ferien.

Was steht auf dem Fahrplan?

WB Activities 11-12

LA Activity 3

WA Activities 9-11

Der Zug steht schon da.

gestern yesterday; *abfahren* to depart; *der Fahrplan* schedule; *das Gleis* track; *umsteigen* to transfer; *die Fahrkarte* ticket; *der Schalter* counter; *frei* available; *die Bahn-Card* reduces the price of the train ticket; *der Imbiss* snack bar; *Mal sehen...* Let's see...; *das Würstchen* hot dog; *genauso...wie* just as; *doch* oh yes; *zurückkommen* to come back; *von einem Wagen zum anderen* from one coach to the next; *das Abteil* compartment; *der Platz* seat

17. *Identifiziere die Wörter!* **Identify the words that are described from the list below.**

Hunger	Abteile	Zug	Fahrkarte
Platz	Gleis	Minuten	Ferien
Probleme	Bahnhof	Imbiss	Fahrplan

1. Wenn alles gut geht, dann hat man wirklich keine ____.
2. Auf einem Fahrplan steht, von welchem ____ der Zug abfährt.
3. Die Reise von Hamburg nach Köln dauert vier Stunden. Da will man nicht stehen. Deshalb ist man froh, wenn man einen ____ findet.
4. An einem ____ kann man eine Cola trinken und ein Käsebrot essen.
5. Petra wartet auf dem Bahnhof. Der ____ soll um 4 Uhr 20 aus Stuttgart ankommen.
6. Familie Hoffmann wird am Wochenende in die ____ fahren.
7. Wenn man mit dem Zug fährt, dann braucht man eine ____.
8. Auf einem ____ gibt es Gleise.
9. Ich habe ____. Deshalb möchte ich jetzt etwas essen.
10. Die Touristen sehen auf den ____. Da steht, um wie viel Uhr die Züge ankommen und abfahren.
11. In zehn ____ fährt der Zug nach Hamburg ab.
12. Jeder Wagen hat ein paar ____.

18. **Beantworte diese Fragen!**

1. Warum fahren Alex und Boris nach Salzburg?
2. Wie lange bleiben sie da?
3. Wie kommen sie dorthin?
4. Warum fahren sie nach München?
5. Um wie viel Uhr fährt der Zug von München nach Salzburg?
6. Wann kommen sie in Salzburg an?
7. Was machen beide an einem Schalter?
8. Was steht auf einer Tafel?
9. Was machen Alex und Boris am Imbiss?
10. Wie alt ist Stefan?
11. Wo ist Stefans Freundin diesen Monat?
12. Müssen Alex und Boris auf den Zug warten?

AC/CD

Übung macht den Meister!

1. *Wir fahren mit dem Zug.* Create your own dialog by using the following information as a guideline. Be as creative as possible.

   You and your friend have arrived at the railroad station one hour before your train is leaving. You have plenty of time. You suggest to your friend that you check the departure time on the schedule board. It shows that the train will depart ten minutes late. Both of you go to the ticket window to buy your tickets. You tell the official that you're buying two second-class tickets to Nürnberg. He or she tells you the cost. Since you have plenty of time, you suggest to your friend that you go to the snack bar and have something to eat and drink.

2. Imagine yourself in the center of a German city giving directions to travelers who need your assistance. Can you come up with different directions for these questions?

   a. *Können Sie mir bitte sagen, wie ich zum Bahnhof komme?*

   b. *Wo gibt es hier ein Café?*

   c. *Wie komme ich von hier zum Rathaus?*

   d. *Ist die Post hier in der Nähe?*

   e. *Wie weit ist das Kaufhaus von hier?*

3. *Wir fahren in die Ferien.* Develop a short narrative or dialog, including the following details.

Your friend is planning a trip. Find out if your friend is going by car or train...when he or she is leaving...where your friend is going...how far it is...what your friend will see there...when he or she will come back.

4. *Können Sie das lesen?* Imagine that while studying the train schedule, an elderly gentleman comes up to you and asks for your help; he has difficulty reading the small print on the *Ankunft* (arrival) schedule. Can you help him out? Here are some of the questions you may have to respond to.

Mann: Können Sie das lesen?

Du: _____

Mann: Meine Enkelin kommt heute aus Münster hier an.

Du: _____

Mann: Nein, sie muss in Düsseldorf umsteigen.

Du: _____

Mann: Ich glaube, der Zug kommt etwas später. Es ist vielleicht der nächste Zug.

Du: _____

Mann: Ja. Es ist ein Intercity.

Du: _____

Mann: Vielen Dank.

Du: _____

Paired Activity: Have students complete the dialog with varied responses. Reverse roles.

Aktuelles

Traveling by Train

The German railway is a quick and reliable means of transportation. Over 30,000 trains crisscross Germany every day. The trains are comfortably equipped and fully air-conditioned.

If you have a reserved seat, you can look at a chart located at your designated track or platform (*Gleis* or *Bahnsteig*) to determine exactly where your train car or coach will stop. This assures you that you won't have to walk much farther once the train arrives and you're ready to get on.

Standard train tickets are valid for one day for distances up to 100 kilometers. For longer distances, a single ticket is valid for four days and a return ticket for one month. Tickets for single and

Was steht schon am Bahnsteig?

Reisen

return trips for distances of 51 kilometers or more are valid on any train, without payment of any supplement. International tickets are valid for two months and a trip may be broken up as often and as long as is desired within that period.

Most Germans travel second class *(Zweite Klasse)*. The second-class sections usually have vinyl seats; they're not luxurious, but fairly comfortable. First-class seats *(Erste Klasse)* are more plush and rather expensive. These accommodations are recommended only if you want to assure yourself of a seat during rush hour if you did not reserve a seat in advance. If you're not sure, you can purchase a second-class ticket and pay the difference after you have boarded the train. Check also to determine whether your car is a *Raucher* (smoking) or a *Nichtraucher* (nonsmoking). Most trains have specially designated cars.

Im ICE gibt's ein Restaurant.

Shortly before departure there will be the final call over the loudspeaker and a warning that the train is ready to depart. Once the train has left the station, you can relax and examine your surroundings. You will find the compartment and the other facilities quite comfortable. Remember, most Germans travel by train and not by plane as in the United States. Therefore, special care is taken to ensure a pleasant environment on trains. If you don't want to bring your own sandwiches, you can have a warm or cold meal in the train car labeled *Restaurant*. Don't be surprised if someone else sits down at your table after asking you *Ist hier noch frei?* This is quite common here and in most German restaurants.

If you want to take a nap, even second-class seats are probably adjustable. They are always adjustable in first-class. On a longer trip, you can reserve sleeping quarters in the *Schlafwagen* (sleeper) or in a *Liegewagen* (couchette) for an additional fee.

Some of the long-distance trains have very modern facilities such as a conference room, a playroom for small children and even a party car called *Gesellschaftswagen* where social functions can be arranged.

The most frequently used train in Germany is the *Intercity (IC)*, which links more than 100 German cities and runs at one-hour intervals between 7 A.M. and 11 P.M. *Intercity* trains that travel beyond the German border are called *Eurocity (EC)*. The various stops are usually posted on some of the cars outside. These *Intercity* trains never stop in small towns. A supplement of six marks is required for travel in the fast and luxurious *Eurocity* and *Intercity* trains. This fee includes a seat reservation *(Platzkarte)*.

Zu den
Gleisen

Information

WC

BAHNHOFS
MISSION

Faced with unrelenting competition from other means of transportation—cars, ships, airplanes—the *Deutsche Bahn* has streamlined and modernized operations. The fastest and most modern train in Germany today is the *Intercity Express (ICE)* which is 1,300 feet long. The *ICE* can cover the distance from Munich to Frankfurt in three hours, with a speed of 150 miles an hour on some sections of its route. This supermodern train has an aerodynamic design and provides travelers with every imaginable comfort. The high-tech *ICE* offers travelers telephones, fax machines, fully equipped offices, videos, audio connections for three radio stations and three preprogrammed audio programs as well as a 40-seat restaurant.

Travelers on the *ICE* have a choice between a standard compartment and open-seating coaches with seats in rows or facing each other. Large tables are fitted between the seats—to work on or, perhaps, play games to pass the time. For passengers who are physically disabled, there is a second-class coach providing wheelchair access.

For business people traveling relatively short distances, the *ICE* and the *IC* trains are very practical and convenient. From downtown locations it is always quicker to get to the main railway station (traditionally in the center of the city) than to the nearest airport.

And, finally, should you fly in or out of Frankfurt—coming from or going to the area around Köln or Stuttgart—Lufthansa, the German airlines, will transport you to your final destination in their Airport Express.

Give five reasons why or why not train travel would or would not be beneficial to you.

Der ICE fährt sehr schnell.

 WB Activity 13

 S Activity 3

Erweiterung

 AC/CD

19. *Bitte schön?* **Pretend to be an official at a railroad station answering questions for tourists who are not familiar with the station or the German train system.**

1. Wo ist der Zug nach Bonn, bitte?
2. Haben Sie einen Fahrplan?
3. Wie lange dauert die Reise nach Bremen?
4. Um wie viel Uhr kommt der Zug aus Österreich an?
5. Wo ist Gleis acht, bitte?
6. Was ist die Entfernung von hier nach Stuttgart?
7. Wann fährt der Zug nach Berlin ab?
8. Wissen Sie, wie viel Uhr es ist?

 WB Activities 14-18

20. ***Wie sagt man's?*** **From the list below, select the appropriate words to complete the various conversational exchanges.**

dauert	Spaß	teuer	Mark	Auswahl
schwimmen	zwanzig	dorthin	Fahrkarte	drüben
stimmt	Hunger	viel	habe	dunkel
Zelt	los	fahrt		

1. Wann kommt der Zug?
   In ____ Minuten.
   Gut, dann ____ ich noch Zeit.
   Ja, das ____.

2. Ja, bitte?
   Eine ____ nach München, bitte.
   Die kostet 55 ____.
   Das ist aber sehr ____.

Wann fährt der Zug ab?

3. Warum ____ ihr wieder zur Ostsee?
   Wir haben letztes Jahr eine tolle Reise ____ gemacht.
   Ist es da im Mai nicht etwas kühl?
   Das stimmt. Wir werden nicht in der Ostsee ____. Das Wasser ist natürlich viel zu kalt.

4. Wann baut ihr denn das ____ auf?
   Wir haben noch ____ Zeit.
   In zwei Stunden wird es aber schon ____ sein.
   Es dauert doch gar nicht so lange.

5. Morgen geht's schon früh ____.
   Warum fahrt ihr nicht etwas später?
   Unsere Reise ____ acht Stunden und wir wollen nicht erst am Abend ankommen.
   Na, dann viel ____!

6. Hast du auch ____?
   Ja, da ____ ist ein Imbiss.
   Die haben wirklich eine gute ____.
   Da hast du recht.

Haben Sie Hunger?

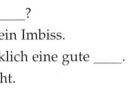

Kapitel 11

21. *Beende diese Sätze!* **Complete these sentences with an appropriate past participle.**

◆ Wem hast du die Ohrringe ____? Meiner Schwester.
◆ Wem hast du die Ohrringe geschenkt. Meiner Schwester.

1. Was habt ihr gestern ____? Wir haben Fußball gespielt.

2. Hat es am Wochenende ____? Nein, es hat geschneit.

3. Katrins Pulli steht ihr gut. Sie hat den heute Morgen im Kaufhaus ____.

4. Wie lange hat eure Reise denn ____? Sechs Stunden.

5. Ich habe Bernd einen Brief ____. Wo wohnt er denn jetzt?

6. Warum hast du den Tisch noch nicht ____? Meine Freunde kommen doch erst um halb sieben.

7. Wir haben bis spät am Abend in der Disko ____. Das hat bestimmt viel Spaß gemacht.

8. Haben Sie schon lange auf den Bus ____? Nein, nur ein paar Minuten.

22. **Etwas Persönliches.**

1. Hast du im letzten Jahr eine Reise gemacht? Wohin?

2. Wohin fährst du gern in die Ferien? Warum?

3. Wie kommst du jeden Tag zur Schule?

4. Wo wohnt dein Freund oder deine Freundin?

5. Wie kommst du von deinem Haus oder deiner Wohnung zum nächsten Kaufhaus?

6. Gibt es in deiner Nähe einen Imbiss? Was kannst du da kaufen?

AC/CD

23. **Provide the proper personal pronouns for the italicized words.**

◆ Ich habe *meiner Freundin* ein Buch geschenkt.
◆ Ich habe ihr ein Buch geschenkt.

1. Seine Freunde bringen *Birgit* ein Geschenk mit.

2. Wir haben *Peters Eltern* eine Karte geschickt.

3. Was hast du *deinem Vater* gesagt?

4. Ich kaufe *seiner Schwester* ein Computerspiel.

5. Warum schenken wir *unserem Lehrer* nicht die CD?

6. Wie geht es *ihrem Großvater*?

AC/CD

24. *Beschreibe jedes Wort.* **Describe each word with a sentence.** *Auf Deutsch, bitte!*

1. Bahnhof
2. Campingplatz
3. Kaufhaus
4. Post
5. Café
6. Schalter
7. Fahrrad
8. Flugzeug

Viele Fahrräder stehen vor dem Hauptbahnhof in Göttingen.

Was weißt du?

1. *Was machst du vor einer Reise?* Describe some of the steps you need to take before going on a trip.

2. *Was gibt's alles auf einem Bahnhof?* Select three items or facilities found at a German railroad station and say at least two sentences about each one.

3. *Wer gebraucht diese?* Select four means of transportation and indicate who among your friends or relatives uses each one and why.

4. *Ich weiß, wie man dorthin kommt.* Pick a place (café, school, post office, etc.) and describe how you get there from your home.

5. *Wen besuchst du?* Imagine that you are planning to visit someone during the summer. Write a short description including such details as whom you are visiting, when you are going, how you get there, how long you will stay and what you will do there.

Was machen die Leute vor der Reise?

Der Zug kommt in ein paar Minuten.

Vokabeln

abbiegen to turn (to)
abfahren to depart, leave
das **Abteil,-e** compartment
alles all, everything
arbeiten to work
aufbauen to pitch (tent), set up, construct
die **Auskunft,-̈e** information
das **Auto,-s** car
die **Bahn-Card,-s** discount and ID card for reduced train ticket
das **Boot,-e** boat
das **Café,-s** café
der **Campingplatz,-̈e** campground
doch sure thing, oh yes
dorthin (to) there
einfach simple
entschuldigen: **Entschuldigen Sie!** Excuse me!
die **Fahrkarte,-n** ticket
der **Fahrplan,-̈e** schedule
die **Ferien** (pl.) vacation; *in die Ferien fahren* to go on vacation
fliegen to fly
das **Flugzeug,-e** airplane

frei free, available
fremd foreign; *Ich bin fremd hier.* I'm a stranger here.
Fuß: zu Fuß on foot
genauso...wie just as
das **Gepäck** luggage, baggage
geradeaus straight ahead
gestern yesterday
gleichfalls likewise; *danke gleichfalls* the same to you
das **Gleis,-e** track
der **Imbiss,-e** snack (bar)
die **Klasse,-n** class; *die Zweite Klasse* second economy class (train)
lang: zehn Tage lang for ten days
letzt- last
links left; *auf der linken Seite* on the left side
mal times; *Mal sehen...* Let's see...
mitnehmen to take along
das **Moped,-s** moped
das **Motorrad,-̈er** motorcycle
das **Museum,- Museen** museum
die **Nähe** nearness, proximity; *in der Nähe* nearby
die **Ostsee** Baltic Sea

packen to pack
der **Platz,-̈e** seat, place
die **Post** post office
rechts right
die **Reise,-n** trip
der **Schalter,-** (ticket) counter
das **Schiff,-e** ship
der **See,-n** lake
die **Seite,-n** side
der **Spaß** fun; *Viel Spaß!* Have lots of fun!
die **Stadtmitte** center of city
der **Strand,-̈e** beach, shore; *Timmendorfer Strand* resort at the Baltic Sea
die **Straßenbahn,-en** streetcar
umsteigen to transfer
das **Verkehrsmittel,-** means of transportation
von: von einem...zum anderen from one to the next
vorbeigehen to go past
der **Wagen,-** coach, car
wieder again
das **Würstchen,-** hot dog
das **Zelt,-e** tent
zurückkommen to come back

Hier ist die Auskunft.

Was kann man hier parken?

ein kleines Zelt

Das macht Spaß!

In this chapter you will be able to:

- talk about weekend activities
- accept or refuse an invitation
- describe talents and abilities
- order from a menu
- talk about past events

AC/CD

Wer geht zum Tanz?

Jürgen: Hallo, Nicole! Hast du Susanne gesehen?

Nicole: Du hast wirklich keine Augen. Die steht da drüben und spricht mit Cornelia.

Jürgen: Weißt du, ob sie am Samstag zum Tanz geht?

Nicole: Hast du noch nicht mit ihr gesprochen?

Jürgen: Nein. Geht sie denn nicht mit Volker?

Nicole: Das glaube ich nicht. Der hat doch eine Freundin.

Die steht da drüben und spricht mit Cornelia.

WB Activity 1

1. Was passt hier?

1e, 2d, 3f, 4b, 5c, 6a

1. Nicole glaubt nicht, dass
2. Jürgen hat
3. Volker hat
4. Nicole sieht
5. Susanne wird
6. Jürgen spricht

a. mit Nicole.
b. Susanne da drüben.
c. nicht mit Volker zum Tanz gehen.
d. nicht mit Susanne gesprochen.
e. Susanne mit Volker zum Tanz geht.
f. schon eine Freundin.

AC/CD

Jürgen: Gehst du am Wochenende zum Tanz?

Susanne: Ich habe keine Lust. Ich bin das letzte Mal da gewesen. Die Band hat nicht gut gespielt.

Jürgen: Die neue Band aus England soll aber ganz toll sein. Und du, Nicole? Was hast du vor?

Nicole: Cornelia und ich gehen bestimmt. Kommst du auch?

Gehst du am Wochenende zum Tanz?

WB Activity 2

WB

Activity 3

WA

Activity 1

Jürgen:	Klar. Wir können ja alle drei zusammen dahingehen.
Nicole:	Treffen wir uns doch noch vor dem Tanz beim Café. So gegen sieben.
Susanne:	Na, dann komm' ich auch. Jürgen und ich treffen euch dort.
Jürgen:	Gut, bis dann.

Jürgen, Susanne, Nicole und Cornelia

2. ***Ergänze diese Sätze!* Complete each sentence with the appropriate forms of the verbs. You will not need all the verbs listed.**

wollen	spielen	sein	gehen
kommen	treffen	haben	werden

1. Nicole und Cornelia ____ bestimmt zum Tanz.
2. Susanne ____ keine Lust, zum Tanz zu gehen.
3. Das letzte Mal hat die Band nicht gut ____.
4. Jürgen ____ mit Nicole und Cornelia zum Tanz gehen.
5. Die Band ____ aus England.
6. Alle vier ____ noch vor dem Tanz zu einem Café gehen.

1. gehen
2. hat
3. gespielt
4. will
5. kommt
6. werden

AC/CD

Cornelia:	Na, endlich! Nicole und ich warten schon lange.
Susanne:	Es tut mir leid. Ich habe noch unseren Wagen gewaschen. Dafür hat mir mein Vater zehn Mark gegeben.
Nicole:	Die Karte kostet sechs Mark. Da kannst du mit deinem Geld nicht viel machen.

Na endlich!

st lade ich euch zu einer Cola und Limo ein.

Susanne:	Das stimmt. Ich habe aber auch noch mein Taschengeld.
Nicole:	Meins habe ich schon ausgegeben.
Jürgen:	Ich hab' ja auch noch etwas Geld. Zuerst lade ich euch zu einer Cola und Limo ein.
Cornelia:	Der Jürgen ist immer solch ein Kavalier!

LA Activity 1

OT Activity 68

Das macht Spaß!

3. *Richtig oder falsch?* Determine whether the following statements are correct or incorrect. If they are incorrect, provide a correct statement. *Auf Deutsch, bitte!*

   1. Susanne hat ein Auto gewaschen.
   2. Jürgen hat schon lange gewartet.
   3. Nicole hat noch etwas Taschengeld.
   4. Eine Karte zum Tanz kostet zehn Mark.
   5. Jürgen wird für die Cola und Limo bezahlen.
   6. Susanne hat von ihren Eltern Taschengeld bekommen.

4. **Beantworte diese Fragen!**

   1. Warum glaubt Nicole, dass Jürgen keine Augen hat?
   2. Was will Jürgen von Nicole wissen?
   3. Wird Susanne mit Volker zum Tanz gehen?
   4. Warum will Susanne nicht zum Tanz gehen?
   5. Ist die Band aus Deutschland?
   6. Um wie viel Uhr kommen alle zum Café?
   7. Warum haben Cornelia und Nicole auf Susanne gewartet?
   8. Was bekommt Susanne jede Woche oder jeden Monat von ihrem Vater oder ihrer Mutter?

Sprichwort

Sie spielt immer die zweite Geige.

(She always plays second fiddle.)

Für dich

More than 6.5 million people (about 8 percent of Germany's population) are from other countries. In increasing numbers since the early 1960s, these immigrants have made Germany their new homeland. For decades there were no racial problems. "Guest workers" (*Gastarbeiter*), initially Italians, began to include Greeks and Spaniards, and later Portuguese, Yugoslavs and Turks.

Viele Türken wohnen in Deutschland.

Since the collapse of the former Soviet Union and other communist governments in eastern countries, hundreds of thousands of people have come to Germany from many eastern bloc countries for political and economic reasons. In recent years, there has been an influx of refugees from the former Yugoslavia (particularly Croatians) who have been displaced by their war-torn country.

Manche Türken haben ihre
eigenen Geschäfte (own stores).

Rollenspiel

With one or two of your classmates talk about an upcoming event such as a dance, sports activity, party, etc. Give them reasons why they should come along. Your reasons could include such things as having lots of fun, meeting others, good food, great music or other entertainment. Respond to their inquiries and questions accordingly. Be as creative as possible. Then reverse roles.

WB Activity 4

Das macht Spaß!

Aktuelles

Foreign Influence in Germany

Due to the break up of the eastern bloc and subsequent turmoil in several countries, many foreigners took advantage of the Basic Law (*Grundgesetz*) which allowed foreigners to apply for asylum. At its

peak in 1992, more than 400,000 foreigners (nearly 80 percent of all people seeking asylum in the entire European Community) came to Germany. As this tremendous influx of people could not be sustained, the Basic Law was changed to allow only victims of political persecution to enter the country.

Was kann man in diesem Geschäft kaufen?

Foreigners who have moved to Germany have made a tremendous impact on the cultural scene for more than 30 years. Among the 6.5 million foreigners, Turks have long been the largest foreign community, followed by people from the areas that belonged to former Yugoslavia. Consequently, it is not surprising to encounter numerous diverse cultural patterns that are indicative of the many ethnic groups which are scattered throughout Germany.

The French influence has long been evident in German clothing. German buyers eagerly await the spring and fall fashion shows in

Paris for the season's first look at the newest French fashions. When it comes to fashion and perfume, Germans look to their style-conscious neighbor to the west to set the trends.

If you like international foods, you won't have to look far. Italian cafés feature delicious ice creams, espressos, and rolls or sandwiches with different fillings. Germans don't have to travel to Italy for a taste of authentic Italian-style pizza. There has been growing interest in Oriental food. And many German restaurants boast Greek culinary influences as well.

Was kann man hier essen?

Of course, the greatest foreign influence is generated by Americans. The American love of fast food has found its way to Germany. Now you can satisfy a craving for hamburgers and french fries from fast-food franchises that are well known to American and German consumers alike. Well-known American soft drinks are also popular among Germans of all ages.

Filme bekommt man in einem Fotogeschäft.

A variety of American products from breakfast cereals to different brands of gum can be found in supermarkets. When you get in line to pay for your items, you'll find the German checkout system very similar to the one in America. German shoppers used to shop daily for their food items. Now many shop less frequently. American-style jeans have been in fashion for years; stores in every German city advertise them. American rock stars dominate the music industry and air waves. Germans buy the latest hits on audiocassettes and CDs.

Man sieht amerikanischen Einfluss (influence) überall.

Computer technology is highly advanced. PCs share shelf space with more sophisticated computers in many stores. Germans have long adored the influence of America's Wild West. Occasionally, American rodeos perform in German cities and towns to the delight of their audience. American films have always been popular as well. They can be seen at nearly every German movie theater.

As a result of the strong American influence on everyday German life, it is not surprising that Germans borrow many words from English. Here are some of the English words with their corresponding articles. The pronunciation of these words in German is usually as close to English as possible, depending on the speaker's familiarity with English.

Das macht Spaß!

die Band	die Party	der Diskjockey	das Popcorn
die City	die Jeans	das T-Shirt	der Computer
der Job	das Hobby	der Teenager	der Manager
die Disco	das Makeup	das Feature	die Snackbar
das Poster	der Ski	das Basketball	der Trend

WB Activity 5

 WA Activity 2

 S Activity 4

Deutscher Einfluss in Amerika (German influence in America). Can you think of German words that have become familiar in this country? Try to find at least ten German words and briefly describe each one. (Example: *Kindergarten*— Before entering first grade, students go to the kindergarten.)

Ergänzung

AC/CD

Was für ein Musikinstrument spielst du?
Ich spiele...

(die) Gitarre   (die) Trompete   (das) Klavier

(die) Blockflöte   (die) Klarinette   (die) Geige   (die) Flöte

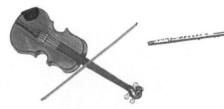

(das) Saxophon   (die) Keyboards   (das) Schlagzeug

Ask other questions:
Spielst du Gitarre?, *Frag Peter, ob er ein Musikinstrument spielt!*
Was für ein Musikinstrument spielt er?
Point out that the article is usually eliminated in a sentence like *Spielst du (die) Gitarre?*

WB   Activity 6

LA   Activity 2

WA   Activities 3-4

OT   Activities 69-70

S   Activity 5

5. Frage deine Schulfreunde!

1. Was für ein Musikinstrument spielst du?
2. Wie viel kostet dieses Musikinstrument neu?
3. Wo spielst du es?
4. Wie lange spielst du schon?
5. Wer spielt in deiner Familie ein Musikinstrument?
6. Gibt es in deiner Schule eine Band? Was für Musikinstrumente gibt es da?
7. Wie heißt deine Lieblingsband? Wie heißen die Rockstars und welche Musikinstrumente spielen sie?

Das macht Spaß!

Praktische Situation

Was für ein Musikinstrument hast du gespielt? You want to find out what musical instruments your classmates played when they were younger. Draw a grid in German of five common musical instruments. Then poll ten of your classmates to determine which instrument(s) they used to play. In your survey:

1. Name each instrument and ask your classmates, one by one, if they played it.

2. As each classmate answers your question, make a mark by the appropriate response.

3. After you have finished asking questions, count the number of students who played each instrument. Figure out the percentage of those asked. Be ready to share your findings with the rest of the class.

Additional words that students might find useful in their responses to this topical question (not covered as yet) are: *zu schnell* (too fast); *romantisch* (romantic); *unmöglich* (impossible); *zu laut* (too noisy); *schrill* (shrill, piercing); *angenehm* (pleasant); *rockig* (rocky, rocklike); *poppig* (poplike); *modern*; *mittelmäßig* (average, mediocre); *schrecklich* (terrible); *zu leise* (too soft); *abartig* (abnormal, weird).

Sag's mal! Wie ist die Musik? Sie ist...

zu schnell*

alt

langweilig

angenehm*   romantisch*

prima

rockig*   neu

abartig*

poppig*   ganz gut   unmöglich*

super

schrill*   zu leise*

modern*

schlecht

schrecklich*

mittelmäßig*   zu laut*

Sprache

Present Perfect Tense (Irregular Verbs)

The irregular verbs, as the term suggests, do not follow the same pattern when forming the past participle as the regular verbs. Some of these verbs use *sein* instead of *haben*. Therefore, you must learn each past participle individually.

❖ *Hast du mit Tanja gesprochen?* Have you spoken with Tanja?

❖ *Sie ist nach Hause gefahren.* She has driven home.

Verbs that use a form of *sein* must both (a) indicate motion or change of condition and (b) be intransitive, i.e., verbs that cannot have a direct object. This is true in cases like *gehen, laufen, kommen, fahren, schwimmen.*

❖ *Hast du schon mit Andrea gesprochen?* Have you already spoken with Andrea?

❖ *Wir sind acht Stunden nach Europa geflogen.* We have flown eight hours to Europe.

Here are the irregular forms for most of the verbs you have learned so far:

Infinitive	Past Participle
backen (to bake)	gebacken
beginnen (to begin)	begonnen
bekommen (to receive, get)	bekommen
bleiben (to stay)	ist geblieben
bringen (to bring)	gebracht
einladen (to invite)	eingeladen
essen (to eat)	gegessen
fahren (to drive)	ist gefahren
finden (to find)	gefunden
fliegen (to fly)	ist geflogen
geben (to give)	gegeben
gefallen (to like)	gefallen
gehen (to go)	ist gegangen
haben (to have)	gehabt
helfen (to help)	geholfen
kennen (to know)	gekannt
kommen (to come)	ist gekommen
laufen (to run)	ist gelaufen
lesen (to read)	gelesen

Students must learn these irregular verbs because most of them will be used frequently.

(continued on next page)

Das macht Spaß!

Infinitive	Past Participle
liegen (to lie, be located)	**gelegen**
scheinen (to shine)	**geschienen**
schießen (to shoot)	**geschossen**
schreiben (to write)	**geschrieben**
schreien (to scream)	**geschrien**
schwimmen (to swim)	**ist geschwommen**
sehen (to see)	**gesehen**
sein (to be)	**ist gewesen**
singen (to sing)	**gesungen**
sprechen (to speak)	**gesprochen**
stehen (to stand)	**gestanden**
treffen (to meet)	**getroffen**
trinken (to drink)	**getrunken**
wissen (to know)	**gewusst**

 Activity 7

 Activity 5

 Activities 3 and 6

Verbs with inseparable prefixes (*bekommen*) do not have the *ge-* in the past participle.

◆ *Dieter hat meinen Brief bekommen.* Dieter has received my letter.

Verbs with separable prefixes have the *ge-* as part of the participle.

◆ *Susi hat mich angerufen.* Susi has called me.

◆ *Wen habt ihr zur Party eingeladen?* Whom have you invited to the party?

The accent or emphasis is always on the separable prefix (*an*gerufen, *ein*geladen).

AC/CD

1. Er hat einen Kuchen gebacken.
2. Er hat seinem Onkel geholfen.
3. Er hat ein Buch gelesen.
4. Er hat Heidi ein Geschenk gebracht.
5. Er hat in seiner Band gesungen.
6. Er hat mit seiner Oma gesprochen.

6. **Was hat Boris an diesem Tag gemacht?**

◆ Was hat Boris am Montag gemacht? (einen Brief schreiben)
◆ Er hat einen Brief geschrieben.

1. Was hat Boris am Sonntag gemacht? (einen Kuchen backen)

2. Was hat Boris am Freitag gemacht? (seinem Onkel helfen)

3. Was hat Boris am Mittwoch gemacht? (ein Buch lesen)

4. Was hat Boris am Samstag gemacht? (Heidi ein Geschenk bringen)

5. Was hat Boris am Donnerstag gemacht? (in seiner Band singen)

6. Was hat Boris am Dienstag gemacht? (mit seiner Oma sprechen)

7. *Habe ich dir das schon gesagt?* Imagine that you are at a party and your friend is filling you in on several events that took place while you were gone. Play your friend's part.

◆ meine Arbeit im Kaufhaus beginnen
◆ Ich habe meine Arbeit im Kaufhaus begonnen.

1. wenig Zeit für Hausaufgaben haben
2. zwei CDs aus Deutschland bekommen
3. zehn Kilometer laufen
4. im Klub Lieder singen
5. am Montag bei meiner Cousine sein
6. in Mathe eine Eins bekommen
7. eine Stunde im See schwimmen
8. einen Film aus Frankreich sehen

AC/CD

1. Ich habe wenig Zeit für Hausaufgaben gehabt.
2. Ich habe zwei CDs aus Deutschland bekommen.
3. Ich bin zehn Kilometer gelaufen.
4. Ich habe im Klub Lieder gesungen.
5. Ich bin am Montag bei meiner Cousine gewesen.
6. Ich habe in Mathe eine Eins bekommen.
7. Ich bin eine Stunde im See geschwommen.
8. Ich habe einen Film aus Frankreich gesehen.

8. *Was ist denn in der Disko los gewesen?* **Tell about what happened at the disco.**

◆ die Jugendlichen / zur Disko gehen
◆ Die Jugendlichen sind zur Disko gegangen.

1. Gisela / ihren Freund vor der Disko treffen
2. Die Musik / schon um halb acht beginnen
3. Viele / in der Disko stehen
4. Ein paar Jungen und Mädchen / Fanta trinken
5. Andere / etwas essen
6. Viele Jugendliche / bis zehn Uhr bleiben
7. Viktor / erst um halb neun kommen

AC/CD

1. Gisela hat ihren Freund vor der Disko getroffen.
2. Die Musik hat schon um halb acht begonnen.
3. Viele haben in der Disko gestanden.
4. Ein paar Jungen und Mädchen haben Fanta getrunken.
5. Andere haben etwas gegessen.
6. Viele Jugendliche sind bis zehn Uhr geblieben.
7. Viktor ist erst um halb neun gekommen.

9. **Provide the correct form of** *haben* **or** *sein.*

1. Wann _____ ihr nach Hause gekommen?
2. Die Jugendlichen _____ Tischtennis gespielt.
3. Es _____ gestern viel geschneit.
4. Angelika _____ mir die Schultasche gebracht.
5. Meine Freunde _____ im Wohnzimmer gewesen.
6. Mein Freund _____ lange vor dem Bahnhof gewartet.
7. Um wie viel Uhr _____ ihr Frühstück gegessen?
8. _____ Sie mit dem Zug gefahren?
9. Was _____ du am Abend getrunken?
10. Wir _____ zur Post gelaufen.

1. seid
2. haben
3. hat
4. hat
5. sind
6. hat
7. habt
8. Sind
9. hast
10. sind

Das macht Spaß!

10. Kombiniere...

Haben	**deine Lehrerin**	**mit dir**		**gewesen**
Hat	**Svens Schulfreund**	**mit den Eltern**		**gefahren**
Sind	**Herr und Frau Stock**	**gestern**	**zu Hause**	**gelaufen**
Ist	**die Jugendlichen**	**in der Schule**	**in die Ferien**	**gesprochen**
			nach Hause	
			am Telefon	

Ergänzung

AC/CD

Have students jot down what they typically eat and drink at breakfast, lunch and dinner. Then ask them to discuss the list with their classmates.

11. *Was haben sie gegessen und getrunken?* Imagine that several of your relatives and/or friends stayed with you over the weekend. Pick three of these people and write a short description of what each one ate and drank for breakfast, lunch and dinner. Be as creative as possible.

Sprache

Possessive Adjectives

A possessive adjective is a pronoun that is used as an adjective to indicate who owns the noun that follows it. It replaces the article in front of the noun and takes on the same endings as those of the indefinite article (*ein*-words). You are already familiar with these possessive adjectives: *mein* (my), *dein* (your, familiar singular), *sein* (his, its), *ihr* (her). The new possessive adjectives are: *sein* (its), *unser* (our), *euer* (your, familiar plural) *ihr* (their) and *Ihr* (your, formal singular and plural).

Nominative	Singular			Plural
	masculine	**feminine**	**neuter**	
ich	mein	meine	mein	meine
du	dein	deine	dein	deine
er	sein	seine	sein	seine
sie	ihr	ihre	ihr	ihre
es	sein	seine	sein	seine
wir	unser	uns(e)re*	unser	uns(e)re*
ihr	euer	eu(e)re*	euer	eu(e)re*
sie	ihr	ihre	ihr	ihre
Sie	Ihr	Ihre	Ihr	Ihre

To simplify the following charts, you may want to take just one of the possessive adjectives and point out the five variations (no ending and adding *-e*, *-en*, *-em*, *-er*) in the various categories.

*The *e* in front of the *r* in *unser* and *euer* is often omitted if the ending begins with a vowel.

◆ *Meine Freundin heißt Angelika.* My friend's name is Angelika.

◆ *Wo ist unser Fußball?* Where is our soccer ball?

Accusative	Singular			Plural
	masculine	**feminine**	**neuter**	
ich	meinen	meine	mein	meine
du	deinen	deine	dein	deine
er	seinen	seine	sein	seine
sie	ihren	ihre	ihr	ihre
es	seinen	seine	sein	seine
wir	uns(e)ren*	uns(e)re*	unser	uns(e)re*
ihr	eu(e)ren*	eu(e)re*	euer	eu(e)re*
sie	ihren	ihre	ihr	ihre
Sie	Ihren	Ihre	Ihr	Ihre

◆ *Kennst du seinen Bruder?* Do you know his brother?

◆ *Ich kaufe ihr Buch.* I'm buying her book.

Dative Singular				Plural
	masculine	feminine	neuter	
ich	meinem	meiner	meinem	meinen
du	deinem	deiner	deinem	deinen
er	seinem	seiner	seinem	seinen
sie	ihrem	ihrer	ihrem	ihren
es	seinem	seiner	seinem	seinen
wir	uns(e)rem*	uns(e)rer*	uns(e)rem*	uns(e)ren*
ihr	eu(e)rem*	eu(e)rer*	eu(e)rem*	eu(e)ren*
sie	ihrem	ihrer	ihrem	ihren
Sie	Ihrem	Ihrer	Ihrem	Ihren

◆ *Kommt ihr zu uns(e)rer Party?* Are you coming to our party?

◆ *Ralf hilft seiner Mutter.* Ralf is helping his mother.

AC/CD

12. *Habt ihr...?* **Imagine you're organizing a club function. You will need a number of items before your meeting. Ask the assembled club members if they have these items.**

◆ Habt ihr eure Gitarre?

1. Habt ihr eure CD?
2. Habt ihr euren Rechner?
3. Habt ihr euer Buch?
4. Habt ihr euren Computer?
5. Habt ihr euer Fahrrad?
6. Habt ihr euer Zelt?
7. Habt ihr eure Fahrkarte?
8. Habt ihr euer Geld?

1.
2.
3.
4.
5.
6.
7.
8.

13. *Wir machen eine kurze Reise.* Your class is planning a short camping trip. Your teacher is asking your class who has specific things that will be needed. Several students are responding.

◆ Wer hat einen Wecker? (Uwe)
◆ Uwe kann seinen Wecker mitbringen.

◆ Wer hat ein Zelt? (Regina)
◆ Regina kann ihr Zelt mitbringen.

1. Wer hat eine Klarinette? (Axel)
2. Wer hat einen Fußball? (Lars)
3. Wer hat eine Kamera? (Christine)
4. Wer hat ein Paar Tennisschuhe? (Cornelia)
5. Wer hat eine Landkarte? (Boris)
6. Wer hat einen Pulli? (Angela)

AC/CD

Divide the class into groups of three or four. Each group member will write down at least five items that he or she would want to take along on a trip. Have each discuss with the others such questions as *Was bringst (nimmst) du mit? Warum?* One student could be the designated recorder who will report to the rest of the class.

1. Axel kann seine Klarinette mitbringen.
2. Lars kann seinen Fußball mitbringen.
3. Christine kann ihre Kamera mitbringen.
4. Cornelia kann ihr Paar Tennisschuhe mitbringen.
5. Boris kann seine Landkarte mitbringen.
6. Angela kann ihren Pulli mitbringen.

14. *Wen besuchen wir noch?* Tell whom else we are visiting.

◆ Schwester / sein
◆ Wir besuchen seine Schwester.

1. Oma / unser
2. Bruder / dein
3. Mutter / euer
4. Onkel / mein
5. Lehrerin / ihr
6. Trainer / sein

AC/CD

1. Wir besuchen uns(e)re Oma.
2. Wir besuchen deinen Bruder.
3. Wir besuchen eu(e)re Mutter.
4. Wir besuchen meinen Onkel.
5. Wir besuchen ihre Lehrerin.
6. Wir besuchen seinen Trainer.

15. *Was brauchst du für deine Ferien?* Several people ask you what items you need to take along on your vacation. Use the cues in your response.

◆ Handschuhe / mein
◆ Ich brauche meine Handschuhe.

1. Fahrkarten / unser
2. Bücher / dein
3. Bälle / euer
4. Tennisschläger / ihr
5. Briefmarken / meine
6. Boot / sein
7. Fahrplan / unser

Briefmarken

AC/CD

1. Ich brauche uns(e)re Fahrkarten.
2. Ich brauche deine Bücher.
3. Ich brauche eu(e)re Bälle.
4. Ich brauche ihren Tennisschläger.
5. Ich brauche meine Briefmarken.
6. Ich brauche sein Boot.
7. Ich brauche uns(e)ren Fahrplan.

Das macht Spaß!

Lesestück

In der Tanzschule

Christian kennt Franziska gut. Beide gehen aufs Konrad Adenauer Gymnasium und wohnen auch in derselben Straße°, nur drei Häuser entfernt°. Jeden Donnerstag gehen Christian und Franziska zur Tanzschule. Dort kommen sie mit anderen Jugendlichen zusammen und lernen alte und neue Tänze.

Christian und Franziska lernen neue und alte Tänze.

Mit dem Tanzen haben Christian und Franziska vor zwei Monaten begonnen. Beim Tanzen muss man etwas locker und koordiniert sein. Die ersten Tänze sind einfach gewesen, aber jetzt sind sie doch etwas schwerer.

Letzte Woche haben die Jugendlichen den Foxtrott gelernt. Herr Müller, der Tanzlehrer, sagt den Jugendlichen immer, sie sollen die neuen Tänze noch einmal zu Hause üben. Christian und Franziska üben ihre Tänze oft vor der Tanzstunde° bei Christian. Christians Mutter, eine gute Tänzerin, sieht manchmal zu° und lacht. Sie sagt beiden, wie sie es besser machen können. Das finden die zwei ganz toll.

Tanzen macht Spaß.

Heute lernen sie in der Tanzschule wieder einen neuen Tanz, die Rumba. Herr Müller zeigt° allen zuerst ohne Musik, wie man die Rumba tanzt. Ganz langsam zeigt er die Schritte°. Dann sagt er Franziska, dass sie seine Tanzpartnerin sein soll. Jetzt können alle die Schritte genau° sehen.

Dann sollen alle Paare diesen Tanz üben. Die Musik spielt und die Jugendlichen tanzen nach dem Rhythmus°. Manche sind schon ganz gut, andere können es noch nicht so gut.

Die Tanzstunde dauert eine Stunde. Während dieser kurzen Zeit üben Christian und Franziska die Rumba und andere Tänze. Beide tanzen sehr gern und sind auch super. Herr Müller sagt allen Jugendlichen, dass sie die Tänze bis nächsten Samstag noch einmal üben sollen, denn an diesem Tag ist der Abschlussball°.

Christians Mutter sieht zu.

Am Samstag kommen die Jugendlichen zur Tanzschule, viele mit ihren Eltern und Freunden. Christian hat seinen dunkelblauen Anzug angezogen. Franziska hat für diesen besonderen Tag ein schönes schwarzes Kleid gekauft. Beide sehen sehr elegant aus°. Christian hat Franziska noch Blumen° geschenkt. Er gibt sie ihr auf dem Abschlussball. Endlich spielt die Musik. Alle tanzen und zeigen, was sie in den letzten Monaten gelernt haben.

 WB — Activities 12-13

 LA — Activity 3

 WA — Activities 9-10

in derselben Straße in the same street; *entfernt* away; *die Tanzstunde* dancing lesson; *zusehen* to watch; *zeigen* to show, demonstrate; *der Schritt* step; *genau* exactly; *nach dem Rhythmus* according to the rhythm; *der Abschlussball* final (graduation) ball; *aussehen* to look like; *die Blume* flower

Was machen sie auf dem Abschlussball?

Das macht Spaß!

16. Was ist hier los gewesen?

1f, 2e, 3b, 4h, 5a, 6g, 7c, 8d

1. Die Musik hat
2. Die ersten Tänze sind
3. Der Tanzlehrer hat
4. Die Jugendlichen haben
5. Christian und Franziska sind
6. Die Tanzstunde hat
7. Franziska hat für den Abschlussball
8. Christian hat seiner Tanzpartnerin

a. Tanzpartner.
b. mit Franziska getanzt.
c. ein Kleid gekauft.
d. Blumen geschenkt.
e. einfach gewesen.
f. gespielt.
g. eine Stunde gedauert.
h. die Rumba geübt.

Was hat Christian Franziska gegeben?

17. Beantworte diese Fragen!

1. Warum kennt Christian Franziska gut?
2. Was machen beide jeden Donnerstag?
3. Wie muss man beim Tanzen sein?
4. Was haben alle das letzte Mal gelernt?
5. Was machen Franziska und Christian oft vor der Tanzstunde?
6. Was für einen Tanz lernen sie heute?
7. Warum soll Franziska mit dem Tanzlehrer tanzen?
8. Sind alle beim Tanzen gut?
9. Warum sollen alle Jugendlichen die Tänze bis nächsten Samstag üben?
10. Was bekommt Franziska von Christian am Samstag?

1. Er geht mit Franziska aufs Konrad Adenauer Gymnasium und wohnt auch in derselben Straße.
2. Sie gehen zur Tanzschule.
3. Locker und koordiniert.
4. Den Foxtrott.
5. Sie üben ihre Tänze.
6. Die Rumba.
7. Dann können alle die Schritte genau sehen.
8. Manche sind gut, andere können es noch nicht so gut.
9. Am Samstag ist der Abschlussball.
10. Blumen.

Übung macht den Meister!

1. *Wir haben einen Schultanz.* Imagine your committee has been put in charge of making the necessary preparations for the next school dance. Make a list of questions that need to be addressed and then ask others in your class. Some of your questions might be:

   a. *Welche Band soll spielen?*

   b. *Wann soll der Tanz beginnen?*

   c. *Wen sollen wir einladen?*

   e. *Was brauchen wir alles?*

   f. *Wie viel soll eine Karte kosten?*

2. *Ich habe nicht genug Geld.* A well-known rock band is in town and your friend wants you to come along to the concert. Tickets are hard to come by; therefore, your friend needs your decision immediately. Unfortunately, you don't have enough money. However, your friend has several solutions. Develop a conversation with one of your classmates in which you discuss the financial situation, and figure out how you can afford to buy a ticket. Reverse roles.

Have students work in groups to develop as many questions as possible. Then present your questions to another group to practice oral proficiency. Reverse roles.

Das macht Spaß!

3. *Kommst du mit zur Disko?* You and your classmates make a list of why you do or do not want to go to the disco this weekend. Give as many reasons as possible.

4. *Spielst du ein Musikinstrument?* Inquire about your classmates' interest in musical instruments. Your questions should include such details as:

> *Was für ein Musikinstrument spielst du?*
>
> *Wie lange spielst du dieses Musikinstrument schon?*
>
> *Wo, wie lange und wie oft übst du?*
>
> *Hast du Musikstunden?*
>
> *Mit wem übst du manchmal zusammen?*

If your classmates don't play an instrument, have them pretend that they do.

Aktuelles

Metric Measurements

The metric system is used in almost all countries of the world. When traveling to Europe, it might come in handy to know the following measurements.

	German Metric	U.S.
1	Gramm (g)	0.035 ounce
28	Gramm	1 ounce
1	Pfund (Pfd)	1.1 pounds
1	Kilogramm or Kilo (kg)	2.2 pounds
1	Zentimeter (cm)	0.3937 inch
2,54	Zentimeter	1 inch
1	Meter (m)	3.281 feet
1609,3	Meter	1 mile
1	Kilometer (km)	1,094 yards
1	Liter (l)	2.113 pints

Metric Units	
1 Pfund	500 Gramm
2 Pfund	1 Kilogramm or 1,000 Gramm
1 Meter	100 Zentimeter
1000 Meter	1 Kilometer

Wo ist das Gasthaus?

Thermometer Readings

German thermometers use the centigrade (Celsius) scale. To convert Fahrenheit to centigrade, subtract 32, then multiply by 5 and divide by 9. To convert centigrade to Fahrenheit, multiply by 9, divide by 5 and add 32. The chart on the right gives some sample readings with the conversions.

Examples:

$20°C = 68°F$ ($20 \times 9/5 + 20 = 68$)
$48°F = 9°C$ ($48 - 32 \times 5 \div 9 = 8.89$)

A simplified (less accurate method) you can use without a calculator: Subtract 30 from Fahrenheit and take half to get centigrade, or to double centigrades and add 30 to get degrees in Fahrenheit.
Example: $60°F = 60 - 30 \div ½ = 15°C$.

WB
Activity 14

S
Activity 2

Beantworte diese Fragen!

1. 12 000
2. 750
3. 160
4. 5°
5. 2
6. 5 600

1. Uwe fährt mit seinem Fahrrad 12 Kilometer. Wie viele Meter fährt er?

2. Frau Breme kauft 1 1/2 Pfund Käse. Wie viele Gramm kauft sie?

3. Martina ist 1,60 Meter groß. Wie viele Zentimeter sind das?

4. In den Alpen ist es heute 41° F. Wie kalt ist das in Celsius?

5. Herr Kowalski kauft im Supermarkt ein Brot. Es wiegt (weighs) 4,4 Pfund. Wie viele Kilo sind das?

6. Wie viele Gramm haben 5,6 Kilo?

Erweiterung

Hier steht, wie weit alles ist.

18. *Kannst du ihnen helfen?* Imagine that you are part of a committee that is in charge of your annual school dance. Several of your classmates are asking you a number of questions. Can you help them?

1. An welchem Tag ist der Tanz?

2. Wo ist der Tanz?

3. Wie viel kostet eine Karte?

4. Welche Band wird da spielen?

5. Um wie viel Uhr beginnt der Tanz?

6. Wer kommt alles zum Tanz?

WB Activities 15-17

Das macht Spaß!

19. *Was ist denn heute bei Gisela los?* **After you have formed sentences with the following words, you will find out what is going on at Gisela's.**

1. es / am/ Freitag / gibt / Party /eine
2. hat / Jugendliche / Gisela / eingeladen / zwanzig
3. werden/ was / sie / machen / dort
4. bestimmt / Gitarre / Gisela / spielt
5. alle / singen / werden / zusammen
6. immer / Spaß / macht / das / viel

20. *Schreibe einen Dialog oder ein Lesestück!* **Write a dialog or a narrative using the following details: Call your friend...ask him or her to go to a dance...provide information about where and when the dance takes place...decide where to meet...ask who is playing. Be as creative as possible.**

21. *Was ist logisch?* **Find the verbs from the list below that best match the phrases.**

ausgeben	warten	trinken	spielen	gehen
waschen	lernen	kaufen	wohnen	glauben

1. deiner Freundin nicht
2. am Wochenende zum Tanz
3. schon eine halbe Stunde auf Freunde
4. dreißig Mark Taschengeld
5. unser Auto
6. eine Kinokarte
7. Schlagzeug
8. alte und neue Tänze
9. eine Fanta
10. in derselben Straße

Beim Tanzen lernen Jugendlic[h] alte und neue Tänze.

22. **Beende diese Sätze!**

1. Geht ihr heute ____?
2. Nein, wir haben ____.
3. Was macht ihr ____?
4. Wir werden ____.
5. Habt ihr denn ____?
6. Ja, ohne ____.

Kapitel 12

23. Etwas Persönliches.

1. Was machst du am Wochenende?

2. Bekommst du jede Woche oder jeden Monat etwas Taschengeld?

3. Kommst du mit deinen Freunden manchmal zusammen? Was macht ihr dann?

4. Musst du manchmal zu Hause helfen? Was musst du dann machen?

Rückblick

1. *Was fehlt hier?* **Complete the dialog using the present perfect tense of the verbs listed.**

warten	sein	helfen	sehen	haben
sagen	lesen	schreiben	machen	dauern

– Warum hast du gestern keine Zeit ____?

– Ich habe Katrina einen Brief ____.

– Warum hast du mir das nicht ____? Ich habe lange auf dich ____.

– Ich habe auch meiner Mutter bei der Arbeit ____. Das hat noch eine Stunde ____.

– Was hast du denn am Abend ____?

– Gegen sieben habe ich einen tollen Film im Fernsehen ____.

– Fernsehen? Ich habe einen Roman ____.

– Hoffentlich ist er so gut wie der Film ____.

2. **Beende diese Sätze!**

1. Nach ____ können wir zum Eiscafé gehen.

2. Wohnt er nicht bei ____?

3. Um wie viel Uhr kommt ihr aus ____?

4. Das Auto steht nicht weit von ____.

5. Sie fahren zu ____.

6. Außer ____ spielt auch der Vater Tennis.

7. Ich fahre mit ____ in die Stadt.

8. Die Touristen fahren von ____ zu ____.

Das macht Spaß!

WA Activity 11

If your students have any difficulties in completing these activities, you may want to go back to the lesson in which the particular grammar point was discussed.

gehabt
geschrieben
gesagt, gewartet
geholfen, gedauert
gemacht
gesehen
gelesen
gewesen

Sample answers:
1. der Schule
2. dem Bahnhof
3. dem Kino
4. der Ecke
5. dem Park
6. der Mutter
7. dem Fahrrad
8. dem Kaufhaus / der Post

3. *Welche Wörter passen hier zusammen?* **Match each word with one of these five categories:** *Sportart, Körperteil, Verkehrsmittel, Musikinstrument, Speisekarte.*

1. Bein
2. Schwimmen
3. Kopf
4. Straßenbahn
5. Geige
6. Nachtisch
7. Fußball
8. Kalte Platte

9. Schulter
10. Klavier
11. Motorrad
12. Stirn
13. Flugzeug
14. Schlagzeug
15. Kartoffeln

4. **Provide an appropriate response in German, making sure the dialog ties together and is meaningful.**

A: Ich möchte heute gern an den See fahren. Kommst du mit?

B: Heute habe ich leider keine Zeit.

A: ____

B: Ich muss mit meinen Eltern zum Bahnhof fahren.

A: ____

B: Mein Onkel und meine Tante.

A: ____

B: Aus Stuttgart.

A: ____

B: Ungefähr drei Wochen.

A: ____

Viele Touristen bleiben ein paar Tage in Berlin.

5. *Etwas von dir.* **A German exchange student is meeting you for the first time and wants to know more about you. Respond to his or her questions.**

1. Welche Sportart treibst du?
2. Was für ein Hobby hast du?
3. Wie kommst du jeden Tag zur Schule?
4. Spielst du ein Musikinstrument?
5. Was für ein Musikinstrument spielst du?
6. Was für Musik hörst du gern?
7. Was isst du und trinkst du gern?
8. Wie lange wohnst du schon hier?
9. Gefällt es dir hier? Warum oder warum nicht?

6. Was haben alle am Wochenende gemacht?

◆ Rainer / seine Tante besuchen
◆ Rainer hat seine Tante besucht.

1. Angelikas Vater / nach Süddeutschland fahren
2. meine Freunde / in die Disko gehen
3. Thomas / ein paar Fernsehprogramme sehen
4. die Jugendlichen / ein Zelt aufbauen
5. ihre Freundin / Tennis spielen
6. seine Schwester / ihre Freundinnen einladen
7. Herr Schreiber / seinen Wagen waschen
8. unser Lehrer / viel arbeiten

1. Angelikas Vater ist nach Süddeutschland gefahren.
2. Meine Freunde sind in die Disko gegangen.
3. Thomas hat ein paar Fernsehprogramme gesehen.
4. Die Jugendlichen haben ein Zelt aufgebaut.
5. Ihre Freundin hat Tennis gespielt.
6. Seine Schwester hat ihre Freundinnen eingeladen.
7. Herr Schreiber hat seinen Wagen gewaschen.
8. Unser Lehrer hat viel gearbeitet.

7. Ergänze die Sätze! Complete the following narrative by adding the proper endings, where necessary.

Fünf Tage die Woche gehen wir schon um halb acht zu unser____ Schule. Mein____ Freundin Karin kommt immer pünktlich. Manchmal kommt sie auch mit ihr____ Schwester. Unser____ Mathelehrer, Herr Dietrich, bringt jeden Montag unser____ Hausaufgaben. Mein____ Note in Mathe ist ganz gut. Karin hat Mathe nicht gern. Deshalb sind ihr____ Noten nicht besonders gut. In der zweiten Stunde haben wir unser____ Englischlehrerin, Frau Braun. Ihr____ Klasse ist immer interessant. Am letzten Freitag im Monat fahre ich mit mein____ Fahrrad zur Schule. An diesem Tag kommt immer mein____ Vater zu Besuch. Dann fahren wir oft mit sein____ Auto zu sein____ Haus. Er wohnt in einer anderen Stadt.

er, e, er, -, e, e, e, e, e, em, -, em, em

8. Supply the German equivalent for the words given in parentheses.

1. Wo wohnt (*your brother*) ____, Herr Weise?
2. (*Their father*) ____ besucht (*my aunt*) ____.
3. Hast du (*your sister*) ____ bei der Arbeit geholfen, Tina?
4. (*Our school*) ____ ist nicht weit.
5. (*My girlfriend*) ____ holt (*her cassette*) ____.
6. Warum kaufst du (*his tickets*) ____?
7. Ich bin ohne (*my books*) ____ in die Schule gegangen.
8. Fährst du mit (*your moped*) ____ in die Stadt, Bernd?
9. Bringt doch (*your ball*) ____, Dieter und Heike!

1. Ihr Bruder
2. Ihr Vater, meine Tante
3. deiner Schwester
4. Uns(e)re Schule
5. Meine Freundin, ihre Kassette
6. seine Karten
7. meine Bücher
8. deinem Moped
9. eu(e)ren Ball

Land und Leute

Die Schweiz

Die Schweiz ist ein sehr beliebtes Land. Jedes Jahr kommen viele Besucher° in die Schweiz. Dieses kleine Land ist halb so groß wie der Staat South Carolina.

die Schweizer Nationalfahne

Die Schweiz hat fünf Nachbarländer: Frankreich, Italien, Österreich, Liechtenstein und Deutschland. Mehr als sechs Millionen Menschen° wohnen in diesem Land. 65% sprechen deutsch, 18% französisch, 12% italienisch und 5% andere Sprachen. Die Nationalfahne ist rot und hat ein weißes Kreuz° in der Mitte.

Der größte Teil der Schweiz liegt in den Bergen. Der Monte Rosa (4 600 m) ist der höchste Berg. Der Rhein ist der längste Fluss. Er fließt 376 Kilometer durch das Land und dann weiter° durch Deutschland und die Niederlande zur Nordsee°.

Die größte Stadt der Schweiz ist Zürich. Diese Stadt liegt am Zürichsee. Die zweitgrößte Stadt ist Basel. Wie Zürich liegt auch Basel im Norden der Schweiz. Der Rhein fließt durch Basel.

Genf ist eine andere große Stadt. Diese Stadt liegt im Süden am Genfer See, direkt an der Grenze zu° Frankreich. Bern, die Hauptstadt der Schweiz, ist die viertgrößte Stadt und liegt im Westen. Dann kommt Luzern. Diese Stadt liegt in der Mitte der Schweiz.

WB Activity 18

Während der Sommermonate besuchen die Touristen die Schweiz sehr gern. Hier können sie viel in den Bergen wandern. Warum kommen auch viele Besucher im Winter in die Schweiz? Während dieser Jahreszeit ist die Schweiz ein Paradies. Tausende fahren in die Schweiz und laufen dort Ski.

Der größte Teil liegt in den Bergen.
(Matterhorn)

der Besucher visitor; *der Mensch* person, human; *das Kreuz* cross; *weiter* further; *die Nordsee* North Sea; *an der Grenze zu* at the border of

Was passt hier?

1. Der längste Fluss ist
2. Die Nationalfahne hat
3. Die zweitgrößte Stadt ist
4. Der höchste Berg ist
5. Ungefähr vier Millionen sprechen
6. Genf liegt
7. Im Winter kann man in der Schweiz
8. Der Rhein fließt
9. Die Schweiz ist
10. Bern ist

1j, 2g, 3b, 4i, 5d, 6h, 7e, 8c, 9a, 10f

Was kann man in der Schweiz im Winter machen?

a. halb so groß wie der Staat South Carolina.
b. Basel.
c. zur Nordsee.
d. deutsch.
e. Ski laufen.
f. die Hauptstadt
g. ein Kreuz in der Mitte.
h. an der Grenze zu Frankreich.
i. der Monta Rosa.
j. der Rhein.

Beantworte diese Fragen!

1. Besuchen viele Touristen die Schweiz?
2. Wie groß ist die Schweiz?
3. Wie viele Nachbarländer hat die Schweiz?
4. Welche sind das?
5. Sprechen alle deutsch?
6. Ist das Land flach?
7. Wohin fließt der Rhein von der Schweiz weiter?
8. Wie heißt die Hauptstadt der Schweiz?
9. Wo liegt Luzern?
10. Kommen Besucher nur im Sommer in die Schweiz?

Wie heißt die Hauptstadt?

AC/CD

1. Ja, viele Touristen besuchen die Schweiz.
2. Die Schweiz ist halb so groß wie der Staat South Carolina.
3. Die Schweiz hat fünf Nachbarländer.
4. Frankreich, Italien, Österrreich, Liechtenstein und Deutschland.
5. Nein, nicht alle sprechen deutsch.
6. Nein, es ist nicht flach.
7. Er fließt durch Deutschland und die Niederlande zur Nordsee.
8. Sie heißt Bern.
9. Luzern liegt in der Mitte der Schweiz.
10. Nein, sie kommen auch im Winter.

Was weißt du?

1. *Ich will wirklich nicht dahingehen.* Your friend is trying to convince you to come along to a school dance. Give five reasons why you are not interested in going.

2. *Wer spielt ein Musikinstrument?* Name four people and describe what musical instruments they play.

3. *Was hast du in den Ferien gemacht?* Write a brief description of what you did during your last vacation. List at least six activities, using the present perfect tense.

4. *Beschreibe, was du zum Frühstück, Mittagessen und Abendessen isst und trinkst.* You may either write a description or develop a list of your typical meals, including beverages.

5. *Was ich noch vor der Party alles machen muss.* Imagine you and your friends are preparing a party for this weekend. Write a short description of what you need to do to ensure a successful party.

 Activities 19-20

 Activity 7

Was machen die Leute im Sommer? (Zermatt)

Und im Winter?

Vokabeln

der **Abschlussball,-̈e** final (graduation) ball
der **Apfel,-̈** apple
  aussehen to look like
die **Banane,-n** banana
die **Band,-s** band
die **Birne,-n** pear
die **Blockflöte,-n** recorder
die **Blume,-n** flower
  dafür for it
  derselbe the same; *in derselben Schule* in the same school
  elegant elegant
  England England
  entfernt away, distant
die **Flöte,-n** flute
der **Foxtrott** foxtrot
der **Fruchtsaft,-̈e** fruit juice
die **Geige,-n** violin
  genau exact(ly)
  geöffnet open
die **Gurke,-n** cucumber
das **Gymnasium,-sien** secondary school

der **Kavalier,-e** gentleman
  leid: Es tut mir leid. I'm sorry.
die **Lust** pleasure, joy; *Ich habe Lust...* I would like to...
das **Mal,-e** time(s); *das letzte Mal* the last time
das **Mineralwasser** mineral water
das **Musikinstrument,-e** musical instrument
der **Nachtisch,-e** dessert
die **Nudelsuppe** noodle soup
  ob if, whether
das **Obst** fruit(s)
der **Orangensaft** orange juice
der **Rhythmus** rhythm; *nach dem Rhythmus* according to the rhythm
die **Rumba** rumba
der **Schritt,-e** step
der **Schüler,-** student (elementary through secondary school)
  solch such
der **Spaß** fun; *Es macht Spaß.* It's fun.

die **Straße,-n** street; *in derselben Straße* in the same street
der **Tanz,-̈e** dance
das **Tanzen** dancing; *beim Tanzen* while dancing
die **Tänzerin,-nen** dancer
die **Tanzlehrerin,-nen** dancing instructor
der **Tanzpartner,-** dancing partner
die **Tanzschule,-n** dancing school
die **Tanzstunde,-n** dancing lesson
der **Tee** tea
  treffen to meet; *Treffen wir uns...* Let's meet...
die **Trompete,-n** trumpet
der **Wagen,-** car
  waschen to wash
  zeigen to show, demonstrate
  zusammen together
  zusehen to watch

viele Blumen

Was gibt's hier?

der Wagen

Das macht Spaß!

Personal Pronouns

SINGULAR	Nominative	Accusative	Dative
1st person	ich	mich	mir
2nd person	du	dich	dir
3rd person	er sie es	ihn sie es	ihm ihr ihm
PLURAL			
1st person	wir	uns	uns
2nd person	ihr	euch	euch
3rd person	sie	sie	ihnen
formal form (singular or plural)	Sie	Sie	Ihnen

Definite Article

	Singular			Plural
	Masculine	Feminine	Neuter	
Nominative	der	die	das	die
Accusative	den	die	das	die
Dative	dem	der	dem	den

Question Words: Wer? Was?

Nominative	wer	was
Accusative	wen	was
Dative	wem	

Indefinite Article

	Singular			Plural
	Masculine	Feminine	Neuter	
Nominative	ein	eine	ein	keine
Accusative	einen	eine	ein	keine
Dative	einem	einer	einem	keinen

Regular Verb Forms — Present Tense

	gehen	finden	heißen
ich	gehe	finde	heiße
du	gehst	findest	heißt
er, sie, es	geht	findet	heißt
wir	gehen	finden	heißen
ihr	geht	findet	heißt
sie, Sie	gehen	finden	heißen

Irregular Verb Forms — Present Tense

	haben	sein	wissen
ich	habe	bin	weiß
du	hast	bist	weißt
er, sie, es	hat	ist	weiß
wir	haben	sind	wissen
ihr	habt	seid	wisst
sie, Sie	haben	sind	wissen

Command Forms

Familiar (singular)	Geh!	Warte!	Sei!	Hab!
Familiar (plural)	Geht!	Wartet!	Seid!	Habt!
Formal (singular/plural)	Gehen Sie!	Warten Sie!	Seien Sie!	Haben Sie!
Wir-form (Let's...)	Gehen wir!	Warten wir!	Seien wir!	Haben wir!

Plural of Nouns

	Singular	Plural
no change or add umlaut	das Zimmer die Mutter	die Zimmer die Mütter
add -n, -en, or -nen	die Ecke der Herr die Freundin	die Ecken die Herren die Freundinnen
add -e or ⸚e	der Tag die Stadt	die Tage die Städte
add ⸚er	das Buch das Fach	die Bücher die Fächer
add -s	das Café das Büro	die Cafés die Büros

Inverted Word Order

1. Formation of questions beginning with the verb
   Spielst du heute Fußball?

2. Formation of questions beginning with a question word
   Wohin gehen Sie heute nachmittag?

3. Command forms
   Komm zu uns rüber!
   Lauft schnell!
   Begrüßen Sie die Gäste!
   Gehen wir ins Kino!

Negation

Verbs (nicht)   *Kommen sie nicht zu uns?*
Nouns (kein)   *Ich habe keine Karte.*

Modal Auxiliaries

	dürfen	können	mögen	müssen	möchten	sollen	wollen
ich	darf	kann	mag	muss	möchte	soll	will
du	darfst	kannst	magst	musst	möchtest	sollst	willst
er, sie, es	darf	kann	mag	muss	möchte	soll	will
wir	dürfen	können	mögen	müssen	möchten	sollen	wollen
ihr	dürft	könnt	mögt	müsst	möchtet	sollt	wollt
sie, Sie	dürfen	können	mögen	müssen	möchten	sollen	wollen

Future Tense (*werden + infinitive*)

ich	werde
du	wirst
er, sie, es	wird
wir	werden
ihr	werdet
sie, Sie	werden

Sie werden dieses Jahr nach Deutschland fahren. Wirst du ins Kino gehen?

Verbs with Stem Vowel Change (2nd & 3rd person singular only)

	a to *ä*	*e* to *i*	*e* to *ie*
ich	fahre	spreche	sehe
du	fährst	sprichst	siehst
er, sie, es	fährt	spricht	sieht
wir	fahren	sprechen	sehen
ihr	fahrt	sprecht	seht
sie, Sie	fahren	sprechen	sehen

Prepositions

Dative	Accusative	Contraction
aus	durch	durch das = durchs
außer	für	für das = fürs
bei	gegen	bei dem = beim
mit	ohne	—
nach	um	um das = ums
seit		—
von		von dem = vom
zu		zu dem = zum/zu der = zur

Verbs Followed by Dative Case

helfen   *antworten*   *gefallen*   *passen*   *glauben*

Gabi hilft ihrer Mutter. Der Anzug gefällt mir.

The verb *glauben* may take either the dative or accusative. If used with a person, the dative follows (*Ich glaube ihm*). If used with an object, the accusative is used (*Ich glaube das nicht*).

Possessive Adjectives

	Singular			Plural
	Masculine	**Feminine**	**Neuter**	
Nominative	mein	meine	mein	meine
Accusative	meinen	meine	mein	meine
Dative	meinem	meiner	meinem	meinen

The endings of possessive adjectives are the same as those of the indefinite article (*ein*-words). Possessive adjectives are *mein, dein, sein, ihr, sein, unser, euer, ihr, Ihr.*

Numbers

0	=	null	11	=	elf	22	= zweiundzwanzig
1	=	eins	12	=	zwölf	30	= dreißig
2	=	zwei	13	=	dreizehn	40	= vierzig
3	=	drei	14	=	vierzehn	50	= fünfzig
4	=	vier	15	=	fünfzehn	60	= sechzig
5	=	fünf	16	=	sechzehn	70	= siebzig
6	=	sechs	17	=	siebzehn	80	= achtzig
7	=	sieben	18	=	achtzehn	90	= neunzig
8	=	acht	19	=	neunzehn	100	= einhundert
9	=	neun	20	=	zwanzig	101	= hunderteins
10	=	zehn	21	=	einundzwanzig		

Time

1:00	Es ist ein Uhr.		11:45	Es ist Viertel vor zwölf.
2:00	Es ist zwei Uhr.		5:10	Es ist zehn Minuten nach fünf.
3:30	Es ist halb vier.		7:58	Es ist zwei Minuten vor acht.
10:15	Es ist Viertel nach zehn.			

Irregular Verbs - Present Perfect Tense (Past Participle)

The following list contains all the irregular verbs used in *Deutsch Aktuell 1*. Verbs with separable or inseparable prefixes are not included when the basic verb form has been introduced (example: *kommen, ankommen*). If the basic verb has not been introduced then the verb with its prefix is included. Verbs with stem vowel changes, as well as those constructed with a form of *sein*, have also been indicated.

Infinitive	Stem Vowel Change	Past Participle	Meaning
abbiegen		ist abgebogen	to turn (to)
anrufen		angerufen	to call up
anziehen		angezogen	to wear, put on
backen	bäckt	gebacken	to bake
beginnen		begonnen	to begin
bekommen		bekommen	to get, receive
bleiben		ist geblieben	to stay, remain
bringen		gebracht	to bring
denken		gedacht	to think
einladen	lädt ein	eingeladen	to invite
essen	ißt	gegessen	to eat
fahren	fährt	ist gefahren	to drive
finden		gefunden	to find
fliegen		ist geflogen	to fly
geben	gibt	gegeben	to give
gefallen	gefällt	gefallen	to like
haben	hat	gehabt	to have
heißen		geheißen	to be called
helfen	hilft	geholfen	to help
kennen		gekannt	to know (person)
kommen		ist gekommen	to come
laufen	läuft	ist gelaufen	to run, walk
lesen	liest	gelesen	to read
liegen		gelegen	to lie, be located
mitnehmen	nimmt mit	mitgenommen	to take along
scheinen		geschienen	to shine
schießen		geschossen	to shoot
schreiben		geschrieben	to write
schreien		geschrien	to scream
schwimmen		ist geschwommen	to swim
sehen	sieht	gesehen	to see
sein	ist	ist gewesen	to be
singen		gesungen	to be
sprechen	spricht	gesprochen	to speak, talk
stehen		gestanden	to stand
treffen	trifft	getroffen	to meet
treiben		getrieben	to do (sports)
trinken		getrunken	to drink
wissen	weiß	gewusst	to know

All the words introduced in *Deutsch Aktuell 1* have been summarized in this section. The numbers or letters following the meaning of individual words or phrases indicate the particular chapter in which they appear for the first time. The letter *E* is for the introductory chapter entitled *Einführung*. For cases in which there is more than one meaning for a word or a phrase and it appeared in different chapters, both chapter numbers are listed. (Example: das that *E*; the 2) Nouns have been listed with their respective articles and plural forms. Words preceded by an asterisk (*) are passive and appear following the *Land und Leute* reading selections in Chapters 4, 8 and 12. All other words are considered active and are used frequently throughout the text.

A

abbiegen to turn (to) 11
der **Abend,-e** evening 7; *am Abend* in the evening 7
das **Abendessen** supper, dinner 6
aber but; *aber nein* of course not 2
abfahren to depart, leave 11
abgeben to pass (ball) 10
Abgemacht! Agreed! 9
abräumen to clear (table) 9
der **Abschlussball,-̈e** final (graduation) ball 12
das **Abteil,-e** compartment 11
acht eight *E*
achtzehn eighteen *E*
achtzig eighty 2
alle all 4; *vor allem* mainly 9
alles all, everything 11
allgemein general(ly) 9
*die **Alpen** Alps 8
also then, so 7; *Also, los!* OK! Let's go! *E*
alt old *E*
Amerika America 3
an at, on, to 2
ander(e) other 9; *die anderen* the others 9
anhaben to have on, wear 7
ankommen to arrive 5
anrufen to call up 8; *Ruf doch...an!* Why don'tyou call...! 8
die **Antwort,-en** answer 4
anziehen to wear, put on 9
der **Anzug,-̈e** suit 7
der **Apfel,-̈** apple 12
der **Apfelsaft** apple juice 6
der **April** April 5
die **Arbeit,-en** work, exam 4; *bei der Arbeit helfen* to help with the work 8
arbeiten to work 11
der **Arm,-e** arm 10
auch also, too 2
auf on, at 5

aufbauen to pitch (tent), set up, construct 11
aufräumen to clean up 9
das **Auge,-n** eye 10
der **August** August 5
aus from, out of 1
ausgeben to spend (money) 9
die **Auskunft,-̈e** information 11
aussehen to look like 12
außer besides 9; except 10
außerhalb out of, outside 9
die **Auswahl** selection, choice 7
das **Auto,-s** car 11

B

backen to bake 8
das **Backgammon** backgammon 10
das **Bad,-̈er** bathroom 8
die **Badewanne,-n** bathtub 8
die **Bahn-Card,-s** discount and ID card for reduced train ticket 11
der **Bahnhof,-̈e** train station 3
der **Ball,-̈e** ball 10
die **Ballkontrolle** ball control 10
die **Banane,-n** banana 12
die **Band,-s** band 12
der **Bass,-̈e** bass 9
der **Basketball,-̈e** basketball 3
basteln to do (handi)crafts 10
beginnen to begin 3
begrüßen to greet 8
bei at, near, by 1; with 10; *beim Park* near the park 1
beide both 7
beige beige 7
das **Bein,-e** leg 10
bekannt well-known 8
bekommen to get, receive 4
Belgien Belgium 5
* **beliebt** popular 8
der **Berg,-e** mountain 7
besonders special, especially 6; *nicht besonders* not especially 6
besser better 5
best- best 9; *am besten* the best 9

bestimmt definitely, for sure 7
der **Besuch,-e** visit 5; *Sie kommt zu Besuch.* She comes to visit. 5
besuchen to visit 5
*der **Besucher,-** visitor 12
das **Bett,-en** bed 8
bezahlen to pay 9
das **Bild,-er** picture 8
die **Biologie** biology 4
die **Birne,-n** pear 12
bis until *E*; *Bis später!* See you later! *E*
bitte please 2; *Ja, bitte?, Bitte schön?* May I help you? 6
blau blue 7
bleiben to stay, remain 5
der **Bleistift,-e** pencil 4
die **Blockflöte,-n** recorder 12
die **Blume,-n** flower 12
die **Bluse,-n** blouse 7
das **Boot,-e** boat 11
die **Bratwurst,-̈e** bratwurst 6
brauchen to need 4
braun brown 7
der **Brief,-e** letter 5
die **Briefmarke,-n** stamp 9
bringen to bring 3; *Bringen Sie mir...* Bring me... 6
das **Brot,-e** bread 6
das **Brötchen,-** hard roll 6
der **Bruder,-̈** brother 2
das **Buch,-̈er** book 2
das **Bücherregal,-e** bookshelf 8
die **Bundesliga** National League 10
bunt colorful 7
das **Büro,-s** office 4
der **Bus,-se** bus 4
die **Butter** butter 6

C

das **Café,-s** café 11
der **Campingplatz,-̈e** campground 11
die **CD,-s** CD, compact disk 2
der **CD-Spieler,-** CD player 8

die **Chance,-n** chance 10
    charmant charming 5
die **Chemie** chemistry 4
die **Cola,-s** cola 6
der **Computer,-** computer 3
das **Computerspiel,-e** computer
    game 3
der **Cousin,-s** cousin (male) 5
die **Cousine,-n** cousin (female) 5

D

da there 1; *da drüben* over there 1;
    Endlich ist der Tag da. Finally,
    the day is here. 8
dafür for it 12
dabei sein to take part, be a
    member, be present 9
dahingehen to go there 9
Dänemark Denmark 5
danke thanks 6
danken to thank 8
dann then 2
das that E; the 2
dass that 8
dauern to take, last 4
decken to cover 8; *den Tisch
    decken* to set the table 8
dein your 1; *Dein(e)...* Your... 7
denken to think 9; *denken an* to
    think about 9
denn used for emphasis 1
der the 2
derselbe the same 12; *in
    derselben Straße* on the same
    street 12
deshalb therefore, that's why 8
deutsch German 5; *Sie spricht
    deutsch.* She speaks German. 5;
    Deutscher Meister National
    Champion of Germany 10
das **Deutsch** German (subject) 4
    Deutschland Germany 2
der **Dezember** December 5
    dich you 8; *für dich* for you E
    die the 2
der **Dienstag,-e** Tuesday 2
    dieser this 4; *diese* (form of *dieser*)
    this 4
    dir (to) you 6
die **Disko,-s** disco 9

doch used for emphasis 3; sure
    thing, oh yes 11
der **Donnerstag,-e** Thursday 2
    dort there 10
    dorthin (to) there 11
    drei three E
    dreißig thirty 2
    dreizehn thirteen E
    du you (familiar singular) E; *Du,
    Steffie...* Say, Steffie... 3
    dunkel dark 7; *dunkelblau* dark
    blue 7
   * **durch** through 8
    dürfen may, to be permitted to 7
der **Durst** thirst 6; *Durst haben* to be
    thirsty 6

E

echt real(ly) 9
die **Ecke,-n** corner 1
    ein(e) a, an E
    einfach simple 11
    einkaufen to shop 9; *einkaufen
    gehen* to go shopping 9
    einladen to invite 8
die **Einladung,-en** invitation 8
    einmal once 8; *noch einmal* once
    more 8; *einmal die Woche* once a
    week 10
    eins one E
    eintönig monotonous, dull 7
*der **Einwohner,-** inhabitant 4
das **Eis** ice cream 6
das **Eiscafé,-s** ice cream parlor,
    café 6
das **Eishockey** ice hockey 10
der **Eistee** ice tea 6
    elegant elegant 12
    elf eleven E
die **Eltern** (pl.) parents 2
    endlich finally 8; *Endlich ist der
    Tag da.* Finally, the day is
    here. 8
    eng tight 7
    England England 12
    englisch English 5; *Er spricht
    englisch.* He speaks English. 5
das **Englisch** English (subject) 4
    entfernt away, distant 12

*die **Entfernung,-en** distance 4; *die
    weiteste Entfernung* the
    farthest distance 4
    **entschuldigen: Entschuldigen
    Sie!** Excuse me! 11
die **Entschuldigung** excuse;
    Entschuldigung! Excuse me! 3
    er he E
das **Erdbeereis** strawberry ice
    cream 6
die **Erdkunde** geography 4
    erfolgreich successful 9
    erst just, only 4; *erst morgen* not
    until tomorrow 6
    es it 1
    essen to eat 6
    etwas some, a little, something 6
    euer your (familiar plural) 12
   * **Europa** Europe 8

F

das **Fach,-̈er** (school) subject 4
    fahren to drive, go 5
die **Fahrkarte,-n** ticket 11
der **Fahrplan,-̈e** schedule 11
das **Fahrrad,-̈er** bicycle 8
der **Fan,-s** fan 8
die **Fanta** brand name of soda
    (orange-flavored) 6
die **Farbe,-n** color 7
der **Februar** February 5
    feiern to celebrate 8
die **Ferien** (pl.) vacation 11; *in die
    Ferien fahren* to go on
    vacation 11
    fernsehen to watch television 3
das **Fernsehen** television 3; *im
    Fernsehen* on television 3
der **Fernseher,-** TV, television set 8
das **Fernsehprogramm,-e** television
    program 3
der **Film,-e** film, movie 9
    finden to find 2; *Wie findest
    du...?* What do you think
    of...? 2
der   **Finger,-** finger 10
der **Fisch,-e** fish 6
die **Fischsemmel,-n** fish sandwich 6
   * **flach** flat 8
    fliegen to fly 11

* **fließen** to flow, run 8
die **Flöte,-n** flute 12
das **Flugzeug,-e** airplane 11
*der **Fluss,-̈e** river 8
die **Form,-en** form, shape 10
das **Fotoalbum, Fotoalben** photo album 8
fotografieren to take pictures 9
der **Foxtrott** foxtrot 12
Frankreich France 5
französisch French 5; *Sie spricht französisch.* She speaks French. 5
das **Französisch** French (subject) 4
die **Frau,-en** Mrs., woman E
frei free, available 11
der **Freitag,-e** Friday 2
fremd foreign 11; *Ich bin fremd hier.* I'm a stranger here. 11
der **Freund,-e** boyfriend 1
die **Freundin,-nen** girlfriend 1
froh glad, happy 4
der **Fruchtsaft,-̈e** fruit juice 12
früh early 2
früher earlier 7
der **Frühling,-e** spring 5
das **Frühstück** breakfast 6
fünf five E
fünfzehn fifteen E
fünfzig fifty 2
für for 4; *für dich* for you E
der **Fuß,-̈e** foot 10; *zu Fuß* on foot 11
der **Fußball,-̈e** soccer, soccer ball 3
der **Fußballplatz,-̈e** soccer field 10
der **Fußballspieler,-** soccer player 10

G

ganz quite 1; *ganz toll* just great (terrific) 2
gar nicht not at all, by no means 8
geben to give 6; *Was gibt's?* What's up? 2; *es gibt* there is (are) 3
gebrauchen to use, make use of 10
der **Geburtstag,-e** birthday 8
der **Geburtstagskuchen,-** birthday cake 8

gefallen to like 5; *Wie gefällt es dir...?* How do you like it...? 5; *Es gefällt mir.* I like it. 7
gegen about, around 2; against 9; *gegen vier Uhr* about four o'clock 2
gehen to go 1; *Wie geht's?, Wie geht es Ihnen?* How are you? 1; *das geht* that's possible, that's OK 2; *Wann geht's los?* When does it start? 3; *Gehen wir doch gleich!* Let's go right away! 6
gehören zu to belong to 9
die **Geige,-n** violin 12
gelb yellow 7
das **Geld** money 6
gemischt assorted, mixed 6; *ein gemischtes Eis* assorted ice cream 6
das **Gemüse** vegetable(s) 6
genau exact(ly) 12
genauso...wie just as 11
das **Genie,-s** genius 4; *So ein Genie!* Such a genius! 4
genug enough 10
geöffnet open 12
das **Gepäck** luggage, baggage 11
geradeaus straight ahead 11
gern gladly, with pleasure 4; *gern haben* to like 3; to like (to do) 4
das **Geschenk,-e** present, gift 8
die **Geschichte** history 4
das **Geschirr** dishes 9
die **Geschirrspülmaschine,-n** dishwasher 8
gestern yesterday 11
die **Gitarre,-n** guitar 3
das **Glas,-̈er** glass 6
glauben to believe, think 7
gleich immediately, right away 1; *gleich um die Ecke* right around the corner 1
gleichfalls likewise 11; *danke gleichfalls* the same to you 11
das **Gleis,-e** track 11
das **Glück** luck 7; *Glück haben* to be lucky 7
die **Glückwunschkarte,-n** greeting card 8
das **Golf** golf 10
grau gray 7

*die **Grenze,-n** border 12; *an der Grenze zu* at the border with 12
groß big, large 4; *so groß wie* as big as 5; *größt-* biggest 4
die **Großeltern** (pl.) grandparents 2
die **Großmutter,-̈** grandmother 2
der **Großvater,-̈** grandfather 2
grün green 7
Grüß dich! Hi!, Hello! E
der **Gruß,-̈e** greeting 7; *Viele Grüße an...* Best regards to... 7
die **Gurke,-n** cucumber 12
gut good, well, OK 1
das **Gymnasium,-sien** secondary school, college preparatory school 12

H

das **Haar,-e** hair 10
haben to have 3
halb half 2
die **Halbzeit** halftime 10
Hallo! Hi! E
der **Hals,-̈e** neck 10
der **Hamburger,-** hamburger 6
die **Hand,-̈e** hand 10
der **Handschuh,-e** glove 7
hart hard 10
*die **Hauptstadt,-̈e** capital (city) 4
das **Haus,-̈er** house 4; *zu Hause* at home 2; *nach Hause gehen* to go home 3
die **Hausaufgabe,-n** homework 4
das **Heft,-e** notebook 4
heiß hot 5
heißen to be called, named E; *Wie heißt du?* What's your name? E
der **Held,-en** hero 10
helfen to help 8; *bei der Arbeit helfen* to help with the work 8
hell light 7
das **Hemd,-en** shirt 7
der **Herbst,-e** fall, autumn 5
der **Herd,-e** stove 8
herkommen to come here 2
der **Herr,-en** Mr., gentleman E
herzlich sincere, cordial 8; *Herzlichen Glückwunsch zum Geburtstag!* Happy birthday! 8

heute today 2; *heute Morgen* this morning 3; *heute Mittag* this noon 3; *heute Nachmittag* this afternoon 3; *heute Abend* this evening 3

hier here 1

das **Hobby,-s** hobby 9

hoch high 10; *höchst-* highest 8

hoffentlich hopefully 8

Holland Holland 5

hören to hear, listen to 3

die **Hose,-n** pants, slacks 7

hundert hundred 2

der **Hunger** hunger 6; *Hunger haben* to be hungry 6

I

ich I E

die **Idee,-n** idea 4; *Gute Idee!* Good idea! 4

ihr you (familiar plural) 1; her 2; their 12

Ihr your (formal singular and plural) 12

der **Imbiss,-e** snack (bar) 11

immer always 4

in in 1; *im Osten* in the east 2

innerhalb within, inside 9

Italien Italy 5

italienisch Italian 5; *Er spricht italienisch.* He speaks Italian. 5

J

ja yes 1

die **Jacke,-n** jacket 7

das **Jahr,-e** year 5

die **Jahreszeit,-en** season 5

der **Januar** January 5

die **Jeans** (pl.) jeans 7

* **jeder** every, each 8

jetzt now 2

jubeln to cheer 10

der **Jugendliche,-n** teenager, young person 9

die **Jugendmannschaft,-en** youth team 10

der **Juli** July 5

der **Junge,-n** boy E

der **Juni** June 5

K

der **Kaffee** coffee 6

der **Kakao** hot chocolate, cocoa 6

kalt cold 5

die **Kalte Platte** cold-cut platter 6

die **Kamera,-s** camera 8

die **Karriere,-n** career 10

die **Karte,-n** ticket, card 3

die **Kartoffel,-n** potato 6

der **Käse** cheese 6

das **Käsebrot,-e** cheese sandwich 6

die **Kassette,-n** cassette 3

kaufen to buy 3

das **Kaufhaus,-̈er** department store 3

der **Kavalier,-e** gentleman 12

kein no 4

der **Kellner,-** waiter, food server 6

die **Kellnerin,-en** waitress, food server 6

kennen to know (person, place) 1

das **Keyboard,-s** keyboard 9

* der **Kilometer,-** kilometer 4

das **Kinn,-e** chin 10

das **Kino,-s** movie theater, cinema 9

klar clear 3; *Klar.* Of course. 3

die **Klarinette,-n** clarinet 9

klasse super, great, terrific 10

die **Klasse,-n** class 4; *die Zweite Klasse* second (economy) class (train) 11

das **Klavier,-e** piano 3

das **Kleid,-er** dress 7

die **Kleidung** clothes, clothing 8

das **Kleidungsstück,-e** clothing item 7

der **Klub,-s** club 10

klug smart, intelligent 4

kommen to come 1; *zu Besuch kommen* to come to visit 5; *rüberkommen* to come over 2; *herkommen* to come here; *Komm mal her!* Come here! 2; *Komm doch zu uns.* Why don't you come to us? 5; *Der Zug kommt pünktlich an.* The train arrives on time. 5

können can, to be able to 7

das **Konzert,-e** concert 9

koordiniert coordinated 10

der **Kopf,-̈e** head 4

der **Körperteil,-e** part of body 10

kosten to cost 3

die **Krawatte,-n** tie 7

die **Kreide** chalk 4

* das **Kreuz** cross 12

der **Krimi,-s** detective story, thriller 3

die **Küche,-n** kitchen 8

der **Kuchen,-** cake 8

kühl cool 5

der **Kühlschrank,-̈e** refrigerator 8

der **Kuli,-s** (ballpoint) pen 4

kurz short 7

L

lachen to laugh 8

die **Lampe,-n** lamp 8

das **Land,-̈er** country 5

die **Landkarte,-n** map 4

lang long 7; *zehn Tage lang* for ten days 11

lange long, long time 5; *längst-* longest 8

langsam slow 4

langweilig boring 2

lassen to leave, let 7

das **Latein** Latin 4

laufen to run, go 9; *Ski laufen* to ski 5

leer empty 4

der **Lehrer,-** teacher (male) 4

die **Lehrerin,-nen** (female) 4

leicht easy 4

leid: Es tut mir leid. I'm sorry. 12

lernen to learn 4

lesen to read 2

letzt- last 11

die **Leute** (pl.) people 9

Liebe(r)... Dear... (letter) 7

lieber rather 3; *Das ist mir lieber.* I prefer that. 3

das **Lieblingsfach,-̈er** favorite (school) subject 4

das **Lieblingslied,-er** favorite song 9

* **Liechtenstein** Liechtenstein 12

das **Lied,-er** song 9

liegen to be located, lie 3

die **Liga, Ligen** league 10

die **Limo,-s** lemonade, soft drink 6

das **Lineal,-e** ruler 4

links left 11; *auf der linken Seite* on the left side 11

die **Lippe,-n** lip 10
locker loose 10
los: Da ist viel los. There is a lot going on. 10
losgehen to start 3; *Wann geht's los?* When does it start? 3
die **Lust** pleasure, joy 12; *Ich habe Lust...* I would like to... 12
Luxemburg Luxembourg 5

M

machen to do, make 2; *Was machst du?* What are you doing? 2; *Mach schnell!* Hurry! 4; *Das macht nichts.* That doesn't matter. 10
das **Mädchen,-** girl E
mähen to mow 9
der **Mai** May 5
mal times 4; *Mal sehen...* Let's see... 11
das **Mal,-e** time(s) 12; *das letzte Mal* the last time 12; *ein paar Mal* a few times 12
man one, they, people, you 5
manche some, a few 10
manchmal sometimes 9
die **Mannschaft,-en** team 10
der **Mantel,-̈** coat 7
die **Mark** mark (German monetary unit) 3
der **Markt,-̈e** market 9
die **Marmelade,-n** jam, marmalade 6
der **März** March 5
die **Mathematik (Mathe)** mathematics (math) 4; *das Mathebuch* math book 4; *die Mathestunde* math class, lesson 4
mehr more 5; *nicht mehr* no more, no longer 5; *mehr...als* more than 8
mein my 1
meins mine 10
meistens mostly 10
der **Meister,-** champion 10; *Deutscher Meister* National Champion of Germany 10 der
Mensch,-en person, human 12
mich me 6
der **Mikrowellenherd,-e** microwave oven 8

die **Milch** milk 6
*die **Million,-en** million 8
das **Mineralwasser** mineral water 12
minus minus E
die **Minute,-n** minute 1
mir (to) me 6
mit with 2
mitbringen to bring along 3
mitkommen to come along 3; *Kommst du mit?* Are you coming along? 3
mitmachen to participate 10
mitnehmen to take along 11
der **Mittag,-e** noon 3
das **Mittagessen** lunch 2
*die **Mitte** center, middle 8
der **Mittwoch,-e** Wednesday 2
möchten would like to; *Ich möchte zum Rockkonzert (gehen).* I would like to go to the rock concert. 3
mögen to like 6
der **Moment,-e** moment; *Einen Moment, bitte.* Just a moment, please. 2
der **Monat,-e** month 5
der **Montag,-e** Monday 2
das **Moped,-s** moped 11
der **Morgen** morning 3
morgen tomorrow 2
das **Motorrad,-̈er** motorcycle 11
der **Mund,-̈er** mouth 10
*die **Münze,-n** coin 9
das **Museum,-seen** museum 11
die **Musik** music 3
das **Musikfest,-e** music festival 8
das **Musikinstrument,-e** musical instrument 12
müssen to have to, must 6
die **Mutter,-̈** mother 2
die **Mutti,-s** mom 2

N

na well 2; *Na ja.* Oh well. 4
nach to, after 3; *nach Hause gehen* to go home 3
das **Nachbarland,-̈er** neighboring country 5
der **Nachmittag,-e** afternoon 8; *Samstagnachmittag* Saturday afternoon 8

nächst- next 9; *das nächste Mal* the next time 9
der **Nachtisch,-e** dessert 12
die **Nähe** nearness, proximity 11; *in der Nähe* nearby 11
die **Nase,-n** nose 10
*die **Nationalfahne,-n** national flag 8
die **Naturwissenschaften** (pl.) natural sciences 4
nebenbei besides that 9
nein no 1
nett nice 5
das **Netz,-e** net 10
neu new 1
neun nine E
neunzehn nineteen E
neunzig ninety 2
nicht not 1
nichts nothing 6
die **Niederlande** Netherlands 5
noch still, yet 6; *noch einmal* once more 8
der **Norden** north 3
*die **Nordsee** North Sea 12
die **Note,-n** grade 4
der **November** November 5
die **Nudelsuppe** noodle soup 12
null zero E
nur only 1

O

ob if, whether 12
das **Obst** fruit(s) 12
oder or 2
oft often 4
* **ohne** without 4
das **Ohr,-en** ear 10
der **Ohrring,-e** earring 8
der **Oktober** October 5
die **Oma,-s** grandma 2
der **Onkel,-** uncle 2
der **Opa,-s** grandpa 2
orange orange 7
der **Orangensaft** orange juice 12
der **Osten** east 2
Österreich Austria 5
der **Österreicher,-** Austrian 8
die **Ostsee** Baltic Sea 11

P

paar: ein paar a few 5

das **Paar,-e** pair, couple 7

packen to pack 11

das **Papier** paper 4

*das **Paradies** paradise 12

der **Park,-s** park 1

die **Party,-s** party 8; *eine Party geben* to give a party 8

passen to fit 7

die **Pasta** pasta 9

die **Physik** physics 4

die **Pizza,-s** pizza 6

das **Pizza-Brot** pizza bread 6

die **Pizzeria,-s** pizza restaurant 6

die **Platte,-n** plate 6; *Kalte Platte* cold-cut platter 6

der **Platz,-̈e** place 8; seat 11; *da ist mehr Platz als...* there is more room than... 8

der **Platz,-̈e** seat, place 11

plus plus E

Polen Poland 5

die **Pommes frites** (pl.) french fries 6

*die **Post** post office 11

das **Poster,-** poster 8

preiswert reasonable 3

prima great 3

das **Problem,-e** problem 4

das **Prozent,-e** percent 8

der **Pulli,-s** sweater, pullover 7

der **Pullover,-** sweater, pullover 7

pünktlich punctual, on time 4

Q

die **Quizshow,-s** quiz show 8

R

das **Rad,-̈er** bike 10; *Rad fahren* to bike 10

der **Radiergummi,-s** eraser 4

das **Radio,-s** radio 8

der **Rasen** lawn 9; *den Rasen mähen* to mow the lawn 9

der **Rechner,-** calculator 4

recht right 4; *Du hast recht.* You're right. 4

rechts right 11

reden to talk, speak 10

regnen to rain 5

die **Reise,-n** trip 11

reisen to travel 5

die **Religion** religion 4

reparieren to repair 9

*die **Republik** Republic 8

das **Restaurant,-s** restaurant 6

der **Rhythmus** rhythm 12; *dem Rhythmus nach* according to the rhythm 12

der **Rock,-̈e** skirt 7

die **Rockgruppe,-n** rock group, rock band 2

das **Rockkonzert,-e** rock concert 3

die **Rockmusik** rock music 3

rosa pink 7

rot red 7

rüberkommen to come over 2

die **Rumba** rumba 12

S

sagen to say, tell 3; *Sagen wir...* Let's say... 3; *Wie sagt man...?* How do you/they say...? 4; *Sag mir...* Tell me... 5

die **Salami** salami 6

der **Salat,-e** salad 6

sammeln to collect 9

der **Samstag,-e** Saturday 2

der **Sauerbraten** sauerbraten (marinated beef) 6

das **Saxophon,-e** saxophone 9

das **Schach** chess 9

schaffen to manage (it), make (it) 10; *Das schaffen wir.* We'll make it. 10

der **Schalter,-** (ticket) counter 11

die **Scheibe,-n** slice 6; *eine Scheibe Brot* a slice of bread 6

scheinen to shine 5

schenken to give a present 8

schick chic, smart (looking) 9

schicken to send 5

schießen to shoot 10

das **Schiff,-e** ship 11

das **Schlafzimmer,-** bedroom 8

die **Schlagsahne** whipped cream 6

das **Schlagzeug** drums, percussion 9

schlecht bad 1

Schlittschuh laufen to ice skate 10

schmecken to taste 6; *Das schmeckt mir nicht.* I don't like it. 6; *Wie schmeckt's?* How do you like it?, How does it taste? 6

der **Schmuck** jewelry 8

schneien to snow 5

schnell fast 4

das **Schokoeis** chocolate ice cream 6

schon already 4

schön beautiful, nice 5

der **Schrank,-̈e** cupboard, closet 8

schreiben to write 5

der **Schreibtisch,-e** desk 8

schreien to scream 10

der **Schritt,-e** step 12

das **Schrittchen,-** small step 9; *ein Schrittchen weiterkommen* to make a little headway 9

der **Schuh,-e** shoe 7

die **Schule,-n** school 3

der **Schüler,-** student (elementary through secondary school) 12

die **Schülerrockband,-s** student rock band 9

der **Schulfreund,-e** schoolmate 6

die **Schultasche,-n** school bag, satchel 4

die **Schulter,-n** shoulder 10

schwarz black 7

die **Schweiz** Switzerland 5

schwer hard, difficult 4

die **Schwester,-n** sister 2

schwimmen to swim 3

sechs six E

sechzehn sixteen E

sechzig sixty 2

der **See,-n** lake 11; *die Ostsee* Baltic Sea 11

das **Segelfliegen** sail gliding 9

sehen to see, look 6; *ein Fernsehprogramm sehen* to watch a TV program 6; *Seht mal!* Look! 6; *Mal sehen...* Let's see... 11

sehr very 1

sein his 4; its 12

sein to be 4

seit since, for 5; *seit fünf Monaten* for five months 5; *seit über...Jahren* for more than...years 9

die **Seite,-n** side 11

der **September** September 5
der **Sessel,-** armchair, easy chair 8
  sie she E; they 1
  Sie you (formal) 1
  sieben seven E
  siebzehn seventeen E
  siebzig seventy 2
  singen to sing 9
  Ski laufen to ski 5
  so so 2; *so gegen vier* at about four (o'clock) 2; *so...wie* as...as 12
die **Socke,-n** sock 7
das **Sofa,-s** sofa 8
der **Sohn,¨e** son 2
  solch such 12
  sollen should, to be supposed to 7
der **Sommer,-** summer 5
*der **Sommermonat,-e** summer month 12
der **Sonnabend,-e** Saturday 2
die **Sonne** sun 5
der **Sonntag,-e** Sunday 2
  sonst besides, otherwise 6; *Sonst noch etwas?* Anything else? 6
  Spanien Spain 5
  spanisch Spanish 5; *Er spricht spanisch.* He speaks Spanish. 5
der **Spaß** fun 4; *Sie haben viel Spaß.* They have lots of fun. 4; *Viel Spaß!* Have lots of fun! 11; *Es macht Spaß.* It's fun. 12
  spät late 2; *später* later 2; *Bis später.* See you later. 2
die **Spätzle** spaetzle (kind of home-made pasta) 6
die **Speisekarte,-n** menu 6
das **Spezi,-s** cola and lemon soda 6
das **Spiel,-e** game 10
  spielen to play 3
der **Sport** sport 4
die **Sportart,-en** kind of sport 10
der **Sportklub,-s** sports club 10
  sportlich athletic, sporty 10
die **Sprache,-n** language 5
  sprechen to speak, talk 5; *Sie spricht deutsch.* She speaks German. 5; *sprechen über* to talk about 8; *sprechen über sich selbst* to talk about themselves 9
das **Spülbecken,-** (kitchen) sink 8
  spülen to wash, rinse 9

*der **Staat,-en** state 8
die **Stadt,¨e** city 1
die **Stadtmitte** center of city 11
der **Star,-s** star (athlete) 10
  staubsaugen to vacuum 9
  stehen to stand, be 7; *Es steht dir gut.* It looks good on you. 7; *Die Mannschaft steht an zweiter Stelle.* The team is in second place. 10; *Es steht...* The score is... 10
  steif stiff 10
die **Stelle,-n** place, spot 10; *Die Mannschaft steht an zweiter Stelle.* The team is in second place. 10
  stimmen to be correct 1; *Das stimmt.* That's correct. 1
die **Stirn,-en** forehead 10
der **Strand,¨e** beach, shore 11; *Timmendorfer Strand* resort at the Baltic Sea 11
die **Straße,-n** street 12
die **Straßenbahn,-en** streetcar 11
der **Strumpf,¨e** stocking 7
der **Stuhl,¨e** chair 4
die **Stunde,-n** hour 4
der **Stundenplan,¨e** class schedule 4
  Süddeutschland southern Germany 3
der **Süden** south 3
  super super, great 2
das **Sweatshirt,-s** sweatshirt 7

T

das **T-Shirt,-s** T-shirt 7
die **Tafel,-n** (chalk)board 4
der **Tafellappen,-** rag (to wipe off blackboard) 4
der **Tag,-e** day E; *Tag!* Hello! E; *Guten Tag!* Hello! E; *am Tag* during the day 7
das **Talent,-e** talent 9
die **Tante,-n** aunt 2
der **Tanz,¨e** dance 12
die **Tänzerin,-nen** dancer 12
  tanzen to dance 3
das **Tanzen** dancing 12; *beim Tanzen* while dancing 12
der **Tanzlehrer,-** dancing instructor 12

der **Tanzpartner,-** dancing partner 12
die **Tanzschule,-n** dancing school 12
die **Tanzstunde,-n** dancing lesson 12
das **Taschengeld** allowance 6
die **Tasse,-n** cup 6
  tausend thousand 2
der **Tee** tea 12
*der **Teil,-e** part, section 8; *zum größten Teil* for the most part 8
das **Telefon,-e** telephone 2; *am Telefon* on the telephone 2
das **Tempo** tempo, speed 10
das **Tennis** tennis 3
der **Tennisplatz,¨e** tennis court 10
der **Tennisschläger,-** tennis racket 10
der **Tennisschuh,-e** tennis (athletic) shoe 7
das **Tennisspiel,-e** tennis game 10
  teuer expensive 7
der **Tip,-s** hint, tip, suggestion 10
der **Tisch,-e** table 4
das **Tischtennis** table tennis 10
die **Tochter,¨** daughter 2
die **Toilette,-n** toilet, restroom 8
  toll great, terrific 2
die **Tomate,-n** tomato 6
das **Tor,-e** goal 10; *aufs Tor schießen* to shoot on goal 10
  Tortellini tortellini (filled pasta) 6
*der **Tourist,-en** tourist 8
die **Tournee,-n** tour 9
der **Trainer,-** trainer, coach 10
  trainieren to train 10
sich **treffen** to meet 9; *Treffen wir uns...* Let's meet... 12
  treiben to do 10; *Sport treiben* to participate in sports 10
  trinken to drink 6
die **Trompete,-n** trumpet 12
die **Tschechische Republik** Czech Republic 5
  Tschüs! See you! Bye! E

U

  üben to practice 10; *zum Üben* for practice 10
die **Übung,-en** exercise, practice 5; *Übung macht den Meister!* Practice makes perfect. 5

die **Uhr,-en** clock, watch 2; *Um wie viel Uhr?* At what time? 2
  um around 1; at 2; *Um wie viel Uhr?* At what time? 2
  umsteigen to transfer 11
  und and E
  * **ungefähr** approximately 4
  unser our 12
die **Unterhaltung,-en** entertainment 9

V

das **Vanilleeis** vanilla ice cream 6
der **Vater,-** father 2
der **Vati,-s** dad 2
*die **Vereinigten Staaten von Amerika** United States of America 4
das **Vergnügen** pleasure, enjoyment 4; *Erst die Arbeit, dann das Vergnügen.* Business before pleasure. 4
das **Verkehrsmittel,-** means of transportation 11
der **Videorekorder,-** VCR, videocassette recorder 8
  viel much 2
  viele many 4; *wie viele* how many 4
  vielleicht perhaps 7
  vier four E
das **Viertel,-** quarter 3; *Viertel nach* a quarter after 3
  vierzehn fourteen E
  vierzig forty 2
der **Volleyball** volleyball 10
  von from 1; *von einem...zum anderen* from one to the next 11
  vor before, in front of 3; *Viertel vor* a quarter before 3
  vorbeigehen to go past 11
  vorhaben to plan, intend 9
der **Vorteil,-e** advantage 10

W

der **Wagen,-** coach 11; car 12
  wahr: nicht wahr? Isn't it true? Isn't that so? 1
  während during 8

wandern to hike 10
wann when 3
warm warm 5
warten to wait 9; *warten auf* to wait for 5
warum why 3
was what 2; *Was gibt's?* What's up? 2; *was für* what kind of 4
waschen to wash 12
das **Waschbecken,-** (bathroom) sink 8
der **Wecker,-** alarm clock 8
  weiß white 7
  weit far 1
  * **weiter** further 12
  weiterkommen to advance, to go further 9
  welcher which 2
die **Welt,-en** world 9
  wenigstens at least 6
  wenn when 6
  wer who E
  werden will, shall 7
der **Westen** west 3
das **Wetter** weather 5
  wie as 6
  wie how, what E; as 6; *Wie heißt du?* What's your name? E; *Wie findest du...?* What do you think of...? 2; *wie viele* how many 4
  wieder again 11
  Wiedersehen: Auf Wiedersehen! Good-bye! E
das **Wiener Schnitzel** breaded veal cutlet 6
  wieviel how much E
der **Winter,-** winter 5
  wir we 1
  wirklich really 2
  wissen to know 6
  wo where 1
die **Woche,-n** week 4
das **Wochenende,-n** weekend 9
  woher where from 1
  wohin where (to) 3
  wohnen to live 1
die **Wohnung,-en** apartment 8
das **Wohnzimmer,-** livingroom 2
  wollen to want to 6
  wünschen to wish 8
das **Würstchen,-** hot dog 11
die **Wurst,-e** sausage 6
das **Wurstbrot,-e** sausage sandwich 6

Z

der **Zahn,-e** tooth 10
  zehn ten E
  zeigen to show, demonstrate 12
die **Zeit,-en** time 2
die **Zeitung,-en** newspaper 9
das **Zelt,-e** tent 11
das **Zimmer,-** room 9
das **Zitroneneis** lemon ice cream 6
  zu at, to, too 2; *zu Hause* at home 2
  zubereiten to prepare (a meal) 8
  zuerst first 3
der **Zug,-e** train 5
die **Zukunft** future 9
  zurück back 10
  zurückkommen to come back 11
  zusammen together 12
  zusammenkommen to get together 10
  zusehen to watch 12
  zwanzig twenty E
  zwei two E
  zwischen between 9
  zwölf twelve E

A

a ein(e) *E*

able: to be able to können *7*

about gegen *2; about four o'clock* gegen vier Uhr *2*

to **advance** weiterkommen *9*

advantage der Vorteil,-e *10*

after nach *3*

afternoon der Nachmittag,-e *3; this afternoon* heute Nachmittag *3; Saturday afternoon* Samstagnachmittag *8*

again wieder *11*

against gegen *9*

Agreed! Abgemacht! *9*

airplane das Flugzeug,-e *11*

alarm clock der Wecker,- *8*

all alle *4;* alles *11; not at all* gar nicht *8*

allowance das Taschengeld *6*

Alps die Alpen *8*

already schon *4*

also auch *2*

always immer *4*

America Amerika *3*

an ein(e) *E*

and und *E*

answer die Antwort,-en *4*

apartment die Wohnung,-en *8*

apple der Apfel, ̈ *12*

apple juice der Apfelsaft *6*

approximately ungefähr *4*

April der April *5*

arm der Arm,-e *10*

armchair der Sessel,- *8*

around um *1; at 2; At what time?* Um wie viel Uhr? *2*

to **arrive** ankommen *5; The train arrives on time.* Der Zug kommt pünktlich an. *5*

as wie *6*

assorted gemischt *6; assorted ice cream* ein gemischtes Eis *6*

at bei *1;* an, zu *2;* auf *5; at home* zu Hause *2; at least* wenigstens *6*

athletic sportlich *10*

August der August *5*

aunt die Tante,-n *2*

Austria Österreich *5*

Austrian der Österreicher,- *8*

autumn der Herbst,-e *5*

available frei *11*

away entfernt *12*

B

back zurück *10*

backgammon das Backgammon *10*

bad schlecht *1*

baggage das Gepäck *11*

to **bake** backen *8*

ball der Ball, ̈-e *10; ball control* die Ballkontrolle *10*

ballpoint pen der Kuli,-s *4*

Baltic Sea die Ostsee *11*

banana die Banane,-n *12*

band die Band,-s *12*

basketball der Basketball, ̈-e *3*

bass der Bass, ̈-e *9*

bathroom das Bad, ̈-er *8*

bathtub die Badewanne,-n *8*

to **be** sein *4; to be present* dabei sein *9*

beach der Strand, ̈-e *11*

beautiful schön *5*

bed das Bett,-en *8*

bedroom das Schlafzimmer,- *8*

before vor *3; a quarter before* Viertel vor *3*

to **begin** beginnen *3*

beige beige *7*

Belgium Belgien *5*

to **believe** glauben *7*

to **belong** to gehören zu *9*

besides sonst *6;* außer *9; besides that* nebenbei *9*

best best- *9; the best* am besten *9*

better besser *5*

between zwischen *9*

bicycle das Fahrrad, ̈-er *8*

big groß *4; as big as* so groß wie *5; biggest* größt- *4*

bike das Rad, ̈-er *10; to bike* Rad fahren *10*

biology die Biologie *4*

birthday der Geburtstag,-e *8; Happy birthday!* Herzlichen Glückwunsch zum Geburtstag! *8; birthday cake* der Geburtstagskuchen,- *8*

black schwarz *7*

blouse die Bluse,-n *7*

blue blau *7*

board: chalkboard die Tafel,-n *4*

boat das Boot,-e *11*

book das Buch, ̈-er *2*

bookshelf das Bücherregal,-e *8*

border die Grenze,-n *12; at the border with* an der Grenze zu *12*

boring langweilig *2*

both beide *7*

boy der Junge,-n *E*

boyfriend der Freund,-e *1*

bratwurst die Bratwurst, ̈-e *6*

bread das Brot,-e *6*

breakfast das Frühstück *6*

to **bring** bringen *3; to bring along* mitbringen *3; Bring me...* Bringen Sie mir... *6*

brother der Bruder, ̈ *2*

brown braun *7*

bus der Bus,-se *4*

but aber *2*

butter die Butter *6*

to **buy** kaufen *3*

by bei *1*

Bye! Tschüs! *E*

C

café das Eiscafé,-s *6;* das Café,-s *11*

cake der Kuchen,- *8*

calculator der Rechner,- *4*

to **call up** anrufen *8; Why don't you call...!* Ruf doch...an! *8*

camera die Kamera,-s *8*

campground der Campingplatz, ̈-e *11*

can können *7*

capital (city) die Hauptstadt, ̈-e *4*

car das Auto,-s *11;* der Wagen,- *12*

card die Karte,-n *3*

career die Karriere,-n *10*

cassette die Kassette,-n *3*

CD die CD,-s *2*

CD player der CD-Spieler,- *8*

to **celebrate** feiern *8*

center die Mitte *8*

chair der Stuhl, ̈-e *4; easy chair* der Sessel,- *8*

chalk die Kreide *4*

champion der Meister,- *10; National Champion of Germany* Deutscher Meister *10* chance die Chance,-n 10

charming charmant 5

to cheer jubeln 10

cheese der Käse 6; *cheese sandwich* das Käsebrot,-e 6

chemistry die Chemie 4

chess das Schach 9

chic schick 9

chin das Kinn,-e 10

chocolate ice cream das Schokoeis 6

choice die Auswahl 7

cinema das Kino,-s 9

city die Stadt,¨e 1; *center of city* die Stadtmitte 11

clarinet die Klarinette,-n 9

class die Klasse,-n 4; *second (economy) class (train)* die Zweite Klasse 11

class schedule der Stundenplan,¨e 4

to clean up aufräumen 9

to clear *(table)* abräumen 9

clear klar 3

clock die Uhr,-en 2; *alarm clock* der Wecker,- 8

closet der Schrank,¨e 8

clothes die Kleidung 8

clothing die Kleidung 8; *clothing item* das Kleidungsstück,-e 7

club der Klub,-s 10

coach *(sports)* der Trainer,- 10

coach *(train)* der Wagen,- 11

coat der Mantel,¨ 7

cocoa der Kakao 6

coffee der Kaffee 6

coin die Münze,-n 9

cola die Cola,-s 6

cold kalt 5

cold-cut platter die Kalte Platte 6

to collect sammeln 9

color die Farbe,-n 7

colorful bunt 7

to come kommen 1; *to come over* rüberkommen 2; *to come along* mitkommen 3; *to come to visit* zu Besuch kommen 5; *to come here* herkommen 2 ; *Why don't you come to us?* Komm doch zu uns. 5; *to come back* zurückkommen 11

compact disk die CD,-s 2

compartment das Abteil,-e 11

computer der Computer,- 3

computer game das Computerspiel,-e 3

concert das Konzert,-e 9

to construct aufbauen

cool kühl 5

coordinated koordiniert 10

corner die Ecke,-n 1

correct: to be correct stimmen 1; *That's correct.* Das stimmt. 1

to cost kosten 3

counter *(ticket)* der Schalter,- 11

country das Land,¨er 5

couple das Paar,-e 7

cousin **(male)** der Cousin,-s 5; *(female)* die Cousine,-n 5

to cover decken 8

cross das Kreuz 12

cucumber die Gurke,-n 12

cup die Tasse,-n 6

cupboard der Schrank,¨e 8

Czech Republic die Tschechische Republik 5

D

dad der Vati,-s 2

dance der Tanz,¨e 12

to dance tanzen 3; *dancing* das Tanzen 12; *while dancing* beim Tanzen 12; *dancing instructor* der Tanzlehrer,- 12; *dancing lesson* die Tanzstunde,-n 12; *dancing partner* der Tanzpartner- 12; *dancing school* die Tanzschule,-n 12

dancer die Tänzerin,-nen 12

dark dunkel 7; *dark blue* dunkelblau 7

daughter die Tochter,¨ 2

day der Tag,-e E; *during the day* am Tag 7

Dear... *(letter)* Liebe(r)... 7

December der Dezember 5

definitely bestimmt 7

to demonstrate zeigen 12

Denmark Dänemark 5

to depart abfahren 11

department store das Kaufhaus,¨er 3

desk der Schreibtisch,-e 8

dessert der Nachtisch,-e 12

detective story der Krimi,-s 3

difficult schwer 4

dinner das Abendessen 6

disco die Disko,-s 9

dishes das Geschirr 9

dishwasher die Geschirrspülmaschine,-n 8

distance die Entfernung,-en 4; *the farthest distance* die weiteste Entfernung 4

distant entfernt 12

to do machen 2; treiben 10; *What are you doing?* Was machst du? 2; *to do (handi)crafts* basteln 10

dress das Kleid,-er 7

to drink trinken 6

to drive fahren 5

drums das Schlagzeug 9

dull eintönig 7

during während 8

E

each jeder 8

ear das Ohr,-en 10

earlier früher 7

early früh 2

earring der Ohrring,-e 8

east der Osten 2

easy leicht 4

to eat essen 6

eight acht E

eighteen achtzehn E

eighty achtzig 2

elegant elegant 12

eleven elf E

empty leer 4

England England 12

English *(subject)* das Englisch 4; *He speaks English.* Er spricht englisch. 5

enjoyment das Vergnügen 4

enough genug 10

entertainment die Unterhaltung,-en 9

eraser der Radiergummi,-s 4

especially besonders 6; *not especially* nicht besonders 6

Europe Europa 8

evening der Abend, -e 7; *this evening* heute Abend 3; *in the evening* am Abend 7

every jeder *8*
everything alles *11*
exactly genau *12*
exam die Arbeit,-en *4*
except außer *10*
excuse die Entschuldigung; *Excuse me.* Entschuldigung! *3*
exercise die Übung,-en *5*
expensive teuer *7*
eye das Auge,-n *10*

F

fall der Herbst,-e *5*
fan der Fan,-s *8*
far weit *1*
fast schnell *4*
father der Vater,- *2*
February der Februar *5*
few: a few ein paar *5*; manche *10*
fifteen fünfzehn *E*
fifty fünfzig *2*
film der Film,-e *9*
finally endlich *8*; *Finally, the day is here.* Endlich ist der Tag da. *8*
to **find** finden *2*
finger der Finger,- *10*
first zuerst *3*
fish der Fisch,-e *6*; *fish sandwich* die Fischsemmel,-n *6*
to **fit** passen *7*
five fünf *E*
flat flach *8*
to **flow** fließen *8*
flower die Blume,-n *12*
flute die Flöte,-n *12*
to **fly** fliegen *11*
foot der Fuß,-e *10*; *on foot* zu Fuß *11*
for für *4*; *for you* für dich *E*; seit; *for five months* seit fünf Monaten *5*; *for more than... years* seit über...Jahren *9*; *for it* dafür *12*
forehead die Stirn,-en *10*
foreign fremd *11*
form die Form,-en *10*
forty vierzig *2*
four vier *E*
fourteen vierzehn *E*
foxtrot der Foxtrott *12*
France Frankreich *5*
free frei *11*

french fries die Pommes frites (pl.) *6*
French (subject) das Französisch *4*; *She speaks French.* Sie spricht französisch. *5*
Friday der Freitag,-e *2*
from aus, von *1*; *from one to the next* von einem...zum anderen *11*
front: in front of vor *3*
fruit juice der Fruchtsaft,-e *12*
fruit(s) das Obst *12*
fun der Spaß *4*; *They have lots of fun.* Sie haben viel Spaß. *4*; *Have lots of fun!* Viel Spaß! *11*; *It's fun.* Es macht Spaß. *12*
further weiter *12*
future die Zukunft *9*

G

game das Spiel,-e *10*
general(ly) allgemein *9*
genius das Genie,-s *4*; *Such a genius!* So ein Genie! *4*
gentleman der Herr,-en *E*; der Kavalier,-e *12*
geography die Erdkunde *4*
German (subject) das Deutsch *4*
German deutsch *5*; *She speaks German.* Sie spricht deutsch. *5*
Germany Deutschland *2*; *National Champion of Germany* Deutscher Meister *10*
to **get** bekommen *4*
gift das Geschenk,-e *8*
girl das Mädchen,- *E*
girlfriend die Freundin,-nen *1*
to **give** geben *6*; *to give a present* schenken *8*
glad froh *4*
gladly gern *4*
glass das Glas,-er *6*
glove der Handschuh,-e *7*
to **go** gehen *1*; *(by vehicle)* fahren *5*; *to go home* nach Hause gehen; *3*; *Let's go right away!* Gehen wir doch gleich! *6*; *to go further* weiterkommen *9*; *to go there* dahingehen *9*; *There is a lot going on.* Da ist viel los. *10*; *to go past* vorbeigehen *11*

goal das Tor,-e *10*; *to shoot on goal* aufs Tor schießen *10*
golf das Golf *10*
good gut *1*
Good-bye! Auf Wiedersehen! *E*
grade die Note,-n *4*
graduation ball der Abschlussball,-e *12*
grandfather der Großvater,- *2*
grandma die Oma,-s *2*
grandmother die Großmutter,- *2*
grandpa der Opa,-s *2*
grandparents die Großeltern (pl.) *2*
gray grau *7*
great super, toll *2*; prima *3*; klasse *10*
green grün *7*
to **greet** begrüßen *8*
greeting card die Glückwunschkarte,-n *8*
greeting der Gruß,-e *7*
guitar die Gitarre,-n *3*

H

hair das Haar,-e *10*
half halb *2*
halftime die Halbzeit *10*
hamburger der Hamburger,- *6*
hand die Hand,-e *10*
happy froh *4*
hard schwer *4*; hart *10*
to **have** haben *3*; *to have to* müssen *6*; *to have on* anhaben *7*
he er *E*
head der Kopf,-e *4*
to **hear** hören *3*
Hello! Grüß dich!, Guten Tag! *E*
to **help** helfen *8*; *May I help you?* Bitte schön? Ja, bitte? *6*; *to help with the work* bei der Arbeit helfen *8*
her ihr *2*
here hier *1*
hero der Held,-en *10*
Hi! Hallo!, Grüß dich! *E*
high hoch *10*; *highest* höchst- *8*
to **hike** wandern *10*
hint der Tip,-s *10*
his sein *4*
history die Geschichte *4*
hobby das Hobby,-s *9*

Holland Holland *5*

home: to go home nach Hause gehen *3*

homework die Hausaufgabe,-n *4*

hopefully hoffentlich *8*

hot heiß *5;*

hot chocolate der Kakao *6*

hot dog das Würstchen,- *11*

hour die Stunde,-n *4*

house das Haus,¨er *4*

how wie *E; as 6; how much* wie viel *E; how many* wie viele *4*

human der Mensch,-en *12*

hundred hundert *2*

hunger der Hunger *6; to be hungry* Hunger haben *6*

I

I ich *E*

ice cream das Eis *6*

ice cream parlor das Eiscafé,-s *6*

ice hockey das Eishockey *10*

to **ice skate** Schlittschuh laufen *10*

ice tea der Eistee *6*

idea *4* die Idee,-n; *Good idea!* Gute Idee! *4*

if ob *12*

immediately gleich *1;*

in in *1; in the east* im Osten *2*

information die Auskunft,¨e *11*

inhabitant der Einwohner,- *4*

inside innerhalb *9*

intelligent klug *4*

to **intend** vorhaben *9*

invitation die Einladung,-en *8*

to **invite** einladen *8*

it es *1*

Italian italienisch *5; He speaks Italian.* Er spricht italienisch. *5*

Italy Italien *5*

its sein *12*

J

jacket die Jacke,-n *7*

jam die Marmelade,-n *6*

January der Januar *5*

jeans die Jeans (pl.) *7*

jewelry der Schmuck *8*

joy die Lust

July der Juli *5*

June der Juni *5*

just erst *4; just as* genauso...wie *11*

keyboard das Keyboard,-s *9*

kilometer der Kilometer,- *4*

kitchen die Küche,-n *8*

to **know** *(person, place)* kennen *1; to know* wissen *6*

L

lake der See,-n *11*

lamp die Lampe,-n *8*

language die Sprache,-n *5*

large groß *4*

to **last** dauern *4*

last letzt- *11*

late spät *2; later* später *2; See you later.* Bis später. *2*

Latin das Latein *4*

to **laugh** lachen *8*

lawn der Rasen *9; to mow the lawn* den Rasen mähen *9*

league die Liga, Ligen *10*

to **learn** lernen *4*

to **leave** abfahren *11*

to **leave** lassen *7*

left links *11; on the left side* auf der linken Seite *11*

leg das Bein,-e *10*

lemon ice cream das Zitroneneis *6*

lemonade die Limo,-s *6*

letter der Brief,-e *5*

to **lie** liegen *3*

Liechtenstein Liechtenstein *12*

light hell *7*

to **like** gern haben *3;* gefallen *5;* mögen *6; How do you like it...?* Wie gefällt es dir...? *5; I like it.* Es gefällt mir. *7; I don't like it (food).* Das schmeckt mir nicht. *6*

likewise gleichfalls *11*

lip die Lippe,-n *10*

to **listen to** hören *3*

to **live** wohnen *1*

livingroom das Wohnzimmer,- *2*

located: to be located liegen *3*

long lang *7; lange 5; longest* längst- *8; no longer* nicht mehr *5*

to **look** sehen *6; Look!* Seht mal! *6; Let's see...* Mal sehen... *11; to look like* aussehen *12*

loose locker *10*

luck das Glück *7; to be lucky* Glück haben *7*

luggage das Gepäck *11*

lunch das Mittagessen *6*

Luxembourg Luxemburg *5*

M

mainly vor allem *9*

to **make** machen *2; to make (it)* schaffen *10; We'll make it.* Das schaffen wir. *10*

to **manage (it)** schaffen *10*

many viele *4; how many* wie viele *4*

map die Landkarte,-n *4*

March der März *5*

mark *(German monetary unit)* die Mark *3*

market der Markt,¨e *9*

marmalade die Marmelade,-n *6*

mathematics (math) die Mathematik (Mathe) *4; math book* das Mathebuch *4; math class, lesson* die Mathestunde *4*

may dürfen *7*

May der Mai *5*

means of transportation das Verkehrsmittel,- *11*

to **meet** sich treffen *9; Let's meet...* Treffen wir uns... *12*

menu die Speisekarte,-n *6*

microwave oven der Mikrowellenherd,-e *8*

middle die Mitte *8*

milk die Milch *6*

million die Million,-en *8*

mine meins *10*

mineral water das Mineralwasser *12*

minus minus *E*

minute die Minute,-n *1*

mixed gemischt *6*

mom die Mutti,-s *2*

moment der Moment,-e; *Just a moment, please.* Einen Moment, bitte. *2*

Monday der Montag,-e *2*

money das Geld *6*

monotonous eintönig *7*

month der Monat,-e *5*

moped das Moped,-s *11*

more mehr *5; no more* nicht mehr 5; *more than* mehr...als 8

morgen tomorrow 2; *not until tomorrow* erst morgen 6

morning der Morgen 3; *this morning* heute Morgen 3

mostly meistens 10

mother die Mutter,- 2

motorcycle das Motorrad,-̈er 11

mountain der Berg,-e 7

mouth der Mund,-̈er 10

movie der Film,-e 9

movie theater das Kino,-s 9

to **mow** mähen 9

Mr. der Herr,-en *E*

Mrs. die Frau,-en *E*

much viel 2

museum das Museum, Museen 11

music die Musik 3

music festival das Musikfest,-e 8

musical instrument das Musikinstrument,-e 12

must müssen 6

my mein 1

N

named heißen, *E; What's your name?* Wie heißt du? *E*

national flag die Nationalfahne,-n 8; *National League* die Bundesliga 10

natural sciences die Naturwissenschaften (pl.) 4

near bei 1; *near the park* beim Park 1

nearness die Nähe 11

neck der Hals,-̈e 10

to **need** brauchen 4

neighboring country das Nachbarland,-̈er 5

net das Netz,-e 10

Netherlands die Niederlande 5

new neu 1

newspaper die Zeitung,-en 9

next nächst- 9; *the next time* das nächste Mal 9

nice nett, schön 5

nine neun *E*

nineteen neunzehn *E*

ninety neunzig 2

no nein 1; kein(e) 4

noodle soup die Nudelsuppe 12

noon der Mittag,-e 3; *this noon* heute mittag 3

north der Norden 3

North Sea die Nordsee 12

nose die Nase,-n 10

not nicht 1

notebook das Heft,-e 4

nothing nichts 6

November der November 5

now jetzt 2

O

October der Oktober 5

office das Büro,-s 4

often oft 4

OK gut 1

old alt *E*

on an 2; auf 5

once einmal 8; *once more* noch einmal 8; *once a week* einmal die Woche 10

one eins *E*; man 5

only nur 1; erst 4

open geöffnet 12

or oder 2

orange orange 7

orange juice der Orangensaft 12

other ander- 9; *the others* die anderen 9

otherwise sonst 6

our unser 12

out of aus 1; außerhalb 9

outside außerhalb 9

P

to **pack** packen 11

pair das Paar,-e 7

pants die Hose,-n 7

paper das Papier 4

paradise das Paradies 12

parents die Eltern (pl.) 2

park der Park,-s 1

part der Teil,-e 8; *for the most part* zum größten Teil 8; *part of body* der Körperteil,-e 10

to **participate** mitmachen 10

party die Party,-s 8; *to give a party* eine Party geben 8

to **pass (ball)** abgeben 10

pasta die Pasta 9

to **pay** bezahlen 9

pear die Birne,-n 12

pen *(ballpoint)* der Kuli,-s 4

pencil der Bleistift,-e 4

people die Leute (pl.) 9

percent das Prozent,-e 8

percussion das Schlagzeug 9

perhaps vielleicht 7

person der Mensch,-en 12

photo album das Fotoalbum, Fotoalben 8

physics die Physik 4

piano das Klavier,-e 3

picture das Bild,-er 8

pink rosa 7

to **pitch** *(tent)* aufbauen 11

pizza die Pizza,-s 6

pizza bread das Pizza-Brot 6

pizza restaurant die Pizzeria,-s 6

place der Platz,-̈e 8; die Stelle,-n 10; *The team is in second place.* Die Mannschaft steht an zweiter Stelle. 10

to **plan** vorhaben 9

plate die Platte,-n 6; *cold-cut platter* Kalte Platte 6

to **play** spielen 3

please bitte 2

pleasure das Vergnügen 4; *Business before pleasure.* Erst die Arbeit, dann das Vergnügen. 4

pleasure die Lust 12

plus plus *E*

Poland Polen 5

popular beliebt 8

post office die Post 11

poster das Poster,- 8

potato die Kartoffel,-n 6

practice die Übung,-en 5; *Practice makes perfect.* Übung macht den Meister! 5

to **practice** üben 10; *for practice* zum Üben 10

to **prepare** *(a meal)* zubereiten 8

present das Geschenk,-e 8

problem das Problem,-e 4

proximity die Nähe 11

pullover der Pulli,-s 7; der Pullover,- 7

punctual pünktlich 4

to **put on** anziehen 9

Q

quarter das Viertel,- 3; *a quarter after* Viertel nach 3
quite ganz 1
quiz show die Quizshow,-s 8

R

radio das Radio,-s 8
rag *(to wipe of blackboard)* der Tafellappen,- 4
to **rain** regnen 5
rather lieber 3
to **read** lesen 2
really wirklich 2; echt 9
reasonable preiswert 3
to **receive** bekommen 4
recorder die Blockflöte,-n 12
red rot 7
refrigerator der Kühlschrank,¨e 8
religion die Religion 4
to **remain** bleiben 5
to **repair** reparieren 9
Republic die Republik 8
restaurant das Restaurant,-s 6
restroom die Toilette,-n 8
rhythm der Rhythmus 12; *according to the rhythm* dem Rhythmus nach 12
right recht 4; *You're right.* Du hast recht. 4; right 11; *right away* gleich 1; *right around the corner* gleich um die Ecke 1
to **rinse** spülen 9
river der Fluss,¨e 8
rock band die Rockgruppe,-n 2
rock concert das Rockkonzert,-e 3
rock group die Rockgruppe,-n 2
rock music die Rockmusik 3
roll das Brötchen,- 6
room das Zimmer,- 9
ruler das Lineal,-e 4
rumba die Rumba 12
to **run** *(river)* fließen 8
sail gliding das Segelfliegen 9
salad der Salat,-e 6
salami die Salami 6
satchel *(school)* die Schultasche,-n 4
Saturday der Sonnabend,-e; der Samstag,-e 2

sauerbraten (marinated beef) der Sauerbraten 6
sausage die Wurst,¨e 6; *sausage sandwich* das Wurstbrot,-e 6
saxophone das Saxophon,-e 9
to **say** sagen 3; *Say, Steffie...* Du, Steffie... 3; *Let's say...* Sagen wir... 3; *How do you/they say...?* Wie sagt man...? 4
schedule der Fahrplan,¨e 11
school die Schule,-n 3
school bag die Schultasche,-n 4
schoolmate der Schulfreund,-e 6
to **scream** schreien 10
season die Jahreszeit,-en 5
seat der Platz,¨e 11
section der Teil,-e 8
to **see** sehen 6; *Bis später!* E; *See you!* Tschüs! E; *Let's see...* Mal sehen... 11
selection die Auswahl 7
to **send** schicken 5
September der September 5
to **set** *(the table)* 8; *to set up* aufbauen 11
seven sieben E
seventeen siebzehn E
seventy siebzig 2
shall werden 7
shape die Form,-en 10
she sie E
to **shine** scheinen 5
ship das Schiff,-e 11
shirt das Hemd,-en 7
shoe der Schuh,-e 7
to **shoot** schießen 10
to **shop** einkaufen 9; *to go shopping* einkaufen gehen 9
shore der Strand,¨e 11
short kurz 7
should sollen 7
shoulder die Schulter,-n 10
to **show** zeigen 12
side die Seite,-n 11
simple einfach 11
since seit 5
sincere herzlich
singen to sing 9
sink *(bathroom)* das Waschbecken,- 8; sink *(kitchen)* das Spülbecken,- 8
sister die Schwester,-n 2
six sechs E

sixteen sechzehn E
sixty sechzig 2
to **ski** Ski laufen 5
skirt der Rock,¨e 7
slacks die Hose,-n 7
slice die Scheibe,-n 6; *a slice of bread* eine Scheibe Brot 6
slow langsam 4
smart klug 4; *smart looking* schick 9
snack (bar) der Imbiss,-e 11
to **snow** schneien 5
so so 2
soccer der Fußball,¨e 3; *soccer ball* der Fußball,¨e 3; *soccer field* der Fußballplatz,¨e 10; *soccer player* der Fußballspieler,- 10
sock die Socke,-n 7
sofa das Sofa,-s 8
some etwas 6; manche 10
sometimes manchmal 9
son der Sohn,¨e 2
song das Lied,-er 9; *favorite song* das Lieblingslied,-er 9
south der Süden 3; *southern Germany* Süddeutschland 3
spaetzle *(kind of homemade pasta)* die Spätzle 6
Spain Spanien 5
Spanish spanisch 5; *He speaks Spanish.* Er spricht spanisch. 5
to **speak**
to **speak** sprechen 5; reden 10; *She speaks German.* Sie spricht deutsch. 5
special besonders 6
speed das Tempo 10
to **spend** *(money)* ausgeben 9
sport der Sport 4; *to participate in sports* Sport treiben 10; *sports club* der Sportklub,-s 10
sporty sportlich 10
spot die Stelle,-n
spring der Frühling,-e 5
stamp die Briefmarke,-n 9
to **stand** stehen 7
star *(athlete)* der Star,-s 10
to **start** losgehen 3; *When does it start?* Wann geht's los? 3
state der Staat,-en 8
to **stay** bleiben 5
step der Schritt,-e 12; *small step* das Schrittchen,- 9
stiff steif 10

still noch *6*
stocking der Strumpf,¨e *7*
stove der Herd,-e *8*
straight ahead geradeaus *11*
strawberry ice cream das
  Erdbeereis *6*
street die Straße,-n *12*
streetcar die Straßenbahn,-en *11*
student *(elementary through*
  secondary school) der Schüler,- *12*
student rock band die
  Schülerrockband,-s *9*
subject *(school)* das Fach,¨er *4*;
  favorite (school) subject das
  Lieblingsfach,¨er *4*
successful erfolgreich *9*
such solch *12*
suggestion der Tip,-s *10*
suit der Anzug,¨e *7*
summer der Sommer,- *5*
summer month der
  Sommermonat,-e *12*
sun die Sonne *5*
Sunday der Sonntag,-e *2*
super super *2*; klasse *10*
supper das Abendessen *6*
supposed: to be supposed to
  sollen *7*
sweater der Pulli,-s *7*; der
  Pullover,- *7*
sweatshirt das Sweatshirt,-s *7*
to **swim** schwimmen *3*
Switzerland die Schweiz *5*

T

T-shirt das T-Shirt,-s *7*
table der Tisch,-e *4*
table tennis das Tischtennis *10*
to **take**, dauern *4*; *to take part* dabei
  sein *9*; *to take pictures*
  fotografieren *9*; *to take along*
  mitnehmen *11*
talent das Talent,-e *9*
to **talk** sprechen *5*, reden *10*; *to talk*
  about sprechen über *8*; *to talk*
  about themselves sprechen über
  sich selbst *9*
to **taste** schmecken *6*; *How does it*
  taste? Wie schmeckt's? *6*
tea der Tee *12*

teacher *(male)* der Lehrer,- *4*;
  (female) die Lehrerin,-nen *4*
team die Mannschaft,-en *10*
teenager der Jugendliche,-n *9*
telephone das Telefon,-e *2*; *on the*
  telephone am Telefon *2*
television das Fernsehen *3*; *on*
  television im Fernsehen *3*;
  television program das
  Fernsehprogramm,-e *3*; *television*
  set der Fernseher,- *8*
to **tell** sagen; *Tell me...* Sag mir... *5*
tempo das Tempo *10*
ten zehn *E*
tennis das Tennis *3*; *tennis shoe* der
  Tennisschuh,-e *7*; *tennis court* der
  Tennisplatz,¨e *10*; *tennis game*
  das Tennisspiel,-e *10*; *tennis*
  racket der Tennisschläger,- *10*
tent das Zelt,-e *11*
terrific klasse *10*
to **thank** danken *8*
thanks danke *6*
that das *E*; dass *8*
the der, die, das *2*; *the same*
  derselbe *12*;
their ihr *12*
then dann *2*
there da *1*; dort *10*; *over there* da
  drüben *1*; *there (to)* dorthin *11*
therefore deshalb *8*
they sie *1*; man *5*
to **think** glauben *7*; denken *9*; *What*
  do you think of...? Wie findest
  du...? *2*; *to think about* denken
  an *9*
thirst Durst *6*; *to be thirsty* Durst
  haben *6*
thirteen dreizehn *E*
thirty dreißig *2*
this dieser *4*; diese
  (form of dieser) *4*
thousand tausend *2*
three drei *E*
thriller der Krimi,-s *3*
through durch *8*
Thursday der Donnerstag,-e *2*
ticket die Karte,-n *3*; die
  Fahrkarte,-n *11*
tie die Krawatte,-n *7*
tight eng *7*

time die Zeit,-en *2*; *on time*
  pünktlich *4*
time(s) das Mal,-e *12*; *the last time*
  das letzte Mal *12*; *a few times* ein
  paar Mal *12*; *long time* lange *5*; *At*
  what time? Um wie viel Uhr? *2*;
  times mal *4*
tip *(suggestion)* der Tip,-s *10*
to zu, an *2*
today heute *2*
together zusammen *12*; *to get*
  together zusammenkommen *10*
toilet die Toilette,-n *8*
tomato die Tomate,-n *6*
tomorrow morgen *2*
too auch, zu *2*
tooth der Zahn,¨e *10*
tortellini *(filled pasta)* Tortellini *6*
tour die Tournee,-n *9*
tourist der Tourist,-en *8*
track das Gleis,-e *11*
train der Zug,¨e *5*; *train station* der
  Bahnhof,¨e *3*
to **train** trainieren *10*
trainer der Trainer,- *10*
to **transfer** umsteigen *11*
to **travel** reisen *5*
trip die Reise,-n *11*
trumpet die Trompete,-n *12*
Tuesday der Dienstag,-e *2*
to **turn (to)** abbiegen *11*
TV der Fernseher,- *8*
twelve zwölf *E*
twenty zwanzig *E*
two zwei *E*

U

uncle der Onkel,- *2*
United States of America die
  Vereinigten Staaten von
  Amerika *4*
until bis *E*
to **use** gebrauchen, *make use of 10*

V

vacation die Ferien (pl.) *11*; *to go*
  on vacation in die Ferien
  fahren *11*

to **vacuum** staubsaugen *9*
  vanilla ice cream das Vanilleeis *6*
  VCR der Videorekorder,- *8*
  veal cutlet *(breaded)* das Wiener
    Schnitzel *6*
  vegetable(s) das Gemüse *6*
  very sehr *1*
  viedocassette recorder der
    Viedorekorder,- *8*
  violin die Geige,-n *12*
to **visit** besuchen *5; She comes to visit.*
    Sie kommt zu Besuch. *5*
  visit der Besuch,-e *5*
  visitor der Besucher,- *12*
  volleyball der Volleyball *10*

W

to **wait** warten *9; to wait for* warten
    auf *5*
  waiter der Kellner,- *6*
  waitress die Kellnerin,-nen *6*
to **want to** wollen *6*
  warm warm *5*
  warum why *3, that's why 8*
to **wash** waschen *12; to wash (dishes)*
    spülen *9*
  watch die Uhr,-en *2*
to **watch** zusehen *12; to watch*
    television fernsehen *3*
  we wir *1*
to **wear** anhaben *7;* anziehen *9*
  weather das Wetter *5*
  Wednesday der Mittwoch,-e *2*
  week die Woche,-n *4*
  weekend das Wochenende,-n *9*
  well gut *1; well* na *2; Oh well.*
    Na ja. *4*
  well-known bekannt *8*
  west der Westen *3*
  what was *2; What's up?* Was
    gibt's? *2; what kind of* was
    für *4; What's your name?* Wie
    heißt du? *E; What do you think*
    of...? Wie findest du...? *2*
  when wann *3;* wenn *6*
  where wo *1; where from* woher *1;*
    where (to) wohin *3*
  whether ob *12*
  which welcher *2*
  whipped cream die Schlagsahne *6*
  white weiß *7*

  who wer *E*
  why warum *3*
  will werden *7*
  winter der Winter,- *5*
to **wish** wünschen *8*
  with mit *2;* bei *10*
  within innerhalb *9*
  without ohne *4*
  woman die Frau,-en *E*
to **work** arbeiten *11*
  work die Arbeit,-en *4; to help with*
    the work bei der Arbeit helfen *8*
  world die Welt,-en *9*
  would like to möchten; *I would*
    like to go to the rock concert. Ich
    möchte zum Rockkonzert
    (gehen). *3; I would like to...* Ich
    habe Lust... *12*
to **write** schreiben *5*

Y

  year das Jahr,-e *5*
  yellow gelb *7*
  yes ja *1*
  yesterday gestern *11*
  yet noch *6*
  you *(familiar singular)* du *E; you*
    (familiar plural) ihr *1; you (formal)*
    Sie *1; you* man *5*
  young person der
    Jugendliche,-n *9*
  your dein *1; Your...* Dein(e)... *7;*
    your (familiar plural) euer *12;*
    your *(formal singular and plural)*
    Ihr *12*
  youth team die
    Jugendmannschaft,-en *10*

Z

  zero null *E*

Index

Aknowledgments

The author wishes to express his gratitude to the following people who assisted in the photography scenes in Germany, Austria and Switzerland:

Friedrich-Wilhelm Becker (Göttingen, Germany)
Axel Dürer (Bremen, Germany)
Dr. Reinhold Frigge (Witten, Germany)
Klaus Hartart and Family (Berlin, Germany)
Volker Held and Family (Bensheim, Germany)
Dr. Wieland Held and Family (Leipzig, Germany)
Guido Kauls (Minneapolis, Minnesota)
Thomas Lustenberger (Lucerne, Switzerland)

Dieter Messner and Family (Lienz, Austria)
Donatus Moosauer (Altenmarkt, Germany)
Uwe Schlaugk and Family (Gräfelfing, Germany)
Frank Schultze (Dortmund, Germany)
Gerfried Stein (Bad Homburg, Germany)
Peter Sternke and Family (St. Augustin, Germany)
Helmut Strunk and Family (Essen, Germany)
Dr. Hartmut Voigt (Odenthal-Glöbusch, Germany)

The author also would like to thank Sarah Vaillancourt and Sharon O'Donnell for editorial and professional advice. Finally, the author would like to thank his wife, Rosie, for showing such tremendous patience and understanding during the development of this series and for her valuable contributions before, during and after the extensive trips throughout German-speaking countries.

The following German instructors provided valuable comments for the new edition of *Deutsch Aktuell:*

Kristine S. Albrecht, St. Charles High School, St. Charles, Illinois; *Marianne Allen*, Northwestern-Lehigh High School, New Tripoli, Pennsylvania; *Eva Arndt*, Morris Catholic High School, Denville, New Jersey; *Gertrud Ashe*, Cholla High School, Tucson, Arizona; *Gabriele Auerbach*, Bettendorf High School, Bettendorf, Iowa; *Fritz A. Baake*, Northwest Global Studies Middle Magnet School, Kansas City, Missouri; *Jim Baggett*, Springstead High School, Spring Hill, Florida; *Ursula Baker*, West Chicago Community High School, West Chicago, Illinois; *Greg Barnett*, Oak Grove High School, San Jose, California; *Brigitte Baur*, Glenbrook North High School, Northbrook, Illinois; *Margrit Bickelmann*, Rochester High School, Rochester, Michigan; *Erin Bierley*, Fernley High School, Fernley, Nevada; *Anneliese Boghossian*, Perth Amboy High School, Perth Amboy, New Jersey; *Rick Brairton*, Chatham High School, Chatham, New Jersey; *Nancy Brock*, Crittenden County High School, Marion, Kentucky; *Mara R. Brogan*, Peoria Notre Dame High School, Peoria, Illinois; *Helga S. Brown*, Basic High School, Henderson, Nevada; *Lynn G. Brown*, Scranton School/Yellowstone Trail Consortium (ITV), Scranton, North Dakota; *Jill Brunner*, Richmond High School, Richmond, Michigan; *Nancy Burbank*, Reno High School, Reno, Nevada; *Jacqueline A. Cady*, Bridgewater-Raritan High School, Bridgewater, North Dakota; *Karin Carl*, Wall High School, Wall, New Jersey; *Phillip Carlson*, New Mexico Military Institute, Roswell, New Mexico; *James P. Carrell*, Albuquerque Academy, Albuquerque, New Mexico; *Chris Case*, McQueen High School, Reno, Nevada; *Marjorie E. Cederlund*, Thomas Middle School, Arlington Heights, Illinois; *Stephanie Christensen*, Flathead High School, Kalispell, Montana; *Sandra Clymer*, Ravenna High School, Ravenna, Nebraska; *Margaret Collier*, Bishop Eustau Preparatory School, Pennsauken, New Jersey; *Susan Davis*, Manchester High School, Manchester, Michigan; *Carol W. Devoss*, St. Charles High School, St. Charles, Illinois; *Maryann De Young*, Miamisburg High School, Miamisburg, Ohio; *Joseph Dowling*, William Penn High School, New Castle, Delaware; *Susan Durkin*, Arbor Park Middle School, Oak Forest, Illinois;

Robert B. Edwards, Metropolitan East Luthern High School Edwardsville, Illinois; *Nancy Ericson*, New Life Academy, Woodbury, Minnesota; *Amy Evers*, Brentwood High School, Brentwood, Tennessee; *Thomas Fischer*, Overbrook Reginal Senior High School, Pine Hill, New Jersey; *Gregory Fruhman*, Clifton High School, Clifton, New Jersey; *Doris Glowacki*, Union High School, Union, New Jersey; *Walter Godecke*, Sacramento High School, Sacramento, California; *K. Joy Gruits*, Reuther Middle School, Rochester Hills, Michigan; *J. Royce Gubler*, Green Valley High School, Henderson, Nevada; *Beth Guhr*, Edgewood High School, Edgewood, Maryland; *John F. Györy*, G.A.R. Memorial Junior Senior High School, Wilkes-Barre, Pennsylvania; *Shawn Harms*, La Salle-Peru High School, La Salle, Illinois; *Mary Hart*, Eddyville High School, Eddyville, Iowa; *Ann Hartman*, New Prague Senior High School, New Prague, Minnesota; *Peri V. Hartzell*, Field Kindley High School, Coffeyville, Kansas; *Victoria Heiderscheidt*, St. Joseph Middle School, Waukesha, Wisconsin; *Arthur Helwing*, Mather High School, Chicago, Illinois; *Arthur P. Herrmann*, White Station High School, Memphis, Tennessee *Nancy Hetzel*, Mark T. Sheehan High School, Wallingford, Connecticut; *Tom Hoffman*, Russell High School, Russell, Kansas; *Judy Horning*, Newark High School, Newark, Ouio; *Patricia Hughes*, Kelliher Public School, Kelliher, Minnesota; *Daniel L. Hunter*, Bald Eagle Nittany High School, Mill Hall, Pennsylvania; *Glenn P. Huntoon*, Wabasha-Kellogg High School, Wabasha, Minnesota; *Terry L. Huth*, Wauwatosa School District, Wauwatosa, Wisconsin; *Kim P. Icsman*, Ursuline Academy of Cincinnati, Cincinnati, Ohio; *Jennifer E. Jacobi*, Haines Middle School, St. Charles, Illinois; *Heinz Janning*, Redwood Valley High School, Redwood Falls, Minnesota; *Wilfried Jarosch*, Thornwood High School, South Holland, Illinois; *Regina Johannson*, Webb School of Knoxville, Knoxville, Tennessee; *Roger P. Johnson*, Elko High School, Elko, Nevada; *Rhonda Jones*, Lane Technical High School, Chicago, Illinois; *Guido Kauls*, Minnehaha Academy, Minneapolis, Minnesota; *Kristine Keller*, Wilton High School, Wilton, Iowa; *Charles King*, St. Joseph High

School, Westchester, Illinois; *Elizabeth Kitamann*, Battle Mountain High School, Minturn, Colorado; *Joanne Kiwak*, Coatesville Area High School, Coatesville, Pennsylvania; *Linda Klein*, Waupaca High School, Waupaca, Wisconsin; *Hans Koenig*, Blake School, Hopkins, Minnesota; *Robert Komar*, North Bergen High School, North Bergen, New Jersey; *Maggie Kornreich*, Mariemont High School, Cincinnati, Ohio; *Nancy Kuechelmann*, Ridge High School, Basking Ridge, New Jersey; *David J. Lane*, The Kiski School, Saltsburg, Pennsylvania; *Erl Langness*, Ishpeming High School, Ishpeming, Michigan; *Ardis D. Larvick*, Stewardson-Strasburg High School, Strasburg, Illinois; *Eric Lassner*, Standley Lake High School, Westminster, Colorado; *Irmgard K. Lindahl*, Lutheran High School, Springfield, Illinois; *Ingrid Luchini*, Mayfield High School, Las Cruces, New Mexico; *Joyce Luekens*, Kawameeh Middle School, Union, New Jersey; *Roger VanMaasdam*, Schaumburg Christian School, Schaumburg, Illinois; *David M. Major*, Colerain High School, Cincinnati, Ohio; *Jean Maley*, New Mexico Military Institute, Roswell, New Mexico; *Ann Mans*, Pine City High School, Pine City, Minnesota; *Ingrid May*, Harding High School and River Valley High School, Marion, Ohio; *Linda R. McCrae*, Muhlenberg High School, Laureldale, Pennsylvania; *Charles Mescher*, Marion Local High School, Maria Stein, Ohio; *Barbara Mieder*, Milton Junior-Senior High School, Milton, Vermont; *Judith Miller*, Hightstown High School, Hightstown, New Jersey; *Jo Anne Miller*, Cumberland Valley High School, Mechanicsburg, Pennsylvania; *Ronald Moore*, Platteview High School, Springfield, Nebraska; *Helga E. Morganstern*, Luther Burbank High School, Sacramento, California; *Karen Mosher*, Alamogordo High School, Alamogordo, New Mexico; *Barbara Muehler*, Providence Catholic High School, New Lenox, Illinois; *Frank Mulhern*, Wissahickon School District, Ambler, Pennsylvania; *Daniel P. Nash*, Evergreen High School, Evergreen, Colorado; *Helga Needham*, Howell High School, Farmingdale, New Jersey; *Jo Ann D. Nelson*, Jacksonville High School, Jacksonville, Illinois; *Rebecca Kettler Nemec*, Maplewood-Richmond Heights Senior High School, St. Louis, Missouri; *Nancy Lorraine Newson*, Lakewood Senior High School, Lakewood, Colorado; *Ronald E. Nocks*, Westerville South High School, Westerville, Ohio; *Joan Nowak*, Oak Creek Senior High School, Oak Creek, Wisconsin; *Patrick O'Malley*, New Prague Senior High School, New Prague, Minnesota; *Mary Loomer Oliver*, Foley Senior High School, Foley, Minnesota; *Barry Olsen*, Timpview High School, Provo, Utah; *Tom Ore*, Pickerington High School, Pickerington, Ohio; *Joan M. Otoupalik*, Cherry Creek High School, Englewood, Colorado; *Lillian Pennington*, Pickerington High School, Pickerington, Ohio; *Sister Mary Perpetua*, Central Catholic High School, Reading, Pennsylvania; *Rosie Peters*, Holt High School, Holt, Michigan; *Connie Popken*, West High School, Sioux City, Iowa; *Ronald Porotsky*, Whitehall High School, Whitehall, Pennsylvania; *Karen Diane Price*, Charlottesville High School, Charlottesville, Virginia; *Lois Purrington*, BDSH High School, Renville, Minnesota; *Susan Rayner*, Foothill Farms Junior High School, Sacramento, California; *Caroline F. Redington*, Dunkirk Middle School, Dunkirk, New York; *David H. Renoll*, Tunkhannock Area High School, Tunkhannock, Pennsylvania; *Dwight Repsher*, Pen Argyl Area School District, Pen Argyl, Pennsylvania; *Rev. Donald R. Rettig*, Elder High School, Cincinati, Ohio; *Albert E. Reynolds*, Cordova High School, Rancho Cordova, California; *Ernest L. Roane*, Huguenot High School, Richmond, Virginia; *Faye Rollings-Carter*, Midlothian High School, Midlothian, Virginia; *Cecil Roth*, Williston High School, Willston, North Dakota; *Don Ruhde*, Iowa Falls High School, Iowa Falls, Iowa; *Runy Runge*, McLane High School, Fresno, California; *Emmerich Sack*, St. John's Preparatory School, Collegeville, Minnesota; *Loretta Saunderson*, Burnet Middle School, Caldwell, New Jersey; *Elaine Schuessler*, Wesclin High School, Trenton, Illinois; *Linda Schwinghammer*, Shakopee Junior High School, Shakopee, Minnesota; *Linda B. Seward*, Loyola Academy, Wilmette, Illinois; *Scott Alan Seyler*, MMI Preparatory School, Freeland, Pennsylvania; *Ramona Shaw*, Steelville R-3 Schools, Steelville Missouri; *Angela Shea*, St. Mary's High School, Stockton, California; *Marsha S. Sirman*, Seaford High School, Seaford, Delaware; *Marcia K. Slosser*, Lloyd C. Bird High School, Chesterfield, Virginia; *Theresa Smejkal*, Loyola Academy, Wilmette, Illinois; *Susan Smith*, Van Hoosen Middle School, Rochester, Michigan; *Ruth Stark*, Chisago Lake High School, Lindstrom, Minnesota; *Mary Stefano*, Seaholm High School, Birmingham, Michigan; *Shirley Swan*, Lakeview High School, St. Clair Shores, Michigan; *Patrick W. Sylvester*, Socorro High School, Socorro, New Mexico; *William Thomas*, Limestone Community High School, Bartonville, Illinois; *Robert S. Thompson*, F. T. Maloney High School, Meriden, Connecticut; *Warren E. Thornock*, Elk Grove High School, Elk Grove, California; *Roswitha Timbrell*, Gulf High School, New Port Richey, Florida; *Tanya Tobin*, Purcell Marian High School, Cincinnati, Ohio; *Ernst Unger*, Paramus High School, Paramus, New Jersey; *Doris Unruh*, Peabody High School, Peabody, Kansas *Joyce Van Ness*, Central Campus High School, Minot, North Dakota; *Archie Walker*, Groveport-Madison High School, Groveport, Ohio; *Nancy S. Walker*, Craigmont High School, Memphis, Tennessee; *Gerald Walta*, Lakeside Lutheran High School, Lake Mills, Wisconsin; *John Walte*, Mount Vernon High School, Mount Vernon, Washington; *Jon Ward*, Rigby High School, Rigby, Idaho; *Deborah E. Weston*, Lindenhurst Junior High School, Lindenhurst, New York; *Eleanor Weston*, Bishop Foley High School, Madison Heights, Michigan; *Gabriele Whittemore*, Manchester Regional High School, Haledon, New Jersey; *Ursula Wilhelm*, John Burroughs School, St. Louis, Missouri; *Robert F. Williams*, Green Mountain High School, Lakewood, Colorado;*Robert Williams*, Waseca High School, Waseca, Minnesota; *Kimberly Winter-McGhee*, Morgan County R-II Schools, Versailles, Missouri; *Diane Wippler*, Proctor High School, Proctor, Minnesota; *William Witney*, Hastings Middle School, Columbus, Ohio; *Spencer H. Wolf*, Middletown High School North, Middletown, New Jersey; *Walter Wolf*, Center High School, Center, North Dakota; *Jan Zamir*, John Hersey High School, Arlington Heights, Illinois; *Georgeanna Zauhoff*, Holland Christian High School, Holland, Michigan

Photo Credits

All the photos in the *Deutsch Aktuell 1* textbook not taken by the author have been provided by the following:

Austrian National Tourist Office: xvi (bottom left and right)), xvii (bottom left and right), 243, 259 (all three), 260, 302 (bottom left), 354 (top)

Berlin-Touristen-Information: xii (bottom), 136 (bottom right), 296 (top)

Chancerel International Publishers: 208 (top)

Deutsche Bahn: 326 (top), 327(right), 347, 349

Deutsches Jugendherbergswerk: 18 (bottom right)

Fremdenverkehrs- und Kongressbetrieb der Stadt Coburg: xiv (top left)

Fremdenverkehrs- und Kongressamt Leipzig: xv (center right), 56, 287 (left)

Fremdenverkehrsverband Franken e.V.: 39

Fremdenverkehrsverband Rheinland-Pfalz e.V.: xiv (bottom left)

Fried, Robert: vii (top), xx (top), 2 (center right), 239

German Information Center: xiii (bottom left), xv (center left), 50, 136 (top right and left), 296 (bottom left and right), 297 (right), 303 (center left)

Gesellschaft für Tourismus und Marketing mbH Kassel: xv (bottom)

Harzer Verkehrsverband e.V.: xv (top left), 67 (right)

Inter Nationes: 301 (top right and left), 302 (top right), 319

Kaerntner Tourismus GmbH: xvi (top)

Kultur- und Verkehrsamt Bad Mergentheim: xii (top), 91 (bottom right)

Kurdirektion Todtnau: 19 (right)

Kurverwaltung Bodenmais: 147 (top left), 262 (bottom right), 327 (left), 355 (right)

Kurverwaltung Garmisch-Partenkirchen: 138 (top)

Kurverwaltung Menzenschwand: xiv (bottom center)

Kurverwaltung Ruhpolding: xv (top right)

Landesfremdenverkehrverband Baden-Württemberg e.V: 296 (bottom center)

Landeshauptstadt Düsseldorf: 262 (top)

Landesverkehrsverband Westfalen e.V.: 301 (bottom)

Lufthansa: 1 (right), 10 (bottom), 256 (left)

Moosauer, Donatus: 193, 249, 250 (all three), 252

Musik + Show: 262 (bottom left), 286, 287 (right), 289 (left)

Postdienst: 371

Salzburger Land Tourismus: 202

Schultze, Frank: viii (top), ix (top), 297 (left), 309, 312, 314, 315 (both), 322, 323, 325 (both), 372 (both), 373 (both), 374, 378

Simson, David: iv (left), ix (bottom), xx (bottom left and right), xii (center and center left), 2 (top and bottom center), 3, 4 (center and bottom left), 14 (bottom), 18 (top), 24, 25, 26, 27, 28, 30, 32, 33, 34 (both), 35, 36 (both), 37, 38, 40 (top and bottom left), 45 (right), 46 (right), 53, 54 (left), 60 (top right), 62, 63, 64, 66 (top), 67 (left), 72 (center right and bottom left), 74, 81, 84, 90 (bottom right), 98, 100, 103 (all four), 112, 117, 120 (both), 139 (right), 145 (right), 147 (center right and left), 148, 157, 167 (right), 168 (bottom right and left, 174 (bottom), 211 (both), 216 (both), 231 (center), 302 (center left and bottom right), 303 (top), 320 (top left), 352 (bottom right and left), 353 (left), 359 (both), 360 (top), 362 (top left)

Specht, Roland: 2 (top left and right, center left, bottom left and right), 4 (top left, center and center right), 16 (right)

Städtische Kurverwaltung Bad Tölz: vi (top), xvii (top left), 163 (left), 326 (bottom left)

Städtische Verkehrsbüro Stadt Bückeburg: xiv (top right)

Sturmhoefel, Horst: 228, 273 (left), 292 (bottom), 341

Switzerland Tourism: xviii (all), xix (all), 142, 303 (center right), 306, 354 (bottom left), 355 (left), 382 (bottom right), 383 (both), 384 (both)

Tourist Information Kiel e.V.: (top left)

Verkehrsamt Breisach: 326 (bottom center)

Verkehrsamt Cochem: xiv (bottom right)

Verkehrsamt Kleinwalsertal: xiii (top right), 163 (right)

Verkehrsamt Reit im Winkl: 219 (bottom), 326 (bottom right)

Verkehrsamt Saarburg: 90 (bottom left)

Verkehrsbüro Blankenheim: xiii (top left)

Verkehrsverein Augsburg e.V.: xii (center right)

Verkehrsverein Naturpark Hann. Münden: 263 (left)

Vorarlberg Tourismus: v (bottom), xvii (center left and bottom), 90 (top right)

Waldinger, Karl-Georg: viii (bottom), 281 (all three), 282 (all three), 283 (both), 289 (right)

Realia Credits

The publisher would like to thank the following sources for granting permission to reproduce certain material on the pages indicated:

Atlantik-Brücke (Meet United Germany): 286

Deutscher Wetterdienst: 149

Kaiserin-Friedrich-Schule, Bad Homburg: 130

Kur- und Verkehrsamt Waldkirch: 291

Kurdirektion des Berchtesgadener Landes: 237, 240

Leipziger Volkszeitung: 319

Städtische Materé-Gymnasium, Meerbusch-Büderich: 107

Stuttgart Marketing GmbH: 143

Verkehrsverein Bad Achen e.V.: 83

Verkehrsverein Helsa e.V.: 257

Verkehrsverein Neunkirchen e.V.: 114

Waldinger, Karl-Georg: 284